EASTERN RELIGIONS
AND
WESTERN THOUGHT

EASTERN RELIGIONS

AND

WESTERN THOUGHT

S. Radhakrishnan

OXFORD UNIVERSITY PRESS
DELHI LONDON NEW YORK

Oxford University Press, Walton Street, Oxford OX2 6DP
NEW YORK TORONTO
DELHI BOMBAY CALCUTTA MADRAS KARACHI
PETALING JAYA SINGAPORE HONG KONG TOKYO
NAIROBI DAR ES SALAAM
MELBOURNE AUCKLAND
and associates in
BERLIN IBADAN

First published 1939
by the Clarendon Press, Oxford
Second edition 1940
First Indian impression 1974
Published by arrangement with
the Clarendon Press
Eighth impression 1988

First published in Oxford India Paperback 1989
Fourth impression 1992

SBN 0 19 562456 4

Printed in India
By Ram Printograph (India), New Delhi 110020
and published by S. K. Mookerjee, Oxford University Press
YMCA Library Building, Jai Singh Road, New Delhi 110001

TO

PROFESSOR J. H. MUIRHEAD

PREFACE

MODERN civilization with its scientific temper, humanistic spirit, and secular view of life is uprooting the world over the customs of long centuries and creating a ferment of restlessness. The new world cannot remain a confused mass of needs and impulses, ambitions and activities, without any control or guidance of the spirit. The void created by abandoned superstitions and uprooted beliefs calls for a spiritual filling.

The world has found itself as one body. But physical unity and economic interdependence are not by themselves sufficient to create a universal human community. For this we require a human consciousness of community, a sense of personal relationships among men. Though this human consciousness was till recently limited to the members of the political States, there has been a rapid extension of it after the War. The modes and customs of all men are now a part of the consciousness of all men. Man has become the spectator of man. A new humanism is on the horizon. But this time it embraces the whole of mankind. An intimate mutual knowledge between peoples is producing an enrichment of world-consciousness. We can no more escape being members of a world community than we can jump out of our own skin. Yet to our dismay we find that the world is anarchical and unruly. Its mind is in confusion; its brain out of hinge. More than ever before, the world is to-day divided and afflicted by formidable evils. The cause of the present tension and disorder is the lack of adjustment between the process of life, which is one of increasing interdependence, and the 'ideology' of life, the integrating habits of mind, loyalties, and affections embodied in our laws and institutions. Education, which has for its aim the transmission not only of skills and techniques, but of ideals and loyalties, of affections and appreciations, is busy in the new world with the old ideals of national sovereignty and economic self-sufficiency. The present organization of the world is inconsistent with the *Zeitgeist* shining on the distant horizon as well as the true spirit of religion. To say that there is only one God is to affirm that there is only one community of mankind. The obstacles to the organization of human society in an international commonwealth are in the minds of men who have not developed the sense of the duty they owe to each other. We have to touch the soul of mankind. 'For soul is Form and doth the body make.' We must evolve ideals, habits, and sentiments which would enable us to build up a world community, live in a co-operative commonwealth working for the faith: 'so long as one man is in prison, I am not free; so long as one community is enslaved I belong to it'.

The supreme task of our generation is to give a soul to the growing world-consciousness, to develop ideals and institutions necessary for the creative expression of the world soul, to transmit these loyalties and impulses to future generations and train them into world citizens. To this great work of creating a new pattern of living, some of the fundamental insights of Eastern religions, especially Hinduism and Buddhism, seem to be particularly relevant, and an attempt is made in these lectures to indicate them. No culture, no country, lives or has a right to live for itself. If it has any contribution to make towards the enrichment of the human spirit, it owes that contribution to the widest circle that it can reach. The contributions of ancient Greece, of the Roman Empire, of Renaissance Italy to the progress of humanity do not concern only the inhabitants of modern Greece or modern Italy. They are a part of the heritage of humanity. In the life of mind and spirit we cannot afford to display a mood of provincialism. At any rate, a mobilization of the wisdom of the world may have some justification at a time when so many other forms of mobilization are threatening it.

I am aware of the scale and difficulty of the problems on which I touch. I am not a trained theologian and can only speak from the point of view of a student of philosophy who has endeavoured to keep abreast with modern investigations into the origin and growth of the chief religions of the world, and it seems to me that in the mystic traditions of the different religions we have a remarkable unity of spirit. Whatever religions they may profess, the mystics are spiritual kinsmen. While the different religions in their historical forms bind us to limited groups and militate against the development of loyalty to the world community, the mystics have always stood for the fellowship of humanity. They transcend the tyranny of names and the rivalry of creeds as well as the conflict of races and the strife of nations. As the religion of spirit, mysticism avoids the two extremes of dogmatic affirmation and dogmatic denial. All signs indicate that it is likely to be the religion of the future.

I have a feeling that it is not quite proper for me to write a book where I have to depend for information at least in part on translations, but I thought that it was no use waiting for a scholar who shall have a proper and critical knowledge of Sanskrit and Hebrew, Greek and Latin, French and German, who alone could get all the sides in proper order, for such a scholar has not yet been born. Even translations could be used with care and judgement. So I felt that it was time that some one with some knowledge got together the main points into order. Again, I wish to lay claim to the task of a historian and not that of a partisan. If I have misrepresented any point of real importance, no one will be more grieved than myself. Those who know the extent and intricacy of the ground traversed will readily pardon less serious errors.

These lectures were given in the years 1936–8, and though they have been revised and slightly expanded for publication, their informal character has been retained. There is inevitably a certain amount of repetition in a book of this kind. I have made no serious attempt to avoid it, partly because it would have tended to spoil the construction of individual lectures and partly because a certain amount of repetition of general principles in different connexions has some value in itself. The book is intended more for the larger public interested in the higher pursuits of the mind and problems of human culture and living than for the professional student of philosophy. Though the book has not the structural perfection which the importance of the theme requires, I hope there is a certain unity of outlook binding the different sections.

I desire to thank the Delegates of the Clarendon Press for

undertaking the publication of the book and for permitting me to use material already published by them, and to thank the staff of the Press for the way in which the publication has been carried out. Sir Richard Livingstone kindly read the proofs and I am greatly indebted to him. Lastly I would take this opportunity to pay a tribute of gratitude to Professor J. H. Muirhead, to whom this work is dedicated and whose critical sense and clear judgement have been my unfailing help in almost all the things that I have written in the last twenty years. Neither he nor Sir Richard Livingstone is, however, responsible for the views contained in this book.

S. R.

CONTENTS

I

THE WORLD'S UNBORN SOUL[1]

WERE I to express adequately my feelings at the honour this ancient University has done me by electing me to this newly founded Chair of Eastern Religions and Ethics, I should be tempted to become somewhat elaborate and perhaps tedious. Permit me therefore to express my gratitude to you with a plain 'Thank you'.

Six years ago I spent a few months in this University. I was, however, a stranger within its gates, in it but not of it. I therefore appreciate the honour of being received into this fellowship of men and women united in their loyalty to the supreme ideal of truth and in their resolution to practise it for the welfare of humanity. When I look at the names of my colleagues and think of the learning and scholarship they represent, I realize my own limitations and can only plead for all the indulgence which they can offer and I very much need.

I

To attempt to understand one's age is an undertaking full of difficulties. No one who is in it can take a detached view of it. However, as rational beings, we cannot help asking what modern life in all its intense activity and rapid change signifies, what the sense of it all is, for, as Socrates tells us, the noblest of all investigations is the study of what man should be and what he should pursue.[2]

Human history is not a series of secular happenings without any shape or pattern; it is a meaningful process, a significant development. Those who look at it from the outside are carried away by the wars and battles, the economic disorders and the political upheavals, but below in the depths is to be found the truly majestic drama, the tension between the limited effort of man and the sovereign purpose of the universe. Man cannot rest in an unresolved discord. He must seek for harmony, strive for adjustment. His progress is marked by a series of integrations, by the formation of

[1] An Inaugural Lecture delivered before the University of Oxford on 20 October 1936.

[2] Plato, *Gorgias*, 487.

more and more comprehensive harmonies. When any particular integration is found inadequate to the new conditions, he breaks it down and advances to a larger whole. While civilization is always on the move, certain periods stand out clearly marked as periods of intense cultural change. The sixth century B.C., the transition from antiquity to the Middle Ages and from the Middle Ages to modern times in Europe, were such periods. None of these, however, is comparable to the present tension and anxiety which are world-wide in character and extend to every aspect of human life. We seem to feel that the end of one period of civilization is slowly drawing into sight.

For the first time in the history of our planet its inhabitants have become one whole, each and every part of which is affected by the fortunes of every other. Science and technology, without aiming at this result, have achieved the unity. Economic and political phenomena are increasingly imposing on us the obligation to treat the world as a unit. Currencies are linked, commerce is international, political fortunes are interdependent. And yet the sense that mankind must become a community is still a casual whim, a vague aspiration, not generally accepted as a conscious ideal or an urgent practical necessity moving us to feel the dignity of a common citizenship and the call of a common duty. Attempts to bring about human unity through mechanical means, through political adjustments, have proved abortive. It is not by these devices, not at any rate by them alone, that the unity of the human race can be enduringly accomplished.

The destiny of the human race, as of the individual, depends on the direction of its life forces, the lights which guide it, and the laws that mould it. There is a region beyond the body and the intellect, one in which the human spirit finds its expression in aspiration, not in formulas, a region which Plato enters when he frames his myths. It is called the soul of a being, the determining principle of body and mind. In the souls of men to-day there are clashing tides of colour and race, nation and religion, which create mutual antagonisms, myths, and dreams that divide mankind into hostile groups. Conflicts in human affairs are due to divisions in the human soul. The average general mind is respectful of the *status quo* and disinclined to great adventures, in which the security and isolation of the past have to be given up. It is not quite convinced by the moral collapse of the present system reposing on a ring of national egoisms held in check by mutual fear and hesitation, by ineffective treaties and futile resolutions of international tribunals. 'Do you imagine', asks Plato in the *Republic*, 'that political constitutions spring from a tree or a rock and not from the dispositions of the citizens which turn the scale and draw all else in their direction? . . . The constitutions are as the men are and grow out of their characters.'[1] A society can be remade only by changing men's hearts and minds. However much we may desire to make all things new, we cannot get away from our roots in the old. Let us go for some distance into the past and trace the ideas which rule the present.

II

The moulding influences of modern civilization, the spirit of science and rationalism, secular humanism and the sovereign State can be traced to the period of classical antiquity.

1. The Greeks laid the foundations of natural science for the European world. To analyse and explore, to test and prove all things in the light of reason, was the ambition of the Greek mind. No part of life is excluded from criticism by the dictates of the State or the scruples of the scriptures. The Greeks were the first to attempt to make life rational, to ask what is the right life for man and to apply the principles of reason and order to the chaos of primitive beliefs. Socrates warned us against the unexamined life and subjected the unanalysed catchwords of his time to careful scrutiny. He had firm faith that it is the nature of man to do right and walk straight. Human nature is fundamentally good, and the spread of enlightenment will abolish all wrong. Vice is only a miss, an error. We can learn to become good. Virtue is teachable.

Plato tells us that the universal or the general idea determines the nature of a particular individual and has greater reality than the latter. The philosopher is one who seeks to escape from the realm of the transient and contemplates the

[1] viii. 544. See Jowett's E.T.

world of real being freed from all confusion and error, which infect the objects of everyday experience. The world of ideas is the only realm of certainty in which man can dwell secure, freed from opinion and probability. The most obvious example of such truth is to be seen in the general propositions of mathematics.

2. Yet the Greek could never forget that his main concern was with man in his full concrete reality. His bodily desires should be given free play, his mental powers full scope. Every side of his nature should be developed so as to produce a harmony in which no part tyrannizes over the rest. Here is a definition of happiness attributed to Solon and approved by Herodotus. 'He is whole of limb, a stranger to disease, free from misfortune, happy in his children and comely to look upon. If in addition to all this he ends his life well, he is of a truth the man of whom thou art in search, the man who may rightly be termed happy.'[1] The Greeks were not famous for their religious genius or moral fervour. We do not come across any hunger for the eternal or any passionate indignation against injustice. The main religion of the Greeks was the worship of the Olympian gods. Originally they were powers or forces of nature, though they soon became representative of human qualities. Dionysus, Aphrodite, Hermes, Artemis, each of them represents some quality of man. They were magnified human beings free

[1] 1–32, Rawlinson's E.T., vol. i, p. 16; Solon prays to the Muses: 'Let me at all times obtain good fortune from the blessed gods and enjoy honourable repute among men.' Ischomachus in the *Economics* of Xenophon reckons among subjects of prayer 'health, bodily strength, good repute in the city, kindly relation with friends, safety in war, increase of wealth'. An echo of this view is found in Aristotle, who defines happiness as 'Prosperity combined with virtue; or independence of life; or that existence which, being safe, is pleasantest; or a flourishing state of prosperity and of body, with the faculty of guarding and producing this; for it may be said that all men allow happiness to be one or more of these things. If then happiness is this sort of thing, these must be parts of it; good birth, the possession of many friends, wealth, the possession of good children, the possession of many children, a happy old age: further the excellence of the body as health, beauty, strength, great stature, athletic power; also good repute, honour, good fortune, virtue. For a man would then be most independent, if he possessed both the personal and the external goods since besides these there are no others' (*Rhetoric*, 1360 b). Jebbs's E.T. Plutarch records a prayer, 'put off old age, thou beautiful Aphrodite'.

from old age and death.[1] Sometimes, as in Aeschylus, their justice and righteousness are insisted upon; but more often, as in Euripides, the gods display their might in a manner that defies all judgement by merely human standards, though it may be in conformity with the ways of natural forces. The sense of mystery was felt strongly in the presence of divine powers so long as they were conceived as natural forces, but it diminished somewhat when they were anthropomorphized. If we measure the nature of a religion by the sense of mystery it induces in its followers, the mythology of the Greeks is not religion of a high quality. The Sophists questioned the right of what religion taught to control man's conduct. It was at best a human convention.[2]

Religious beliefs, however, were useful for political purposes. Some god or other guards every city with special care. The religious festivals were open to the Greeks and closed to others. If Socrates was executed and Anaxagoras exiled for attacking traditional beliefs, it was because of their unpatriotic impiety. It was more political oppression than religious persecution. If the Sophists did not for long subvert the piety of the ancients, if Epicurus admitted the existence of the gods, even while he denied them any part in the government of the world, if the Stoics with the most pronounced rationalism still employed the old religious dynamic, it was because they knew the social value of religion.[3]

[1] Sophocles, *Oedipus Coloneus*, 607–15.

[2] Protagoras expresses clearly the easy view of the Sophists: 'I do not know whether God exists or does not exist, nor what is his nature; there are many obstacles to such knowledge, the obscurity of the subject and the shortness of man's life' (*Fr.* 4).

[3] The essentially subordinate part played by religion in the Greek view can be illustrated by a reference to the doctrine of future life. Even Plato on occasions felt uncertain about life after death, whether it is immortality or dreamless sleep (*Republic*, ii. 363, iii. 387). Aristotle is not clear on the subject, for he suggests that when a man is dead, neither good nor evil affects him any more (*Nichomachean Ethics*, 1115 a. 25). The Stoics denied personal immortality though on occasions they affirmed the survival of the soul till the general conflagration. The Greeks played with the belief of future life, though they were little affected by it. In its great days the Greek mind remained positivist and humanistic and was indifferent to the fate of the soul. An ordinary young Athenian Glaucon in Plato's *Republic* answers the question 'Have you not heard that our soul is immortal?': 'No, really I have not' (608).

It is true that in Pythagoras and Plato, the Orphics and the Neoplatonists, mystic elements were found, but these tendencies were by no means representative of the Greek spirit. Pindar and Pericles, Thucydides and Socrates, who represent the Greek genius at its best, with their visions of art and science, with their conceptions of civic life and aspiration, were essentially humanist thinkers.[1] The mystery religions believed in the deification of man, and the typical Greek has no use for it. Pindar writes: 'Two things alone there are that cherish life's bloom to its utmost sweetness amid the fair flowers of wealth—to have good success and to win therefor fair fame. Seek not to be a God; if the portion of these honours falls to thee, thou hast already all. The things of mortals best befit mortality.'[2] There are passages in Plato which ask us to mistrust our nature, to see in it an incurable taint, and exhort us to live in the world of the unseen, but in them Plato is not voicing the Greek spirit.[3]

3. Devotion to the city-State filled the spiritual vacuum in the Greek consciousness. The city was the unit of Greek society and claimed the devotion of its citizens. No Greek city was willing to submit to the leadership of another.[4] The funeral oration of Pericles proclaims service of the *polis*, which is both Church and State in one, as the highest duty. Since each city had a consciousness of its own superiority, the Greeks failed to develop a larger loyalty towards a union of the whole Greek world. They could not organize and act

[1] 'Supposing Plato and Pindar to have a vein of Orphism and Pythagoras's queer ideas on numbers, supposing Aeschylus to be touched with mysticism and Euripides with mysticism and morbidity, the student of the Greek genius has a right to disregard their peculiarities, if he feels that he has his hand on an essential quality in Hellenism and that they are inconsistent with it' (Livingstone, *The Greek Genius and its Meaning to Us*, 2nd ed., 1915, p. 21; see also p. 22).

[2] *Isthm*. 4. 12.

[3] *Laws*, 918. Rohde says in *Psyche* (1925), E.T., chap. xiii, that the Platonic spirit is an alien phenomenon in Greece. Sir Richard Livingstone writes: 'Though in a thousand ways Plato is a Greek of the Greeks, in all that is most distinctive in his thought, he is a heretic' (op. cit., p. 183). For a different view see W. R. Inge, *The Philosophy of Plotinus* (1918), vol. i, pp. 71–4.

[4] Grote writes: 'In respect to political sovereignty complete disunion was among their most cherished principles. The only source of supreme authority to which a Greek felt respect and attachment was to be sought within the walls of his own city' (*A History of Greece*, vol. iii, p. 41).

together, and their lives were spent in violent conflicts of the mutually repellent autonomies. Plato, it is true, dreamed of an ideal society, but it was conceived as a city-State, not a commonwealth of mankind. Greek civilization came to an end mainly on account of its adherence to the false religion of patriotism.[1] While it gave Europe the habit of disinterested pursuit of knowledge,[2] it also left her a negative legacy of the untenability of holding up patriotism as the highest virtue. With the disappearance of the city-State, Greek patriotism died or survived as public spirit. Rome, which succeeded Greece, was powerful for a time, but her religion had a special relation to the State. Worship was a public duty or civic function carried out by an official priesthood. The citizens may have their own private beliefs, so long as they publicly acknowledge the religion of the State. New worships were readily accepted and Rome soon became a museum of strange faiths. Besides, the dignity of the gods was greatly prejudiced when wielders of supreme power in the State like Julius Caesar and Augustus were deified.[3] The political apotheosis removed the last shred of mystery from religion and made it into a 'national anthem'. Such a religion could neither satisfy the immortal longings of man nor supply the spiritual unity which could bind the different provinces of Rome. Each of them had its own religious forms and practices and despised those of its neighbours, and in the hour of her trial localism prevailed and Rome failed. By the time the old tradition broke down the new current of Christianity had set in.

III

The vital urge to the development of medieval culture, which attained high and beautiful expression in the twelfth and thirteenth centuries, was derived from the Judaic-Christian conception of life. Some Hellenists are inclined

[1] 'This state worship was the spiritual disease that Hellenism died of' (A. J. Toynbee, *Essays in Honour of Professor Gilbert Murray* (1936), p. 308).

[2] 'Men differ from beasts and the race of the Hellenes from barbarians in that they are better educated for thought and for its expression in words' (*Isocrates*, xv. 293).

[3] In the last part of his rule Commodus believed in his identity with the god Hercules, whose reincarnation he pretended to be.

to suggest that this movement is an unhappy interruption of human progress. It is said that Europe would have been a very different place, more humane and peace-loving, less given to national and racial feuds, cultural and religious strife, if the essential rationality and cosmopolitanism of the Stoics had been allowed to leaven the European world, if the persecutions of Marcus Aurelius had exterminated the Christian creed. Such speculations are profitless, for history has taken a different course. Nature obviously had a different intention.

Rome's military conquests brought her into contact with other communities and her spiritual poverty exposed her to foreign religious influences. After a period of struggle, Christianity won. Even as Justinian's closure of the schools of Athens defined the end of the ancient world, the conversion of Constantine gave an official recognition to the victory of Christianity. While retaining the Jewish beliefs in a living God and passion for righteousness, it absorbed Greek thought and Roman traditions.

1. Its two chief contributions to European thought are an insistence on the insufficiency of the intellectual and the importance of the historical. Both Judaism and Christianity take their stand on revelation. While for the most spiritual of Greek thinkers God was the 'Idea of the Good', 'The First Mover', 'The Ruling Principle', Reason or Logos, for the Jews and the Christians, God is a supreme person who reveals His will to His lawgivers and prophets. Christians believe in addition that God took the form of man and led a human life on earth. Again, while the greatest of Hellenic thinkers had no conception of history as a purposive process with a direction and a goal, but believed it to be a cyclic movement, the Jews had faith in an historical fulfilment.[1] The Jewish consciousness lived in the intense expectation of some great decisive event which will be the definitive solution of the historical problem. The Messianic idea, which is the determining factor in Jewish history, survived in

[1] Cf. Isaiah: 'This is the purpose that is purposed upon the whole earth: and this is the hand that is stretched out upon all the nations. For the Lord of hosts hath purposed, and who shall disannul it? and his hand is stretched out, and who shall turn it back?' (xiv. 26–7).

Christianity. The Christian view represents a blend of the Greek and the Jewish conceptions of the historical. In the works of St. Augustine, who stood at the meeting-point of the two worlds, the classical and the Christian, we find the struggle between the two conceptions. When he saw the great catastrophe happening before his eyes, the decay and death of the Roman Empire, the end of what seemed the most stable structure the world had seen, he pointed to the transcendent reality of God, the one changeless being above all the chances and changes of life. This is the central idea in his *Confessions*. The Jewish emphasis on the historical, and the Christian doctrine of incarnation are difficult to reconcile with the absolute and non-historical character of the Godhead. The vigorous intellectual life of the Middle Ages was devoted to the explication of this problem and the finding of credible justifications for the other doctrines of the faith. In the theological writings of Thomas Aquinas we find an impressive attempt to build a system of Christian theology with the aid of the cold logic of the Aristotelians. In spite of these great attempts, however, the problem still remains unsolved.[1]

The very completeness of the edifice of thought raised by the Middle Ages left little room for undiscovered facts and paralysed thought.

2. When righteousness is practised, not for its own sake but because it is the will of God, it is practised with a fervour and a fanaticism that are sometimes ungodly. When the will of God is known, we feel driven to pass it on and think it intolerable that it should be disobeyed. 'The Lord God

[1] A great Russian theologian, Nicholas Berdyaev, refers to this difficulty thus: 'According to the dogma of the Church and its prevailing philosophy, the possibility of a movement or of an historical process in the depths of divine life would appear to be incompatible with the Christian consciousness. There exists, indeed, a wide-spread Christian doctrine which denies that the principle of movement and of tragic destiny can affect the nature of the Divine Being. But I am deeply convinced that the Christian doctrine of the immobility and inertia of God and the Absolute, and of the effectiveness of the historical principle only in the creative and relative world that differs essentially from the Absolute is a purely exoteric and superficial doctrine. And it ignores what is most inward and mysterious, the esoteric truth implicit in the doctrine of the divinity' (*The Meaning of History*, E.T. (1936), p. 47).

hath spoken, who can but prophesy?'[1] While such a belief gives definiteness, conviction, and urgency to the ethical message, which no abstract logic could give, it at the same time shuts the door against all change and progress.

The Jews first invented the myth that only one religion could be true. As they, however, conceived themselves to be the 'Chosen People',[2] they did not feel a mission to convert the whole world. The Jews gave to Christianity an ethical passion and a sense of superiority; the Greeks gave the vague aspirations and mysteries of the spirit a logical form, a dogmatic setting; the Romans with their practical bent and love of organization helped to institutionalize the religion. Their desire for world dominion transformed the simple faith of Jesus into a fiercely proselytizing creed. After the time of Constantine, authorities, clerical and secular, displayed systematic intolerance towards other forms of religious belief, taking shelter under the words 'He that is not with me is against me, and he that gathereth not with me, scattereth'.

Add to this the idea that the Kingdom is not of this world and Augustine's distinction of the Two Cities and the world becomes a fleeting show, beauty a snare, and pleasure a temptation. The highest virtue is abstinence and mortification. 'If any man come to me, and hate not his father, and mother, and wife, and children, and brethren, and sisters, yea, and his own life also, he cannot be my disciple.' Under the shadow of this great renunciation social impulses declined and intellectual curiosity slackened.

3. The doctrine of the State as a divine creation was supported by the apostles and the Primitive Church. 'Render unto Caesar the things that are Caesar's.' 'The powers that be are ordained of God.' It was one of the elementary duties of the Christians to pray for princes and other powers. The supremacy of the State obtained religious support.

The conquests of the Romans imposed unity on a large part of Europe and gave it a characteristic civilization with its laws and languages. Roman law still forms the basis of the codes of several European countries. Before the close of the fifth century the Roman Empire of the West had

[1] Amos iii. 8. [2] Deuteronomy xiv. 2.

fallen before the arms of the northern invaders, and though a shadow of Rome's ancient power and name still survived at Constantinople, Europe had lost its former political unity. But the idea of cultural unity was sustained to some extent by the Holy Roman Empire. Though there were local and feudal anarchy and a good deal of fighting in the Middle Ages, her greatest representatives, Charlemagne and Otto, Barbarossa and Hildebrand, Aquinas and Dante, believed in one Church and one Empire. The capture of Constantinople by the Turks in 1453 destroyed the last remains of the Roman Empire in the East and ushered in a new era.

While medieval Christianity gave to Europe a sure sense of the reality of the unseen, which holds the key to the destiny of man and the clue to right conduct, and thus redeemed even the intellectual and artistic pagans from an easy, self-centred, and self-complacent superficiality, it imposed on Europe religious bigotry, which stifled free intellectual inquiry and fostered narrowness and obscurantism. But people whose physical and mental powers are unexhausted cannot remain content with such an order. The elements of a freer life gradually asserted themselves. Though the Middle Ages had lived in the shadow of antiquity and were more concerned with its forms than the spirit, still through a gradual inward ripening of the mind the easy and natural thought of the ancient Greeks, their exactitude of conception and experiment, attracted attention. The scholastic movement itself prepared the way for a rationalist revival. The greatest minds had a perception of the interrelations of the divine and the human. Dante tells us that divine providence has set before man two ends: blessedness of this life, which consists in the exercise of his natural powers, and blessedness of eternal life, which consists in the fruition of the vision of God. Religion and humanism are not opposites. Each needs the characteristic gifts and graces of the other. This recognition prepared the way for the belief in the perfectibility of man and society which was later raised to the rank of a dogma.

IV

The Renaissance is the great age of disintegration and rebirth, when for good or ill the organic unity of life of the

Middle Ages, derived from its religious orientation, passed away, and the new world of Copernicus and Columbus, of Luther and Calvin, of Galileo and Descartes, of Machiavelli and Henry VIII, came to birth. The history of the last four hundred years in Europe has been a simultaneous growth in political freedom, economic prosperity, intellectual advancement, and social reform, but it has also been a slow and sure decay of traditional religion, morality, and social order. If in one sense it has been a progress, in another it has been a reaction, marked by a departure from the authentic foundations of life. A new civilization, based on the three Greek ideals of rationalist philosophy, humanist ethics, and nationalist politics, has been growing up.

1. The Renaissance gave back to Europe the free curiosity of the Greek mind, its eager search for first principles as well as the Roman's large practicality and sense for the ordering of life in harmony with social utility. These were pursued with a passion, a seriousness, an almost religious ardour, which Europe acquired during the long centuries of medieval religious discipline.

Under the influence of the new movement aiming at a complete rehabilitation of the human spirit, science started on its unfettered career. The sky changed with Copernicus, and the habitable world with the explorers. The scientific and technological achievements cast the world into a closely knit unity and modern history slowly grew into the stature of world history.

Philosophical thought was moulded by the prestige of science. The reassertion of the mental habits of the Graeco-Roman world dates from Descartes, who rejects all that his intellect cannot include. He tries to put an end to the capricious multifariousness of opinion by the practice of the critical method. Truth is contained only in that which can be recognized clearly and distinctly. What is unclear and mysterious is not true. Truth lies where all men think alike, in judgements of universal validity. Mathematics is the great example of ideal truth. Spinoza, like Kant, aimed at a strictly scientific metaphysics and clothed his thoughts in the form of geometrical propositions. Metaphysics should be strict science and contain no arbitrariness. 'Truth', says

Spinoza, 'would be eternally hidden from the human race, had not mathematics, which deals, not with ends, but with the nature and properties of figures, shown to man another norm of truth.'[1] So he treats of God, understanding, and human passions as though they were circles and triangles. Nature becomes an enormous silent machine which is indifferent to the values of man. Even if we call the former by the name of God, it does not come nearer the human being. 'For the reason and will which constitute God's essence must differ by the breadth of all heaven from our reason and will, have nothing in common with them, except the name; as little, in fact, as the dog star has in common with the dog, the barking animal.' Leibniz breaks up the one world of Spinoza into an infinitely large number of parts which move according to eternally existing laws and have neither the right nor the power to alter by a hair's breadth, the order which is independent of them. Kant raises the question whether a science of metaphysics with a logical structure like that of the well-established mathematical and natural sciences is possible. These latter have acquired a scientific character on account of the universal rules, the synthetic *a priori* judgements, which they employ. Since these rules are applicable only within the limits of possible experience, metaphysics, which aims at the transcendent, is an impossibility. The passion for law, for rule, dominates Kant's philosophy. Rule expresses truth and justifies conduct. An action is right if we so act that the principle of it can be made a general rule. Hegel does not ask whether it is necessary for metaphysics to be a science, but strengthens the belief in the autonomy of reason. For him philosophy is the self-development of the spirit, its natural and necessary unfolding.

The English school of empiricism would get rid of all ideas which do not correspond to actual facts, of all propositions which cannot be tested by experience. Locke wished to rid philosophy of futile speculations into the inscrutable. In his hands even natural science becomes uncertain. 'In physical things', says he, 'scientific knowledge will still be out of our reach.' Sense is the only way of knowing, and it

[1] *Ethics*, pt. 1, Appendix.

cannot give us certainty. Though his intellectual successor Berkeley imparted a theological impulse to his empiricism and admitted the reality of spirits, human and divine, Hume developed the logical implications of the empirical attitude when he left us with a world of impressions and ideas about whose origin and significance we know next to nothing. The successors of the rationalist and empirical schools to-day are dominated by the scientific method. Some of the recent writings of realists remind us of Humian analysis and scepticism. A contemporary German thinker, Husserl, says that it is his desire 'to discover a radical beginning of a philosophy which, to repeat the Kantian phrase, will be able to present itself as science', 'to furnish philosophy with a scientific beginning'.[1] The infallibility of the Church had yielded to the infallibility of scientific reason. As it in its turn seems to be failing us, we are in a tide of reaction against it. The different philosophical tendencies of voluntarism, pragmatism, and vitalism are indications of the transition from the predominantly rationalistic period of human development.

2. To conserve the ancient wisdom and practise the ancient virtue was the ambition of the humanist thinkers of the fifteenth and sixteenth centuries. They aimed at an escape from a life regulated by rigid ecclesiastical tradition into one of joyous freedom and unfettered spontaneity. Earthly life becomes the object of all striving and action. The critical spirit helps us to see the relativism of all moral codes. We refuse to be satisfied by mere statements about right and wrong, but ask for their reasons. We long for freedom from convention, mistaking it for real freedom. Conventions are said to be mere inhibitions and habits an orthodoxy. A cold dissection of the deepest things men have lived by ends in libertarian experiments in morals. Intellectual and artistic refinement places no check on brutal lusts and savage passions. The faith that the spread of reason will abolish all irrational outbursts has disappeared. There is more violence, oppression, and cruelty than there used to be. Man tries to rule his conduct by means external to himself,

[1] *Ideas*, by E. Husserl, E.T. by W. R. Boyce Gibson, pp. 27 and 30 (1931). See also Ayer, *Language, Truth, and Logic* (1936).

by technique and not self-control. Morality as an individual regeneration, an inner transformation, is not accepted.

Under the influence of the democratic conception of the right of all individuals as members of the society to the full life and development of which they are individually capable, the old landed economy of feudalism broke up, and the new money economy with the beginnings of economic individualism and the promise of modern industrialism developed. The release of the middle classes, which was effected by the abolition of privilege and feudalism, was succeeded by the claim of the working classes to a fair share in the wealth they produce. Liberal attempts to free the workers from their ignorance, isolation, and poverty by gradual humanitarian legislation and increased taxation seemed to be very slow, and a new programme of abolishing capitalism, which is said to be the root cause of all political and social evils, by persuasion and constitutional methods if possible and by violence and revolution if necessary, became more popular. Everywhere a tendency towards State absolutism has been growing. The pressure of society on the individual is not less effective to-day than it was in the days of barbarism. The view that social discipline is intended to assist the development of the innate goodness in man, which he does not altogether abandon even when his nature is heated by passion, finds little support. Coercion becomes justified both within and without the State.

The influence of the Renaissance aided the breaking of the power of the Papacy, in the establishment of Protestantism, and the right of free inquiry. Luther put the Bible in place of the infallible Church and held it to be an unerring expression of God's relation to man. The Reformation insists on the right of the individual reason to determine the sense of the inspired scripture. Though in theory the interpretation of the Bible was left to the individual thinker, in practice the members of the different Churches were required to accept their varying interpretations of the contents of the Bible. Each Church thought itself to be the special depositary of the only true exposition of the perfect will of God.

From the philosophical side, attacks were made on the

traditional religion. If the world is an expression of law, if the universe is mechanical in character, God is necessary perhaps to set up the machinery which can work of itself. He is only the architect of the world. The theism of the Middle Ages lapses into deism. If the machine can work of itself it can also set itself up and start working.

While the philosophers of the Enlightenment and German Idealism attempt to reconcile Christian truth with the findings of reason, Schleiermacher sets out to prove that it is in conformity with the conditions of religious consciousness. Ritschl tries to establish that it is consistent with the cultural ethos. Thus Christian theology, which was once based on a sovereign act of God transcending all human powers of comprehension, gets steadily rationalized and is recommended on the ground that it can be reconciled with scientific truth and ethical values. The latter thus become more important than the revelation itself. The new spirit, which questioned the conventional forms of religion and the mediation of the priesthood between God and man, could not fail to go forward and question the scripture itself, and then all sense of the supernatural.

Humanism is the religion of the majority of the intellectuals to-day. Most of us who profess to be religious do so by habit, sentiment, or inertia. We accept our religion even as we do the Bank of England or the illusion of progress. We profess faith in God but are not inclined to act on it. We know the forms of thought but do not have the substance of conviction. When men have lost the old faith and have not yet found anything solid to put in its place, superstition grows. The long-starved powers of the soul reassert their claims and shift the foundations of our mind. The weak, the wounded, and the overstrained souls turn to psycho-analysis, which deals with the problems of the soul under the guise of rationality and with the prestige of science. It tells us that man is only rational in part. The authoritarian creeds, which take us back to pre-Renaissance days, appeal to those who find the life of pure reason so utterly disconcerting. Revivals overtake us, and we yield to them in the faith that something is better than nothing. The age is distracted between new knowledge and old belief, between the cheap godless naturalism of the intellectuals and the crude revivals of the fundamentalists. As piety in any real sense has been effectively destroyed for large numbers, the national State absorbs all their energies and emotions, social, ethical, and religious.

3. The State which is the most powerful organization is least hampered by inner scruples or outer checks. Man in the community is at least half-civilized, but the State is still primitive, essentially a huge beast of prey. We have no strong public opinion, or effective international law, to restrain the predatory State. The fear of defeat or of a disastrous break-down is all that prevents an outburst.

Nations have become mysterious symbols to whose protection we rally as savages to fetishes. They claim to be enduring entities each sufficient to itself and independent of the rest. They are trained to believe that there would be no impoverishment of the world if other nations perished and they themselves were left intact. Speaking of Athens, Pericles says: 'We of the present generation have made our City in all respects most self-sufficient to meet the demands of peace or war.'[1] If the modern Frenchman, German, or American is sincerely convinced of his own immeasurable superiority to the 'lesser breeds without the law' and proclaims himself as the source and consummation of world civilization, he is only the spiritual heir of the Greeks and the Jews. While Plato knew that patriotism was not enough, that it was something of a pious fraud, he yet commended it on grounds of social expediency.[2] For him barbarians were enemies by nature, and it was not improper to wage war on them even to the point of enslaving or extirpating them.[3] The influence of the Jews, who were intensely conscious of being not as other men are, helped to strengthen the sacred egoism of the nation. Paul reaffirmed the dichotomy when he divided 'vessels of mercy afore prepared into glory' from 'vessels of wrath fitted to destruction' on the basis of religion, and patriotism used it for its purposes. The antitheses of the Greek and the barbarian, of the Jew and the Gentile, of Nordic and non-Nordic, have all a family likeness. Only the other day did we hear a great leader declare that 'Germany is

[1] Thucydides, ii, E.T. by Marchant.

[2] *Republic*, 414 b.

[3] *Republic*, v. 470 c–471 a.

our religion', the glory of the blood and soil of 'eternal Germany' is the sole purpose of existence justifying any sacrifice of individual liberty and thought. These resounding appeals for national hegemony and racial domination have a common origin and accent.

V

What then is the position to-day? Uncertainty, a fundamental agnosticism, a sense of uneasiness that we are hastening confusedly to unknown ends. In his famous cartoon *The Twentieth Century Looks at the Future*, Max Beerbohm depicts a tall, well-dressed, somewhat stooping figure looking out over a wide landscape at a large question-mark which hangs over the distant horizon like a malignant star. The future is incalculable. We do not know what we want. In previous periods men had a clear conception of the goal they were aiming at. It is either a life of reason or a triumph of religion or a return to old perfection. We are aware of the emptiness and the profaneness of our life, but not of a way of escape from it. Some advise us to retain our respect for reason and submit to fate. Others tell us that the task is too much for man and we are only to wait for a saviour who alone can set right the disorder in the heart of things. Some gaze back in spirit to the mellow vistas of the nineteenth century, of industrial prosperity, colonial expansion, and liberal humanitarianism, honestly persuaded that the world was better off under the guidance of men of birth and breeding, and are prepared to fight a last battle for authority and order. A vision of the medieval order with Church and theocracy, militarism, and despotism for its principles is sometimes held up before us. All these efforts are irrelevant to our times. They are like doses of morphia which give us temporary relief but cause permanent injury to the health. Neither a contented fatalism nor religious expectancy nor reversions to the past can give meaning to a world which is in search of its soul. The slow dying of the old order need not fill us with despair, as it is the law of all nature that life comes only by death. Every civilization is an experiment in life, an essay in creation, to be discarded when done with. With the infinite patience of one who has endless time and limitless resources at her absolute command, Nature slowly, hesitatingly, often wastefully, goes on her triumphant way. She takes up an idea, works out its form till, at the moment of its perfect expression, it reveals some fundamental flaw, and then breaks it up again to begin anew a different pattern. Yet in some way the wisdom and spirit of all past forms enter into those which succeed them and inspire the gradual evolution of the purpose of history.

To-day the soul of man no longer rests upon secure foundations. Everything round him is unsteady and contradictory. His soul has become more complicated, his spirit more bitter, and his outlook more bewildered. But his unrest is not a mere negative force. He is not only oppressed by new doubts but is inspired by new horizons, new perspectives, and a thirst for new relations with fellow men. He has reached a more advanced state of spiritual maturity, and so the dogmas of traditional religions are no longer able to answer his questions or overcome his doubts. The present profound *malaise* is really a form of growing-pains. The new world for which the old is in travail is still like an embryo. The components are all there; what is lacking is the integration, the completeness which is organic consciousness, the binding together of the different elements, making them breathe and come to life. We cannot live by instinct, habit, or emotion. We need a rational faith to sustain a new order of life and rescue us from our mental fag and spiritual anxiety.

The great periods of human history are marked by a widespread access of spiritual vitality derived from the fusion of national cultures with foreign influences. If we take Judaism we find that Abraham came from Mesopotamia and Joseph and Moses from Egypt. Later, Judaism shows the influence of Hellenism. Asia Minor and Egypt exercised considerable influence over the Greek development. The creative genius of the medieval world came from Palestine. The transition to the modern world was marked by the recovery of the ancient. In times of trouble we draw the profoundest inspiration from sources outside us, from the newly recovered past or the achievement of men under different skies. So, perhaps, the civilizations of the East, their religions and ethics, may offer us some help in negotiating difficulties that we are up against. The only past known to the Europeans emerging from the Middle Ages was the Biblical, and the Graeco-Roman and their classics happen to be the subjects studied in the great universities founded in that period. Now that we have the whole world for our cultural base, the process of recovery and training in classics cannot cease with listening to the voices of Isaiah and Paul, Socrates and Cicero. That would be an academic error, a failure of perspective. There are others also who have participated in the supreme adventure of the ages, the prophets of Egypt, the sages of China, and the seers of India, who are guide-posts disclosing to us the course of the trail. Of the living non-European civilizations, the chief are the Islamic, the Chinese, and the Hindu. The Islamic has the same historical background as Judaism and Christianity, which is well known in the West. The humanist civilization of China was considerably affected by the religious conceptions of India, especially the Buddhist. Religion, however, has been the master passion of the Hindu mind, a lamp unto its feet and a light unto its path, the presupposition and basis of its civilization, the driving force of its culture, and the expression—in spite of its tragic failures, inconsistencies, divisions, and degradations—of its life in God. In the West, even in the most sympathetic quarters, Hindu thought is in general a subject for respectful but in every sense distant homage, not of living concern. The institution of this Chair by the far-sighted generosity of Mr. and Mrs. Spalding—which is a sign of the times, pregnant with meaning—and the unprecedented appointment of an Asiatic to an Oxford Chair are motived, I take it, by a desire to lift Eastern thought from its sheltered remoteness and indicate its enduring value as a living force in shaping the soul of the modern man.

VI

1. Hinduism adopts a rationalist attitude in the matter of religion. It tries to study the facts of human life in a scientific spirit, not only the obvious facts, the triumphs and defeats of men who sleep in spiritual unconsciousness, but the facts

of life's depths. Religion is not so much a revelation to be attained by us in faith as an effort to unveil the deepest layers of man's being and get into enduring contact with them.

The religions of the world can be distinguished into those which emphasize the object and those which insist on experience. For the first class religion is an attitude of faith and conduct directed to a power without. For the second it is an experience to which the individual attaches supreme value. The Hindu and the Buddhist religions are of this class. For them religion is salvation. It is more a transforming experience than a notion of God. Real religion can exist without a definite conception of the deity but not without a distinction between the spiritual and the profane, the sacred and the secular. Even in primitive religion, with its characteristic phenomena of magic, we have religion, though not a belief in God. In theistic systems the essential thing is not the existence of the deity, but its power to transform man. *Bodhi*, or enlightenment, which Buddha attained and his followers aim at, is an experience. Perfect insight (*sambodhi*) is the end and aim of the Buddhist eightfold path. There are systems of Hindu thought like the Sāṁkhya and the Jaina which do not admit God but affirm the reality of the spiritual consciousness. There are theists like Rāmānuja for whom the spiritual consciousness, though not God Himself, is the only way in which God can be known. All, however, are agreed in regarding salvation as the attainment of the true status of the individual.[1] Belief and conduct, rites and ceremonies, authorities and dogma, are assigned a place subordinate to the art of conscious self-discovery and contact with the divine. This distinctiveness of the Hindu religion was observed even by the ancients. Philostratus puts in the mouth of Apollonius of Tyana these words: 'all wish to live in the nearness of God, but only the Hindus bring it to pass'.[2]

[1] 'ātmaprāptilakṣaṇam mokṣam.'

[2] About spiritual experience, Sir Charles Eliot writes that 'it has been confirmed by the experience of men whose writings testify to their intellectual power and has commanded the respect of the masses. It must command our respect too, even if it is contrary to our temperament, for it is the persistent ideal of a great nation and cannot be explained away as hallucination or charlatanism' (*Hinduism and Buddhism*, vol. i (1921), p. lxii).

Brahman, which is the Sanskrit word for the Absolute, is the principle of search as well as the object sought, the animating ideal and its fulfilment.[1] The striving of the soul for the infinite is said to be Brahman. The impulse that compels us to raise the question of the true, the divine, is itself divine. Brahman stands for the breath, 'the breath of the power of God', as it is said in the Wisdom of Solomon. It is man's sense of the divine as well as the divine, and the two meanings coalesce. The transcendent self stoops down as it were and touches the eyes of the empirical self, overwhelmed by the delusion of the world's work. When the individual withdraws his soul from all outward events, gathers himself together inwardly and strives with concentration, there breaks upon him an experience, secret, strange, and wondrous, which quickens within him, lays hold on him, and becomes his very being. Even if God be an idea and has no reality apart from one's ideation, that which frames the idea of God and strives to realize it is itself divine.[2] Our longing for perfection, our sense of lack, our striving to attain consciousness of infinity, our urge to the ideal, are the sources of divine revelation. They are to be found in some measure in all beings. The very fact that we seek God clearly proves that life cannot be without Him. God is life. Recognition of this fact is spiritual consciousness.

To say that God exists means that spiritual experience is attainable. The possibility of the experience constitutes the most conclusive proof of the reality of God. God is 'given', and is the factual content of the spiritual experience. All other proofs are descriptions of God, matters of definition, and language. The fact of God does not depend on mere human authority or evidence from alleged miraculous events. The authority of scripture, the traditions of the Church, or

[1] *Indian Philosophy*, 2nd ed. (1929), vol. i, p. 163 n.

[2] The Apostle has given the classical expression to this paradox: 'Work out your own salvation with fear and trembling; for it is God who worketh in you both to will and to do of his good pleasure' (Phil. ii. 12–13). 'When a soul truly desires God, it already possesseth Him' (St. Gregory). When Pascal uttered the anguish of his soul in the silence of the night, he heard the answer: 'Be comforted, thou wouldst not have sought Me unless thou hadst found Me.'

the casuistries of schoolmen who proclaim but do not prove, may not carry conviction to many of us who are the children of science and reason, but we must submit to the fact of spiritual experience, which is primary and positive. We may dispute theologies, but cannot deny facts. The fire of life in its visible burning compels assent, though not the fumbling speculations of smokers sitting around the fire.

While realization is the fact, the theory of reality is an inference. There is difference between contact with reality and opinion about it, between the mystery of godliness and belief in God. A man may know much about theology but yet be lacking in the spirit of religion. The Hindu thinkers warn us against rationalistic self-sufficiency. The learned run far more risks than the unlearned.[1] There are two ways in which we deceive ourselves: the easy way of the unlearned who believe that the world we see is all, and the laborious way of the learned who establish the truth of naturalism and are deceived by the definite. Both of them succeed in shutting us away from the reality of our being.

The process of self-discovery is not the result of intellectual analysis but of the attainment of a human integrity reached by a complete mastery over nature. The old faith in mere reason that we will act properly if we think rightly is not true. Mere knowledge is of the nature of a decoration, an exhibit with no roots. It does not free the mind. In the *Chāndogya Upaniṣad* Nārada confesses that all his scriptural learning has not taught him the true nature of the self, and in the same Upaniṣad, Svetaketu, in spite of his study of the scriptures for the prescribed period, is said to be merely conceited and not well instructed.[2] Spiritual attainment is not the perfection of the intellectual man but an energy pouring into it from beyond it, vivifying it. The *Kaṭha Upaniṣad* says: 'As the self existent pierced the openings of the senses outward, one looks outward, not within himself. A certain thoughtful person, seeking immortality, turned the eye inward and saw the self.'[3] It is seeing with the spiritual eye of the pure in heart, who have overcome the passions of greed and envy, hatred and suspicion, that is here insisted

[1] *Bṛhadāraṇyaka Upaniṣad*, iv. 4. 10; *Īśa Up.* ix.
[2] vi. 1. 3.
[3] iv. 1.

on. This is the fulfilment of man's life, where every aspect of his being is raised to its highest point, where all the senses gather, the whole mind leaps forward and realizes in one quivering instant such things as cannot be easily expressed. Though it is beyond the word of tongue or concept of mind, the longing and love of the soul, its desire and anxiety, its seeking and thinking, are filled with the highest spirit. This state of being or awareness to which man could attain is the meaning of human life. It is religion, and not mere argument about it, that is the ultimate authority for one's ideas of God and life. God is not an intellectual idea or a moral principle, but the deepest consciousness from whom ideas and rules derive. He is not a logical construction but the perceived reality present in each of us and giving to each of us the reality we possess. We are saved not by creeds but by gnosis, *jñāna*, or spiritual wisdom. This is the result of the remaking of man. Logical knowledge is comparable to a finger which points to the object and disappears when the object is seen. True knowledge is awareness, a perception of the identity with the supreme, a clear-sighted intuition, a dawning of insight into that which logic infers and scriptures teach. An austere life turns knowledge into wisdom, a pundit into a prophet.[1]

This is not, however, to attribute strength to sentiment, or derive illumination from ignorance. The truth of the experience does not arise from the mystery of its origin or the delight it causes in us. It is due to the fact that it satisfies our wants, including the intellectual, and thus gives peace of mind to the individual and contributes to the social harmony of the community. He who enters into an awareness of the real is the complete man whose mind is serene and whole being at rest. It is essential for us to seize and sift our intuitions, for the dangers of mistaking paradoxes for discoveries, metaphors for proofs, and words for truth are quite serious. If we are suspicious of the claims of intel-

[1] See *Bṛhadāraṇyaka Up.* iv. 4. 21. Ruysbroeck says: 'If we desire to taste God in our own selves we must pass beyond reason. . . . We must remain despoiled and free of all images. . . . We go on to a state of ignorance and darkness to suffer the higher information of the Eternal word, the image of the Father' (*The Ring*, chap. ix).

ligence we will land in a self-satisfied obscurantism. Any experience which does not fit in with tested knowledge must be rejected as hocus-pocus. To be spiritual is not to reject reason but to go beyond it. It is to think so hard that thinking becomes knowing or viewing, what we might call creative thinking. Philosophy and religion are two aspects of a single movement.

2. This view is humanistic in a deeper sense. It looks upon religion as a natural development of a really human life. Man, no doubt, is the measure of all things; only his nature contains or reflects every level of reality from matter to God. He is a many-levelled being. He may identify himself with his animal nature, the physical and the physiological, or with the self-conscious reason. The subrational vital aims, however indispensable and valuable in their own place, cannot without disaster take control of a being who after all is not and cannot be a mere animal. In the thought and life of the modern man self-conscious intellect, with its clear analysis and limited aims, takes the highest place, and suicidal scepticism is the result; for while it accepts the evidence of the senses and the results of judgement and inference, it rejects as spurious and subjective the deeper intuitions which discursive reason must take for granted. Faith in conceptual reason is the logical counterpart of the egoism which makes the selfish ego the deadliest foe of the soul. True humanism tells us that there is something more in man than is apparent in his ordinary consciousness, something which frames ideals and thoughts, a finer spiritual presence, which makes him dissatisfied with mere earthly pursuits. The one doctrine that has the longest intellectual ancestry is the belief that the ordinary condition of man is not his ultimate being, that he has in him a deeper self, call it breath or ghost, soul or spirit. In each being dwells a light which no power can extinguish, an immortal spirit, benign and tolerant, the silent witness in his heart. The greatest thinkers of the world unite in asking us to know the self. Mencius declares: 'Who knows his own nature knows heaven.' St. Augustine writes: 'I, Lord, went wandering like a strayed sheep, seeking thee with anxious reasoning without, whilst thou wast within me. . . . I went round the streets and squares of the city of

this world seeking thee, and I found thee not, because in vain I sought without for him who was within myself.' We make a detour round the universe to get back to the self. The oldest wisdom in the world tells us that we can consciously unite with the divine while in this body, for this is man really born. If he misses his destiny, Nature is not in a hurry; she will catch him some day and compel him to fulfil her secret purpose. Truth, beauty, peace, power, and wisdom are all attributes of the divine self which awaits our finding.

What is our true self? While our bodily organization undergoes changes, while our thoughts gather like clouds in the sky and disperse again, the self is never lost. It is present in all, yet distinct from all. Its nature is not affected by ordinary happenings. It is the source of the sense of identity through numerous transformations. It remains itself though it *sees* all things. It is the one thing that remains constant and unchanged in the incessant and multiform activity of the universe, in the slow changes of the organism, in the flux of sensations, in the dissipation of ideas, the fading of memories. Our personality, which we generally take for our self, is conscious only by fits and starts. There are large gaps in it, without consciousness. The seer always exists. Even if death comes, the seer cannot die. 'When the sun and the moon have both set, the fire has gone out, and speech has stopped, Yājñavalkya, what serves as the light for a man? The self serves as his light (*ātmaivāsya jyotir bhavati*). It is through the light of the self that he sits, goes out, works, and returns.'[1] Nothing on the object side can touch the subject. Feelings and thoughts are on the same plane as objects and events in so far as they are observable. Things can be different from what they are without the self being different from itself. This persisting self which is universal seer to all things seen, this essential awareness which nothing has the power to suppress, which knows nothing of having been born as it knows nothing of dying, which is the basis of all knowledge, of dreams and ecstasies, is, says Saṁkara, not capable of proof, nor does it need any, for it is self-proven (*svasiddha*). Though itself inconceivable, it is the

[1] *Bṛhadāraṇyaka Up.* iv. 3. 6.

ground of every possibility of conceiving, of every act of knowledge. Even he who denies it presupposes it in so far as he thinks. It is not an organ or a faculty but that which vivifies and disposes every organ and every faculty, the vast background of our being in which all organs, intellect, and will lie. Body, mind, and the world are almost arbitrary restrictions imposed on this consciousness. This universal self is in our ordinary life obscured by psychological impurities and fluctuations and becomes confused with the empirical self. The latter, which is a system of energies, psychological and logical, lays claim to perfect independence and individuality, little knowing that it can conserve itself only by perpetual change. We take our personality to be our most intimate and deepest possession, our sovereign good. But it belongs to the object side, itself shaped by relative happenings, mutable and accidental, as compared with the self. We can think about it, calculate its interests, sacrifice them on occasions. It is a sort of psychological being that answers to our name, is reflected in the looking-glass (*nāmarūpa*), a number in statistical tables. It is subject to pleasure and pain, expands when praised, contracts when criticized, admires itself, and is lost in the masquerade.[1] The *Muṇḍaka Upaniṣad* makes a distinction between the two birds which dwell in the same tree, one eating the sweet fruit and the other looking on without eating.[2] The former is the empirical self and the latter the transcendental self.

The phenomenal character of the empirical self and the world answering to it is denoted by the word *māyā*, which signifies the fragility of the universe. *Māyā* does not mean that the empirical world with the selves in it is an illusion, for the whole effort of the cosmos is directed to and sustained by the one supreme self, which though distinct from everything is implicated in everything. The criticism that Hindu thought is pantheistic makes out that the supreme being, which is complete and impenetrable, is yet filled with things which live, breathe, and move each according to its nature. Nothing can be born, exist, or die in any degree, nothing can have time, place, form, or meaning, except on this universal background.

[1] *Chāndogya Up.* viii. 3. 12. [2] ii. 1. 2.

Māyā is a term employed also to indicate the tendency to identify ourselves with our apparent selves and become exiled from our spiritual consciousness with its maximum of clarity and certainty. This tendency is the expression of the working of self-conscious reason. Intellectual activities are a derivation, a selection, and, so long as they are cut off from the truth which is their secret source, a deformation of true knowledge (*avidyā*) which has its natural result in selfishness. The aim of all human living is self-definition. It is to isolate the substantial permanence which each finite life possesses deep down from the strife of empirical happenings. We can exceed the limits within which human consciousness normally functions. Man can abstract from his body and flesh, from his feelings and desires, even from thoughts which rise like waves on the surface of his mind, and reach a pure awareness, the naked condition of his pure selfhood. By steady discipline he can be led back to the pure being, the subject that reflects, and reach that state of immediacy and unity in which all chaos disappears. When we break through the ring of smoke round the self, unwrap the sheaths which cover it, we achieve here and now in the flesh the destiny of our being. The 'I', the *ātman*, the universal self, infinitely simple, is a trinity of transcendent reality (*sat*), awareness (*cit*), and freedom (*ānanda*). Such is the way in which we formulate in intellectual terms the truth of our own being to which our ordinary consciousness is now alien. We recommend to others this truth by conceiving of it as pure superpersonality or cosmic personality manifesting the universe. The negative method which requires us to give up the creaturely, to divest ourselves of all qualities, push slowly out beyond all distinctions, reveals the inexpressible sanctity of the experience. This exaltation, this motionless concentration, this holy calm and deep serenity which is like the state of a deep sea at rest, reflecting heaven on its surface, or, in the image of the *Bhagavadgītā*, 'still as a flame in a windless place', bathed as it were in an incomprehensible brightness (*tejas*), is hard to describe. An austere reticence or a negative account is all that is open to us. When, however, we lapse back from this state into our ordinary consciousness, we represent the self as another with its transcendent majesty. We quake and shiver, bleed and moan with a longing gaze at it. We dare not even lift up our eyes. We are filled with a desire to escape from the world of discord and struggle. In this mood we represent the supreme as the sovereign personality encompassing this whole world, working through the cosmos and ourselves for the realization of the universal kingdom. If the personal concept is more prominent, the individual seeks his development in a humble, trustful submission to God. We may adopt the mode of *bhakti* or devotion, or the method of *jñāna* or contemplation by which the self, set free from all that is not self, regains its pure dignity. The attainment of spiritual status when refracted in the logical universe appears as a revelation of grace.

Śaṁkara brings out clearly the distinction between the absolute self, the divine person, and the human individual:

> 'Therefore the unconditioned self, being beyond speech and mind, undifferentiated and one, is designated as "not this, not this"; when it has the limiting adjuncts of the body and organs which are characterized by imperfect knowledge, desire, and work, it is called the empirical individual self; and when the self has the limitation of the creative power manifesting through eternal and unlimited knowledge, it is called the inner ruler and divine person. The same self, as by its nature transcendent, absolute, and pure, is called the immutable and supreme self.'[1]

When we seek to grasp the reality superpersonal in itself, personal from the cosmic end, by conceptual methods, we must note that logically precise formulas are at best provisional and incomplete. The definiteness and transparency of the symbols do not mean that the thing signified has been grasped completely. Those who have no contact with reality, no insight into truth, accept the relative symbol for the absolute truth. In their self-confident jugglery with symbols and definitions they forget the thing itself. Only the background of reality can transform the empty sounds of words into

[1] 'tasmān nirupādhikasyā'tmano nirupākhyatvān nirviśeṣatvād ekatvācca neti neti ti vyapadeśo bhavati. avidyākāmakarmaviśiṣṭakāryakaraṇopādhir ātmā saṁsārī jīva ucyate. nityaniratiśaya jñānaśaktyupādhir ātmā' ntaryāmīśvara ucyate. sa eva nirupādhiḥ kevalaḥ śuddhaḥ svenasvabhāvenākṣaram para ucyate' (Śaṁkara on *Bṛhadāraṇyaka Up.* iii. 8. 12).

significant expressions of truth. Our pictures of God have no reality save a spiritual one. They are not in things outside ourselves. 'The mortal made the immortal', says the *Ṛg Veda*. The Indian monk Bodhidharma, in the sixth century of our era, said to the emperor Leang Wu Ti: 'There is no Buddha outside the spirit. Save the reality of the spirit all is imaginary. The spirit is the Buddha and the Buddha is the spirit. To imagine a Buddha outside the spirit, to conceive that he is seen in an external place is but delirium.'[1] The distinction of superpersonal and personal, *nirguṇa* and *saguṇa*, is found in all mysticism, Eastern or Western. If Śaṁkara distinguishes Brahman from Īśvara, Eckhart contrasts the Godhead (*Deitas*) with God (*Deus*). While God is the personal triune God of Church doctrine, which 'becomes and dis-becomes', the pure Godhead stands high above God, and is the ground of the possibility of God, who is absorbed in the Godhead, which is beyond being and goodness.

The two familiar criticisms that for Hindu thought the world is an illusion (*māyā*), that it is divine (pantheism) cancel each other and point out that the Hindu is aware of both the upward and the downward movements. The way to the knowledge of the divine has two sides, the negative and the positive. The negative takes us to the spiritual consciousness, the silent witness which dissolves all form and thought, what Plotinus, the Neoplatonic Christian mystic called Dionysus the Areopagite, Eckhart, Ruysbroeck aim at, the 'Divine Darkness', 'the nameless, formless nothing'. But there is the way of affirmation by which the God-conscious man affirms that the great silent sea of infinity, in whose mysterious embrace the individual loses his name and form, is also the over-mastering, all-embracing life. Here is the refrain of the *Chāndogya Upaniṣad*:[2] 'This whole world has that being for itself. That is reality. That is the self. That art thou, O Śvetaketu.' The self is the core of being, the inner thread by being strung on which the world with all its variety exists. It is the real of the real, *satyasya satyam*. The manifold universe is not an illusion; it is being, though of a lower order, subject to change, waxing and waning,

[1] Wieger, *A History of the Religious Beliefs and Philosophical Opinions in China*, E.T. (1927), p. 524.

[2] vi. 10 ff.

growing and shrinking. Compare again, 'He who dwells in the Earth, who is other than the Earth, whom the Earth does not know, whose body the Earth is, who controls the Earth from within, he is yourself, the inner controller, the immortal.' This is said to be true of all things in the world, subjective and objective, which are the manifestations of the 'unseen seer'.[1] Even Śaṁkara admits that 'This whole multiplicity of creatures existing under name and form in so far as it has the supreme Being itself for its essence is true; if regarded as self-dependent is untrue'.[2] Everything everywhere is based on reality.[3] For the Hindu thinkers, the objective world exists. It is not an illusion. It is real not in being ultimate, but in being a form, an expression of the ultimate. To regard the world as ultimately real is delusion (*moha*).

While the criticism regarding the illusory nature of the world suggests the superpersonal restful character of the supreme, that of pantheism brings out its ceaseless self-expression or active creativity. It is not true to contend that the experience of the pure realm of being, timeless and perfect, breeds in us contempt for the more familiar world of existence, which is unhappily full of imperfection. Reality and existence are not to be set against each other as metaphysical contraries. Nothing on earth is utterly perfect or utterly without perfection. Those who have the vision of perfection strive continually to increase the perfection and diminish the imperfection. Life is for ever striving for its fuller creative manifestation. For one who has the vision of the supreme, life, personality, and history become important. The life of God is the fullness of our life.

When man apprehends the supreme being, returns to the concrete, and controls his life in the light of its truth, he is a complete man. He reaches an almost inconceivable universality. All his powers which have been hitherto bound up with narrow pursuits are liberated for larger ends. The doctrine of *māyā* tells us that we fall away from our authentic being if we are lost in the world of empirical objects and

[1] *Bṛhadāraṇyaka Up*. iii. 7.

[2] 'sarvam ca nāmarūpādivikārajātam sadātmanā eva satyam, svatas tu anṛtam' (Śaṁkara on *Chāndogya Up*. vi. 3. 2).

[3] 'sadāspadam sarvam sarvatra' (Śaṁkara on *Bhagavadgītā*, xiii. 14).

earthly desires, turning our back on the reality, which gives them value. They are so alluring that they provoke ardent desires, but they cannot satisfy the inner being, and in the world outside they break forth into frantic disorder. This does not mean that we have to neglect worldly welfare or despise body and mind. The body is a necessity for the soul. A system which believes in rebirth cannot despise bodily life, for every soul has need of it. Personal life is not to be repressed in order to gain the end of religion. It is to be re-created and purified in the light of the higher truth. He in whom the spark of spirit glows grows into a new man, the man of God, the transfigured person. The divine penetrates his self, wells up and flows through him, absorbing him and enriching him within it. God is not for him another self, He is the real self closer than his own ego. 'I live, yet not I, but it is Christ who liveth in me.' In the order of nature, he keeps up his separate individuality; in the order of spirit, the divine has taken hold of him, remoulding his personality. The pride of a self-conscious individual yields to the humility of a God-centred one. He works in the world with the faith that life in its pure quality is always noble and beautiful and only its frustration evil.

3. The fundamental truths of a spiritual religion are that our real self is the supreme being, which it is our business to discover and consciously become, and this being is one in all. The soul that has found itself is no longer conscious of itself in its isolation. It is conscious rather of the universal life of which all individuals, races, and nations are specific articulations. A single impulsion runs beneath all the adventures and aspirations of man. It is the soul's experience of the essential unity with the whole of being that is brought out in the words, 'Thou in me and I in thee'. Fellowship is life, lack of fellowship death. The secret solidarity of the human race we cannot escape from. It cannot be abolished by the passing insanities of the world. Those who are anxious to live in peace with their own species and all life will not find it possible to gloat over the massacres of large numbers of men simply because they do not belong to their race or country. Working for a wider, all-embracing vision they cut across the artificial ways of living, which seduce us

from the natural springs of life. Our normal attitudes to other races and nations are no more than artificial masks, habits of thought and feeling, sedulously cultivated by long practice in dissimulation. The social nature of man is distorted into queer shapes by the poison poured into his blood which turns him into a hunting animal. Racialism and nationalism, which require us to exercise our baser passions, to bully and cheat, to kill and loot, all with a feeling that we are profoundly virtuous and doing God's work, are abhorrent to the spiritually awakened. For them all races and nations lie beneath the same arch of heaven. They proclaim a new social relationship and serve a new society with civil liberties for all individuals, and political freedom for all nations, great and small.

VII

The collapse of a civilization built on the audacities of speculative doubt, moral impressionism, and the fierce and confused enthusiasms of races and nations need not dishearten us, for it has in it elements of an antisocial and antimoral character, which deserve to perish. It is directed to the good, not of mankind as a whole, but of a powerful privileged few among individuals as well as nations. Whatever is valuable in it will enter into the new world which is struggling to be born. In spite of all appearances to the contrary, we discern in the present unrest the gradual dawning of a great light, a converging life-endeavour, a growing realization that there is a secret spirit in which we are all one, and of which humanity is the highest vehicle on earth, and an increasing desire to live out this knowledge and establish a kingdom of spirit on earth. Science has produced the necessary means for easy transport of men and communication of thought. Intellectually the world is bound together in a web of common ideas and reciprocal knowledge. Even the obstacles of religious dogma are not so formidable as they were in the past. The progress of thought and criticism is helping the different religions to sound the note of the eternal, the universal, the one truth of spirit which life obeys, seeks for, and delights in at all times and in all places. We are able to see a little more clearly that the truth of a religion is not what is singular and private to it, is not the mere letter of the law which its priests are apt to insist on, and its faithful to fight for, but that part of it which it is capable of sharing with all others. Humanity's ultimate realization of itself and of the world can be attained only by an ever-increasing liberation of the values that are universal and human. Mankind is still in the making. Human life as we have it is only the raw material for human life as it might be. There is a hitherto undreamt-of fullness, freedom, and happiness within reach of our species, if only we can pull ourselves together and go forward with a high purpose and fine resolve. What we require is not professions and programmes but the power of spirit in the hearts of men, a power which will help us to discipline our passions of greed and selfishness and organize the world which is at one with us in desire.

II

THE SUPREME SPIRITUAL IDEAL: THE HINDU VIEW[1]

I

WHEN we enter the world of ideals the differences among religions become negligible and the agreements striking. There is only one ideal for man, to make himself profoundly human, perfectly human. 'Be ye perfect.' The whole man, the complete man, is the ideal man, the divine man. 'You are complete in the godhead', said St. Paul. The seeking for our highest and inmost self is the seeking for God. Self-discovery, self-knowledge, self-fulfilment is man's destiny.

From the beginning of her history India has adored and idealized, not soldiers and statesmen, not men of science and leaders of industry, not even poets and philosophers, who influence the world by their deeds or by their words, but those rarer and more chastened spirits, whose greatness lies in what they are and not in what they do; men who have stamped infinity on the thought and life of the country men who have added to the invisible forces of goodness in the world. To a world given over to the pursuit of power and pleasure, wealth and glory, they declare the reality of the unseen world and the call of the spiritual life. Their self possession and self-command, their strange deep wisdom their exquisite courtesy, their humility and gentleness of soul, their abounding humanity, proclaim that the destiny of man is to know himself and thereby further the universal life of which he is an integral element.

This ideal has dominated the Indian religious landscape for over forty centuries. If we wish to know the spirit of a religion which has had a long and continuous evolution, we cannot get at it by taking a cross-section of it at any one stage. It is not to be found either in its earlier phases or in its later developments Any historical process can be understood

[1] An Address delivered before the World Congress of Faiths at Queen's Hall, London, on 6 July 1936.

only by surveying the whole growth and grasping that inner meaning which is struggling for expression at every stage, though never expressed perfectly at any stage. This is the spirit which binds together the different stages of its history, which is present in the earliest as well as in the latest. What is this meaning, this spiritual core of the Hindu religion?

If we turn to the Indus valley civilization which archaeologists have unfolded for us in recent times, we see that among the relics of a religious character found at Mohenjo-daro are not only figurines of the mother goddess but also figures of a male god, who is the prototype of the historic Śiva. Obviously many of the features of modern Hinduism are derived from very early primitive sources. Sir John Marshall tells us that the god, who is three-faced, is seated on a low Indian throne in a typical attitude of *yoga*, with legs bent double beneath him, heel to heel, with toes turned downwards, and hands extended above the knees. He has a deer throne and has the elephant, the tiger, the rhinoceros, and the buffalo grouped round him.[1] This figure of Śiva, the great Yogi, has been there from nearly 3250 B.C. (if not earlier), the date which archaeologists give to the Indus valley civilization; calling upon all those who have ears to hear, the inhabitants of the native land as well as the invaders from outside who frequently pass and repass, to be kings not over others, but over themselves. Perfection can be achieved only through self-conquest, through courage and austerity, through unity and brotherhood in life.

We hear nowadays a good deal about *yoga* even in the West. It means the process, as well as the result, of balancing the different sides of our nature, body, mind, and spirit, the objective and the subjective, the individual and the social, the finite and the infinite. A passage in the *Bhagavadgītā* makes out that this world has its roots above in heaven while its branches spread out earthward.[2] The human being has his roots in the invisible though his life belongs to the passing stream of the visible. While he moves in the order of things visible, tangible, measurable in reference to time and space, while his life is subject to succession and change,

[1] *Mohenjo-daro and the Indus Civilisation*, by Sir John Marshall, vol. i, pp. 52–3 (1931).

[2] 'ūrdhvamūlam adhaḥśākham', xv. 1.

corruption and death, he is also a spirit belonging to the invisible and intangible world, which we can in no way comprehend, though we think and speak of it in symbols and metaphors drawn from the things of our world. If we think that our nature is limited by the little wave of our being which is our conscious waking self, we are ignorant of our true being. The relation of our life to a larger spiritual world betrays itself even in the waking consciousness through our intellectual ideals, our moral aspirations, our cravings for beauty, and our longing for perfection. Behind our conscious self is our secret being without which the superficial consciousness cannot exist or act. Consciousness in us is partly manifest and partly hidden. We can enlarge the waking part of it by bringing into play ranges of our being which are now hidden. It is our duty to become aware of ourselves as spiritual beings instead of falsely identifying ourselves with the body, life, or mind. While we start with the immediate and the actual, our limited self-consciousness, we can constantly increase and enrich it, gathering into it all that we can realize of the seen and the unseen, of the world around us and above us. This is the goal of man. His evolution is a constant self-transcending until he reaches his potential and ultimate nature which the appearances of life conceal or inadequately express. We are not, through this process, abolishing our individuality but transforming it into a conscious term of the universal being, an utterance of the transcendent divine. The instinctive and the intellectual both attain their fruition in the spiritual personality. The flesh is sanctified and harmonized with the spirit; the intellect is illumined and harnessed to the realm of ends. Body and mind, instinct and intellect become the willing servants of spirit and not its tyrannical masters.

The uniqueness of man among all the products of nature lies in this, that in him nature seeks to exceed itself consciously, no longer by an automatic or unconscious activity, but by a mental and spiritual effort. Man is not a plant or an animal, but a thinking and spiritual being set to shape his nature for higher purposes. He seeks to establish order and harmony among the different parts of his nature and strives after an integrated life. He is unhappy so long as he does not succeed in his attempt at reaching an organic wholeness of life. There is always a mental and moral ferment in him, a tension between what he is and what he wishes to become, between the matter which offers the possibility of existence and the spirit which moulds it into significant being.

II

The present crisis in human affairs is due to a profound crisis in human consciousness, a lapse from the organic wholeness of life. There is a tendency to overlook the spiritual and exalt the intellectual. It can be traced chiefly to the influence of the Greeks, who determined the bent of the Western mind towards science and the pursuit of truth for its own sake. Greek civilization was a magnificent achievement of the human reason and it was by no means one-sided. The Greek inheritance has enabled the West to remake the world. Earth, sea, and air have been made to yield to the service of man. Though the triumphs of intellect are great, its failures are not less great. Some of the finest things of life have escaped its meshes, which the uncouth and unlettered peasants, who lived more naturally and professed animistic conceptions of life, had possessed. Pitiful and sordid as had been their estate, they had a hope in their hearts, a spark of poetry in their lives, and a feeling of exaltation in their human relationships. Ignorant and superstitious they might have been, but wholly forsaken they were not. Their lives were not empty and devoid of content. They had their deep affections, a sense of the great value of the little things of life, love, companionship, and family attachments, an element of mystery in their make-up, a faith in the unseen which is the consolation of their dreams. The business of intellect is to dispel the mystery, put an end to the dreams, strip life of its illusions, and reduce the great play of human life to a dull show, comic on occasions but tragic more frequently. The primitive cults which helped their adherents to live healthily and happily on their own plane are dismissed as crude superstitions. Everything is stripped of soul, of inner life. This world is all, and we must rest content with it.

Religion, however, cannot be so lightly disposed of. When man gets a feeling or a fear that after all life means nothing, leads nowhere, and at bottom no one is really necessary and nothing worth while, he cannot live. Even if life be aimless, man must pursue some dream. To deny him hope is to take away his interest in life. Religions exploit this need, this fundamental insufficiency of an all-pervading positivism, this primitive hunger for fellowship. The fugitive character of life makes man fondly hope that his life is not at an end with the death of the body, that it cannot be true that the suffering of the innocent meets with no reward and the triumph of the wicked with no requital. It must be that man does count. Religions attempt to satisfy this fundamental need of man by giving him a faith and a way of life, a creed and a community, and thus restore the broken relationship between him and the spiritual world above and the human world around. While the prophet founders of religions declare that the community is world-wide and make no distinctions between the Jew and the Gentile, the Greek and the barbarian, the traders in religion declare that the greatness of one's own creed and group is the end and coercion and violence are the ways to it. They develop group loyalties at the expense of world loyalty. Such a bellicose condition is the only one in which life becomes worth while for a large number of people. There is not much to choose between these religions, which exalt belief, bigotry, and preservation of group loyalties and vested interests, and the older, cruder, primitive cults. The later, which are the more sophisticated, are the more dangerous, for they are constructions of intellect interfering with the natural relations of man.

Left to himself, man feels kinship with the whole universe, especially with living things and human beings. The sense of community is latent in the hearts of men. Even in this artificial world, where intellect has imposed on us the restrictions of tribe, race, and nation, the fundamental humanity of man wells up on occasions. When there is an earthquake in Japan or a famine in India, an explosion in a mine in Great Britain, or a crash of an airship on the Atlantic, our hearts go out to the victims. When there is an act of heroism or daring, an achievement of genius in science or art, we feel elated and do not pause to ask the religion or the race to which the author belongs. We salute spontaneously the great ones of the world and do not wait to know whether a Ranji or a Robeson is of our group or race. One touch of nature makes the whole world kin. The feeling of fellowship with the whole of humanity is implanted in our nature. We are members of a world community. It is our intellectual consciousness that breeds in us the feeling of separatist individuality, and this unnatural development is checked by artificial devices to bring men back into communal relations. Unfortunately, instead of strengthening the invisible bonds which bind man to man, irrespective of colour or race, the natural feeling of the oneness of humanity, these attempts keep men in separate camps hostile to one another. We are educated into the mystic worship of race and nation. By force and fraud, by politics and pseudo-religions, diplomats and priests exploit the baser passions of fear and greed and impose on us the deadly restraints of blood, race, and nation, and thus accentuate the division in man's soul. Political dictatorships and religious dogmatisms have no understanding of the profound identity of human beings, their passions and reactions, their ideals and aspirations in all ages and in all places. Religions, by propagating illusions such as the fear of hell, damnation, and arrogant assumptions of inviolable authority and exclusive monopolies of the divine word, and politics, by intoxicating whole peoples with dreams of their messianic missions, by engendering in them false memories, by keeping the old wounds open, by developing in them megalomania or persecution complex, destroy the sense of oneness with the world and divide humanity into narrow groups which are vain and ambitious, bitter and intolerant. By getting mixed up with politics, religion becomes degraded into a species of materialism.

We believe that we have conquered nature, simply because science has pushed the boundaries of the unknown farther from us, yet we are as far as ever from having conquered our own nature. The problems of outer organization are not so pressing in some respects, but so long as our passions of greed and selfishness are unconquered, our outer conquests will only be the material for the exercise of our inner barbarisms. Thanks to centuries of one-sided training, the barbarous occupies a large place in our nature, ready to prostrate itself before all representations of power that are external. Brute force attracts it, not moral law or spiritual ideal. It compels our respect, on account of our fear and greed, our selfish passions and crudity of mind. The tragedies of the world, individual and national, are due, in the main, to the fact that we are gripped by ruinous and explosive passions, the burden of which could not be easily shaken off, and they take us inevitably to our doom.

Life to-day, in spite of our material possessions and intellectual acquisitions, in spite of our moral codes and religious doctrines, has not given us happiness. If we knew the deepest thoughts of men to-day, we should find that there are millions who are dissatisfied with themselves and with the pursuits that absorb their energies. They have lost the radiance and gladness of life, they have no hopes to inspire, no ambitions to realize, no happiness to which they can look forward, no faith to live by. Their minds are distracted and so their action is fragmentary and futile. Let us take, for illustration, the one problem which is now demanding all our attention and effort, how to make the world safe for peace and humanity. This great country is in two minds about that question. It is unable to decide between power politics and peace politics, between binding secret agreements and the League Covenant, between international anarchy and international order and justice. We are thoroughly convinced of the futility, the horror of war and its dreadful consequences for civilization, and yet we are drifting towards it, overpowered by the machine which we have built up, as if we were not reasonable human beings but mere victims of forces blind and deep, slow and irresistible, bearing all things away. The condition of the world to-day reminds one of Joseph Conrad's *Typhoon*, the story of the adventure of a vessel carrying Chinese coolies who begin to murder each other in the midst of a terrific storm on account of some missing money. We are prepared to pay the price, run the risk of collective suicide, for the sake of national glory and honour, which are 'fictional abstractions', idols of the market-place, but are not prepared to pay the price for world peace by way of surrender of control over subject nations, a submission of national sovereignty to international control, the transformation of backward areas into mandates. Nations, like individuals, are made, not only by what they acquire, but by what they resign. We are on the eve of gigantic changes and are witnessing a struggle between clashing sets of ideas. Why should nations which have the moral leadership of the world continue to serve discredited ideals? Is it necessary to wade through war, to pass through hell, before we can settle down and adjust in a spirit of reasonableness and equity the conflicting claims of the different nations? A peace concluded at the end of a war, when passions run high, is bound to be of an unjust character, a source of bitterness and humiliation to the vanquished, like the Treaty of Versailles. It is possible to take a just view of the whole situation, and work for a constructive peace when, as yet, there is no war to disturb and distract. Wars scarcely ever achieve the ends for which they are undertaken, and even if they do, the other results they produce are so mischievous that even the victors gain little from their achievements. If only we can visualize the misery and devastation, the pain and the horror which the armaments we are piling up will cause to common people, when they go off! Statistics which give us estimates hide the sorrow of human hearts and the tension of human minds. They speak as if they were dealing with earth and water, and not flesh and blood. Will humanity declare itself to be bankrupt of all statesmanship and wisdom and transfer the future to the decision of a disastrous war? Are we, after ages of enlightenment, to admit the defeat of reason and accept a reversion to the Dark Ages, a relapse into barbarism?

We live on the surface and are afraid of thinking because it is all so confused and disordered; we suffer from conflicts. We are divided from our real nature, cut off from the universal in us by our egoistic impulses and separatist tendencies. Rodin has created that wonderful statue called *The Thinker*, the striking figure of a man sitting with his head bent, his eyes staring out into space, his brows wrinkled with thought, his face furrowed with suffering and tense with concentration, and looking at . . . what? Looking down the ages, age after age, world after world, he finds man advancing along the corridors of time, trying to control his difficult, discordant, divided self and asking, Shall we never escape from this division? Must we go on for ever aiming at the high and doing the low? Is it our fate to be for ever split selves, with bewildered outlooks, aspiring after ideals of universal human decency and practising policies which lead us to universal barbarism? Why, why cannot we have the courage and the selflessness, the vision and the generosity to regulate our affairs on principles of equity and justice?

Hindu and Buddhist thinkers with a singular unanimity make out that *avidyā* or ignorance is the source of our anguish, and *vidyā* or wisdom, *bodhi* or enlightenment is our salvation. The former is intellectual knowledge which produces self-consciousness and self-will. Our anxieties are bound up with our intellectuality, whose emergence at the human level causes a fissure or cleavage in our life. The break in the normal and natural order of things in human life is directly traceable to man's intellectuality, the way in which he knows himself and distinguishes himself from others. *Firstly*, he thinks and imagines an uncertain future which rouses his hopes and fears. The rest of nature goes on in absolute tranquillity. But man becomes aware of the inevitability of death. This knowledge of death produces the fear of death. He worries himself about ways and means by which he can overcome death and gain life eternal. His cry is, Who shall save me from the body of this death? Though he is born of the cosmic process he feels himself at enmity with it. Nature, which is his parent, is imagined to be a threat to his existence. An overmastering fear thwarts his life, distorts his vision, and strangles his impulse. *Secondly*, man's naïve at-oneness with the living universe, his essential innocence or sense of fellow feeling, is lost. He does not submit willingly to a rational organization of society. He puts his individual preferences above social welfare. He looks upon himself as something lonely, final, and absolute, and every other man as his potential enemy. He becomes an acquisitive soul, adopting a defensive attitude against society. *Thirdly*, the knowledge of death and the knowledge of isolation breed inner division. Man falls into fragmentariness. He becomes a divided, riven being, tormented by doubt, fear, and suffering. His identity splits, his nucleus collapses, his naïveté perishes. He is no more a free soul. He seeks for support outside to escape from the freezing fear and isolation. He clings to nature, to his neighbours, or to anything. Frightened of life, he huddles together with others. The present nervousness of mankind, where fear is the pervasive element of consciousness, where we are always taking precautions, avoiding entanglements, where life is always on the defensive, where man has lost his community with nature and man, is another name for spiritual death. The world in which we live to-day, the world of incessant fear (*bhaya*) and violence (*hiṁsā*), of wars and rumours of wars, where we are afraid of everything, suspect mines under our feet, snipers in thickets, poison in the air we breathe and the very food we eat, is nothing but the ordinary life of ignorance hurried up, intensified, and exaggerated. The tragedy is that we are not conscious of our ignorance. The more sick, the less sensible.

This view, that the problem of religion is inherent in the nature of man, that it arises from the division in man's soul, is supported by high authority. According to the familiar legend human history began with a grave tension in the dimness of remote antiquity, starting the dialectic movement which we witness to-day. As a result of the first transgression, the spirit of discord entered. A tremendous upheaval of the human consciousness brought about a revolution in natural relations. The Fall symbolizes the disintegration of the harmony, the lapse from the primeval condition into division, from a unitive life into a separate self-centred one. A reintegration of human nature is the meaning of salvation.

Religion is the conquest of fear, the antidote to failure and death. The fear which is an expression of man's rationality cannot be removed by any change in his circumstances. It is not an instinctive fear which can be displaced by the stimulation of other instincts. We cannot get rid of it by slipping into a subrational animal existence, by attempting to abolish altogether the reason which gives rise to the affliction. Man cannot shake off his rationality. We cannot still our doubts by drugging ourselves with myths and illusions. We can obtain a kind of psychological peace, but it will not endure. True freedom from fear can be reached only by *jñāna* or wisdom, the truth that casteth out fear. So long as religions themselves are an expression of fear, the security and protection they afford us are purchased at a terrible price and end in distorting human life. The dogmas lead to mutual destruction; the devotions become a trap for fruitless self-immolation. By demanding loyalty to warring creeds equally arbitrary and unverifiable we turn men against one another. The ideal elements of religion which make for universalism and the current beliefs and institutional practices which make for narrow group loyalties do not fit each other.

What we need is a religion of freedom, which stimulates faith not fear, spontaneity not formalism, abundant life not the monotony of the mechanical, the mechanization of mind which is dogmatism, the mechanization of ends which is conformity. When one is in contact with the universal source of life, one is filled with vitality and freedom from fear. When we discover the secret seed of spirit which lies concealed within the coatings of our nature and live by it, life becomes a pure flame full of light and happiness. 'Knowing the bliss of Brahman, he does not fear anything.'[1] 'By knowing him alone, one surpasses death.'[2] 'What sorrow, what delusion is there for him who perceives this unity?'[3] The soul is no more lonely or isolated. It becomes one with the enveloping world and is saved from despair and defiance. It enters a spiritual context in which its life finds a new and deeper significance and purpose. *Abhaya*, or freedom from fear, is a temper of mind, not the acceptance of a belief or the practice of a rite. Under the insight of such a faith our fellow men become something more than creatures of time and place separated from us by the accidents of nature, set against us by the necessities of animal existence. To be religious is to apprehend the reality of other souls. The law of love is obeyed not because it is known or willed but because life which has been more fully revealed consists in

[1] *Taittirīya Up.* ii. 8. 'May I reach the light on reaching which one attains freedom from fear' (*Ṛg Veda*, ii. 27).

[2] *Śvetāśvatara Up.* vi. 15.

[3] *Īśa Up.* 7.

loving. When the Upaniṣad says 'yasmin sarvāni bhūtāni ātmaivābhūd vijānataḥ', it means that he who realizes the universal self sees all human beings as belonging to a kingdom of ends. Spirits in unity with themselves must in the end be in unity with one another. To live as selfish individuals is to miscarry the purpose of creation. *Ahiṁsā* or fellow feeling for all living things, enfolding in its merciful arms even the lowest forms of animal life, is the natural fruit of *abhaya* or spiritual life.

The marks of genuine religion are *abhaya* or freedom from fear, expressing itself in harmony, balance, perfect agreement between body and soul, between the hands and the brain, and *ahiṁsā* or love. *Abhaya* and *ahiṁsā*, awareness and sympathy, freedom and love, are the two features, theoretical and practical, of religion. The free individual does not suffer from any conflicts. He does not give way to anger or depression—not even to what is called righteous indignation. For those who are opposed to us are our brothers from whom we happen to be estranged, and they can be won over by love and understanding. A Gandhi who declares that 'if untruth and violence are necessary for furthering the interests of my country, let my country go under' shows himself to be more religious than the so-called religious who tell us that it is sometimes our religious duty to kill![1] They are then talking as politicians, not as religious men. In this imperfect world it may be an urgent political duty to make our defences as secure as possible against attack, but under no circumstances can it be one's religious duty to slaughter one's fellow men. Nations and civilizations are not eternal. They live and die. Man is to live for the eternal values of spirit, truth, and goodness. The free man has that sovereign loyalty which belongs to true spiritual liberty.

Life is a supreme good and offers the possibility of happiness to every one. No generation has ever had so much

[1] The Bishop of London in his sermon in Westminster Abbey on 28 November 1915 said: 'Everyone that puts principle above ease, and life itself beyond mere living, is banded in a great crusade to kill Germans, not for the sake of killing, but to save the world, to kill the good as well as the bad, to kill those who have shown kindness to our wounded as well as the friends' (*The Potter and Clay*, by the Rt. Rev. A. W. Ingram (1917)).

opportunity. Yet the blessings of the earth have turned into curses on account of the maladies which afflict us, envy and hatred, pride and lust, stupidity and selfishness. Man, as he exists to-day, is not capable of survival. He must change or perish. Man, as he is, is not the last word of creation. If he does not, if he cannot, adapt himself and his institutions to the new world, he will yield his place to a species more sensitive and less gross in its nature. If man cannot do the work demanded of him, another creature who can will arise.

We need not lose hope of changing our ideals and re-ordering our life. We are not by nature savage and violent; we are highly suggestible and sensitive. We must endeavour to preserve our natural characteristics, and use our intellect to confirm, not cripple, them; we must consciously recover and retain the sense of reality and kinship with the universe, the essential solidarity of the human race. When the Hindu thinkers ask us to free ourselves from *māyā*, they are asking us to shake off our bondage to the unreal values which are dominating us. They do not ask us to treat life as an illusion or be indifferent to the world's welfare. They are asking us to escape from the illusion which holds us by the throat and makes us pursue physical satisfaction or corporate self-seeking as the highest end. It is the function of religion to reaffirm the intuitive loyalty to life and solidarity of human nature, to lift us out of the illusion of isolation and take us back to reality. The religious soul does not seek for release from suffering in the present life or a place in paradise in the next life. His prayer, in the words of the Upaniṣad, is 'Lead me from the unreal to the real, lead me from darkness to light, lead me from death to immortality'.[1] The resurrection is not the rise of the dead from their tombs but the passage from the death of self-absorption to the life of unselfish love, the transition from the darkness of selfish individualism to the light of universal spirit, from falsehood to truth, from the slavery of the world to the liberty of the eternal. Creation 'groaneth and travaileth in pain', 'to be delivered from the bondage of corruption into the liberty of the glory of the children of God'.

[1] 'asato mā sad gamaya, tamaso mā jyotir gamaya, mṛtyor mā amṛtam gamaya.'

III

How can we rise above the present vision of the world with its anarchic individualism, its economic interpretations of history, and materialist views of life? This world of *māyā* has thrown our consciousness out of focus. We must shift the focus of consciousness and see better and more. The way to growth lies through an increasing impersonality, through the unifying of the self with a greater than the self. Prayer, worship, meditation, as well as philosophy, art, and literature, help to revive and purify the inner being and predispose it to the contact with the divine. The discipline has different stages which are not clearly marked off from one another. Speaking roughly, three stages may be distinguished: purification, concentration, and identification.

They answer to the *via purgativa*, *via contemplativa*, and *via unitiva*. They are not successive steps but different points of view. The path to perfection is more a slope than a staircase. The first stage insists on the ethical preparation, which is an essential prerequisite for spiritual insight. The mind must be rid of its impurities and made a clean mirror in which the divine can be reflected. Not only the ordinary obligations but the more austere vows of chastity and poverty are taken as helpful to the development of a pure moral life. He who has no possessions is relieved of many worries; if he is vowed to obedience to a teacher, which is sometimes abused by teachers, he has no casuistical problems to puzzle out. If ascetic practices are adopted, they are for disciplining one's nature and strengthening the will and not for pleasing an angry deity or imitating a past model. Absence of cares and preoccupations is essential for spiritual life. In the *Yoga Sūtra*, which is the classic on the subject, this moral training is included under the first two heads of *yama* and *niyama* of the eightfold means (*aṣṭāṅga*) of *yoga*.[1] The obstacles to perfection are the common defects of sensuality, avarice, glut-

[1] *Yama* is negative, consisting of non-injury (*ahiṁsā*), truth-speaking (*satya*), integrity or abstinence from appropriating the property of others (*asteya*), celibacy (*brahmacarya*), and not having possessions (*aparigraha*). *Niyama* signifies the cultivation of positive virtues. It includes purity (*śauca*), contentment (*saṁtoṣa*), austerity (*tapas*), study (*svādhyāya*), and devotion to God (*īśvara praṇidhāna*). In *Yoga Sūtra*, i. 23, devotion to God is represented as one, and not the only, way of attaining *samādhi*.

tony, envy, and sloth, and they must be put to rest. The next three stages of yogic training are designed to restrain the mind from the physical side. They are bodily posture (*āsana*), control of breath (*prāṇāyāma*), and withdrawal of the senses from the objects (*pratyāhāra*). These are the aids of the contemplative life. A comfortable posture of the body and regulation of breath help to ease the mind. When we withdraw the senses from the objects, the mental discipline starts. If people sometimes go to hill-tops or monasteries, deserts and caves, it is because they are places which help to draw the soul away from its familiar surroundings. This withdrawal from the world into a solitary retreat is not essential, though it is helpful. For a disciplined mind ordinary life or familiar surroundings are no distraction. *Pratyāhāra* is what is generally known as abstraction. The three remaining stages are *dhāraṇa* or concentration, *dhyāna* or meditation, and *samādhi* or unification. It is assumed that the real nature of man, his inherent capacity for the divine, cannot be obliterated. We can reach the depths of our nature by bursting through the outer strata. Deep down in his own self is the divine secret, which we must reach. All the forms, superficial and alien, imposed and forced upon it from without, are secondary, and the spirit in us which is a constant affirmation of our oneness with the whole universe is the primary fact. The process of reaching the spirit in us is, in Plato's expression, an act of recollection, for it is there already[1] and we have only to recognize it. The process starts with a quiet introspection, the tiny beginning of spiritual contemplation. By a repetition of a text, or by focusing the mind on an external object such as an image, we try to banish intruding thoughts and collect ourselves. *Dhāraṇa* is concentration. It is the control of will, of attention. To chain the mind, which is generally compared to a restless monkey, to a single object is not easy. Irrelevant thoughts will drift in, desires and worries will disturb, and only with an effort can we fix our mind on the chosen object. When attention becomes less discursive and concentration deepens and mind ceases to wander we get into the state of

[1] 'I will put my law in their inward parts and in their heart will I write it' (Jeremiah xxxi. 33).

dhyāna or meditation. The soul becomes empty of every thought except the one meditated on, which takes possession of it. When it is awake only to the reality to which it is directed and all else is forgotten, *ekāgratā* or one-pointedness arises. Out of the brooding darkness, illumination is won.

While outer knowledge can be easily acquired, inner truth demands an absolute concentration of the mind on its object. So in the third stage of *samādhi* or identification, the conscious division and separation of the self from the divine being, the object from the subject, which is the normal condition of unregenerate humanity, is broken down. The individual surrenders to the object and is absorbed by it. He becomes what he beholds. The distinction between subject and object disappears. Tasting nothing, comprehending nothing in particular, holding itself in emptiness, the soul finds itself as having all. A lightning flash, a sudden flame of incandescence, throws a momentary but eternal gleam on life in time. A strange quietness enters the soul; a great peace invades its being. The vision, the spark, the supreme moment of unification or conscious realization, sets the whole being ablaze with perfect purpose. The supreme awareness, the intimately felt presence, brings with it a rapture beyond joy, a knowledge beyond reason, a sensation more intense than that of life itself, infinite in peace and harmony. When it occurs our rigidity breaks, 'we flow again', and 'are aware, as at no other time, of a continuity in ourselves' and know more than 'the little section of it that is our life in this world'.[1] When we find the real in our own heart, we feel exalted and humbled. The memory of the eternal illumination has enduring effects and calls for renewal. Plotinus gives a glowing description of this state.

'Since in the vision there were not two things, but seer and seen were one, if a man could preserve the memory of what he was when he was mingled with the divine, he would have in himself an image of God. For he was then one with God, and retained no difference, either in relation to himself or to others. Nothing stirred within him, neither anger nor concupiscence nor even reason or spiritual perception or his own personality, if we may say so. Caught up in an ecstasy, tranquil and alone with God, he enjoyed an imperturbable calm, shut up in his proper essence he declined not to either side, he turned not

[1] See Charles Morgan, *Sparkenbroke* (1936), p. 71.

even to himself; he was in a state of perfect stability; he had become stability itself. . . . Perhaps we ought not to speak of vision; it is rather another mode of seeing, an ecstasy and simplification, an abandonment of oneself, a desire for immediate contact, a stability, a deep intention to unite oneself with what is to be seen in the sanctuary.'[1]

The development of this power which, in the words of Plotinus, all have but few use[2] is not anything distinct from the normal operations of the mind but is acquired by a whole-hearted concentration of these on the supreme being. It is not a mystical faculty, as there is a continuous development from sense perception to the vision of the real. The different steps are not meant to enable men to find the truth by successive steps as in a process of logical demonstration but to bring them into that condition of mind in which truth reveals itself in and to them.

This process of vital realization of God is not a comfortable one for those of us who are given to the delights of the flesh and love of visible things. Natures which are marred by self-conceit and self-will will find it extremely hard to tread the path to the mountain-top. Ignorance is in the centre of the soul, has become connatural to it, and it must be burned in the fire of knowledge and annihilated. The complexes in the unconscious must be broken up. The passions and imperfections which are as old as Adam are confounded with our very selves. Their whole substance must groan and travail, must liquefy itself in order that it may reach the life eternal. All must be surrendered. Annihilation is the condition of abundance, death of life.[3] Our lack of possessiveness and proprietorship must be absolute.

In *samādhi* or ecstatic consciousness we have a sense of immediate contact with ultimate reality, of the unification of the different sides of our nature. It is a state of pure apprehension, in which the whole being is welded into one. To make this complete subjection of the whole personality

[1] *Enneads*, vi. 9. 7.

[2] Cf. John Wesley: 'I pretend to no extraordinary revelation or gifts of the Holy Ghost, none but what every Christian may receive, and ought to expect and pray for.'

[3] 'To win to the being of all, wish not to be anything', says St. John of the Cross.

to the divine a settled habit, a permanent condition, and not merely a fleeting and transitory episode, is the aim of religious discipline. Ecstasy or emotional excitement is not the goal of religious striving. The unitive life, the integration of the self which the contact brings, must become an abiding possession of the soul.

The methods adopted by religions such as contemplation and service are intended to stabilize our nature and aid the systematic purification of our whole being, essential for an integral reflection and taking in of the divine reality. Our powers are by force of habit adjusted to a life of claims and counterclaims, and if they are to be adapted to a life of universalism, a drastic process of change is necessary. When religion succeeds in making us spiritual, our conflicts are resolved, and we find ourselves in the great current of life. Nothing human is alien to us. We are no more members of this or that particular group, but belong to humanity as a whole. We have the primary patriotism which is the love of humanity. We have respect for the diversity which is natural to the constitution of things and understand the unity underlying it all. We feel in our deeper selves our oneness with our fellows and unity with life. We realize the idea in the mind of God of what each individual is meant to be. The unity of all life, which is the intellectual assumption of science, becomes the consuming conviction of the sage. He feels and acts as he knows. By his self-mastery and purity he attains that contentment in the depths, that serenity in the soul, that profound peace which is not mere emotion, what the Hindus call *śānti*, which enables its possessor to say: 'I have overcome the world.' However wicked the world may be, whatever pain and misery it may contain, he is not ruffled, for he has seen that at rock bottom things are good, and there is a power which is ceaselessly overcoming evil and transforming it into good. He is aware of the central drive of the universe. It drives through him and he has a vision of what it is driving at, the transformation of the indwelling of God into a conscious fact, of the possibility or hope of God for every man into a realization. He has the sense of power by which he creates meaning and beauty out of the conficts of human desires and passions. For the sake of his sanctities he would embrace poverty and exile and would much rather have his tongue plucked out than shape it to a lie. He does not remain proudly on the mountain-top apart from the world but devotes his energies to its spiritualization and raising it to its highest levels. No one, not at any rate he who has perfected himself, can be at ease when the world cries for help. The well-being of others becomes his deepest concern. He loves his fellows with a tenderness and depth unknown to others. He can no more help loving humanity than a sunflower can help pointing to the sun. To be saved is not to enter a region of blissful ease and unending rest. The saved one becomes an elemental force of nature, a dynamo of spirit, working at a stupendously high velocity. The renunciation he has practised does not require him to flee from the world of works but only to slay the ego sense. Eternal life is here and now. It is the life of the eternal part of us, of the light within us, of intelligence and love, whose objects are incorruptible.

The soul in solitude is the birthplace of religion. Moses on the lonely Mount of Sinai, Buddha under the *bodhi* tree lost in contemplation, Jesus by the Jordan in the stillness of prayer, Paul in the lonely sojourn in the desert, Mohammad on a solitary mount at Mecca, Francis of Assisi in his prayers in the remote crags of the highlands of Alverno, found the strength and the assurance of the reality of God. Everything that is great, new, and creative in religion rises out of the unfathomable depths of the soul in the quiet of prayer, in the solitude of meditation.

IV

Now and again the criticism is brought against the Hindu ideal that it is not sufficiently ethical in character. It is difficult to know what exactly this criticism means. An ideal which requires us to integrate ourselves, to maintain a constant fight with the passions which impede the growth of the soul, to wage war on lust, anger, and worry, cannot but be deeply ethical. The power to perceive reality, to absorb it and be absorbed by it, is the reward of a severe and sustained process of self-purification.

Nor can it be said that the saint does not believe in the

efficacy of human action, in the power of suffering and sacrifice to redeem the world. Those who realize that every soul belongs to God cannot help working for the divinization of the world. The great march of humanity towards the far-off divine ideal is directed and held together in the central lines by the effort and example of the saints, who are the natural leaders of mankind. Religion is not for them a refuge from reality. They do not escape to a world of fantasy and thus evade the responsibilities of life. The Hindu ideal affirms that man can attain his immortal destiny here and now. The Kingdom of God is within us and we need not wait for its attainment till some undated future or look for an apocalyptic display in the sky. It is true that the deepest secret of spiritual life is hidden from the common view and can be attained only with an effort. This effort is a lonely one, a flight of the alone to the alone. It is also true that when the world tires us we go back to ourselves, plunge into the deep wells of our spiritual being and return from it refreshed, serene, satisfied, and happy. On that account, we cannot say that life has become individualistic. As a matter of fact it is an escape from individualism. When the perfected individual works for the world, he is the channel through which the divine influence flows. He is only the instrument (*nimittamātram*). He works in the spirit of the words 'I, yet not I' (*kartāram akartāram*).

The criticism has obvious reference to the political failure of India despite her profession of exalted spiritual ideals. Her leaders dwelt in prayer and let the legions pass by. Solitude and isolation were the roots of their existence. At best they fed the deer and held converse at night with the stars, healed the sick, and preached the word of God.

The criticism, which is partly justified, amounts to this, that India did not till recently take to the cult of the nation. We did not make our country a national goddess, with an historic destiny, a sacred mission, and a right of expansion. We did not worship Mother India (*bhāratmātā*) as others do, 'Britannia', 'La France', 'The Fatherland'. We did not tell the people that the enemy of India is the enemy of God and if the enemy said he, too, had a god, he could only be a false god. Our leaders disdained to become leaders of hosts, proclaiming to the people that we are the finest people on earth, the chosen race of the universe.

Secondly, let us remember that conquests and empires do not result from the exercise of religious virtues. It will do good to be reminded of William Watson's lines:

> Best by remembering God, say some,
> We keep our high imperial lot;
> Fortune, I fear, hath oftenest come
> When we forgot—when we forgot.

May it not be that the Evil One offered the nations security and aggrandizement as the price of their soul? 'All these things will I give thee if thou wilt fall down and worship me' in the guise of the Nation-State. External success and frightfulness did not attract the Indian temperament at its best.

While independence for every country is its legitimate right, there is something vulgar and philistine about aggressive nationalism which lapses into imperialism. When it overtakes us, it spoils our sight, torments our rest, confuses our values, and makes the transitory seem more important than the permanent. In the present crisis, Great Britain is not able to see clearly or act honestly on account of her imperial interests and ambitions. The world of independent sovereign nations with a mystic significance is in dissolution and will soon be a past chapter in man's history, like the world of feudalism. Let us prefer to be human.

All the same, Indian culture has failed to give political expression to its ideals. The importance of wealth and power to give expression to spirit, though theoretically recognized, was not practically realized. India has suffered for this negligence. Though she affected deeply even the strangers who came to conquer but stayed behind, politically she has failed. Thanks to the contact with the West, her people are to-day infected with the nationalistic passion, and some of them feel justified in adopting the methods of organized violence sanctified in the history of the world, for gaining political freedom, if it is not conceded to the demands of justice. The arguments which are employed the world over to justify militarism, that war is the nursery of heroic virtues like fidelity and restraint, courage and cohesiveness, health and vigour, are not unfamiliar in India. But her religious leader, who is, happily, also her leader in politics, has evolved a method to free India from political domination, which is in consonance with the religious traditions and mental background of the country. This method, which has not yet been tried on a large scale, can well serve as the moral equivalent for war in William James's words. It gives us the virtues of war without its horrors. In a famous article on 'The Doctrine of the Sword', Gandhi says:

> 'I do believe that when there is only a choice between cowardice and violence, I would advise violence. . . . I would rather have India resort to arms in order to defend her honour than that she should in a cowardly manner become or remain a helpless victim to her own dishonour. But I believe that non-violence is infinitely superior to violence, forgiveness more manly than punishment. Kṣamā vīrasya bhūṣaṇam. . . . Non-violence is the law of our species as violence is the law of the brute. The spirit lies dormant in the brute and he knows no law but that of physical might. The dignity of man requires obedience to a higher law, to the strength of the spirit. The *rishis* who discovered the law of non-violence in the midst of violence, were greater geniuses than Newton. They were themselves greater warriors than Wellington. Having themselves known the use of arms, they realized their uselessness and taught a weary world that its salvation lay not through violence but through non-violence. Non-violence in its dynamic condition means conscious suffering. It does not mean meek submission to the will of the evildoer, but it means the putting of one's whole self against the will of the tyrant. Working under this law of our being, it is possible for a single individual to defy the whole might of an unjust empire, to save his honour, his religion, his soul and lay the foundation for that empire's fall or regeneration. . . . And so I am not pleading for India to practise non-violence because she is weak. I want her to practise non-violence being conscious of her strength and power. I want India to recognize that she has a soul that cannot perish and that can rise triumphant above any physical weakness and defy the physical combination of a whole empire.'

With all her poverty and degradation, her suffering and subjection, India still bears witness to the cult of the spirit.

It is not right to complain that India has failed because she has followed after things spiritual. She has failed because she has not followed after them sufficiently. She has not learned how to make spirit entirely the master of life, but has created in recent times a gulf between spirit and life and has rested in a compromise. Some of our holy men are inclined to become creatures set apart, beings who take flight from the temporal in order to cling to the heart of the eternal. If, in our eagerness to seek after God, we ignore the interests of humanity, we may produce a few giants but we will not elevate the race. We have shown how high individuals can rise by spiritual culture and how low a race can fall by its one-sidedness. To master life, to accept it and improve it, is a difficult task for the individual and more difficult for the race. Harmony of the social order is an essential aim of the spiritual man.

To be inspired in our thoughts by divine knowledge, to be moved in our will by the divine purpose, to mould our emotions into harmony with divine bliss, to get at the great self of truth, goodness, and beauty to which we give the name of God as a spiritual presence, to raise our whole being and life to the divine status, is the ultimate purpose and meaning of human living. Some exceptional individuals have achieved this status and harmony. They are the highest type of humanity yet reached and indicate the final shape which humanity has to assume. They are the forerunners of the new race.

These men with wisdom and vitality, constant awareness and unremitting social effort, are not members of limited groups based on blood and soil but citizens of a world yet unborn, still in the womb of time.

Whatever the individual has done, the race, too, may and should eventually succeed in doing. When the incarnation of God is realized, not only in a few individuals but in the whole of humanity, we will have the new creation, the new race of men and women, mankind transformed, redeemed, and reborn, and a world created anew. This is the destiny of the world, the supreme spiritual ideal. It alone can rouse our deepest creative energies, rescue us from cold reason, inspire us with constructive passion, and unite us mentally, morally, and spiritually in a world fellowship.

III

MYSTICISM AND ETHICS IN HINDU THOUGHT[1]

I

THOUGH the British have been in India for many decades and Christian missionaries from this country are to be found there in large numbers, Indian culture occupies less space in their thoughts and studies than in those of some other countries of the West. The ordinary Englishman is interested in law and order, in political and economic relations, and is indifferent to the life and thought which alone can bind peoples together. He thinks that he has comprehended India because he has conquered it. Sir George Birdwood, with his keen sense of inquietude for Indian culture and his imaginative understanding, is an exception to the general rule. If these two great sections of humanity, Great Britain, which represents the best of Europe, and India, which is the ultimate East, with their distinctive temperaments and traditions can live together in a political system whose keynote is equality and friendship, and not dominion or subjection, it will be the greatest achievement of history. An appreciation of cultural values and psychological differences is essential if the present connexion between the two countries is not to end in a tragedy of cross-purposes. We have a proper approach to the Indian problem in the writings of Sir George Birdwood, who realized that religion represents the essential motive of Indian life.

The place of religion in the life of mankind has of late become the subject of keen and anxious discussion among the thoughtful. The hurry and distraction of our life are obvious; the deep faith in the reality of eternal values and the earnest endeavour to live, individually and socially, in the light of that faith escape notice. The indifference to

[1] The Sir George Birdwood Memorial Lecture given at the Royal Society of Arts, London, on 30 April 1937.

organized religions is the product not so much of growing secularism as of deepening spirituality.

Scrupulous sensitiveness in our search for truth is making it difficult for us to accept doubtful authority or half-heard traditions. If genuine religious belief has become for many a phenomenon of the past, it is because religions confound eternal truth with temporal facts, metaphysics with history. They have become largely a traffic with the past. For example, in Christendom theology is busy with such questions as, Are the Scriptures inspired? How shall we explain the divergencies in the accounts of the life of Christ? How shall we reconcile the Biblical account of creation with modern science? Were the Old Testament prophecies fulfilled? Shall we believe in the New Testament miracles? Acute thinkers spend their time and energies in finding modern ideas in ancient texts or reading meanings into them which are not there. So long as the life of Jesus is regarded as a mere event in history which occurred nineteen hundred years ago there can be no understanding of what that life should mean to us. A study of comparative religion has broken down the barriers behind which dogmatists seek to entrench themselves and show that their own religion is unique. Besides, the anthropomorphic conceptions which look upon God as king or conqueror, father or lawgiver, the good shepherd or the righteous judge possessing to a transcendent degree the qualities of power and virtue which we most admire in human beings, seem to many somewhat archaic and crude. They tend to hide the central truth that God is Spirit and that the only real worship is that which is in spirit and truth. We cannot say that definiteness in conception makes for depth in religion. The image narrows the thought of the divine being within human limits and works against a more spiritual conception of Godhead. As we have to live on earth, the spectacle of an incarnate God has great religious value, but a sharply defined anthropomorphism makes for narrowness and intolerance and takes us sometimes to absurd lengths. When the *Titanic* was going down, it is said that an American millionaire retired to his cabin, not to say his prayers, but to put on his dinner clothes. When asked, he explained that he wished to go before his Maker looking like a gentleman. We cannot be satisfied with gods who are inconstant and fickle, easily moved to love or anger, revengeful for trifling provocations and vexed at small things. If we educate men in the belief that God is like a father in a patriarchal society, who has His favourite children to whom He communicates His mind, we cannot blame simple people if they assume that some persons possess divine knowledge through mysterious agencies. If the Roman Catholics accept the Pope's Encyclical on Marriage, the National Socialists accept the decrees of Hitler as Holy Writ. Those who question the true faith are thrown into concentration camps, and Dante and Milton tell us in detail much that we know about them.[1]

Again, religion as a way of life is the seeking of the eternal. It is more behaviour than belief. If we believe in God we must act in the light of that faith. There are many who feel that outward conformity is all that is expected of them. We are said to be religious if we go through the round of ceremonies from baptism at birth to the solemn commitment of the body to the grave at death, even though this process is unaccompanied by any intense inward discipline or spiritual experience. If we repeat the phrases and make the gestures, we need not bother about the rest. Many of those who affirm belief in God or in future life act as if neither existed. There is a difference between what we think we believe and what we really believe. We are familiar with the story of the clergyman who asked the captain of the ship, when a storm broke out, what he was doing. The captain said: 'We have done all we could and now we can only trust in God.' The clergyman replied: 'Is it as bad as all that?' Religion is not to-day an operative force in men's lives or public affairs. Countries which stand at the head of civilization do not hesitate to slaughter thousands and thousands of human beings for the sake of their political programmes. Lady Macbeth remarked of the murder of Duncan, 'A little water clears us of this deed.' A sprinkling of holy water and the muttering of a formula will put to flight all the

[1] Is it an accident that Hitler and Mussolini have been brought up in Roman Catholic societies, where it is blasphemous to criticize infallible authority?

agonies and cruelties of the world. The difficulties of the situation are due to the substitution of religion for God, of an infallible Church or book for personal effort. If religion is to revive, it must be founded on verifiable truth. The centre should shift from reliance on external direction, whose validity is becoming more and more questionable, to a trust in experience, intimate and personal. There is a fervent desire to replace the religion of dogma by a religion of life, and the worship of the Nation-State by loyalty to a world community.

Religion begins for us with an awareness that our life is not of ourselves alone. There is another, greater life enfolding and sustaining us. Religion as man's search for this greater self will not accept any creeds as final or any laws as perfect. It will be evolutionary, moving ever onward. The witness to this spiritual view is borne, not only by the great religious teachers and leaders of mankind, but by the ordinary man in the street, in whose inmost being the well of the spirit is set deep. In our normal experience events happen which imply the existence of a spiritual world. The fact of prayer or meditation, the impulse to seek and appeal to a power beyond our normal self, the moving sense of revelation which the sudden impact of beauty brings, the way in which decisive contacts with certain individuals bring meaning and coherence into our scattered lives, suggest that we are essentially spiritual. To know oneself is to know all we can know and all we need to know. A spiritual as distinct from a dogmatic view of life remains unaffected by the advance of science and criticism of history. Religion generally refers to something external, a system of sanctions and consolations, while spirituality points to the need for knowing and living in the highest self and raising life in all its parts. Spirituality is the core of religion and its inward essence, and mysticism emphasizes this side of religion.

Mysticism is a word ill favoured by the rationalist as well as by the dogmatic theologian. It is criticized as a tendency to see things cloudily, in a golden or sentimental haze, to justify the habit of the human mind to entertain contradictory beliefs at the same time, to exalt confusion of thought. Mysticism is none of these things. It is the admission of mystery in the universe.[1] It cannot be regarded as a reproach in a world which is by all rational accounts mysterious. If we were only what we seem to be to our normal self-awareness there would be no mystery; if the world were only what it can be made out to be by the perceptions of the senses and the analysis of reason, there would be no riddle. At any rate, the mystery will not be deep, nor the riddle difficult. In our rationalistic consciousness we are ignorant of ourselves because we know only that which changes in us from moment to moment and not that which is enduring; we are ignorant of the world because we are aware of its appearances and not its true being. Mysticism is opposed to the naturalism which categorically denies the existence of God and the dogmatism which talks as if it knew all about Him. Both agree in abolishing all mystery in the world. In his exaltation of scientific integrity the rationalist can at times be as vehement, as dogmatic, and as narrow as any of the creeds which he believes himself to have supplanted. Without a sense of awe in the presence of the unknown, religion would be a petty thing.[2] There is a well-known story of St. Augustine which relates that, while meditating on his book *De Trinitate* by the sea-shore, he saw a child engaged in filling a shell from the ocean and then pouring it out into a hole he had dug in the sand. In answer to his question as to what he was doing, the child replied that he meant to empty all the water of the sea into his hole. When the great theologian gently rebuked the child about the futility of such a task, the child retorted, 'What I am doing is more likely to be accomplished than what you are trying to do, that is to understand the nature of the divine being.' In mystic religion God is not a logical concept or the conclusion of a syllogism but a real presence, the ground and possibility of all knowledge and values. Mysticism, which lays stress on

[1] Etymologically considered, the mystic is one who closes his eyes to all external things and keeps silent about the divine mysteries into which he has been initiated.

[2] Einstein puts the point thus: 'The fairest thing we can experience is the mysterious. It is the fundamental emotion which stands at the cradle of true art and true science. He who knows it not can no longer wonder, no longer feel amazement, is as good as dead, a snuffed out candle' (*The World as I See It*).

the personal experience of God, direct contact with the creative spirit, is what Bergson calls 'open religion'. The closed religions are the credal, ritualistic ones which give a sense of security to frightened children. Only an open religion which requires us to enter the spiritual stream where our spirit can refresh and restore itself can save humanity, which is half crushed by the weight of its own progress.

The criticism that mysticism is an effective spiritual instrument in the hands of political reaction points to its abuse. The mystic or the intuitive consciousness is not to be confused with the instinctive. It is not a flight to unreason or a glorification of ignorance and obscurity. It assumes the indivisible oneness of human life, whose apprehensions cannot be contrary to reason.

Pascal's well-known classification of the three ways to belief, custom, reason, and inspiration, suggests the three stages of mental evolution, sense, reason, and intuition, though they are not to be regarded as chronologically successive and separate. In the lowest stage of infancy the senses are most active. In youth we rise from the empirical to the dialectical stage when we argue and derive conclusions from observed data. At a more mature stage we obtain a synthetic and intuitive knowledge of reality by means of an experience which embraces the whole soul. But intuition, though it includes the testimony of will and feeling, is never fully attained without strenuous intellectual effort. It cannot dispense with the discipline of reason and the technique of proof. Religion itself may take three forms, primitive or sensuous, reflective, and mystical. Religion in the mystic sense is not a mere speculation of reason or a feeling of dependence or a mode of behaviour. It is something which our entire self is, feels, and does; it is the concurrent activity of thought, feeling, and will. It satisfies the logical demand for abiding certainty, the aesthetic longing for repose, and the ethical desire for perfection. In the great mystics, the *rsis* of the Upanisads, Buddha, Saṁkara, and hundreds of others, holiness and learning, purity of soul, and penetration of understanding are fused in an harmonious whole.

II

A study of the classic types of mystical experience discloses an astonishing agreement which is almost entirely independent of race, clime, or age.[1] An ultimate inward similarity of the human spirit does not mean an absolute identity of mystical experience. There are individual variations within the large framework. In the East, for example, the mysticisms of the Upaniṣads, of the *Bhagavadgītā*, of Śaṁkara, of Rāmānuja, of Rāmakṛṣna, of Zen Buddhism, of Jalāluddin Rūmi are different one from the other. Similarly in the West, the mysticisms of Plato and Paul, of Proclus and Tauler, Plotinus and Eckhart differ from one another. The variations are not determined by race, climate, or geographical situation. They appear side by side within the same circle of race or culture, developing different tendencies and traditions.

Unfortunately, a tendency has grown up of late to distinguish Eastern mysticism from that of the West, or, to be more precise, Hindu mysticism from the Christian, by contrasting the immense ethical seriousness of the latter with the ethical indifference of the former. Christian thought, it is said, is dynamic and creative. It affirms the reality of the world and the meaningfulness of life. Hindu thought, on the other hand, is said to deny the reality of the world, despair of human life, poison the very springs of thought and activity, and exalt death and immobility. It does not create power and purpose directed to high ends.

A characteristic statement of this contrast is found in Dr. Schweitzer's account of Indian thought, which we shall consider for two reasons.[2] Firstly, the author is a thinker of great influence and importance whose writings, whatever faults we may find in them, are nevertheless entitled to our

[1] Cf. Dr. Inge: 'Mysticism is singularly uniform in all times and places. The communion of the soul with God has found much the same expression whether the mystic is a Neo-platonic philosopher like Plotinus, a Mohammadan Sufi, a Catholic monk or a Quaker. Mysticism, which is the living heart of religion, springs from a deeper level than the differences which divide the Churches, the cultural changes which divide the ages of history' (*Freedom, Love, and Truth* (1936), pp. 25–6).

[2] *Indian Thought and its Development*, E.T. (1936).

respect and gratitude. Secondly, his account brings together in a convenient form the chief criticisms urged against Hindu thought. His argument is based mainly on the antagonism of the two attitudes which he calls 'world and life affirmation' and 'world and life negation'. The former accepts the reality and value of world and life, while the latter denies any real existence to the world and the life in it. These are said to be meaningless and sorrowful. In this scheme the individual is required to 'bring life to a standstill in himself by mortifying his will to live and to renounce all activity which aims at improvement of the conditions of life in this world'.[1] World and life affirmation results in social service, whilst the other takes no interest in a world which it dismisses as a stage play or at best a puzzling pilgrimage through time to eternity. The latter view is bound to make compromises, since 'ethical world and life negation is in itself a contradictory and non-realizable idea. For ethics comprise world and life affirmation.'[2] The instinctive will to live is in us and it operates in the direction of world affirmation.

It is interesting to compare with this the almost identical phrases in which another great German theologian, Professor Heiler, commends the prophetic as against the mystical religion in his book on *Prayer*.[3] He, however, recognizes the presence of the two types both in India and the West, and his contrast is not geographical.

'The fundamental psychic experience in *mysticism*', says Heiler, 'is the denial of the impulse of life, a denial born of weariness of life, the unreserved surrender to the Infinite, the crown and culmination of which is ecstasy. The fundamental psychic experience in *prophetic* religion is an uncontrollable will to live, a constant impulse to the assertion, strengthening and enhancement of the feeling of life. Mysticism is passive, quietist, resigned, contemplative; the prophetic religion is active, challenging, desiring, ethical.'

'Mysticism flees from and denies the natural life and the relish of life in order to experience an infinite life beyond it; prophetic piety, on the contrary, believes in life and affirms it, throws itself resolutely and joyfully into the arms of life. On the one side we have an uncompromising denial of life; on the other an unconquerable belief in life.'

'Mysticism is the religion of feminine natures. Enthusiastic surrender, a delicate capacity for feeling, soft passiveness are its

[1] Op. cit., pp. 1–2. [2] Ibid., p. 111. [3] E.T. (1932).

characteristics. Prophetic religion, on the contrary, has an unmistakably masculine character, ethical severity, bold resoluteness, and disregard of consequence, energetic activity.'

Prophetic religion is severe, militant, uncompromising, intolerant, while mystic religion is renouncing, other-worldly, peaceful.

'"Personality affirming" and "personality denying" religion, the experience of God which values history and that which ignores it, "revelation and ecstasy", prophetism and monasticism, transformation of the world and flight from the world, preaching of the gospel and contemplation—these contradictions are too great to give us the right to assert an essential identity of both types.'[1]

While Heiler admits that Christianity and Hinduism have both these types, he argues that the mystic tendency in Christianity is derived from Indian sources, while the prophetic tendency is based on the Jewish revelation. In other words, he indirectly supports Schweitzer's contention that Indian religion, which is predominantly mystical, is other-worldly and life-denying, while the Western development of Christianity is self-assertive and voluntaristic. It enshrines, according to both these thinkers, 'an irresistible will to live, an uncontrollable impulse toward the expression, mastery and exaltation of the sense of living'. The religious man in the West believes in life, affirms life, and throws himself with joy and resolution into the tasks of life. While the mystic is lost in the contemplation of God, the Western man is engaged in the vindication of personal worth; he directs all his energies to our joys and sorrows, our troubles and fears, our plans and confidences. I hope I have not misrepresented by these extracts writers who have few equals in the sphere of theology, but it is hard to resist the conclusion that their conceptions of prophetic and world-affirming religions have more in common with neo-pagan faiths than with the self-denying, self-forgetful genius of Christianity whose symbol is the Cross. There are many who will not agree with Heiler's characterization of Christian mysticism but will grant that it is possibly true of Hindu mysticism and thus support Schweitzer's views.

[1] Op. cit., pp. 142, 146, 163, 170–1.

This type of criticism and contrast has been so pervasive and persistent that there is no little danger of its being accepted without much examination as an incontrovertible truth. Large historic movements cannot be forced into exaggerated symmetry. Nature refuses to be regulated according to our prescription. If we start with the idea of fitting history into neat patterns, we shall find it difficult to resist the temptation of overlooking essential facts or twisting them out of shape. Schweitzer defines world and life affirmation and world and life negation as antitheses or alternatives which exclude each other, whereas they are only phases which are emphasized more or less. He is compelled by the evidence of facts to admit in Hindu thought aspects which are of a world-affirming character and in Christian thought aspects of a world-negating character. On account of his starting-point he is obliged to regard them as inconsistencies.

There are certain central features in Hindu thought such as the four stages of life (*āśramas*), the second of which is that of the householder, the doctrines of Karma and rebirth which imply action in a real world. In the earliest Hindu thought as found in the *Ṛg Veda* and the Upaniṣads these characteristic views are set forth and Schweitzer can only say that 'Brāhmanism has the courage to be inconsistent'.[1] Again, Buddhist ethics with their pity for suffering and sympathy for every form of sentient life are incompatible with world negation. Buddha's thinking was as clear and objective as his feeling was warm and tender. He would spend hours alone in the forest, 'causing', as he said,

> 'the power of benevolence which fills my mind to extend over one quarter of the world, in the same way over the second quarter, over the third, over the fourth, above, below, across, on all sides, in all directions. Over the entire universe I send forth the power of benevolence which fills my spirit; the wide, the great, the immeasurable feeling which knows naught of hate, which doeth no evil.'

Buddha insists on an active and systematic cultivation of the spirit of goodwill for all kinds and conditions of men and even for animals and all other sentient creatures.[2] This

[1] Op. cit., p. 38.

[2] In the second Rock Edict of Aśoka we read: 'Everywhere his sacred and

whole exalted conception of compassion not only for mankind but for all living things does not trouble Schweitzer, who observes 'the commandment not to kill, not to harm does not arise . . . from a feeling of compassion but from the idea of keeping undefiled from the world. It belongs originally to the ethic of becoming more perfect, not to the ethic of action.' It is difficult to know why we should regard perfection and action as antithetical. We find in the Epics of the *Rāmāyaṇa* and the *Mahābhārata* stress laid on the joy of life and the dignity of man, an eager desire for personal pre-eminence and love of adventure. The *Bhagavadgītā* exalts the idea of action as the way to God, but Schweitzer reminds us that such action was to be empty of all motive. It is essentially a form of inactivity. We are not told, however, when action is really action. If Rāmānuja and the long line of theists who came after him affirm the reality of the world and the efficacy of action, they are to be treated as a departure from the main tradition. If Gandhi and Tagore to-day adopt an ethical view of life, it is certainly to be traced to their contact with the Christian West. The whole development of Indian thought is described as a gradual weaning from 'world and life negation' to the more rational 'world and life affirmation'.

It is not easy to argue that Christian thought insists on the reality of the world, the value of life, and the necessity for social service. As an historical critic of Christianity, Schweitzer took the same view as Johannes Weiss, Loisy, and Baron von Hügel, that Jesus predicted His own coming in power within a very short time, a prediction with which the event failed to correspond. The eschatological teaching of Jesus that the end of the world was at hand reveals an attitude of world and life negation in so far as He did not assume that the Kingdom of God would be realized in this natural world but expected its sudden and startling inauguration by supernatural power.[1] In the coming Kingdom

gracious Majesty has made curative arrangements of two kinds, curative arrangements for men and curative arrangements for animals.'

1 When the rich young man came to Jesus saying, 'What shall I do that I may inherit eternal life?' he was first asked about his knowledge of the commandments. When the young man replied, 'All these things have I observed

the State and the other earthly institutions and conditions shall either not exist at all or shall exist only in a sublimated form. The only ethic that Jesus can preach is a negative one, to enable man to free himself from the world and fit himself for the Kingdom. It is a penitential discipline and not a humanist ethic. Earthly goods are emptied of any essential value. Our highest ideals and noblest impulses are to be swept away, as the new world is wholly other than that which now is. As it is to be realized by the unmediated and catastrophic activity of God, our attitude to this world must be one of uncompromising hostility. Jesus did not think that the Kingdom of God is something embryonically present in human nature and society to be brought into realization by steady progress. No good can come except by direct divine intervention. It is possible to cite many texts which support the legitimacy of earthly joys and ideals and the value of natural beauty, domestic happiness, and civil order, but Schweitzer is definite that 'his acceptance of the world is but the last expression of the completeness with which he rejects it'. 'The teaching of the historical Jesus was purely and exclusively world-renouncing.'[1] For the late Bishop Gore the Sermon on the Mount

'is a proclamation of unworldliness in its extremest form. It is the poor, or those who have no care at all for wealth, those whose concessiveness or submissiveness to injustice knows no limit, and who have no desire for place or power or distinction, and those who take up their burden of misery most readily, who are to enjoy the blessings of the kingdom. These negative characteristics—expressing an extreme renunciation of "the world" and all its normal desires—are constantly emphasized.'[2]

Even an 'interim ethic' is inherently inconsistent with the eschatological teaching that the end is at hand. There is no

from my youth', Jesus said: 'Go and sell whatsoever thou hast, and give to the poor, and thou shalt have treasure in heaven' (Mark x. 17–22). 'So likewise, whosoever he be of you that forsaketh not all that he hath, he cannot be my disciple' (Luke xiv. 33). 'Love not the world, neither the things that are in the world. If any man love the world, the love of the Father is not in him' (1 John ii. 15). These statements may be interpreted as the extreme negation of all possible kinds of social values.

[1] *The Quest of the Historical Jesus*, E.T. (1910), pp. 248, 249.

[2] *New Commentary on Holy Scripture*, pt. iii, pp. 287–8.

denying that Jesus had a real and acute feeling of the immediate nearness of the end. In the Gospels we find that even while Jesus was living the vision of His disciples is fixed upon the future in a second coming of the Master. St. Peter, writing to the converts widely scattered through the provinces of Asia Minor, has no doubt that 'the end of all things is at hand'. When the delay in the return awakened doubts as to the certainty of the coming of the Messianic Kingdom, the writer of the Epistle to the Hebrews exhorts believers not to give up hope but to remain steadfast to the end.[1] When the sceptics asserted that the return of Christ would not take place at all, the Second Epistle of Peter points out that God's reckoning of time is not like man's, for a thousand years are in his sight as a single day. If he still delayed it was to give men more time for repentance.[2] The Apocalypse of John closes with the words, 'Surely I come quickly. Amen. Come, Lord Jesus.'[3] Ignatius in his Epistle to the Ephesians (about A.D. 110) holds that 'the last times have come'. Justin says to Trypho, 'You have only a short time now in which to attach yourself to us; after the return of Christ your remorse and weeping will be of no avail; for he will not listen to you.'[4] This thought of the second coming 'within the lifetime of those now living' became an obsession and proved disastrous to normal life. The Christians give away their property because they will have no use for it 'in the day of the Lord'. They are not encouraged to marry or give in marriage since it is foolish to establish households and conceive children when the end of all things is at hand. As the hope of the second coming began to fade, another hope, more remote but not less certain, that of meeting Jesus beyond the grave, took its place. By the third century the great body of Christians were living for this future life. Four centuries after the death of Jesus Augustine saw the capture and destruction of Rome and wrote his *City of God*, in which he comforted himself and the people of the Empire with the thought that the destruction of our earthly cities was a matter of no importance, since there was a spiritual city of God triumphant here and in the world to come, which

[1] vi. 11–12; x. 23, 35; xii. 12–14.
[2] iii. 4–9.
[3] Revelation xxii. 20.
[4] *Dial.* xxviii. 2.

was destined to endure for ever.[1] For Augustine the builder of this world was Cain and its head the Devil.[2] Through the centuries the preparation for the life that is to come, the heaven or hell that is to follow after death has been the key-note of Christian doctrine and discipline. St. Basil says: 'We consider this human life of ours to be of no value whatsoever; nor do we think or call anything absolutely good which is profitable to us while we are here . . . but we run forward in hope, and act in everything with a view to another life.'[3] The typical Christian attitude in this matter is beautifully set forth in Bunyan's *The Pilgrim's Progress*. In this text-book of Christian faith the hero of the story, significantly named Christian, discovers that he is living in a city which is doomed to imminent destruction. Filled with alarm, he wonders what he shall do and encounters a man named Evangelist, who counsels him to fly. Immediately Christian begins to run away. His wife and children, frightened at his precipitate departure, 'began to cry after him to return', but Christian 'put his fingers in his ears, and ran on crying "Life! Life! Eternal Life!" '. His friends and neighbours tried to stop him, but Christian would not so much as even pause for a moment to tell them the doom that was upon the city and bid them to fly as well. He was thinking only of himself, of his own salvation. So far as the city was concerned, it might disappear together with his wife and children, and all his friends and neighbours, but there was no need to worry if only he were saved.

Austerities, flagellations, and fastings were adopted by many religious people as means for controlling the body. In many cases they were desired for their own sake.[4] A

[1] Mr. Edwyn Bevan points out that certain forms of Christianity were world-negating: 'To turn from the wearying transitoriness of earthly things to the contemplation of the eternal and the unchanging—that seems widely to have been felt in Eastern Christianity as the core or the highest goal of religion—renunciation and tranquillity—though this is hardly anything distinctively Christian, but common to Eastern Christianity with Neoplatonism and Indian religion' (*Christianity* (1932), p. 141).

[2] *The City of God*, xv. 1 (2).

[3] *A Monument to St. Augustine* (1930), p. 133.

[4] Cf. St. Theresa: 'Suffering alone, from now on, can make life supportable to me. My dearest wishes all lead to suffering. How often from the bottom of

glorification of suffering led to the exaltation of martyrdom in the early Church. St. Jerome writes to the priest Heliodorus bidding him break away from all contact with the world and leave his mother's house, adding these words: 'Should your little nephew hang on your neck, pay no regard to him. Should your mother, with ashes on her head and garments rent, show you the breasts at which she nursed you, heed her not. Should your father prostrate himself on the threshold, trample him underfoot and go your way.' The extravagances with which we are familiar in the East are not unknown in the West. Some endeavoured to subdue the body by spending nights in ditches and brooks, others made their abodes in holes and cisterns. Some exposed themselves to the scorching heat of the day and the bitter cold at night. Some stood on one leg, wore heavy chains, and carried weights. Describing the life of Dorotheus, Sozomen says that he limited himself to six ounces of bread and a few vegetables each day and drank only water. 'He was never seen to recline on a mat or bed, nor even to place his limbs in an easy attitude, or willingly surrender himself to sleep.' To the question why he was destroying his body his reply was: 'Because it is destroying me.'[1] The lives of Suso and Marguerite Marie, the founder of the Society of the Sacred Heart, are marked by an excessive emphasis on self-denial and suffering. In the eighteenth century Rousseau wrote:

> 'Christianity is an entirely spiritual religion concerned solely with heavenly things: the Christian's country is not of this world. He does his duty, it is true; but he does it with a profound indifference as to the good or ill success of his endeavours. Provided that he has nothing to reproach himself with, it matters little to him whether all goes well or ill here below. If the State flourishes, he scarcely dares to enjoy the public felicity. If the State declines, he blesses the hand of God which lies heavy on his people.'[2]

Many social idealists in whose hearts a real faith for service of humanity burns are turning away from Christianity on account of its ascetic tradition. The Communists declare

my heart have I cried out to God, O Lord, to suffer or die is the only thing I ask.'

[1] *Ecclesiastical History*, bk. vi, chap. xxix. See also Madame Guyon's *Life*, by Upham, chap. xix, p. 140. [2] *The Social Contract*, bk. iv, chap. viii.

that they adopt the religion of the love of one's neighbour in a more thoroughgoing way than Christianity ever did.[1] It is not easy to make out that Christianity's principal concern is with world and life affirmation and that world and life negation is merely an accidental or peripheral error.

When confronted with historical evidence of the world-negating character of Christianity, Schweitzer contends that the Christian form of negation denies not the world as such but only the imperfect world in expectation of the perfect world yet to come. It is not easy to establish this view. St. John tells us, 'The whole world lieth in wickedness.' Christian theology takes the account of the Fall in the third chapter of Genesis and the Platonic theory as literal facts and exaggerates man's alienation from God and the depravity of human nature. As a consequence of Adam's disobedience, it is impossible for sinful man to fulfil the moral law by his own effort and attain salvation. For St. Paul 'flesh and blood cannot inherit the Kingdom of God'.[2] Man can be saved only by God's grace. About the year A.D. 400 Pelagius dared to assert that man is created good and is free to fulfil God's commandments, the implication being that the grace of God is an aid and not a necessity for man's salvation. Augustine, when he shook himself free from the influence of Plotinus, held against Pelagius that man is inherently evil and helpless and that only the grace of God can save him. He looked upon life not merely as imperfect but as utterly corrupt. Man's salvation is a miracle of divine grace. Even the faith by which the individual is inclined to accept the proffered prevenient grace is divinely bestowed on him. The complete depravity of man gives the opportunity for the divine plan of salvation through Christ. The Church decided that Augustine was right and Pelagius wrong. Luther accepts this view, and it persists in Calvin and Knox. The movement of Jansenism in the Roman

[1] Dr. Needham says of the religion of the Communists: 'Their doctrine may be described as the highest form which religion has yet taken. . . . They alone have noted the Apostle's warning "He that despiseth man, despiseth not man but God". Religion must die to be born again as the holy spirit of a righteous social order' (*Faiths and Fellowship*, being the proceedings of the World Congress of Faiths (1937), pp. 135–6).

[2] See Romans ix. 15–21.

Catholic Church, and the mystical intensity of seventeenth-century quietism, are expressions of the same type of thought. The utter inability of man to do anything for himself, to discover God, promote his own salvation, or be an organ of spiritual values has received new emphasis in the Crisis Theology of Karl Barth and his followers. For them the nature of God is for ever unrevealable in terms of human life and thought. The whole point may be put in another way. For the orthodox Christian, the coming of the Kingdom is catastrophic and not the peaceful outcome of an ever-widening process of evolution, an intervention of God cutting right *into* history and not springing *from* it. He despairs of earth and lives in apocalyptic hopes of divine intervention. There is, of course, the other emphasis in Christianity brought out by the parables of the leaven and the grain of mustard seed and utterances like 'The Kingdom of God is within you'.

All immense simplifications of the complicated patterns of reality are misleading. To divide peoples into those who will not accept the world at all and those who will accept nothing else is hardly fair. The many reservations which Schweitzer is obliged to make in applying his scheme of world affirmation and world negation as opposite categories of which one or the other must be denied show that it is not adequate to the facts. A very different view is expressed by Sir George Birdwood when he says:

> 'European Christianity, unfortunately through the accident of the impatience of some of its early converts of the military discipline of Rome, was at its beginning placed in opposition to the general philosophical, literary, artistic and scientific culture of the Gentile world, and thenceforward in more or less marked antagonism also to the modern secular life of the west. Happily in India . . . the Brāhmanical religious life has never sundered itself from the daily working life of the laity, but is a component part of it and indissolubly bound up with it.'

He concludes his chief work, *Sva*, with the hope that

> 'India may yet be destined to prepare the way for the reconciliation of Christianity with the world, and through the practical identification of the spiritual with the temporal life, to hasten the period of that third step forward in the moral development of humanity, when there will be no divisions of race, or creed, or class, or nationality, between men, by whatsoever name they may be called, for they will all be one

in the acknowledgment of their common brotherhood, with the same reality, and sense of consequent responsibility, with which two thousand years ago, they recognised the Fatherhood of God, and again, two thousand years before that an exceptionally endowed tribe of Semites, in the very heart of Anterior Asia, formulated for all men, and for all time, the inspiring and elevating doctrine of his unity.'[1]

In other words, Sir George Birdwood believes that while the Hebrews gave the world the conception of the unity of Godhead and the Christians that of the Fatherhood of God, the Hindus will help to make these truths effective in life and thus to achieve the brotherhood of man. While Schweitzer, whose knowledge of India is based on books, holds that Hinduism makes us fugitives from life, Birdwood, who spent a lifetime among the Indians, hopes that Hinduism will yet reconcile the truths of Judaism and Christianity with earthly life.

The contrast to my mind is not so much between Hinduism and Christianity as between religion and a self-sufficient humanism. While religion is taken more seriously in the East, humanism is the predominant feature of Western life. Hindu religion, like all true religion, is essentially 'otherworldly'. It pictures the world as a mere vestibule and training-ground for another in which alone life is real, rich, and abiding; yet it moves men to the most impressive and sustained demonstrations of human courage, power, and persistence and has woven for itself a secular vesture. Its adherents describe themselves as strangers and pilgrims on earth. Its most illustrious representatives are saints and martyrs.[2]

[1] *Sva* (1915), pp. 354–6.

[2] The contrast between the Eastern and the Western points of view is brought out vividly in Arnold's well-known lines. He gives us first the impact of Europe drunk with power on Asia:

> The East bow'd low before the blast,
> In patient, deep disdain
> She let the legions thunder past
> And plunged in thought again.

A Europe grown weary of humanism and secular development heeded the voice of the East, when she accepted Christianity:

> She heard it, the Victorious West,
> In sword and crown array'd
> She felt the void that mined her breast!
> She shivered and obey'd.

Religion and humanism do not exclude each other. If we wrongly identify religion with world and life negation, and ethics with humanism and social progress, the two become quite different and require to be pursued on their own separate lines and in obedience to their own separate principles. They are, on the contrary, organic to each other. While the chief value of religion lies in its power to raise and enlarge the internal man, its soundness is not complete until it has shaped properly his external existence. For the latter we require a sound political, economic, and social life, a power and an efficiency which will make a people not only survive but grow towards a collective perfection. If a religion does not secure these ends, there is a defect somewhere, either in its essential principles or in their application. A spiritual view is sustained not only by insight but by a rational philosophy and sound social institutions.

III

Let us now consider the chief arguments which Schweitzer advances in support of his thesis. (1) The emphasis on ecstasy in Hindu thought naturally tends to world and life negation. (2) Hindu thought is essentially other-worldly, and humanist ethics and other-worldliness are incompatible with each other. (3) The Hindu doctrine of *māyā*, which declares that life is an illusion, contains the flaw of world and life negation, and in consequence Hindu thought is non-ethical. (4) The best that the Hindu has to say about the origin of the world is that it is a game played by God. (5) The way to salvation is *jñāna* or self-discovery. This is different from moral development, and so Hindu religion is non-ethical. (6) The goal of human endeavour is escape, not reconciliation. It is the deliverance of the soul from the bonds of finitude, not the conversion of the finite into the organ and manifestation of the infinite. Religion is a refuge from life and its problems, and man has no hope of better things to come. (7) The ideal man of the Hindu religion is raised above the ethical distinctions of good and evil. (8) The ethics of inner perfection insisted on by Hindu thought conflict with an active ethic and wide-hearted love of one's neighbour.

IV

'The real belief of the Brāhmins', says Schweitzer, 'is that man does not attain to union with Brahman by means of any achievement of his natural power of gaining knowledge, but solely by quitting the world of the senses in a state of ecstasy and thus learning the reality of pure being.'[1] The suggestion here is that Christian mysticism represents the enrichment of personality, the heightened expression of spiritual life, and Hindu mysticism requires one to run away from oneself. This is another example of over-simplification. As a reading of Hindu mysticism it is far from correct. For the Hindu, the spiritual is the basic element of human nature. Spiritual realization is not a miraculous solution of life's problems but a slow deposit of life's fullness, a fruit which grows on the tree of life when it is mature. The soul, in the state of ecstasy, enters the stream of life, is borne along in the flowing current of it, and finds its reality in the larger enveloping life. This life of spirit, where freedom from the sense of bodily or even mental limitations and emergence into a space of unlimited and infinite life are felt, is not the same as magical mysticism.

What Schweitzer regards as the supernatural or the magical, the spasm of the human mind in contact with pure spirit, is the supremely normal, though most of us are feeble-minded or more or less insane compared with this ideal of sanity.

Ecstasy is a word which covers a multitude of things, from alcoholic intoxication and possession by demons to the raptures of Plotinus.[2] Ecstasy of the quiet contemplative type is different from the wild excitement induced by physical means and indulged in for its intoxicating effects. All experience of God when it becomes intense is ecstatic, though every ecstatic emotion is not an experience of God. It is true, however, that there is a certain temperament which predisposes its subject to emotional exaltation which is quite different from a convulsed state. This is not

[1] Op. cit., p. 38.

[2] On the ecstatic as a sign of communion with God, see W. James, *The Varieties of Religious Experience* (1906), pp. 379–422; R. H. Thouless, *An Introduction to the Psychology of Religion* (1924), pp. 230–2, 249–51.

surprising in view of the obvious fact that something of the same kind is true of poets and philosophers, painters and musicians. If we do not say that the genius of the artist is due to mental degeneration or nervous instability, religious geniuses need not be treated differently. A sense of rapture is a frequent accompaniment of mystic states, but it by no means implies a disintegration of the self. To be rapt is not to pass beyond one's self but to be intensely one's self, not to lose self-consciousness but to be greatly conscious. Man is not torn out of the ordinary setting of his earthly life. He still has a body and mind, though he knows them to be instruments of his higher life. He does not exult in his own intelligence or seek for his own soul, for he has it no more. If he has gained a transcendent personality and an independence which nothing in this world can touch, it is because not he but the Super-spirit lives in him, making him illimitable. While mystic experience has something in common with the delight of the artist or the ecstasy of love, which exceed all law and restriction and indicate the possibility of a real communion with life, it is not a mere glow of feeling. Excited emotionalism, which seeks and strives after sensations and rapturous states of a sensual character, is quite different from perfect insight (*samyag-darśana*). The contemplative saints assign a subordinate position to images and other sensible presentations. These are symbols which we use to understand, and the symbol is different from experience or understanding. *Jñāna* or *vidyā* is cool, clear-sighted vision. In ecstasy the soul feels itself, or thinks it feels itself, in the presence of God, being irradiated by the light; but we must go beyond it to a stage where the consciousness of being at unity with the divine becomes constant. To have an ecstasy is to look upon the promised land but not to set foot on its soil. It is not beatitude or the perfect spiritual possession of divine reality but is its beginning, the first step here below. After the tremendous experience of the celestial vision in chapter xi of the *Bhagavadgītā* the book does not end. The illumination must be transformed into the spiritual union of man with infinite being. When the ecstasy dies out, the soul stands alone and feels desolate, dissatisfied with its incomplete union. Accustomed for a time to dazzling light, it now gropes in gloom, striving for the purity of heart and the chastity of mind essential for that spiritual life which is the gradual penetration of the human consciousness by the divine. The effort to conquer the will and subdue it entirely is unceasing, until the union is absolute, until the personality is permanently changed, until it becomes a God-moved soul.[1]

Ecstasy is not the only way to spiritual life. It is often a perversion of mysticism rather than an illustration of it. As there is a tendency to mistake it for spiritual life, we are warned against it. The spiritual mystics the world over regard ecstasy, visions, auditions as things to be avoided and of secondary importance. They are the anomalies of the life of mystics from which they sometimes suffer, and are the results of an imperfect adaptation to a changed inner world. When the personality of the mystic rises to a level which is disconcerting to his normal self-centred life, certain disorders show themselves. The experience throws an intense strain on the organism. When the seed of the oak is planted in earthen vessels, they break asunder. When new wine is poured in old bottles, they burst. Man must become a new vessel, a new creature, if he is to bear the spiritual light. That is why the Hindu system of *yoga* insists on the development of healthy nerves.

Ecstatic phenomena are not peculiar to Hinduism. We have a case of ecstasy in the book of Numbers in the Balaam narrative: 'seeing the vision, falling down and having his eyes open'.[2] Trance visions initiated the prophecies of Isaiah and Ezekiel.[3] St. Paul speaks of spiritual rapture independent of the senses and was only reminded of their existence by the 'sting of the flesh'. The experience of gifts in the early Church, 'speaking with tongues' and the 'interpretation of tongues', messages given by the prophets,[4] are more

[1] Cf. St. Theresa, for whom ecstasy is betrothal leading up to the spiritual marriage 'in which the soul always remains in its centre with God' (*The Interior Castle*, Seventh Mansion, chap. ii, secs. 2–4).

[2] xxiv. 4. See also Isaiah vi.

[3] Ezra vi. 32.

[4] See Acts of the Apostles and the First Letter to the Corinthians. See also Mark i. 12; Luke iv. 1. 'The great prophets do not depart from the conception of inspiration common to the whole of Semitic antiquity; for them

invasions from beyond than developments from within. Montanism, which prevailed in the second and third centuries, was definitely ecstatic. St. Theresa and St. Catherine of Genoa, among others, suffered from visions and ecstasies. Any argument based on ecstatic phenomena will apply to all religions alike.

V

Any ethical theory must be grounded in metaphysics, in a philosophical conception of the relation between human conduct and ultimate reality. As we think ultimate reality to be, so we behave. Vision and action go together. If we believe absurdities, we shall commit atrocities. A self-sufficient humanism has its own metaphysical presuppositions. It requires us to confine our attention to the immediate world of space and time and argues that moral duty consists in conforming to nature and modelling our behaviour in accordance with the principles of her working. It attempts to perfect the causes of human life by purely natural means. The subject of ethics is treated as a branch of sociology or a department of psychology. Scientific materialism and mystical nationalism are two types of humanist ethics, interpreted in a narrow sense. They look upon man as a purely natural phenomenon whose outlook is rigorously confined by space and time. They encourage a cynical subservience to nature and historical process and an acquiescence in the merely practicable. Renunciation, self-sacrifice, disinterested service of humanity are not stimulated by the workings of natural law.

An abundance of material things will not help to make life more interesting. The rich of the world are among those who find life stale, flat, and unprofitable. Even the social conscience that urges us to extend the benefits of a material civilization cannot be accounted for by the principles of scientific naturalism. The material basis, while essential, is still too narrow for real living. The collective myths of Nazism, Fascism, and Communism propose to make life seem rich and significant by asking us to banish all considerations of reason and humanity and to worship the State.

it is the invasion of a human personality by a power foreign to it, which they usually call the spirit or the word of Yahweh.' Adolphe Lods: *The Prophets and the Rise of Judaism* (1937), p. 53.

Man is not merely an emotional being. The Nation-State falls short of the human and the universal and constitutes a deadly menace to the growth of the universal in man which is postulated with increasing force by the advance of science and which the well-being of human society demands.

The question has its centre in the nature of man. Is he only a body which can be fed, clothed, and housed, or is he also a spirit that can aspire? The feeling of frustration experienced even by those who are provided with all the comforts and conveniences which a material civilization can supply indicates that man does not live by bread or emotional excitement alone. Besides, progress is not its own end. If it is the ultimate reality, it cannot ever be completed. We can draw nearer and nearer the goal, but cannot reach it. Its process has neither a beginning nor an end. It starts nowhere and leads nowhere. It has no issue, no goal. Senseless cycles of repetition cannot give meaning to life. It may be argued that, although the universe may have no purpose, items in the universe such as nations and individuals may have their purposes. The rise and fall of nations, the growth and crash of individuals may be quite interesting, and the universe may be viewed as an infinite succession of finite purposes. This cannot be regarded as a satisfactory goal of ethics. Does not the humanist hope to build a terrestrial paradise inhabited by a perfect race of artists and thinkers? What is the good of telling us that though our sun, moon, and stars will share in the destruction of earthly life, other suns, moons, and stars will arise? We long for a good which is never left behind and never superseded. Man's incapacity to be satisfied with what is merely relative and remain permanently within the boundaries of the finite and empirical reality cannot be denied. Man stands before the shrine of his own mystery. He enters it the moment he becomes aware of his own eternity. Apart from eternity there is nothing that can, strictly speaking, be called human. A meaningful ethical ideal must be transcendent to the immediate flow of events.

Again, in view of the enigmatic character of the actual, is moral life possible? There are some thinkers who exhort us to do what is right even though we may not know whether it can be realized or not. Moral enthusiasm is possible only if our motive includes the expectation of being able to contribute to the achievement of moral ideals. If we are not certain that active service of the ideals will further their actualization, we cannot be sure of their worthwhileness.

We cannot help asking ourselves whether our ideals are mere private dreams of our own or bonds created by society, or even aspirations characteristic of the human species. Only a philosophy which affirms that they are rooted in the universal nature of things can give depth and fervour to moral life, courage and confidence in moral difficulties. We need to be fortified by the conviction that the service of the ideals is what the cosmic scheme demands of us, that our loyalty or disloyalty to them is a matter of the deepest moment not only to ourselves or to society, or even to the human species, but to the nature of things. If ethical thought is profound, it will give a cosmic motive to morality. Moral consciousness must include a conviction of the reality of ideals. If the latter is religion, then ethical humanism is acted religion. When man realizes his essential unity with the whole of being, he expresses this unity in his life. Mysticism and ethics, other-worldliness and worldly work go together. In the primitive religions we have this combination. Other-worldliness appears as *māna*, which the savage derives from an innate sense of some mysterious power within the phenomena and behind the events of the visible world, and morality appears as taboo, and the sense of sacredness in things and persons, which with its inhibitions controls the whole range of his conduct. In the higher religions of mankind, belief in the transcendent and work in the natural have grown together in close intimacy and interaction. Religion is the soul's attitude, response, and adjustment in the presence of the supreme realities of the transcendent order; ethics deal with the right adjustment of life on earth, especially in human society. Both are motived by a desire to live in the light of ideals. If we are satisfied with what exists, there is no meaning in 'ought'; if we are a species of passing phenomena, there is no meaning in religion. Religion springs from the conviction that there is another world beyond the visible and the temporal with which man has dealings, and ethics require us to act in this world with the compelling vision of another. With our minds anchored in the beyond we are to strive to make the actual more nearly like what it ought to be. Religion alone can give assurance and wider reference to ethics and a new meaning to human life. We make moral judgements about individual lives and societies simply because we are spiritual beings, not merely social animals.

If there is one doctrine more than another which is characteristic of Hindu thought, it is the belief that there is an interior depth to the human soul, which, in its essence, is uncreated and deathless and absolutely real. The spirit in man is different from the individual ego; it is that which animates and exercises the individual, the vast background of his being in which all individuals lie. It is the core of all being, the inner thread by being strung on which the world exists. In the soul of man are conflicting tendencies: the attraction of the infinite, which abides for ever, changeless, unqualified, untouched by the world; and the fascination of the finite, that which like the wind-beaten surface of the waters is never for a moment the same. Every human being is a potential spirit and represents, as has been well said, a hope of God and is not a mere fortuitous concourse of episodes like the changing forms of clouds or the patterns of a kaleidoscope. If the feeling for God were not in man, we could not implant it any more than we could squeeze blood from a stone. The heart of religion is that man truly belongs to another order, and the meaning of man's life is to be found not in this world but in more than historical reality. His highest aim is release from the historical succession denoted by birth and death. So long as he is lost in the historical process without a realization of the super-historical goal, he is only 'once born' and is liable to sorrow. God and not the world of history is the true environment of our souls. If we overlook this important fact, and make ethics or world affirmation independent of religion or world negation, our life and thought become condescending, though this condescension may take the form of social service or philanthropy. But it is essentially a form of self-assertion and not real concern for the well-being of others. If goodwill, pure love, and disinterestedness are our ideals, then our ethics must be rooted in other-worldliness. This is the great classical tradition of spiritual wisdom. The mystery cults of Greece had for their central doctrine that man's soul is of divine origin and is akin to the spirit of God. The influence of these mystery cults on Socrates and Plato is unmistakable. When Jesus tells Nicodemus that until a man is begotten from above he cannot see or enter the Kingdom of God,[1] when Paul declares that 'he that soweth to the flesh shall of the flesh reap corruption; but he that soweth to the spirit shall of the spirit reap everlasting life',[2] they are implying that our natural life is mortal and it is invaded by sin and death,[3] and that the life of spirit is immortal. St. John in the First Epistle says: 'the world passeth away, and the lust thereof: but he that doeth the will of God abideth for ever.'[4] We are amphibious beings, according to Plotinus. We live on earth and in a world of spirit.

VI

Although the view about the coexistence of the human and the divine in close intimacy and interpenetration may be true, does not Hindu thought declare that life is empty and unreal, and that it has no purpose or meaning? Schweitzer tells us that for the Upaniṣads 'the world of the senses is a magic play staged by the universal soul for itself. The individual soul is brought into this magic play under a spell. By reflection about itself it must become capable of seeing through the deception. Thereupon it gives up taking part in the play. It waits quietly and enjoys its identity with the universal soul until, at death, the magic play for it ceases to be.'[5] 'Man cannot engage in ethical activity in a world with no meaning.'[6] 'For any believer in the māyā doctrine ethics can have only a quite relative importance.'[7] This account is by no means a fair representation of the position of the Upaniṣads. The long theistic tradition interprets the doctrine of the Upaniṣads in a way directly opposed to this account. Śaṁkara adopts the doctrine of *māyā*, and it is doubtful whether Schweitzer's view is adequate to Śaṁkara's thought. Religious experience, by its affirmation that the basic fact in the universe is spiritual, implies that the world of

[1] John iii. 5. [2] Galatians vi. 8. [3] Romans vi. 23. [4] 1 John ii. 17.
[5] Op. cit., p. 59. [6] Ibid., p. 60. [7] Ibid., p. 65.

sound and sense is not final. All existence finds its source and support in a supreme reality whose nature is spirit. The visible world is the symbol of a more real world. It is the reflection of a spiritual universe which gives to it its life and significance.

What is the relation of absolute being to historical becoming, of eternity to time? Is succession, history, progress, real and sufficient in its own right, or does man's deep instinct for the unchanging point to an eternal perfection which alone gives the world meaning and worth? Is the inescapable flux all, or is there anything which abides? Religious consciousness bears testimony to the reality of something behind the visible, a haunting beyond, which both attracts and disturbs, in the light of which the world of change is said to be unreal. The Hebrews contrasted the abidingness of God with the swift flow of human generations. 'Before the mountains were brought forth or ever Thou hadst formed the earth and the world even from everlasting to everlasting, Thou art God.'[1] The Psalmist cries to his God: 'They [i.e. heaven and earth] shall be changed: but Thou art the same, and Thy years shall have no end.'[2] The Christian exclaims: 'The things which are seen are temporal; but the things which are not seen are eternal.'[3] The mutability of things which is part of the connotation of the word *māyā* is a well-known theme in the world's literature. The saying that 'time and chance happeneth to them all' of Ecclesiastes is the refrain we hear often.[4]

[1] Psalms xc. 2. [2] Psalms cii. 26 and 27. [3] 2 Corinthians iv. 18.

[4] Shakespeare in his Sonnet 65 speaks of the mortality of things:

Since brass, nor stone, nor earth, nor boundless sea,
But sad mortality o'ersways their power,
How with this rage shall beauty hold a plea,
Whose action is no stronger than a flower?
O, how shall summer's honeybreath hold out
Against the wreckful siege of battering days,
When rocks impregnable are not so stout,
Nor gates of steel so strong, but Time decays?

Milton writes:

Then all this earthly grossness quit,
Attired with stars, we shall forever sit,
Triumphing over Death and Chance and thee, O Time.

[*Note cont. overleaf.*]

Gauḍapāda argues that 'whatever is non-existent at the beginning and in the end is non-existent in the middle also'.[1] In other words, the things of the world are not eternal. The world is *māyā*, i.e. passes away, but God is eternal. Change, causality, activity are finite categories and the Eternal is lifted above them. God is not a mere means to explain the universe or improve human society.

Śaṁkara, who is rightly credited with the systematic formulation of the doctrine of *māyā*, tells us that the highest reality is unchangeable,[2] and therefore that changing existence such as human history has not ultimate reality (*pāramārthika sattā*). He warns us, however, against the temptation to regard what is not completely real as utterly illusory. The world has empirical being (*vyāvahārika sattā*) which is quite different from illusory existence (*prātibhāsika sattā*). Human experience is neither ultimately real nor completely illusory. Simply because the world of experience is not the perfect form of reality, it does not follow that it is a delusion, without any significance. The world is not a phantom, though it is not real.[3] Brahman is said to be the

Shelley's lines in the *Adonais* are well known:

Life, like a dome of many-coloured glass,
Stains the white radiance of Eternity,
Until Death tramples it to fragments.

So Kingsley:

They drift away—ah, God, they drift for ever;
I watch the stream sweep onward to the sea
. . . Ah, God, my God, Thou wilt not drift away.

Sometimes we say with Faber:

O Lord, my heart is sick,
Sick of this everlasting change;
And life runs tediously quick
Through its unresting race and varied range.
Change finds no likeness of itself in Thee
And makes no echo in Thy mute eternity.

[1] 'ādāvante ca yannāsti vartamānepi tat tathā.' *Kārikā* on *Māṇḍūkya Up.* ii. 6.

[2] In the tenth chapter of Revelation the angel who comes down from heaven declares: 'There should be time no longer.'

[3] Even Gauḍapāda says: 'māyāmātram idam dvaitam advaitam paramārthataḥ.' This duality is phenomenal; non-duality is the supreme reality (i. 17). *Māyā* is not non-existence. For 'the non-existent cannot be born either really

real of the real, *satyasyasatyam*. In all objective consciousness, we are in a sense aware of the real.

Similarly, all knowledge presupposes the knower who is constant, while the known is unsteady. When Plato tells us that we bring universal ideas with us from the world in which we lived before our birth, he is referring to the non-phenomenal, time-transcending power in us which belongs to a different world from the observed phenomena. The 'nous' which organizes the facts of experience and interprets them is not itself a fact of experience. It must have had its origin in and belong to another world. It beholds by virtue of its own nature eternal realities. This presence in us is an assurance that we are in touch with reality. Spirit is real being and the rest its limited activity. The spirit is pure existence, self-aware, timeless, spaceless, unconditioned, not dependent for its being on its sense of objects, not dependent for its delight on the gross or subtle touches of outward things. It is not divided in the multitude of beings. Śaṁkara's *advaita* or non-duality has for its central thesis the non-difference between the individual self and Brahman. As for difference or multiplicity (*nānātva*), it is not real. Its self-discrepant character shows that it is only an appearance of the real. All schools of *advaita* are agreed on these two propositions. Differences arise when the nature of the actuality of the manifold world as distinct from the reality is described. Śaṁkara accepts the empirical reality of the world, which is negated only when perfect insight or intuition of the oneness of all is attained. Until then it has empirical validity or pragmatic justification. There are *advaitins* who argue that the world of difference has not even empirical validity. Śaṁkara, however, tells us that so long as we are in the world of *māyā* and occupy a dualistic standpoint, the world is there, standing over against us, determining our perceptions and conduct.

Besides, the world we see and touch is not independent and self-sufficing. It carries no explanation of itself. It is a world reflecting the condition of our minds, a partial construction made from insufficient data under the stress of self-

or through māyā. For the son of a barren woman is born neither in reality nor through māyā' (ii. 28).

conscious individuality with its cravings and desires. What is perceived and shaped into meaning depends on the powers of apprehension we employ and the interests we possess. Our passion-limited apprehension gives us the world of common sense. Take the apparent facts of the universe. Matter is not primal. It is a thing made, not self-existent. It is not unreal but being as it forms itself to sense. It is not a baseless fiction but at the lowest a misrepresentation of truth; at the highest an imperfect representation or translation of the truth into a lower plane. Even as our knowledge implies the presence of a constant consciousness, the object of our knowledge implies the reality of pure being. Our conceptions of the universe answer to our degrees of consciousness. As our consciousness increases in its scope, we see more clearly. We now see partly as an animal and partly as a human being. Sometimes the world is viewed as one of self-satisfaction, at other times as an object of curiosity and contemplation. To see it in truth, one has to free oneself from sense addiction and concentrate the whole energy of one's consciousness on the nature of reality. It is the only way by which we can attain a clear consciousness of reality as it is and get a true picture of the world instead of partial sketches. Knowledge which we now obtain through senses and reason cannot be regarded as complete or perfect. It is flawed with antinomies and contradictions. Through the force of *avidyā* (not knowing) we impose on the reality of the one the multiplicity of the world. Being which is one only appears to the soul as manifoldness, and the soul beholds itself as entangled in the world of *saṁsāra*, in the chain of birth and death. This *avidyā* is natural (*naisargika*) to the human mind, and the world is organically connected with it. It is not therefore mere waking dream.

Māyā is not solipsism. It does not say that suns and universes are the invention of the solitary mind. Śaṁkara proclaims his opposition to *Vijñānavāda* or mentalism. He argues that waking experiences are distinct from dream-states, though neither can be regarded as real metaphysically. Our world of waking experience is not the ultimate reality, but neither is it a shadow-show. We are surrounded by something other than ourselves, which cannot be reduced to states of our own consciousness. Though the world is always changing, it has a unity and a meaning. These are revealed by the reality present all through it. This reality lies not in the facts but in the principle which makes them into a whole. We are able to know that the world is imperfect, finite, and changing, because we have a consciousness of the eternal and the perfect. It is by the light of this consciousness that we criticize ourselves or condemn the world. Even as the human individual is a complex of the eternal and the temporal, the world which confronts him contains both. It is for Śaṁkara a mixture of truth and illusion.[1] It partakes of the characteristics of being and non-being (*sadasadātmaka*). Although, therefore, it has a lower form of reality than pure spirit, it is not non-existent. While Śaṁkara refuses to acquiesce in the seeming reality of the actual, he does not dismiss it as an unreal phantasmagoria. It is not determinable either as real or as unreal.[2] Its truth is in being, reality, truth (*sat*); its multiplicity and division, its dispersal in space and time is untrue (*an-ṛtam*). In the world itself we have change. Śaṁkara does not tell us that the process of the world is perpetual recurrence, in which events of past cycles are repeated in all their details. If everything is recurrent, perpetually rotating, and governed by a law of cyclic motion, there is nothing new, no meaning in history. But there is an historical fulfilment and destiny for the cosmic process. Mankind is engaged in a pursuit that tends towards a definite goal. Truth will be victorious on earth, and it is the nature of the cosmic process that the finite individual is called upon to work through the exercise of his freedom for that goal through ages of struggle and effort. The soul has risen from the sleep of matter, through plant and animal life, to the human level, and is battling with ignorance and imperfection to take possession of its infinite kingdom. It is absolute not in its actual empirical condition but in its potentiality, in its capacity to appropriate the Absolute. The historical process is not a mere external chain of events, but offers a succession of spiritual opportunities. Man has to attain a mastery over it and

[1] 'satyānṛte mithunīkṛtya . . .'

[2] 'sadasadbhyām anirvacanīyam.'

reveal the higher world operating in it. The world is not therefore an empty dream or an eternal delirium.

VII

To the question why the supreme spirit makes individual souls and the world arise from itself Schweitzer informs us that the Hindus have no better answer than that the whole thing is just a play. 'So it is impossible for them to attribute real importance to ethics.'[1] This brings us to the problem of the relation between the unchanging real and the changing world. Whatever the nature of the world may be, finite or infinite, it is contingent. The question remains, Why does the world exist at all? To say that it is a mystery is perhaps true, but it can hardly be called an answer.[2] No theory can be logically satisfactory since the question itself is not logically framed. It involves a confusion of standpoints. We are using temporal terms with reference to an order which is essentially non-temporal. The Psalmist tells us, 'God is in heaven, and thou upon earth; therefore let thy words be few.'[3] When Augustine was asked, 'What was God doing before He made heaven and earth?' he answered, 'Preparing hell for the over-curious.' Time was with creation, and so the question of 'before' has no meaning. As to how the primal reality in which the divine light shines everlastingly can yet be the source and fount of all empirical being, we can only say that it is a mystery, *māyā*. If we still raise the question, our answers are bound to be riddled with difficulties. Why should there arise an imperfect process of becoming from a being who is perfection itself? If we answer with Plato that God was not jealous and He wished to share His goodness with others, other difficulties arise. Is the creation different from perfection or not? If it is not, we have no creation but only repetition. If it is, in what sense is it so? Is it good or bad? If it is bad, then perfection has produced something imperfect. If it is good,

[1] Op. cit., p. 158.

[2] Schweitzer himself admits that 'ethical mysticism humbly leaves unanswered the question in what manner the world spirit exists within the poor human spirit and in it attains to consciousness of itself' (ibid., p. 264).

[3] Psalms cii. 25–7.

then it is not new, for perfection by definition includes all that is good. If it is said that God is not perfect without His creation, and that creation is necessary to His full expression, then God is not perfection or absolute reality. The two together, God and the world, make up the total reality. God by Himself is imperfect. A being who is perfect and eternal cannot depend on anything fragmentary and temporal. If God is bound by the necessity to create, He is dependent on the worshippers and so cannot be an object of worship. And yet there is a world of becoming which in a sense is other than God. How can God and the world both be real? If God is always complete reality without the world, how can anything else arise?

The explanation offered by Śaṁkara admits that the universe is dependent on the Absolute, though not the Absolute on the universe. A distinction is made between manifestation or transformation (*pariṇāma*) and one-sided dependence (*vivarta*). The illustrations used for explaining the latter type of dependence suggest the illusory theory of the world. The world is said to depend on the Absolute, even as the appearance of snake depends on the rope, or that of a mirage on shining sand particles, or that of silver on a conch-shell. The point of these illustrations is to affirm that the production and cessation of the appearances make no difference to the reality of which they are the reflections. In the case of transformation, the substance itself is changed. When the effect is destroyed, the cause also is destroyed. If the supreme itself were modified into the world, then the immortal would become mortal.[1] So it is said that it does not itself become many but seems to have become many through *māyā*. Aristotle tells us that the world depends on God, though God is completely unaware of and unaffected by it. The temporal yields a real apprehension of the eternal, though it does not contain or exhaust the eternal. The eternal does not take part in the temporal process as though it were one with it. We see the eternal through the temporal, not face to face but under a veil. Becoming is an imperfect representation of being. The doctrine of one-sided depen-

[1] 'martyatām amṛtam vrajet.' Gauḍapāda (*Kārikā* on *Māṇḍūkya Up.* iii. 19); see also iii. 20–4; iv. 6–8.

dence is hostile to ideas of organic relationship between God and the world, which are popular to-day. Evolution is introduced into the life of God. For William James, God 'may draw vital strength and increase of very being from our fidelity'.[1] Bergson's life-force and Alexander's emergent deity are finite self-educating gods. For Nicholas Berdyaev the process of history belongs to the inmost depths of the divine.[2] For him God is susceptible of change and even suffering. Hindu thought is emphatic in asserting that the changes of the world do not affect the integrity or perfection of the Absolute. Evolution and novelty do certainly exist, but they belong solely to the cosmic side of the picture, and their function is to reveal the immutable presence of an Absolute to which they add nothing. Advaita Vedānta proclaims that this cosmos is not the final end of the Absolute, which is independent of creation. When we look at the Absolute from the cosmic end, not as it is in itself, but as it is in relation to the world, the Absolute is envisaged as Īśvara or personal God who guides and directs the process by His providence. In the Upaniṣads the Absolute is said to have nothing of empiric being about it. It is perfection itself, though personality is attributed to it. Śaṁkara explains that there are two different doctrines in the Upaniṣads, one representing the esoteric truth that Brahman is the impersonal, unknowable Absolute without attributes, the other exoteric, that Brahman is the God who manifests Himself in the universe. The Upaniṣads believed that there was only one doctrine. Theistic philosophy conceives Brahman as a personal God. Śaṁkara makes out that impersonal Brahman beyond all word and thought becomes personal Īśvara through combining with the limitation of wisdom.[3] God has in His own being eternal values which human history tries to realize on the plane of space-time-cause. Creation is a necessary part of God's being. God needs it for the fullness of His being. God, the self-conscious Īśvara, is the great *māyin* who produces the world. The world has its roots in God.

The analogy of play (*līlā*) is employed to suggest the free

[1] *The Will to Believe, and other Essays.*

[2] *The Meaning of History*, E.T. (1936), pp. 45–6.

[3] Commentary on *Aitareya Up.* v. 3.

overflow of the divine into the universe. It does not mean that there is nothing real or significant going on all the time. The world is the profoundest expression of the divine nature. Gauḍapāda mentions different theories of creation. Some attribute it to the wondrous power (*vibhūti*) of God; others look upon it as of the same nature as dream and illusion (*svapnamāyāsarūpa*); some assign it to the mere will of God (*icchāmātram prabhoḥ sriṣṭiḥ*); others declare time to be the manifester of all beings (*kālātprasūtim bhūtānām*). Some think that creation is for the enjoyment of God (*bhogārtham*); others attribute it to mere diversion (*krīḍārtham*). But the truth is that it is of the very nature of the supreme being, for what desire can he whose desires are fulfilled have?[1] The analogy is not intended to suggest that the universe is a meaningless show made in a jest.[2] The world is created by God out of the abundance of His joy.[3]

VIII

Schweitzer declares: 'If the reality of the world is denied, then ethics altogether cease to have any importance. The only thing that remains for man to do is to see through the delusion of believing in a material world.'[4] Again, 'for any believer in the māyā doctrine ethics can have only a quite relative importance'.[5] The second statement is somewhat different from the first, since it affirms the compatibility of ethics with the *māyā* doctrine, though the first denies it altogether. While this doctrine suggests that the world may not be worthy of being lived in, it holds that life in it is worth living if it is directed by spiritual ideals. Enthusiastic service of humanity is possible only if we have faith in a transcendent goal. Mere morality without spiritual conviction or *jñāna* is incapable of giving us satisfaction.

[1] 'devasyeṣa svabhāvoyam āptakāmasya kā spruha' (*Kārikā*, i. 7–9). The theory that the world is of the nature of dream or illusion is set aside by Gauḍapāda.

[2] The Qur'ān asks, 'Thinkest thou that I have made the heavens and the earth and all that is between in a jest?'

[3] Cf.: sṛṣṭyādikam harir naiva prayojanam apekṣyatu
kurute kevalānandāt yathā mattasya nartanam.

[4] Op. cit., p. 60.

[5] Ibid., p. 65.

Jñāna, or seeing through the veil of *māyā*, is the spiritual destiny of man. It is something more than ethical goodness, though it cannot be achieved without it. The difference is that between perfection and progress, between eternal life and temporal development, between time suspended and time extended. One is an improvement of human nature, while the other is a reorientation of it. We cannot reach perfection by means of progress any more than we can reach the point where the clouds touch the horizon by running.

The old sage Yājñavalkya, in order to follow the way of salvation, gives up his possessions, leaving them to his two wives. But his wife Maitreyī refuses these riches of the world with the words, 'What are these to me if I am not thereby to gain life eternal?'[1] All activity only helps that which is perishable; the seeker after perfection is not satisfied by it. A well-known Sanskrit verse asks: 'What if a man has all the wealth to realize his ends? What if he defeats his enemies; what if he helps his friends by gifts to them all? What if he continues to live endlessly in an embodied existence?'[2] We can become perfect only by overcoming selfishness. The moral man battles with selfishness but works all the time under the illusion of egoism. The saint 'covers himself with the truth of the universal self'. If we take our stand on unreality we may grow better or worse, but not perfect.

The view which regards the multiplicity as ultimate is deceptive (*māyā*), for it causes the desire to live separate and independent lives. When we are under the influence of *māyā*, we think we are completely separate entities, sharing little and mistaking individuality, which is one of the conditions of our life in space-time, for isolation and not wishing to lose the hard outlines of our separate existence. *Māyā* keeps us busy with the world of succession and finitude. It causes a certain restlessness in our souls, fever in our blood. It tempts us to accept, as real, bubbles which will be broken,

[1] 'yena na amṛtāsyām, kim tena kuryām.'

[2] prāptāś śriyas sakalakāmadhugās tataḥ kim
nyastam padamśirasi vidviṣatām tataḥ kim
sampāditāh praṇayino vibhavais tataḥ kim
kalpam sthitam tanubhritām tanubhiḥ tatah kim.

cobwebs which will be swept away. This wearing of masks, this playing of roles, this marionette performance of ourselves, is mistaken for truth. We forget that we are more closely allied in spirit than we suspect, that we share infinitely more than we realize. If this life were all, if our brief little existence on the little lighted stage were the grand reality, if there were no invisible sphere, no great communion of minds, no shared adventures of spirit, we would not have the feeling of moving through a haunted world. Compared with those who have seen the truth of things, the awakened spirits, we are sleep-walkers. There is a saying of Goethe that error stands in the same relation to truth as sleep to waking. The *Bhagavadgītā* tells us that 'the wise one is awake when it is night for all others and he looks upon that as night in which other living beings are awake'.[1] The genuineness of one's awakening is directly proportionate to one's apprehension of truth. Wisdom liberates while ignorance binds, and the inner change is essential to perfection.

This self-finding or becoming one with the infinite, Schweitzer complains, is 'a pure act of the spirit which has nothing to do with ethics'.[2] Progress is represented as a growing out of ignorance into knowledge. This knowledge is not merely intellectual any more than ignorance is error. Ignorance (*avidyā*) and selfish desire (*kāma*) are two phases of one phenomenon. Patañjali traces the karmas which bind us to the cycle of birth and death to ignorance (*avidyā*), egoism (*asmitā*), attachment (*rāga*), hatred (*dveṣa*), and self-love (*abhiniveśa*). These five are different expressions of the fundamental ignorance. Only when a man rises to dispassion and acts without selfish attachment is he really free. The ego is the knot of our continued state of ignorance, and so long as we live in the ego we do not share in the delight of the universal spirit. In order to know the truth we must cease to identify ourselves with the separate ego shut up in the walls of body, life, and mind. We must renounce the narrow horizon, the selfish interest, the unreal objective. This is an ethical process. Truth can never be perceived except by those who are in love with goodness. Again, the delivery from the illusion is not achieved by means of

[1] ii. 69. [2] Op. cit., p. 43.

abstract knowledge. Intellectual progress helps us to clear the mental atmosphere of chimeras and phantoms, of errors and illusions. When these hindrances are removed, the truth of spirit is revealed, self-supported and indubitable, filling our entire horizon. An inward change alone fits souls for eternal life. Besides, our apprehension of reality is by no means final, until it is total. It must embrace the whole of our nature, thought, feeling, and will. Wherever the apprehension is only partial, in thought or feeling or will, there will be discontent and unrest in the midst of repose. The individual strives to make God-control entire by throwing off all that is impure and selfish. All this means effort. Wisdom is not cheaply won. It is achieved through hard sacrifice and discipline, through the endurance of conflict and pain. It is the perfection of human living, the ceaseless straining of the human soul to pierce through the crushing body, the distracting intellect, the selfish will, and to apprehend the unsheathed spirit. It is intent living, the most fruitful act of man by which he tries to reach reality behind the restless stream of nature and his own feelings and desires. The destiny of the human soul is to realize its oneness with the supreme. There is a difference between the substantial immanence and the conscious union which requires of the creature voluntary identification. If the substantial reality of the human soul abides in that quality which we call spirit, growth or spiritual life means conscious realization of the fundamental truth. The *Bṛhadāraṇyaka Upaniṣad* tells us that when the individual soul (*puruṣa*) is embraced by the all-embracing spirit (*prajñenātmanā*) he attains his proper form in which his desire is fulfilled (*āptakāmam*), in which his desire is the spirit (*ātmakāmam*); he is without desire (*akāmam*), apart from grief (*śokāntaram*).[1] The heart is released from its burden of care. The sorrows and errors of the past, the anxiety of unsatisfied desire, and the bitterness of resentment disappear.

IX

In another way Hindu thought is said to be non-ethical. Systematic ethical reflection cannot be found in it, for the

[1] iv. 3. 21.

obvious reason that the supreme end is release from the constitutive conditions of actuality. 'Deliverance from reincarnation can only be attained through freedom from the world and freedom from the will to live.'[1] Śaṁkara tells us that the end of all discipline is to secure the full riddance of the causes which make for rebirth.[2] The question relates to the 'constitutive condition of actuality'. It is the ego sense, the illusion that each of us is an exclusive unity sharply marked off from whatever lies outside his body in space and beyond his experience in time. So long as the illusion of a separate ego persists, existence in the temporal process is inevitable. Negatively, release is freedom from hampering egoism; positively, it is realization of one's spiritual destiny. The abandonment of the ego is the identification with a fuller life and consciousness. The soul is raised to a sense of its universality. It leaves behind its existence for itself alone and becomes united with the spirit of the universe. No longer has it any private wishes of its own. In Gethsemane, Christ as an individual felt that the cup should pass away. That was His personal desire. The secret of the Cross is the crucifixion of the ego and the yielding to the will of God. 'Thy will be done.' Every man by merging his will in the will of God, by losing his self in submission to God, finds the truth of his own self. The burden of experience is laid upon us in order to purify us from egoism.

Eternal life is one in which the universal spirit is all in all. The *jñāni* or the seer does not abstain from the work of the world but does it with his eyes fixed on the eternal. Religion is not a flight from the world, a taking refuge in the ordered serenity of heaven, in despair over the hopeless disorder of earth. Man belongs to both orders, and his religion is here or nowhere. Life eternal consists in another kind of life in the midst of time. Religious life is a rhythm with moments of contemplation, and of action, of refreshment and restoration in the life of spirit, and of action with a sense of mission in the world. Action of the seer is more efficient since it springs from conviction and depth and is

[1] p. 42.
[2] 'sahetukasya saṁsārasya atyantoparamam'.

carried out with poise and serenity. The man of wisdom is interested in promoting the welfare of all created beings according to the *Bhagavadgītā* (*sarvabhūtahiterataḥ*). Holiness is known by the happiness it sheds. The test of authentic spiritual insight is an increased integration of the personal life, quickened sensibility, heightened power, and universal tenderness. The fusing of the finite and the infinite, of the surface consciousness and the ultimate depths, gives the sense of a new creation. To live consciously in the finite alone is to live in bondage, with ignorance and egoism, suffering and death. By drawing back from an ignorant absorption in ourselves, we recover our spiritual being, unaffected by the limitations of mind, life, and body, so that the finite in which we outwardly live becomes a conscious representation of the divine being. Thus does it escape from its apparent bondage into its real freedom.

Freedom, love, light, and power are not to be confused with dejected looks or depression of mind. Spirit without mind or spirit without body is not the aim of human perfection. Body and mind are the conditions or instruments of the life of spirit in man, valuable not for their own sake but because of the spirit in them. In the *Maitri Upaniṣad* the knower of the self is compared to a smokeless fire burning as it were with glow.[1] The body becomes a transparency through which the spirit shines, a glass for its indwelling flame. The spiritual tendency does not move in the region of the abstract, but has its grip on the actual and embraces the complexity of thought and the richness of life. Body and mind are the conditions and instruments of the life of spirit in man.

The dualism between body and spirit is not radical. Without maltreating the body we can attain to the freedom of spirit. In a famous passage we are called upon to make body and the senses, speech and thought worthy of the infinite spirit which dwells in them. 'May the earth, water, fire, air and ether that compose my body become purified; may sound, touch, vision, taste and smell become purified . . . may my thought, speech, actions become purified . . . may my soul become purified so that I may become the effulgent

[1] i. 2.

spirit, free from sullying passion and sin.'[1] The distinctive feature of the Hindu view is that it does not look upon the development of mind, life, and body as the primary ends of life. Health and vigour of the body are essential for vital energy and mental satisfaction. As the expression of the spiritual, the perfection of the physical is an integral part of man's complete living. While it is desired to some extent for its own sake, it is desired more for its capacity to further human activity which has for its aim the discovery and expression of the divine in man (*dharmasādhanam*). Similarly, we are not called upon to crush the natural impulses of human life or ignore the intellectual, emotional, and aesthetic sides of man's being, for they are a part of man's finer nature, and their development not only satisfies the individual but helps to express the spirit in him. The aim of ascetic discipline is the sanctification of the entire personality. Again, morality, individual and social, is not a mere rational ordering of man's relations with his fellows but is a means for his growing into the nature of spirit. This is true of all our aims and activities. The Upaniṣad tells us that health and wealth, husband and wife are dear to us not for their own sake but because of the spirit in them (*ātmanastu kāmāya*). The power of the spiritual truth casts its light on the natural life of man and leads it to flower into its own profound spiritual significance. Such a view does not take away from the value of ordinary life, which becomes supremely important when it is felt to be instinct with the life of the spirit and a support for its expression.

Mysticism has its fanatics who look upon the real as spiritual freedom and contrast it with the actual in its bondage, declaring that birth is an error of the soul and our chance of liberation lies in shaking off these shackles. The theory of *māyā* has been interpreted in this negative sense so as to lend support to the doctrine that man's life has no real meaning, that it is a mistake of the soul, an error that

[1] pṛthivyāpas tejo vāyur ākāśā me śuddhyantām . . .
śabda sparśa rūpa rasa gandhā me śuddhyantām . . .
mano vākkāya karmāṇi me śuddhyantām
ātmā me śuddhyantām, jyotir aham virajā
vipāpmā bhūyāsam. (*Taittirīya Āraṇyaka*, x. 66.)

has inexplicably crept into being. Since the real is the supreme Brahman, the only thing to do is to get away from all existence, celestial or terrestrial. The illusion is real to itself and it binds us so long as we rest in it. Our true aim should be to get rid of the error and thus of life. *Mokṣa* or release is the extinction of the individual, his annulment in the Absolute. Since the world is an illusion, it is a waste of energy to spend labour and heroism in battling with its merely illusory events. Our duty consists in putting up uncomplainingly with its annoying semblance of reality. By adopting an ethic of quietism and resignation we are enabled to enter in some measure into the peaceful being of the Absolute, which knows nothing of errors and illusions and is tirelessly at rest. If this view is accepted, the path of the universe becomes an aimless one. The world of history and the wheel of rebirth are parts of a mechanism of self-deception. The will not to live is the highest good, the one desirable result of all living.

Such exaggerations are to be met with in mysticism, Eastern as well as Western. But Śaṁkara has nothing in common with people who will not accept the visible world any more than with those who will accept nothing else. Exclusive absorption in a super-historical goal often produces the feeling that all things temporal are so fragile and fleeting that they are hardly worth our serious attention. But the eternal is not out of all relation to the world of history. Though caught in the finite, we aspire for the infinite. The long series of births and rebirths, though in one sense a chain of bondage, is in another sense a means to self-knowledge. To develop out of a materialized being into a spiritualized one is the crown of human evolution. It is to live in the immortality of spirit though attached to a mortal body. It consists in a self-finding, a self-becoming. We have to outgrow much and exceed many of our limitations in order to attain this, but the transfiguration to which we aspire is the very law of our nature. Ignorance and imperfection of self-knowledge conceal this fact from us.

The liberated individual works for the welfare of the world. The *Bhagavadgītā* tells us, 'Man does not attain to the state of being without work by undertaking no work, nor does he reach perfection by simply shunning the world.' It is improper for man to remain without sharing in the work of the world even when God consents to work for the universe. Besides, so long as man lives, he cannot remain even for an instant without activity.[1] Love to God expresses itself in love to creation.[2] The sage is not egocentric in the sense of caring for his own soul, or altruistic in the sense of caring for others, or theocentric in the sense of wishing to enjoy God in the solitude of his soul. He is at the heart of the universe in which he himself and others live, move, and have their being. He is conscious of the wider destiny of the universe. The question is not, What shall I *do* to be saved? but In what *spirit* shall I do? Detachment of spirit and not renunciation of the world is what is demanded from us. The knowers of Brahman remake the world according to the *Bṛhadāraṇyaka Upaniṣad*.[3] Action done in a disinterested spirit does not bind or sully the soul (*na karma lipyate nare*). Until this cosmic process is terminated, the saved individuals along with the world soul continue to function. This cosmic process from the world soul to the lowest objects is a phenomenon, an historical series,[4] which when it reaches its end disappears into the Absolute. Until this consummation is attained, the freed individuals share, though in a disinterested spirit, in the work of the world. Religion has no secret which absolves us from living.

Schweitzer forgets that the great text 'That art Thou' (*tat tvam asi*) is bound up with an ethic of active service. He writes: 'Easy as it would be to turn the doctrine of tat tvam asi in an ethical direction, they nevertheless neglect to do it.'[5] At the end of his Indian tour Dr. Paul Deussen said to a gathering at Bombay: 'The Gospels quite correctly establish as the highest law of morality, "Love your neighbour as yourselves." But why should I do so since by the order of nature I feel pain and pleasure only in myself, not in my neighbour? The answer is not in the Bible . . . but it is in the Veda, in the great formula That art Thou which

[1] iii. 8. [2] xii. 13–14. [3] iii. 5.

[4] Śaṁkara on *Bṛhadāraṇyaka Up.* i. 1. 'evam brahmādyā sthāvarāntā svabhāvikāvidyādidoṣavato dharmādharmasādhanakṛtā saṁsāragatir nāmarūpa-karmāśrayā.'

[5] Op. cit., p. 43.

gives in three words the combined sum of metaphysics and morals. You shall love your neighbour as yourselves because you are your neighbour.' In the words of the *Bhagavadgītā*: 'He who knows himself in everything and everything in himself will not injure himself by himself.' Every person round me is myself at a different point of space and time and at a different grade of being. When one realizes that all beings are but the self (*ātmaivābhūt*), one acts not selfishly but for all beings.

X

Schweitzer thinks that 'Brāhmanic mysticism has nothing to do with ethics. It is through and through supra-ethical.'[1] When the individual soul is liberated from egoism and attains spiritual freedom, it is at spontaneous unity with universal will. It acts in an impersonal way without effort or expectation. It has become a passive instrument of the divine, itself without initiative, *sarvārambhaparityāgi*. Ordinarily, action distracts us from our true self. Man in affirming himself by his actions thinks himself to be the agent. Such action tends to be an escape from the deeper reality of his own nature. As we have seen, the action of the seer is of a different kind. It is creative living where external authority gives place to inward freedom. Only in this sense do the Upaniṣads declare: 'The immortal man overcomes both the thoughts "I did evil" and "I did good". Good and evil, done or not done, cause him no pain.'[2] 'Give up good and evil, truth as well as untruth. Having given up truth and untruth, give up the consciousness that you have given them up.'[3] Even self-consciousness is an obstacle. The liberated individual is lifted beyond the ethical distinctions of good and evil. When the Upaniṣad says that 'sin does not cling to a wise man any more than water clings to a lotus leaf' it does not mean that the sage may sin and yet be free,

[1] Op. cit., p. 43.
[2] *Bṛhadāraṇyaka Up.* iii. 4.
[3] tyaja dharmam adharmam ca
ubhe satyānṛte tyaja
ubhe satyānṛte tyaktvā
yena tyajasi tat tyaja.
(*Mahābhārata*, xii. 337. 40.)

but rather that any one who is free from worldly attachments is also free from all temptation to sin. So long as a man is a creature of desire, he will do as he wills to be, and act in accordance with his will. 'He will become pure by good acts and impure by evil acts. Whatever deed he does, of that will he reap the fruit.' Good and evil are the most real things in his existence, but when he has shaken off his egoism, then the moral distinction has no longer any point. 'Whosoever is begotten of God cannot sin.'[1] Augustine shows by the example of the mind of God that liberty in its perfect state has no place for wrong choosing but is at one with righteousness. Green argues that the freedom is a choice of right, not wrong. It is not a choice between right and wrong. The passionate physico-mental individual is not the real man. It is the envelope encompassing the person's real self. When the individual spirit realizes his divine nature and acts from it, he transcends the distinctions of good and evil. Not that he can do evil and yet be free from sin, but that it is impossible for him to do wrong, for he is no more the agent or the enjoyer. Good and evil presuppose the basis of egoism. Good acts are those which aim at the well-being of oneself and others, and evil ones are those which interfere with the well-being of oneself and others. Where exactly the line between self and others falls depends on convention. The essence of evil lies in invading what is regarded as another's sphere. While all kinds of actions based on the conception of a separate self are in essence evil, the term wrongdoing is reserved for those actions in which one's egoism goes so far as to break from its own sphere into that of another in order to deny it. From ethical ór non-ethical conduct higher or lower forms of rebirth ensue. By the constant practice of goodness is finally attained the highest form of existence in which man becomes capable of the experience of union with the universal soul. While ethical life can give rise to a better existence, it by itself cannot effect release, which requires the shifting of the very basis of all life and activity. Schweitzer is right when he contends that 'ethical conduct is only an aid to a better reincarnation but does not effect redemption'.[2] Ethics presuppose the separatist view

[1] 1 John iii. 9.

[2] Op. cit., p. 165.

of life. When we transcend it, we get beyond ethical laws.[1] The followers of Śaṁkara repudiate the Mīmāṁsā view that works lead to salvation and argue that spiritual insight (*jñāna*) is the only way to it. When the theory of 'put a penny in the slot and pull out a pardon' became fashionable in Christianity, Luther held justification is by faith alone and not by works. Release is eternal, while pursuit of works is transient. The latter is helpful in hindering the hindrances to spiritual life. The conception of saintliness which is beyond good and evil is not an invitation to practise unethical conduct. *Kaṭha Upaniṣad* declares that 'he who has not ceased from immoral conduct cannot obtain God through intelligence'.[2] Immoral conduct (*duścarita*) and spiritual life are incompatible, since the eternal is pure and free of all evil (*apahatapāpmā*). That pure being (*tat śubhram*) can be apprehended only by those 'whose nature is purified' (*viśuddhasattva*, *vītarāga*).[3] God is both truth and virtue.[4] 'Only when one's whole nature is purified are the bonds released which keep the soul from God.'[5]

This contention is based upon the conception of God as superior to the categories of the world. We cannot speak of Him as doing right and wrong. In its inmost being reality is neither good nor evil, neither moral nor immoral, just as it is neither high nor low, neither coloured nor colourless. These distinctions belong not to reality as such but to the human world which is a part of this cosmic process, which is itself a phase in which being is alienated from itself. Not that the distinctions of good and evil are arbitrary or conventional; they are certainly reasonable and natural, and they express absolute truths of the moral order, but they are fundamentally the categories of this world. They are symbolic, not images or shadows. The symbolism is not artificial, accidental, or false. It tells us about the ultimate reality, but darkly, reflected as it were in the mirror of the world. As good and evil belong to this world, and as the real is beyond good and evil, the problem for man is to pass

[1] St. Paul says: 'If ye are led by the Spirit, ye are not under the law.' See also 1 John iii. 6, 9, 14.

[2] i. 2. 24.

[3] *Muṇḍaka Up.* ii. 2. 7.

[4] *Bṛhadāraṇyaka Up.* ii. 5. 11.

[5] *Chāndogya Up.* v. 10. 7.

from symbols to reality. When he succeeds in his attempt he is beyond good and evil. In the life of spirit, all symbolism is overcome.

XI

The last criticism which we shall deal with is that Hindu ethics treat inner perfection and inward calm as of more importance than outer activity. Schweitzer contrasts 'the inactive ethic of perfecting the self alone' with the active enthusiastic love of one's neighbour.[1] Hindu ethics hold 'before man as the highest aim that he should endeavour to attain to the right composure, the right inwardness, the right ethical attitude of mind and the true peace of soul'.[2] He forsakes the arena, abandons action, and withdraws into himself. He is, in the words of Bishop Creighton, 'as good as gold and fit for heaven but of no earthly use'. Hindu ethics will plead guilty to this charge. The motive behind ethical practices is that of purging the soul of selfish impulses so that it may be fitted to receive the beatific vision. Spiritual strenuousness, meditation, the freeing of the mind from hatred, anger, and lust are emphasized. We must seek the eternal with all our power, with purified emotion, illumined mind, and reflective will. The perfecting of self is to pass from the narrow, constricted, individual life to the free, creative, spiritual life. It is to get our tangled lives into harmony with the great movement of reality. It is not to be unsocial, or to despise the natural relationships of life or end in a type of self-centred spiritual megalomania. The *Mahābhārata* says: 'For a knower of Brahman there is no wealth comparable to unity, sameness, truthfulness, virtue, steadfastness, non-injury, candour, and withdrawal from all activities.'[3]

There is no reason why we should regard self-perfecting as a species of inactivity. To harness the restless steeds of

[1] Op. cit., pp. 5, 8–9.

[2] Ibid., p. 9. M. Bergson supports this contention when he says that Hindu thought 'did not believe in the efficacy of human action' (*Two Sources of Morality and Religion*, E.T. (1935), p. 192).

[3] naitādṛśam brāhmaṇasyāsti vittam yathaikatā samatā satyatāca
śīlam sthitir daṇḍanidhānam ārjavam tataścoparamaḥ kriyābhyaḥ.
(xii. 176. 37.)

the senses, to subdue the passions and evil impulses which lead us away from our real nature, is an essential part of ethics. The root of all evil is desire, which determines will and act. Desires torment the soul, bind it in chains, reducing it to a servitude. They darken and blind the intellect. It cannot be said that those who aim at perfecting themselves are doing something non-ethical simply because they are not 'troubled over many things'. What appears to be passivity is intense concentration of consciousness where the soul lays hold immediately and ineffably on divine reality.

While normally the individual is called upon to develop the universal life through social institutions, the love of contemplative life has prompted men to abandon the world, surrender all ties, and live in solitude. But these hermits and anchorites are not confined to Hinduism.

Asceticism is associated with all religions and represents a basic need of human nature. It is the outgrowth of the demand that the highest religion requires the surrender of the individual claim and identification with the universal life. Subject to this primary demand, Hinduism recognizes the value of simple human relationships. The noblest love can grow in and through the simple love of a father or a mother. We must climb to the love of the universal through the staircase of human love, though even a strong earthly love demands self-control and self-surrender. The essential quality of asceticism is the denial of the individual desires, which is a part of religious life. Ascesis is training, and a religious man is in training all his life. Ascetic practices are adopted for different reasons. Some take to them in order that they may escape from the corruption of society, which makes life in the world almost intolerable to gentle spirits. Others are prompted by the desire to achieve invulnerability. Still others hope that the mystic vision which they wish to enjoy may sometimes be induced by physical buffetings. The wish to harden the will against the temptation of the senses is also among the motives of asceticism.

For the sake of self-knowledge, some enter monasteries and hermitages not because they are afraid of life or are cowardly, but in order that they may train themselves for the work of the world and approach it with an inextinguishable hope, a vision of divine purpose at work, with a deeper peace in the acceptance of sorrow and a beauty of holiness. If they do not at once rush into the world, it is because they are afraid of losing these. Asceticism has entered far too deeply into the texture of religious life for it to be regarded as a mistake, though our critics would now generally look upon any attempt to withdraw from the life of the world in order to gain greater purity of motive and energy of spirit as a case of forsaking our duties to our neighbour. Morality is not merely a question of laws and conventions but one of purity of mind with action as its outward manifestation.

The opposite of outward action is not inaction but inward action. Buddha went to a rich farmer of Benares and asked alms of him. He said to Buddha, 'I having ploughed and sowed eat; you, on the other hand, propose to eat without ploughing and sowing.' Buddha replied that he was engaged in an even more important tillage of the spirit. 'Faith is the seed, penance the rain, understanding my yoke and plough, modesty the pole of the plough, mind the tie, thoughtfulness my ploughshare and goad. . . . Exertion is my beast of burden carrying me without turning back to the place, where, having gone, one does not grieve. . . . So this ploughing is ploughed; it bears the fruit of immortality.'[1] What is called passivity is not inertia. The Hindu emphasis on inner life seems to many leaders of our generation, apostles of success and efficiency, a sheer waste of time. We are asked to get out and do something. The man who bakes bread or builds a house is said to be doing something useful, while he who paints pictures or composes music is doing something selfish. A variation of this astonishing doctrine animates the work of social uplifters. The royal road to the Golden Age is the road of economic reform or military conquest or armed revolution or the dictatorship of the proletariat: all these methods insist on social machinery and organization. They have resulted in a coarsening of fibre and a cheapening of life. Humanity is plunged to the depths in external things, class and nation, State and society. Man is treated as a part of the objective world and is not permitted to remain himself, have his own inner being. The

[1] Hardy, *Manual of Buddhism*, p. 215.

emphasis on negative virtues such as gentleness and love, passivism and lack of aggressiveness, which makes one surrender one's rights rather than fight for them, appears to those engaged in the busy life of politics and sport to be weakness and cowardice. There are many in India who believe that the gentleness of the strong who refuse to push their way in a crowd is prompted by fear and cowardice.[1] But like all Eastern religions Christianity also preaches a gospel of renunciation, of passivity, of withdrawal from the traffic of external things. The Cross signifies that progress is achieved not by those who fight for it but by those who suffer for it. It appealed to the Western mind in the turbulent times of the Roman Empire, when life was insecure and injustice rife. Are we to believe that insistence on negative virtues is attractive only when the glitter and glamour of life fade, when power becomes a burden and nerve fails?

The perfection of a human being differs from that of an instrument or a machine. We may judge the latter by its capacity to produce certain goods which are external to it, by its speed and efficiency in its productivity. We are not right in judging human civilization by the same standards of energy and efficiency, though we actually do so. Peaceful nations whose wheels are not turning at an excessive speed, which look upon insensate strife and savage slaughter as inhuman, are dismissed as worthless, anaemic, politically backward, senile civilizations, whose veins are not flooded by the sap of youth.

The great teachers are united in thinking that the soul of man is more precious than the immensity of the world and its growth is effected in moments of leisure and meditation. To grow more profound, to grasp essential truth, is the special privilege of man. But this is not to shirk living or run away from life.

There is no inconsistency between mysticism and the most exalted ethics. It is a one-sided view of contemplation that makes it exclusive of moral activity. Inner perfection and outer conduct are two sides of one life. Contemplation and action, the *yoga* of Kṛṣṇa and the *dhanus* of Arjuna, are

[1] Cf. 'yad evam kṣamayā yuktam aśaktam manyate janaḥ' (*Mahābhārata*, Śāntiparva, clx. 34).

two movements merged in one act. Love is organic to spiritual life. While the eyes are lifted up to the Eternal, the arms are stretched out to embrace the whole creation. Some of the greatest contemplatives were those who were most intensely active in the service of others. There are extremists among mystics—and they are not confined to one religion—who are intent on becoming one with God and indifferent to suffering bodies and broken hearts, but the normal mystic has a burning passion for social righteousness. In spite of our strong dislike of monasticism, it is well to remember that the Christian monks took the leading part in rebuilding European civilization after the barbarian hordes had almost destroyed it. The lamp of knowledge was kept burning in the Dark Ages in the monasteries by the teachers and scholars who sought the deep places of truth and counted all else as dross. The life and work of Dr. Schweitzer are themselves an example of disciplined asceticism at a time when both purpose and discipline are lacking in the world.

India, however, is full of mendicant ascetics who wander from one part of that vast continent to the other, leaving the world around to its fate. But these are not the true representatives of the genius of India, who, with a perception of the unity of things (*ekatvam anupaśyati*), move at ease in the world of spirit and the world of sense.

The semblance of truth which this view of the world-negating character of Hinduism has is due to the impression that Hindu culture has not resulted in a strong and successful organization of life such as Europe shows to us. Because India has blundered in life and failed to make the best of her material resources, she is said to be a nation of unpractical dreamers, world-shunning ascetics, patient and docile, inept and inefficient. Because the West has recently made marvellous progress in science and technology, social reform and political advancement, Christian religion, which is professed in the West, is said to be world-affirming in character. Any such sharp contrast confuses different questions. What is civilized life? Is the great Western civilization the only measure and standard by which we judge human achievement? Do the East and the West happen to be what they are on account of the religions they profess? Are they guided in their actual lives and public affairs by religious considerations, and if so, to what extent? Are the insane ambitions which make of life a hideous reign of terror attributable to religion or to a betrayal of it? Have there been fundamental differences between the East and the West till three or four centuries ago? Reality is never so clear-cut in its differences as the rubrics under which we dismember it for neat handling.

XII

What we need to-day, when executive man has far outreached reflective man, is increase of depth and the power of life. We have exalted ideals but not the power to operate them. The world commonwealth has been for some time on the agenda of mankind, but the soul that can shape the body is not there. The world over, religious theory goes one way and the drift of social tendencies is in another way. The great religions have had every opportunity which power, prestige, and wealth could give, and yet the world is as far as ever from an age of mutual helpfulness, peace, and joy. There is a general tradition of dishonesty which even honest men do not wish to notice. As they are afraid of losing their sanity and peace, they, like the pious priest and orthodox Levite of the parable, carefully pass by on the other side. We profess ourselves to be religious while we wallow in brutishness and lawless violence. We live a double life on utterly different moral levels.

Tolstoi relates that when he was in the Army he saw one of his brother officers strike a man who fell out from the ranks during a march. Tolstoi said to him: 'Are you not ashamed to treat a fellow human being this way? Have you not read the Gospels?' The other officer replied, 'Have you not read the Army Orders?' Those who lead men to the conquest of material things do not seem to feel the need for justice and charity. Religion does not possess us with a grip that is born of first-hand conviction. Our inner lives are empty. We have little initiative and less imagination, and have made ourselves so passive-minded that we are the helpless victims of all forms of publicity and propaganda.

If we do not pull ourselves together another dark age will cover the world.

Religion itself must be reborn. It has compromised with the world; there has been a good deal of world affirmation in it. By withdrawing from politics on the assumption that it deals with the salvation of souls, and politics with the preservation of society, it betrayed civilization to its worst enemy. The withdrawal of vision from life is a phenomenon of some seriousness. The romantic who is very much with us tends to look upon God as a name for his own scheme of improvement. We are satisfied that religion is compatible with militarism and imperialism, with mass murders and the crushing of human decencies. Organized religions bless our arms and comfort us with the belief that our policies are just and inevitable. In every age, religion adjusted itself to the follies and cruelties of men. If the Thugs dedicated their swords to Kāli, if chapels are attached to bull-rings and matadors do their ghastly work in the name of their favourite saint, are they in principle different from the habit of blessing wars encouraged by our religious leaders? I do not deny that, in this imperfect world, force is a sad necessity. I am not reproaching the religious teacher for exhorting us to kill. I can understand his devotion to his country. I am only uneasy when he tries to pretend that his exhortation is not in conflict with his religion. In exhorting us to kill he is violating the law of religion, and he cannot overlook it. The real distinction between the two positions is brought out by the remark of Cardinal Lavigerie, who was asked, 'What would you do if some one slapped your right cheek?' and who replied, 'I know what I ought to do, but I do not know what I should do.' Whatever he may do, he knows what he ought to do. The modern world is like the brigand in one of Tolstoi's stories who made his confession to a hermit and the hermit said in amazement: 'Others were at least ashamed of being brigands: but what is to be done with this man, who is proud of it?'

We have to-day to fight against not nature's death but man-made death. There are the great catastrophes of famine, flood, and earthquake. They cause suffering and devastation, and yet is not Gibbon right when he says that 'Man has much more to dread from the passions of his fellow creatures than from the convulsions of the elements'? Gibbon wrote many years ago, but have we improved since his time? Have we abolished the rivalries of mankind? Is not economic competition quite as ruthless as war itself, though less dramatic and spectacular? Slow-grinding starvation is not less deadly in its effects than bombs and bullets. Religion has to fight against wars, military and economic, even though it may mean loss of dividends to a few individuals.

We need not reaffirm the major temptations of our age, which sets a high value on a life of action. The prominence given to conation in psychology, pragmatism in philosophy, and social gospels in religion is leading us away from the inner life of the soul, the need for self-possession. It is an age in which power and speed are held to be more important than comprehension and love, an age of the tyranny and the futility of success. We are preoccupied with gospels of world affirmation, to the exclusion of world negation. We are unable to control the 'here and now' because we have lost conscious contact with a sphere of existence that transcends our own. The creeds which are anxious to save the world take many forms: Neo-paganism, Fascism, Nazism, Bolshevism, conventional religion. They are all marked by violence and brutality. Civilization is comradeship. It is to be civil, friendly, and not hostile to one's neighbours. Brave Italians machine-gun ignorant Abyssinians who have been blinded with mustard gas by gallant young airmen. Russian Communists liquidate Russian peasants and aristocrats, loyalists and heretics impartially. Blond Germans brutally beat Jews for the great fault of not having fair hair and blue eyes. Spaniards slay Spaniards with a savagery unheard of even among savages. The Arab and the Jew have for their daily recreation shooting one another. The military forces of Japan attack with immunity defenceless Chinese, inflicting on them untold suffering and misery, and the world looks on helpless, unable to check or modify the course of events. All these groups of world-affirmers proclaim the noble purpose of the redemption of the world. They would save the world in their own way or blow it to bits. This indifference to suffering, this callous disrespect of the stuff of life, shows the decadence of the moral sense of mankind, the attrition of ethical values. The civilized man who operates a machine-gun and massacres unarmed women and children is not in moral nature an improvement on the savage who raped and slew without turning back. Hate is spreading like a vast black cloud. Terror has become the technique of States. Freedom won by centuries of effort is lightly surrendered. Fear is over the world, and our hearts are failing us. We protest a little too much our desire for peace, while preparing for war. It is like professing vegetarianism while running a butcher's shop.

But why? There is nothing finer in our murderous species than this noble curiosity, this restless and reckless passion to understand. We cannot help asking why we are unable to save ourselves; why this incomprehensible world is so savage and stupid and suffering; why we make ourselves responsible for such queer happenings and monstrous contrasts. It is the selfishness of man and his worship of abstractions of race, nation, empire. When we get to the root of the matter we find that the individual spirit is the creator of world conditions. From within our natures comes all that will exalt or defile a man. Out of the heart are the issues of life.[1] The passions of the heart upset the balance of the mind and the even course of the world. It is the human heart that is decadent and mercenary, brutal and selfish. Pater's Marius the Epicurean was one day watching the butcheries of the gladiators in ancient Rome. What was wanting, he thought, was the *heart* that would make it impossible to witness all this: and the future would be with the forces that could beget that heart. The world can be saved only if men and women develop a heart that will make it impossible for them to witness with equanimity mutual slaughter and suffering of people. The fallen nature of man is the source of the disastrous disintegration of humanity. Until the dignity of life, the importance of human happiness, and a horror of

[1] Jeremiah says: 'The heart is deceitful above all things and is desperately sick: who can know it?' (xvii. 9). Jesus says: 'Out of the heart of men evil thoughts proceed, fornications, thefts, murders, adulteries, covetings, wickednesses, deceit, lasciviousness, and evil eye, railing, pride, foolishness' (Mark vii. 21, 22).

subjection under any guise become functioning realities, our economic, our racial, and our national Utopias will remain inhuman monstrosities demanding the murder of bodies and souls. All else is sophistry and deception. The coming struggle is not so much between Fascism and Communism as between empires of material values, supported by organized religions and provincial patriotisms, and the sovereignty of spiritual ideals. Those who tell us that asceticism is superfluous, that contemplation is perilous, and the precept 'be perfect' means 'make a success of life and attend if possible to the perishing moment', do not understand the high destiny of man. A reborn living faith in spiritual values is the deepest need of our lives. Only religion which demands as its first principle individual change, the substitution of the divine for the dark image in the soul, can create that new heart in the peoples, can give them the courage and the faith to be consistent and change their life and institutions which are so barbarous, in a thousand details which loyalty to their religion demands.

IV

INDIA AND WESTERN RELIGIOUS THOUGHT: GREECE

I

THOUGH Asia and Europe are different, they are not so completely different as to disallow an interchange of goods, material and spiritual. This interchange has occurred throughout the centuries and points to the underlying unity of the human mind. India, which is, in a sense, representative of the Asiatic consciousness, has never been isolated from the Western continent in spite of geographical, linguistic, and racial barriers. Its influence or, at any rate, connexion with Western thought, though not constant and continuous, has been quite significant. We cannot speak of India as we do of Assyria or Egypt, Crete or Babylon, for its history is still being made and its civilization is still in progress.

The West is passing through a new Renaissance due to the sudden entry into its consciousness of a whole new world of ideas, shapes, and fancies. Even as its consciousness was enlarged in the period of the Renaissance by the revelation of the classical culture of Greece and Rome, there is a sudden growth of the spirit to-day effected by the new inheritance of Asia with which India is linked up. For the first time in the history of mankind, the consciousness of the unity of the world has dawned on us. Whether we like it or not, East and West have come together and can no more part. The spatial nearness is preparing the way for a spiritual approximation and interchange of treasures of mind and imagination. If we are nurtured exclusively on the past of Europe or of Asia we cannot consider ourselves to be cultivated. The thought and experience of one-half of humanity cannot be neglected without peril. If we are to correct the narrowness resulting from a one-sided and exclusive preoccupation with either Eastern or Western thought, if we are to fortify our inner life with the dignity of a more perfect and universal experience, an understanding of each other's cultures is essential. It is a foolish pride that impels some of us to combat all external influences. Every spiritual or scientific advance which any branch of the human family achieves is achieved not for itself alone, but for all mankind. Besides, there is no power possessed by any race of men that is not possessed in some measure by all. The difference is one of degree. The mysticism of ancient India or the rationalism of modern Europe is only a fuller development of something which belongs to man as man. To the observer of the essential drifts of the dawning world, it is clear that we are in an age when cultures are in fusion. To penetrate to the heart of a civilization we ought to study its secret springs of thought, its religious ideals. Religion has been from the beginning the bearer of human culture. It is the supreme achievement of man's profound experience. It is the deepest kind of life reflecting the different phases, complex and conflicting, of human living. Millions of minds, their thoughts and dreams, go to make a religion. A large part of the world received its religious education from India. In spite of continuous struggle with superstition and theological baggage, India has held fast for centuries to the ideals of spirit.[1]

II

In this short sketch it is impossible to give even an outline of either Eastern or Western thought. My object is a very limited one,to refer to the mystic tendencies in the two streams and indicate their affinity of type more than their identity of origin. My endeavour is to argue that mystical aspiration is a genuine part of human nature and it assumes the same general forms wherever it is developed. Even this

[1] 'It is true that even across the Himalayan barrier India has sent to us such questionable gifts as grammar and logic, philosophy and fables, hypnotism and chess, and above all our numerals and our decimal system. But these are not the essence of her spirit; they are trifles compared to what we may learn from her in the future. As invention, industry, and trade bind the continents together, or as they fling us into conflict with Asia, we shall study its civilisation more closely, and shall absorb, even in enmity, some of its ways and thoughts. Perhaps, in return for conquest, arrogance and spoliation, India will teach us the tolerance and gentleness of the mature mind, the quiet content of the unacquisitive soul, the calm of the understanding spirit and a unifying, pacifying love for all living things' (Will. Durant, *The Story of Civilisation: Our Oriental Heritage* (1935), p. 633).

can only be done in a cursory manner. The proportions of treatment, therefore, will be widely different from those which are proper in a complete study of the philosophical and religious problems. If this seems to be unsatisfactory I must beg the reader to look upon this treatment only as an introduction to the subject.

Hindu civilization goes back to the period of the Indus valley in which were found great cities of well-planned houses built with baths and sanitary arrangements. Only two of the ruined cities have been explored so far, Mohenjo-daro on the Indus, and Harappa on the Ravi. They are four hundred miles apart, though the civilization of the two is astonishingly homogeneous.[1] The same forms of architecture and town planning, of metal tools and weapons, are found in both. The members of the civilization which flourished in the fourth millennium B.C. cultivated fields of grain, raised cattle, tamed the horse, harnessed the bullock to two-wheeled carts, and taught the elephant to carry burdens. Tools of copper and bronze were in use and craftsmen worked in silver and understood the art of glazing. A form of picture writing was in use. This civilization resembled in essential features those of Sumer, Egypt, and Minos.

According to Sir John Marshall, the four cultures seem to have had a common parent in the Afrasian Chalcolithic culture of which they are the articulations. He says 'each no doubt had its own particular type of civilisation which was adopted to suit local conditions. But between them all was a fundamental unity of ideas which could hardly have been the result of mere commercial intercourse.'[2] He gives as illustrations, (1) the idea of using picture signs to represent objects, concepts, and actual sounds; (2) the discovery of spinning and weaving; (3) painted pottery. The Indus civilization developed on this basis, in a way peculiar to itself. As Professor Childe puts it: 'The Indus civilisation represents a very perfect adjustment of human life to a specific environment that can only have resulted from years of patient effort.

[1] 'The area embraced by the Indus civilisation must have been twice that of the old Kingdom of Egypt and probably four times that of Sumer and Akkad' (Childe, *New Light on the Most Ancient East* (1934), p. 206).

[2] *Mohenjo-daro and the Indus Civilisation* (1931), vol. i, pp. 93–5.

And it has endured; it is already specifically Indian and forms the basis of modern Indian culture.'[1] When we speak about the religious and social doctrines of the Indus people we are in the region of conjecture. From the isolated sculptural works we can infer the presence of the Śiva cult, Śakti worship, and *yoga* method. An apparent polytheism and a technique of psychological development found also among Hermetic groups in Egypt are indicated. From the skeletal remains and figurines of several physically distinct types, primitive Australoid, Eurafrican, Alpine, and Mongoloid,[2] we may infer that the social order was not based on any racial or religious exclusiveness. It permitted the worship of more than one God, exalted yogic perfection, and tolerated different racial groups. Obviously its philosophy of life, if it had one, must have been profoundly social and profoundly religious. This culture is linked up with that of Sumer, which changed into Babylonia and forms along with it the tradition which Europe has inherited.

III

The second stage of Indian civilization, the period of the *Ṛg Veda*, takes us to the second millennium B.C., and we find close agreements between the language and mythology, religious traditions and social institutions, of Indians and Iranians on the one hand, and those of the Greeks, Romans, Celts, Germans, and Slavs on the other. The gods of Father Heaven (*dyauspitar*, Jupiter), Mother Earth, the wide expanse of heaven (*varuṇa*), the Dawn (*aurora*, Usas), the Sun (*sūrya*), are common to the Greeks and the Indians, and they were conceived primarily as powers or causes working in nature. Though they have some human attributes, they were not clearly anthropomorphized. The Olympian religion of the Greeks and Vedic beliefs had a common background. There is also striking similarity between the social life described in the Homeric poems and that of the Veda. Both are patriarchal and tribal. These agreements indicate that the two peoples must have been in close contact at some early period, but neither possessed any recollection of those

[1] *New Light on the Most Ancient East* (1934), p. 220.

[2] Ibid., pp. 208–9.

times, and they met as strangers within the Persian Empire. Thus in the *Ṛg Veda* the European will find memorials of his own racial inheritance.[1] For a considerable period after their separation from their Western kinsmen, the Indians and Iranians lived together. The most prominent figure among the deities of the *Ṛg Veda* is Varuṇa, wise and all-powerful, who rules heaven and earth and the underworld by his holy ordinance, *ṛta*, the right. He is the protector of the moral order. Nothing is hidden from his eye. He is holy and pure-minded (*pūtadakṣa*).

> What is between heaven and earth and what is above,
> Everything Varuṇa, the King, sees clearly—
> The very blinking of men's eyes he numbers.
> He who moves, he who stands, he who hides himself,
> He who slips away or secretly steals into hiding,
> That which two, sitting together, secretly debate,
> That is known by Varuṇa, the King, as third.

He has his kingdom, spiritual and truthful, 'which he leads to victory against all opposition',[2] an idea which receives emphasis in Zoroastrianism in the struggle of Ormuz against Ahriman, in the contest of the divine light with demonic darkness.[3] Varuṇa's kingdom is the anticipation of the Kingdom of God (*brahmaloka*) and the Kingdom of Heaven.

The Vedic hymns were, however, composed after the separation of the Indians from the Iranians, and at the time of their composition[4] their place of abode was the territory of the Sindhu (Indus).

[1] Cf. Max Müller: 'In so far as we are Aryans in speech, that is, in thought, so far the *Ṛg Veda* is our own oldest book.' 'If one will only take the trouble to project himself into the life and thought, the poetry and action, of a people and age, which best display the first development of intellectual activity in our own race, he will find himself attracted by these hymns on many sides. . . .' See Kaegi, *The Ṛg Veda* (1898), p. 25.

[2] *Ṛg Veda*, vii. 87.

[3] 'Here first arises the important conception of a being who is by nature opposed to God, not only in the sense of a demonic abomination generally, but in the sense of an adversary of the holy spirit of the deity with which he is in fundamental conflict. This idea did not arise upon the soil of Israel, but came down from Aryan times' (Rudolph Otto, *The Kingdom of God and the Son of Man*, E.T. (1938), p. 272). The idea of a divine warfare is to be met with in the Book of Enoch, in the Assumption of Moses (x. 1, 2).

[4] Max Müller gives 1500–1200 B.C. as the period of composition of the Vedic hymns, *Chips*, I. 11; Weber the sixteenth century B.C. (*History of Indian*

Twice the Persian gods all but conquered the West. On the first occasion they were stopped at Salamis. Centuries later, under the dynasty of the Arsacids, the god Mithra found his way into the Roman world. The hymns of the Vedas and the Avesta celebrate his name, and the Vedic Mitra and the Iranian Mithra have so many points of resemblance that there is not any doubt about their identity. For both religions he is a god of light invoked together with Heaven, who is called Varuṇa in the Vedas and Ahura in the Avesta. He is the protector of truth and the enemy of falsehood and error. Mitra-Varuṇa and the five other Ādityas such as the Mithra-Ahura and the Amshaspands are not to be found in the original Aryan pantheon. They seem to have grown up at a later stage when the Hindus and Persians were still together. In Zoroastrianism, Mithra acquired greater importance. 'Ahuramazda established him to maintain and watch over all this moving world.'[1] A distinction is made between the supreme deity who dwells in perpetual serenity above the stars and an active deity engaged in ceaseless combat with the spirit of darkness. The fame of Mithra extended to the borders of the Aegean Sea, and his name was well known in Ancient Greece. Artaxerxes popularized his worship in his different capitals at Babylon, Damascus, and Sardis, as well as at Susa, Ecbatana, and Persepolis. In Babylon the official clergy (Magi) became more powerful than the indigenous priests. They looked upon Mithra as the mediator between Ormuz, or light, and Ahriman, or darkness. They soon crossed Mesopotamia and penetrated into the heart of Asia Minor. They swarmed into Pontus, Galatia, and Phrygia. After the break-up of the Persian Empire, in the religious fermentation caused by the Macedonian conquest, Mithraism received a definitive form. Hellenic and Iranian beliefs came to be identified; Ahuramazda with Zeus, Verethraghna with Heracles, Anāhita, to whom the bull was consecrated, with Artemis Tauropolos, and Mithra with

Literature, p. 2); Haug 2400–1400 (Introduction to *Aitareya Brāhmaṇa*, i. 47 f.); Whitney 2000–1400 B.C. (*Oriental and Linguistic Studies*, p. 21); Kaegi 2000–1500 B.C. (*The Ṛg Veda* (1898), p. 11). He holds that the collection of the Vedic hymns was closed about 1500 B.C. (p. 22).

[1] *Yasht*, x. 103.

Helios. The mysteries of Mithra found their way into the Roman Empire. Nero (A.D. 54–68) wished to be initiated into the ceremonies by the Magi. Mithra became linked up with the Great Mother Isis and secured the official protection which the latter enjoyed. Commodus (A.D. 180–92) became an adept and participated in the ceremonies. In A.D. 270 Aurelian won his victories in the name of Mithra. In the year A.D. 307, Diocletian, Galerius, and Licinius dedicated at Carnuntum on the Danube a temple to Mithra, 'the protector of their Empire', and the last pagan who occupied the throne of the Caesars, Julian the Apostate, was an ardent votary of Mithra. The worship of Mithra proved the most dangerous rival to the Christian Church before its alliance with Constantine. No wonder Renan observed: 'If Christianity had been stopped in its growth by some deadly disease, the world would have been Mithraist.' Then in the cathedrals the Bull would have supplanted the Cross.

Commerce between the mouth of the Indus and the Persian Gulf was unbroken down to Buddhist times. We have evidence of trade by sea between the Phoenicians of the Levant and western India as early as 975 B.C., when Hiram, King of Tyre, imported 'ivory, apes and peacocks' for decorating the palaces and the temple of King Solomon.[1]

Trade between the Indus valley and the Euphrates seems to be very ancient, for we find in the cuneiform inscriptions of the Hittite kings of Mittani in Cappadocia belonging to the sixteenth or fifteenth century B.C., the names of the Vedic gods Indra, Mitra, Varuṇa, and the Asvins, whom they call by the Vedic title Nāsatyā. The Hittite kings bore Aryan names.[2]

The ethical and religious speculations of the Jews derive largely from the culture which was common to Sumer, Egypt, and the Indus. The Hebrews first appear in history in the letters of Tell-el-Amarna, which date from 1400 B.C. They relate how Hebrew nomads drifted into Palestine, which was then under Egyptian control, and entered the military service of the Egyptians. The Jews then were a barbarous nomad people with only the most rudimentary

[1] 1 Kings x. 22.
[2] *Cambridge History of India*, vol. i (1922), p. 320.

social forms. Apparently the Hebrew nomads who took refuge in Egypt were subjected to slavery, from which they were delivered by a leader of notable gifts, whose name has come down to us. Moses persuaded the Hebrews to give up polytheism. The great Egyptologist Professor Breasted tells us that the Book of Proverbs and a large part of the Psalms are based on older Egyptian literature, and the code exemplified in Deuteronomy is largely a degraded version of the Hammurabi Code.

IV

We get to the third stage of Indian civilization in the older or canonical Upaniṣads,[1] which are pre-Buddhistic (900 to 600 B.C.). They set forth the fundamental concepts of Hindu thought, which still dominate the Indian mind. The highest wisdom is to know the self (*ātmānam viddhi*). What is the self? The Upaniṣads answer that it is the primal spirit, pure awareness, distinct from bodily states and mental happenings. By a process of analysis, the self can be discriminated from the not-self. The self is assumed to be that which remains identical in the varied experiences of life. It cannot be the body, which is subject to constant change. Nor can it be identified with the dreaming self, which, though relatively free from association with external objects, is subject to changes like pains and pleasures, suffering and joy. Nor can it be confused with the state in dreamless sleep, for the self in such a condition seems to be non-existent. The *Chāndogya Upaniṣad*[2] where this analysis of self is undertaken concludes by asserting that the self which is the basis of the stream of changes is the supreme light by which we see and hear, think and meditate. The *Māṇḍūkya Upaniṣad* confirms this account. It distinguishes four states of consciousness: ecstatic or transcendental consciousness (*turīya*), dreamless sleep (*suṣupti*), dream (*svapna*), and waking (*jāgrat*). In the waking state the self is brought into relation with the physical environment by the functioning of the body, but the body is

[1] The word *Upaniṣad* means etymologically *upa* near by, *ni* devotedly, *ṣad* sitting; and later came to signify secret (*rahasya*) instruction imparted at private meetings.

[2] viii. 7–12.

not the self, for the sense of self persists even when our bodies are injured and brains affected. The self which is aware of possessing the body cannot be the same as the body. In the state of dreams, the self is aware of other worlds than the physical. In dreamless sleep the self subsists, even though it is not aware of the physical world of waking experience or the subtler world of dreams. The principle of objectivity is there, though it is unmanifest. Neither body nor mind can function but for the principle of self. Though it is the intellect that gives rise to the consciousness of the ego, in another sense, it is itself its product. The psychological ego is a composite of ideas and imaginations, memories and affections, desires and habits. It is not the self, for we look upon our hopes and fears, our loves and disappointments, as waves on the stream which we can objectify or dramatize by means of the inward light. The self is more than the ego; personality is truly a mask. The self is the silent eternal witness, a light which no power can extinguish, whose attributes are truth and beauty, peace and wisdom, our true being which we do not perceive on account of the cloud of ignorance which covers our eyes. We can, however, see it in the empty space of the heart (*hṛdayākāśe*), in the bare room of the inner man (*antarbhūtasya khe*). When the interior darkness is illuminated there is the reflection in our consciousness of that principle which is the foundation of our life, which by its continuous presence sustains the broken parts of life and correlates them. It is the mysterious depth in which the spirit turns back on itself, its most secret dimension. This spiritual consciousness is not a metaphysical fantasy but one that can be realized by each of us. In this transcendental consciousness, where the body is still, the mind attains quiescence, and thought comes to rest, we are in contact with the pure spirit of which the states of waking, dream, and sleep are imperfect articulations. It is, according to the Upaniṣad, unseen (by sense organs), unrelated to the things of the world, incomprehensible (by the mind), devoid of marks (which can be the basis of inference), unthinkable, indescribable, essentially of the nature of consciousness which constitutes the character of the self, negation of all phenomena, the tranquil, the blissful, the 'non-dual'.[1] This negative knowledge is not mere ignorance. To know that the supreme spirit is not to be confused with any object that can be apprehended in this life is the most perfect knowledge of it. Even when we say that it remains unknown it is known by us. We affirm that it is unrelated to objects external as in waking experience, or internal as in dreams, and is a state which transcends all ordinary experience,[2] though it is its basis. Reality is not an object of knowledge but is knowledge. For when knowledge is objectified, the knower and the known are mutually alien. In such cases we cannot know an object but only know about it. In true knowledge of the real, we must know the real and not merely ideas about it. We should know the spirit and by the spirit (*ātmānam ātmanā*). And this is not possible if the spirit were an object. The moment we make it into an object, we distort its nature.

Answering to the four states of the self are the four views of reality. Brahman is the impersonal Absolute to which no finite signs or symbols are applicable. It is beyond all the similitudes of our limited understanding. The *via negativa* or the way of negation is prominent in the Upaniṣads.[3] We can only say 'I am that I am'.[4] 'That in which one sees nothing else, hears nothing else, knows nothing else is the infinite.'[5] On this Nārada asks, 'Where does the infinite exist?' (*sa kasmin pratiṣṭhitaḥ*). He who raises such a query has not comprehended the nature of the infinite. So Sanatkumāra says, 'He exists in his majesty' (*sve mahimni*), and, afraid that his answer might suggest a distinction between the infinite and his majesty, adds: 'or rather he does not exist in his majesty' (*yadi vā na mahimneti*). The Upaniṣads require us to adopt an attitude of utter silence in regard to the nature of the absolute spirit. If, however, any description is permitted, it can only be in negative terms. This does not mean that the absolute is non-being, for the very fact that the

[1] 'adṛṣṭam, avyavahāryam, agrāhyam, alakṣaṇam, acintyam, avyapadeśyam, ekātmapratyayasāram prapañcopaśamam, śāntam, śivam, advaitam' (*Māṇḍūkya Up*. i. 7).

[2] 'avastu, anupalambham, lokottaram.' Gauḍapāda's *Kārikā* on *Māṇḍūkya Up*. iv. 88.

[3] See *Bṛhadāraṇyaka Up*. ii. 3. 1.

[4] 'so'hamasmi.' *Īśa Up*. 16.

[5] *Chāndogya Up*. vii. 24. 1.

self of man is able to know it indicates its kinship with the deepest in man. Brahman is Ātman. That art thou. If a more detailed description is required, it is said to be pure being, awareness, and bliss (*saccidānanda*).

Evidently the authors of these writings are aware that the highest reality thus conceived seems to the ordinary intelligence to be that which has the least content, the thinnest of all abstractions. For the religious consciousness, God as pure being is not of much importance. While insisting that the nature of the supreme being cannot be adequately expressed in terms familiar to our finite mind, the Upaniṣads ascribe qualities such as oneness, wisdom, perfection to the object of their worship. 'He who is one, above all distinction of colour, who dispenses through his varied powers the hidden needs of men of many colours, who knows all things from beginning to end, may he unite us with the sacred wisdom.'[1] This conception of the real as the divine self answers to the state of dreamless sleep.

In the state of dreamless sleep the principle of objectivity from which the dream and waking states arise is present, though it is inactive. So also when Brahman becomes Īśvara the personal god, he is confronted by the principle of objectivity. The repose of Brahman is dissevered into the duality of subject and object, self-conscious intelligence facing the principle of objectivity which is in an unmanifested (*avyākṛta*) form in the state of world dissolution when all distinctions disappear. If our feeble minds are to form any conception of the inconceivable beginning of things, we may think of the cosmos as arising from a self-division of the Absolute. In the undivided Absolute, time is not, and there is no history. God negates Himself in order that there may be a world. The sundering of the Absolute into the personal God and object is creation's dawn. The object is regarded as the void, the mere framework of space-time. We can think away all objects, all worlds, but the vast void cannot be thought away. It is the abyss, the unfathomable night, the *tamas* which is

[1] ya eko'varṇo bahudhā śaktiyogāt
varṇān anekān nihitārtho dadhāti,
vicaiticānte viśvam ādau sa devaḥ
sa no buddhyā śubhayā saṁyunaktu.

mentioned in the *Nāsadiya sūkta* of the *Ṛg Veda*. The whole universe shrivels into nothingness, though it has limitless possibilities which will be roused into activity by the divine overlord, the spirit of God floating on the waters. The supreme is compared to light which shineth in darkness, and yet light presupposes the infinity of darkness.

The contemplation of sheer nothingness as a possibility leads to the perception that any kind of existence requires an absolute being which would overcome utter non-being. Even the minimum of being involves the defeat of non-being by positive being. The existence of anything at all presupposes absolute positivity, eternal being, activity, and form which actualizes potentialities. At the stage of duality the Supreme is conceived as a personal being whose knowledge and will are not dependent on anything outside himself and who is in turn identical with the Absolute being itself. 'He is the lord of all, the knower of all, the controller within, the source of all, that from which all things originate, and in which they finally disappear.'[1] He is the Logos, the knower of all beings ever present in the hearts of all (*sarvasya hṛdi samsthitam*). If we start from the cosmic end, it is true to say 'In the beginning was the Logos', the personal creator God. The dualism of God and matter, good and evil, eternity and time, is not ultimate as with some Gnostics and Manichaeans. It is subordinate to a fundamental monism. Yet the problem of evil is a real problem.[2] In the view of the Upaniṣads, the Absolute is not the creator of the world. God the creator facing nothingness is the first act and the rest of creation is secondary. The world is created by God because nothing can become something, something new that never existed before, only through the dynamism of being. From the womb of nature (*prakṛti*) the self (*puruṣa*) creates. Creative-

[1] *Māṇḍūkya Up.* i. 6.

[2] It is not traced to the abuse of freedom with which God endowed his creatures. Such an explanation is not free from difficulties. If God gave us freedom which we used to choose evil, the giver of such a fatal gift is the cause of pain and evil. As He is omniscient, He would have foreseen the suffering and evil of the world and yet created man and gave him this source of all perdition. Calvinist theology, which affirms that God has from all eternity predetermined some to eternal salvation and others to eternal damnation, follows as a natural corollary from the omniscience of God.

ness is out of the freedom of being; birth or production is from nature or non-being. Self is the father who creates; not-self is the mother who generates. The two principles interact and supplement one another. The free human individual is a child of God as well as the product of non-being from out of which God creates the world. He is both being and non-being, and the progress of man consists in the awakening of spirit and the overcoming of the abyss of non-being in his own nature. Creation of the world cannot be deduced from the Absolute (Brahman), which is perfectly self-sufficient, beyond all distinctions of the world, but the world implies movement in God (*Īśvara*), and its relation to God is not accidental or unnecessary.[1]

In the stage answering to the dream, Iśvara the personal God becomes Hiraṇyagarbha the world-soul, which is said to be the first-born son of God.[2] The conception of the world-soul affirms not only the oneness of the cosmos but the organic unity of humanity and the significance of its social destiny. When the world is manifested as in the waking state, we have Virāṭ or the cosmic person. We thus have the supreme Absolute which is the first principle, from which both the personal God (nous) and world-soul arise to mediate between the Absolute and the world. The symbol Aum, including the three sounds A U M, represents the supreme with its three gross, subtle, and causal aspects. Even as the totality of man's experience includes the three states of waking, dream, and dreamless sleep,[3] the reality of Brahman includes the gross, subtle, and causal aspects of the universe. As the Upaniṣad says: 'All that is past, present and future is verily Aum; that which is beyond these three modes of time is also Aum.'[4] There is no justification for confusing the Brahman of the Upaniṣads with the *Ens abstractissimum*. The pure being of Brahman is not the last residue of analysis and abstraction, which is almost identical with pure nothing-

[1] This view has led to the misconception in Gnostics like Marcion who contend that the evil world was created by an evil god, Demiourgos.

[2] See *Śvetāśvatara Up.* iii. 4; iv. 12; vi. 18.

[3] Gauḍapāda, i. 2: 'tridhā dehe vyavasthitah.' See also 'triṣudhāmasu yat-tulyam sāmānyam', i. 22.

[4] 'bhūtam bhavad bhaviṣyad iti sarvam aumkāra eva, yaccānyat trikālātītam tadapy aumkāra eva.' *Māṇḍūkya Up.* i. 1. See also i. 8–11.

ness, but the one Transcendent Fact in which all other facts are held. It is incomprehensible not because it is empty but because it is full (*pūrṇam*), as the Upaniṣad has it.[1] It exceeds our powers of comprehension. Every idea or image we form of the highest reality is in a sense an abstraction. The most concrete idea we can form of it, viz. divine personality, is also an abstraction, however comprehensive it may be. The supreme reality is incomprehensible in the sense that it cannot be expressed in logical propositions but it is increasingly apprehensible by the purified mind. This apprehension is reached not so much by the exercise of reason as by the purification of the heart, by the process of turning the attention of the soul to its own central necessities. The conception of the ground of all existence in God and of the kinship of the human spirit to the divine is at the basis of the idea that the human soul is an exile always longing for home. It is the source of the urge in the heart towards union with the beloved.

The world of our daily experience is different from the real world, whose existence we are able to infer from the empirical facts of direct intuition. The world of multiplicity (*nānātva*) is declared to be less real than the Absolute. He who has attained an insight into reality will see that the world of multiplicity is the non-dual Brahman, pure, free, and ever illumined. When God is defined as the sole reality, there is a tendency to do less than justice to the existence of creatures. The status of the world is an interpretation and not a fact of experience as the being of God is. All mystic experience involves an experience of the comparative unreality of everything else, including the finite individual. The relative non-being of creatures is the fact of experience which is interpreted in different ways by systems of philosophy. It is to theists nothing more than utter dependence on God. The view of the Upaniṣads does not destroy the sense of the reality and importance of the historical process.

[1] It is unfortunate that this point should be persistently misunderstood. Cf. Father Tyrrell: 'Heaven and earth are not more asunder than Oriental and Christian mysticism: the one looking to nonentity as the Summum Bonum the other to the Fulness of Infinite existence' (M. D. Petre, *Von Hügel and Tyrrell* (1937), p. 38).

History is not a meaningless repetition but a creative process determined by the free acts of the individuals. The spiritual world is more real than the material world, and we can remake the earth in its likeness if we truly believe and practise the life of spirit.

The Upaniṣads protest against the exclusive sway of the dialectical spirit, against the rigid limitation of experience to the data of sense and reason. They believe in the possibility of a direct intercourse with the central reality, intercourse not through any external media such as historical revelations, oracles, answers to prayers, and the like, but by a species of intuitive identification in which the individual becomes in very truth the partaker of the divine nature. Since that which is sought is one, he who would have the vision of it must get back to the principle of unity in himself. He must become one instead of being many. Life in the physical body which casts its glamour over us is not our real self. Senses and intellect are only means, for the self is the witness of both. We must empty and exhaust ourselves if we would be filled. It is in that strange experience when we check the stream of thoughts and desires that we get into touch with our real self. This state is not one of waking, dream, or sleep. The contemplative act is accomplished more in receiving than in seeking. To contemplate is to see, and the manner of our seeing varies with the state of our souls. It is the intuition of our true selfhood, which is neither a prisoner in the body nor a captive in the cage of passing thoughts and fleeting passions, but a free universal spirit. These memorable moments of our life reveal to us the truth that we are, though we soon lapse from them into the familiar life of body, sense, and mind; and yet these moments of our divine existence continue to guide us the rest of our lives as 'pillars of cloud by day, pillars of fire by night'. The soul is led through a succession of states until in the depths of its own being it experiences the touch of divinity and feels the life of God. By breaking through the entanglements of created things, the veils of sense and of intellect, the soul establishes itself in the nudity of spirit. The seer no longer distinguishes himself from that which is seen. He is one with the centre which is the centre of all. It is the flight of the alone to the alone of Plotinus, the meeting of naked substances, the soul and God of St. John of the Cross.[1] God ceases to be an object external to the individual and becomes a consuming experience.

In the *Taittirīya Upaniṣad* it is argued that the human individual is the microcosm. The same structure is found on a large scale in the universe and on a small scale in the individuals, who reproduce the whole in miniature, mirror every level and form of being from inanimate matter to God. All grades of being intersect in man.[2] He stands on the frontier between impersonal nature, where operation is determined by rigid law and the domain of spiritual freedom. This paradoxical character of man is suggested by the statement that he is a fallen creature, an earthly being preserving memories of heaven. The reflection of the divine light is in him. He is the highest of all created beings, who can share consciously the creative freedom of spirit. Matter (*anna*), life (*prāṇa*), consciousness (*manas*), intelligence (*vijñāna*), and bliss (*ānanda*) constitute a ladder of increasing reality which passes from the negative pole of pure nonentity to the positive pole of God's absolute being. Man is essentially an intellectual being, though he shares the vital subpersonal life of the animals, and is united with spirit. A healthy animal by its sound instincts is able to lead a normal life, but man can attain normality not merely by the development of his intellect with its productions of arts and crafts but by the acceptance of the world of spirit with its non-utilitarian values. Man hungers and thirsts not only for bread but for the bread of eternal life, for truth, beauty, goodness, and holiness. To achieve harmony is the aim of his existence.[3] If he purifies himself, he becomes divine; if he is still impure, he will sink into lower forms of life. Man's will is free to assert

[1] St. John of the Cross says: 'In order that God should bring the soul to this union in his own way, the sole worthy action is that which unloads and empties the faculties, which makes them renounce their natural jurisdiction and operations in order that they may receive the infusion and the illumination of the supernatural' (*Ascent of Mount Carmel*, bk. iii, chap. 2).

[2] Cf. Proclus: 'All things are in all things, but in each according to its proper nature' (*Elements of Theology*, prop. 103).

[3] Human beings are distinguished into three classes: *sāttvika*, *rājasa*, and *tāmasa*, according as one or the other quality preponderates.

itself against the universal order. If he does so, it will assert itself against him. An inner disharmony between his self-will and the spiritual impulse of his nature produces disquiet.

So long as the soul is held captive in the body and the senses and is not their master, there is an internal conflict of good and evil, light and darkness. This dualism is a part of ethical struggle and religious consciousness, but it is not ultimate. Evil is not a positive malignant thing incapable of control and change. If good and evil are regarded as absolute, then their opposition and struggle will be without end and meaning. *Avidyā*, which is more a functional disorder of the human mind than an organic defect of the universe, can be removed and evil overcome. We must win a victory over our self before we can win it over the environment.

All the things of the world are there to be enjoyed by man, but in a spirit of detachment. 'Enjoy by renunciation', says the Upaniṣad.[1] What matters is not the possession or the non-possession of things but our attitude towards them. The question relates to the desires and the appetites, not to the things to which they are directed. It is what a man *is*, not what he has, his frame of mind that matters. The *Bṛhadāraṇyaka Upaniṣad* asks us to use the resources of the world for the unfolding of the spirit. All things are dear, not for their own sake but for the sake of the spirit. To be detached is never to want anything for oneself. If we cannot be satisfied with the beauty of the flower until we pluck it and put it in our buttonhole, we cannot be at peace. From detachment comes wisdom, harmony with the environment, peace. The higher vision is possible only for those who have organized their natures. *Jñāna* or wisdom is a function of being. The path to it is as hard 'as the sharp edge of a razor'.

The individual is already in possession of the truth. The part of the teacher is that of the midwife, to assist to bring the truth to clear consciousness. To become conscious of the world of spirit is to be reborn. *Brahmacarya* or initiation into *gāyatrī* marks the second birth.[2] While the first birth into the physical environment involves disunion and separation, submission to necessity, the second birth represents the

[1] 'tyaktena bhuñjītha' (*Īśa Up.*).

[2] Cf. the Upaniṣad, 'tad dvitiyam janma, mātā sāvitrī, pitātu ācāryaḥ'.

victory over the constraint of necessity and the attainment of union and liberty. It is life at a deeper level. The *jñāni* or the man of insight has liberated himself from the bondage of fear of life and of death, from the prejudices of his time and place, of his age and country. As one with the universal self, he has the utmost charity and love for all creation. Things of the world do not tempt him, for he is freed from the bondage of selfish desires and passions.[1] He does not look upon himself as his own. He has emptied himself of all selfishness.[2] In a famous image, the Upaniṣads declare that the released souls become one with Brahman even as the rivers losing their name and form become one with the ocean.[3] Another image is that of a lump of salt dropped into water and dissolved in it.[4] The *Taittirīya Upaniṣad* makes out that the liberated soul feels his oneness with God but is not absorbed in the Absolute. It is unity of spirit but not of substance.[5] It is the infinite love of God that is lived by the soul. It is a unity of spirit between the individual and God, so long as the cosmic process lasts.[6] The highest life is an incomparable plenitude and infinite liberty. The free man is not bound by laws, for he has become more than the law, the lawmaker, a king (*svarāṭ*).[7]

[1] *Bṛhadāraṇyaka Up.* iv. 4. 23.

[2] In representing the relation between the soul and God, St. John of the Cross has recourse to the classic image of the flame and the wood. So long as the wood keeps its own native humidity, it smokes, it crackles. It is changing but is not changed. Only when it becomes pure flame is it completely changed. (*Living Flame*, Str. 1, v. 5.)

[3] Cf. St. Theresa: 'One might speak of the water from the sky, which falls into a river or a fountain, and is so lost in it that we cannot any longer divide or distinguish which is the water of the river and which the drop from the sky. Or better, of a tiny brook which throws itself into the sea, and which it is impossible to separate from thence' (*Interior Castle*, Seventh Mansion, chap. ii).

[4] *Bṛhadāraṇyaka Up.* ii. 4. 12.

[5] Cf. St. John of the Cross: 'Mine are the heavens and mine is the earth, mine are mankind and the just and the sinners; the angels are mine and the Mother of God, and all things are mine; and God himself is mine and for me; for Christ is mine and all for me. Truly then what seekest thou for, my soul, and what doest thou ask for? All that is is thine and is all for thee' (*Spiritual Maxims and Sentences*, cited in Maritain, *The Degrees of Knowledge* (1937), pp. 446–7).

[6] See *An Idealist View of Life*, 2nd ed. (1937), pp. 306–10.

[7] *Bṛhadāraṇyaka Up.* iv. 4. 23.

'Whoever knows I am Brahman becomes all this.'[1] This supreme aim of eternal life is accessible here below, even before the dissolution of the pitiable flesh,[2] in this perishable and fleeting existence itself. It is the state of *jīvanmukti*. The individual reflects from his personal centre the vitality, the fire, the light, the intelligence, the inexhaustible energy of the primordial source. He does not lose his individual being so long as the cosmic process lasts.

The distinction between *parāvidyā*, or higher wisdom, and *aparāvidyā*, or lower knowledge, is made in the Upaniṣads.[3] While a few are capable of the effort required to attain enlightenment, the large majority are incapable of such effort and for them the lower knowledge, with its belief in ritual and traditional ceremonial, is intended. While it has to be transcended by those who seek enlightenment, it is a useful aid for the ordinary people. Those who are not saved are bound to the wheel of rebirth governed by the law of Karma or moral causation.

For the first time in the history of thought, the Upaniṣads indicate a religious view which has for its integral elements: the supremacy of the Absolute spirit; the reality of mystic consciousness; the distinction between intellect soberly contemplating the intelligible and intellect rapt into enthusiasm and borne above itself; higher and lower knowledge; the *via negativa* as the way of approach to the mystic consciousness; the non-ultimateness of the pluralistic universe with its independent existents, some with life, some with consciousness; insistence on ascetic discipline; rebirth determined by the law of Karma, until the destiny of man is realized which is release or deliverance. This religious outlook seems to have affected the thought of the West from very early times.[4]

The rise of philosophical reflection in Greece and the revolt against the traditional Homeric religion belongs to this period. India and the West were brought into closer

[1] Ibid. i. 4. 10. [2] Ibid. iv. 4. 7.

[3] *Muṇḍaka Up.* i. 1. 4–5.

[4] 'Especially does there seem to be a growing probability that, from the historical standpoint at any rate, India was the birthplace of our fundamental imaginings, the cradle of contemplative religion and the nobler philosophy' (Stuckfield, *Mysticism and Catholicism* (1925), p. 31).

political, economic, and cultural connexion in the sixth century B.C. The outstanding event of the period was the rise of Persia. Babylon fell in 538 B.C., and Cyrus founded the Persian Empire. About 510 B.C., his successor Darius made the Indus valley a part of his empire, which also included Greece.[1] The Iranians, who ruled the empire from the Mediterranean to the Indus, were themselves kinsmen of the Vedic Aryans. The community of interest and ideals between the kindred peoples received emphasis during the centuries preceding the invasion of India by Alexander the Great, when Persia exercised sway over north-western India. While Indians took part in the invasion of Greece in 480 B.C., Greek officials and soldiers served in India also. The Indians knew the Greek Ionians (*yāvanas*)[2] as early as the period when north-west India was under Persian rule. The earliest speculations, which questioned the simple eschatology of Homer and sought for a more rational explanation of the meaning of life, originated with the Ionian Greeks of Asia Minor, who were in touch with Persia. Though Thales of Miletus was the father of Greek philosophy, the foundations of Greek metaphysics were laid by the Eleatic school, Xenophanes, Parmenides, and Zeno. The merchant seamen who established Greek colonies broke down the seclusion of Greek life and brought to their native cities knowledge of many strange things from other lands. Anaxagoras, the chief forerunner of Socrates, came from the Ionian Clazomenae of Asia Minor, and Xenophanes was a homeless wanderer. There is great agreement between the teaching of the Upaniṣads on the nature of reality and the Eleatic doctrine, between the Sāṁkhya teaching and the views of Empedocles and Anaxagoras. Much has been made of these resemblances, though it is quite possible that the Greeks and the Indians reached similar conclusions independently of one another.

[1] The first Greek book about India was perhaps written by Scylax, a Greek sea-captain whom Darius commissioned to explore the course of the Indus about 510 B.C. (Herodotus, iv. 44).

[2] Cf. Pāṇini, who speaks of the Greek script as *yāvanāni lipi*, iv. 1. 49 The Prākrit equivalent of *yāvana*, viz. *yona*, is used in the inscriptions of Aśoka to describe the Hellenic princes of Egypt, Cyrene, Macedonia, Epirus, and Syria.

The case is somewhat different with the mystery cults and the teaching of Pythagoras and Plato. In them we find a decisive break with the Greek tradition of rationalism and humanism. The mystic tradition is definitely un-Greek in its character.[1] A reference to the Orphic and Eleusinian mysteries and the doctrines of Pythagoras and Plato will help to elucidate the distinctive character of this tradition in Greek thought.

Orpheus, said to be a Thracian, appears in Greek history as the prophet of a religious school or sect with a code of rules of life, a mystical theology, and a system of purificatory and expiatory rites.[2] His teachings are embodied in a collection of writings to which there are frequent references in Greek literature.[3] Dionysus is the god of the cult. Faith in the inherent immortality of the soul is a cardinal feature of the Orphic religion.[4] In the phenomenon of ecstasy the soul 'steps out of the body' and reveals its true nature. Orgiastic religions share the conviction that the worshippers of God are possessed by God.[5] When we are possessed by God, we are for the moment lifted to the divine status. What can become divine even for a time cannot be different in essence from the divine, though it is not, however, divine when it is enclosed in the body. There is no insuperable gulf between God and the soul. The release of the divine from the non-divine elements is the objective of the Orphic

[1] Nietzsche looks upon Plato's thought as 'anti-Hellenic'. See his *Will to Power*, ed. by Dr. Oscar Levy, vol. i (1909), p. 346.

[2] Plato, *Phaedrus*, 69 c.

[3] In the *Hippolytus* of Euripides, Theseus taunts his son with the ascetic life he leads through having taken Orpheus for his lord. In the *Alcestis* the chorus lament that they have found no remedy for the blows of fate, 'no charm on Thracian tablets which tuneful Orpheus carved out'. Orphism is mentioned in Plato's *Cratylus*, 402 b; *Laws*, ii. 669 d, viii. 829 d; *Republic*, ii. 364 e; *Ion*, p. 536 b.

[4] Herodotus, ii. 81.

[5] Orphism was a reformation of the Dionysian religion. 'The great step that Orpheus took was that, while he kept the old Bacchic faith that man might become a god, he altered the conception of what a God was and he sought to obtain that godhead by wholly different means. The grace he sought was not physical intoxication but spiritual ecstasy; the means he adopted, not drunkenness but abstinence and rites of purification' (J. E. Harrison, *Prolegomena to the Study of Greek Religion* (1903), p. 477).

religion. The soul is not a feeble double of the individual as in Homer, but is a fallen god which is restored to its high estate by a system of sacraments and purifications.

If the soul is divine and immortal in essence, and if it is not at once freed from bondage at death, then it must remain in an intermediate state or in other animal and human forms until release is attained. Man is required to free himself from the chains of the body in which the soul lies bound like a prisoner in the cell. It has a long way to go before it can find its freedom. The death of the body frees it for a little while, but it passes on to a new body. It continues the journey perpetually, alternating between an unfettered separate existence and an ever-renewed embodiment traversing the great circle of necessity in which it assumes many bodies. Birth is not the beginning of a new life but admission into a new environment. This wheel of birth goes on until the soul escapes from it by attaining release.[1] It becomes divine, as it was before it entered a mortal body.[2] To seek to become like the gods is to the orthodox Greek the height of insolence, though it is of the essence of the Orphic religion. We have the typical Greek reaction to the fine abandon of the Orphic 'God am I, mortal no longer' in Pindar. 'Seek not to become a god.' 'Seek not to become Zeus . . . mortal things befit mortals best.' 'Mortal minds must seek what is fitting at the hands of the gods, recognising what is at our feet, and to what lot we are born. Strive not, my soul, for an immortal life, but do the thing which it is within thy power to do.'[3] The concern of the Orphic is not so much with the future of the soul as with the attainment of perfect purity.

[1] Cf. Campagno, Gold Tablets, No. 5. 'I have flown out of the sorrowful weary wheel' (*Prolegomena to the Study of Greek Religion*, J. E. Harrison (1903), p. 670).

[2] See Plato, *Phaedrus*, 62 b; *Cratylus*, 400 b: Herodotus speaks of a Thracian tribe, the *Getai*, who believe in 'men made immortal', iv. 93–4. They accept the doctrine of rebirth also. See Rohde, *Psyche*, p. 263.

[3] W. K. C. Guthrie, *Orpheus and Greek Religion* (1935), pp. 236–7. '*Genuine* Greek religion knows no mystical striving after a blessed union with God in ecstasy after an abolition of the limits of individuality in a realm beyond the conscious life. Prophetic austerity and mystic indifference are alike foreign to it' (Heiler, *Prayer*, E.T. (1932), p. 76).

The possibility of salvation or the germ of divinity lies within each of us. Its existence does not assure one of perfection, for it may be suppressed by a life of sinfulness. To become actually what we are now potentially, to shake off our earthly trammels, we must lead the Orphic life. The source of evil is in our appetites and passions, which must be subdued. Ascetic practices are prescribed, such as abstinence from beans, flesh, and certain kinds of fish, wearing ordained clothes, and avoidance of bloody sacrifices. In the Orphic mysteries we find in addition to baptism such rites as the Sacred Marriage, the Birth of the Holy Child, and these perhaps led to later Christian sacraments.[1] Union with the body and its desires is regarded as a thwarting hindrance to the immortal abiding life of the soul. Orphism does not insist on the civic virtues characteristic of Greek morality.[2] The Orphic cult transcends the limits of blood groups. It affirms that all men are brothers. The sense of solidarity not only includes all mankind but embraces all living things. All life is one, and God is one. The pictures of Orpheus in which wild and tame animals were represented as lying down in amity side by side all alike, charmed by the notes of his lyre, illustrate the unity of all living creation.[3] The influence of the Orphic cult was on the side of civilization and the arts of peace. Orpheus was entirely free from warlike attributes, and his lyre was used to soften the hearts of men. Orphic religion is different from the anthropomorphic worship of the Greeks. Its adherents are organized in communities based on voluntary admission and initiation. Orphic cosmogony and eschatology are foreign to the Greek

[1] 'The early Christians owed some of their noblest impulses to Orphism.' J. E. Harrison, *Prolegomena to the Study of Greek Religion* (1903), p. 504; see also p. 549.

[2] Rohde observes: 'It does not enjoin the practice of the civic virtues, nor is discipline or transformation of character required by it; the sum total of its morality is to bend one's course towards the deity and turn away, not from the moral lapses and aberrations of earthly life, but from earthly existence itself' (*Psyche*, ii. 125). 'This was a religion of an entirely different kind from the civic worship to which the ordinary Greek professed his allegiance' (Guthrie, op. cit., p. 206).

[3] They may be the symbol of the Good Shepherd of the Christians and remind us of Kṛṣṇa with the flute.

spirit. Homer is not troubled by the problem of the origin of things. He knows of no world egg which plays a prominent part in many cosmogonies and in Orphism. Those who are familiar with the Vedic hymn of creation will note that the conceptions of night and chaos and the birth of love, as well as that of the cosmic egg, are accepted by the Orphics.[1]

In later times Orphic theology was studied by Greek philosophers, Eudemus the Peripatetic, Chrysippus the Stoic, and Proclus the Neoplatonist. It became a favourite study of the grammarians of Alexandria. While much of the Orphic literature that has come down to us is of a late date, 'the thin gold plates, with Orphic verses inscribed on them discovered at Thourioi and Petelia, take us back to a time when Orphicism was still a living creed'.[2] 'From them we learn', says Professor Burnet, 'that it has some striking resemblances to the beliefs prevalent in India about the same time', though he finds it 'impossible to assume any Indian influence in Greece at this date'. The beliefs held in common are those of rebirth, the immortality and godlike character of the soul, the bondage of the soul in the body, and the possibility of release by purification. If we add to them metaphors like the wheel of birth and the world egg, the suggestion of natural coincidence is somewhat unconvincing.[3]

[1] The most popular of all Orphic theogonies holds that Chronos or Time, 'who grows not old', first existed, and from it sprang ether and the formless chaos. From them was formed an egg which bursting in due time disclosed Eros or Phanes, the firstborn, at once male and female and having within himself the seeds of all creatures. Phanes creates the Sun and Moon and Night, and from Night arise Uranos and Gaea (Heaven and Earth). These two give birth to the Titans, among whom is Kronos, who defeats his father Uranos and succeeds to his throne. He is in turn deposed by Zeus, who swallows Phanes and thus becomes the father of gods and men (Legge, *Forerunners and Rivals of Christianity* (1925), vol. i, p. 123; see Aristophanes, *The Birds*, 693 ff.). For the Vedic theory of creation, see *Indian Philosophy*, 2nd ed., vol. i (1929), pp. 100 ff.

[2] Burnet, *Early Greek Philosophy* (1930), p. 82.

[3] There are certain striking resemblances in the matter of the passage to heaven. In the *Ṛg Veda* heaven is the home of the soul to which, after death, it returns purified (x. 14. 8); before reaching heaven it has to cross a stream (x. 63. 10) and pass by Yama's watchful dogs, 'the spotted dogs of Saramā' (x. 14. 10).

The Eleusinian cult is akin to the Orphic and uses Orphic hymns. While the Orphic cult imposes an ascetic regimen, no such claim is made for Eleusis. Its root idea seems to be more magical than ethical.[1] If we perform the correct ritual the great goddess will protect us here and hereafter. Yet, so far as the theoretical background is concerned, it is not different from that of the Orphics. It believes that the divine dwells in man. Dark shrouds are wrapped round it and we must unwrap them. Initiation was considered to be of great importance. Any one who has not had initiation is only a half-man. Through it we enter into an awareness of our real selfhood, which is divine. This is to be twice born. Our first birth is the physical one; the second is unto what is real in us, to be changed in our nature. The yearning of religion is the desire for union with our true self. At the conclusion of the rites, the last words heard by the initiates were 'Go in peace'.[2] They were to depart with their minds serene and souls at rest. 'The initiated', said Aristotle, 'are not supposed to learn anything, but to be affected in a certain way and put into a certain frame of mind.'[3] Even Alexander and Julius Caesar availed themselves of these initiatory rites. God is not a word or a concept but a consciousness we can realize here and now in the flesh. Religion is more than worship of a personal God. These doctrines inspired the *Bacchae* of Euripides, as in the oft quoted line—'Who knows if life be death and death be life?' It is fairly certain that only a small proportion of those who attended the ceremonies grasped the full meaning of what they saw and heard. 'Many are the thyrsus bearers,' quotes

[1] Sophocles wrote: 'Thrice happy are those mortals who see these rites before they depart for Hades; for to them alone is it granted to have true life on the other side. To the rest, all there is evil.' To this Diogenes the cynic is said to have retorted: 'What! Is Pataikion the thief to have a better lot after death than Epaminondas, just because he has been initiated?' (Plutarch).

[2] Cf. 'om śāntiḥ śāntiḥ śāntiḥ'; also, 'Peace I leave with you, my peace I give unto you.'

[3] *Fr.* 45 (1483 a. 19); see also *Fr.* 15. 'Those who are being initiated are not required to grasp anything with the understanding, but to have a certain inner experience, and so to be put into a particular frame of mind, presuming that they are capable of this frame of mind in the first place' (Jaeger, *Aristotle*, E.T. (1934), p. 160).

Plato, 'but few are the mystes.'[1] These mystic cults were well known to and favoured by the tragic poets, Aeschylus, Sophocles, and Euripides. They exercised great influence until they were proscribed by the Christian emperors.[2]

There was a close analogy between these cults and the teaching of Pythagoras, which was noticed by Herodotus.[3] Pythagoras lived and taught in the second half of the sixth century B.C. at Kroton. He looked upon Orpheus as the chief of his patrons. The great musician of legend impressed Pythagoras, who was led by his experiments in music to the understanding of numerical ratios and hence to the foundation of mathematical science. For Pythagoras the universe is not only an order or observance of due proportions but a 'harmonia' or being in tune. The human soul must also strive to imitate the orderliness of the universe. Pythagoras enjoined an ascetic way of living. Abstention from meat was a principal requirement. He believed in rebirth. The earliest reference to Pythagoras is in a few verses quoted by Xenophanes in which we are told that Pythagoras once heard a dog howling and appealed to its master not to beat it, as he recognized the voice of a departed friend.[4] Another anecdote which has become famous through Ennius and Horace tells us that Pythagoras was gifted with the power of remembering his former births, and he claimed to have been Euphorbus among others. Pythagoras believed not only in rebirth but in purification of the soul. The cycle of births is regarded as a means for the growth of man's higher nature. The theoretic is for him the highest form of life. He was also known as an important scientific man.[5] According to

[1] *Phaedrus.*

[2] F. Legge, *Forerunners and Rivals of Christianity* (1915), vol. i, p. 123. Julian the Apostate was initiated at Athens into the mysteries of Eleusis. Sir W. M. Ramsay affirms that the Eleusinian mysteries constituted 'the one great attempt made by Hellenic genius to construct a religion that should keep pace with the growth of thought and civilisation in Greece' (*Encyclopaedia Britannica*, 9th ed., vol. xvii, p. 126).

[3] ii. 81.

[4] *Fr.* 7:

Once he was passing by an ill-used pup,
And pitied it, and said (or so they tell)
'Stop, do not thrash it! 'tis a dear friend's soul:
I recognized it when I heard it yell.'

(*Oxford Book of Greek Verse in Translation* (1938), p. 226.)

[5] Heraclitus, *Fr.* 17; Herodotus, iv. 95.

Aristotle, Pythagoras first busied himself with mathematics and numbers. The only mention of Pythagoras in Plato is in the *Republic*,[1] where he tells us that Pythagoras won the affection of his followers by teaching them a way of life which was still called Pythagorean.[2] A peculiar feature in the asceticism of the Pythagoreans from the fourth century at least seems to have been silence. The Pythagorean order was a religious fraternity. Admission to the fraternity was gained by initiation, i.e. by purification followed by the revelation of truth. Purification consisted not only in the observance of rules of abstinence from certain kinds of food and dress but also in the purification of the soul by *theoria*, or the contemplation of the divine reality. Plato in the *Phaedo*[3] states as the Pythagorean doctrine the view that men are strangers to the world and the body is the tomb of the soul, and yet we must not escape from it by suicide. For Pythagoras, pure contemplation is the end of man, the completion of human nature. To the question what are we born for he replied, 'To gaze upon the heavens.'[4] When by the contemplative process the soul is perfected, that is, purified from the taint of its subjection to the body, there would be no need of further rebirths. Pythagoras is believed to have reached this threshold of divinity.[5] Professor Burnet says: 'If we can trust Herakleides, it was Pythagoras who first distinguished the "three lives", the Theoretic, the Practical, and the Apolaustic, which Aristotle made use of in the *Ethics*.'[6] Pythagoras held, as the early

[1] x. 600 b. [2] *Republic*, vii. 530 d. [3] 62 b.

[4] Jaeger, *Aristotle*, E.T. (1934), p. 75.

[5] Aristotle, *Fr.* 192. Aristoxenus says of Pythagoras and his followers: 'Every distinction they lay down as to what should be done or not done aims at communion with the divine. This is their starting point; their whole life is ordered with a view to following God and it is the governing principle of their philosophy' (see F. M. Cornford, 'Mysticism and Science in Pythagorean Tradition', *Classical Quarterly* (1922), p. 142).

[6] *Early Greek Philosophy* (1930), p. 98. 'The doctrine is to this effect. We are strangers in this world and the body is the tomb of the soul, and yet we must not seek to escape by self-murder; for we are the chattels of God who is our herdsman, and without his command we have no right to make our escape. In this life there are three kinds of men, just as there are three sorts of people who come to the Olympic games. The lowest class is made up of those who come to buy and sell and next above them are those who come to

Upaniṣad thinkers did, that all souls are similar in class and the apparent distinctions between human and other kinds of beings are not ultimate. Iamblichus[1] informs us that Pythagoras held that the islands of the blest were the sun and the moon. In the Upaniṣads the moon is mentioned as the dwelling-place of spirits.[2]

Being a mathematician, Pythagoras expressed his cosmogony in mathematical terms. The primal Monad takes the place of the world egg. The world is a mixture of light and darkness, the formless and the form. The mathematical and mystical sides were side by side in Pythagoras and, according to tradition, a split occurred within the school between the *Mathematikoi* or the rationalists, whose interest was in the theory of numbers, and the *Akusmatikoi*, who followed up the religious side of the movement. We have in Pythagoras a rare combination of high intellectual power and profound spiritual insight.

Herodotus suggests that Pythagoras got the doctrine of rebirth from the Egyptians,[3] but 'the Egyptians did not believe in transmigration at all and Herodotus was deceived by the priests or the symbolism of the monuments'.[4] Even if the theory be a development from the primitive belief in the kinship of men and beasts, it is difficult to account for the other parts of the system, taboos on certain kinds of food,[5] the rule of silence which the members of his fraternity were required to observe, the ascetic emphasis and insistence on release assured to those who are initiated. Iamblichus, the biographer of Pythagoras, tells us that he travelled widely, studying the teachings of Egyptians, Assyrians, and Brāhmins.[6] Gomperz writes: 'It is not too much to assume

compete. Best of all, however, are those who come to look on. The greatest purification of all is science and it is the man who devotes himself to that, the true philosopher, who has most effectually released himself from the "wheel of birth".'

[1] *Vit. Pyth.* 82.

[2] See Deussen, *Philosophy of the Upaniṣads*, E.T. (1906), pp. 326 ff.

[3] ii. 123.

[4] Burnet, *Early Greek Philosophy* (1930), 4th ed., pp. 88–9.

[5] 'Timaios told how at Delos, Pythagoras refused to sacrifice on any but the oldest altar, that of Apollo the Father, where only bloodless sacrifices were allowed' (ibid., p. 93).

[6] Professor H. G. Rawlinson writes: 'It is more likely that Pythagoras was

that the curious Greek, who was a contemporary of Buddha, and it may be of Zoroaster too, would have acquired a more or less exact knowledge of the East in that age of intellectual fermentation, through the medium of Persia.'[1]

Whether or not we accept the hypothesis of direct influence from India through Persia on the Greeks, a student of Orphic and Pythagorean thought cannot fail to see that the similarities between it and the Indian religion are so close as to warrant our regarding them as expressions of the same view of life. We can use the one system to interpret the other.

Though Socrates (470–399 B.C.) was a great advocate of rational self-discipline, he was a deeply religious man. He often talked of his 'inner voice', which would forbid him on occasions to do something which he planned to do. Being something of a mystic he would occasionally fall into deep meditation. Once when he was serving in the army in northern Greece, he was observed standing still meditating in the early hours of the morning. Deep in thought he stood there all day and all night, and with the return of light he offered a prayer to the sun and went on his way. For him religion was quite different from the ritualistic religion of the Greeks. He was aware of the supernatural world and felt himself a member of the heavenly city. The world might kill, but it has not the last word.

'If you should say to me, "O Socrates, at the moment we will not

influenced by India than by Egypt. Almost all the theories, religious, philosophical and mathematical taught by the Pythagoreans, were known in India in the sixth century B.C., and the Pythagoreans, like the Jains and the Buddhists, refrained from the destruction of life and eating meat and regarded certain vegetables such as beans as taboo' (*Legacy of India* (1937), p. 5). 'It seems also that the so-called Pythagorean theorem of the quadrature of the hypotenuse was already known to the Indians in the older Vedic times, and thus before Pythagoras' (ibid.). Professor Winternitz is of the same opinion: 'As regards Pythagoras, it seems to me very probable that he became acquainted with Indian doctrines in Persia' (*Viśvabhārati Quarterly*, Feb. 1937, p. 8). It is also the view of Sir William Jones (*Works*, iii. 236), Colebrooke (*Miscellaneous Essays*, i. 436 ff.), Schroeder (*Pythagoras und die Inder*), Garbe (*Philosophy of Ancient India*, pp. 39 ff.), Hopkins (*Religions of India*, pp. 559 and 560), and Macdonell (*Sanskrit Literature*, p. 422). Professor A. Berriedale Keith is needlessly critical of this view. See his article on 'Pythagoras and the Doctrine of Transmigration', *J.R.A.S.*, 1909, pp. 569 ff.

[1] *Greek Thinkers*, vol. i, p. 127.

hearken to Anytus, but we release you on this condition, that you no longer abide in this inquiry or practise philosophy—and if you are caught still doing this, you will be put to death", if then you would release me on these conditions, I should say to you, "You have my thanks and affection, men of Athens, but I will obey the God rather than you and, while I have breath and power, I will not desist from practising philosophy." '[1]

He perhaps accepted the Orphic view that the soul is immortal and that happiness means the achieving of immortality by renunciation of the world, and that all men are brothers whatever their conditions be.

The mystic tradition finds its full expression in Plato (427–347 B.C.). Plato does not adopt the Greek view of rationality. For him truth cannot always be proved. Sometimes it can only be suggested and grasped by the mind in a wordless dialectic. It appeals to the whole nature of man and not simply to the intellect. Plato speaks of the poet as 'a light and winged and holy thing, one whom God possesses and uses as his mouthpiece'.[2] He finds the empiricist view that Forms are present in sensible things and our knowledge of them is conveyed through the senses unsatisfying. The world of intelligible forms is separate from the things our senses perceive, and it is the rational soul that has a knowledge of them. The Forms must always be what they are. The many things that we perceive are perpetually changing. There are two orders of reality: the unperceived, exempt from all change, and the perceived, which change perpetually. The soul is unperceived, simple, indissoluble, immortal; the body is complex, dissoluble, mortal. When the soul is mixed up with the senses, it is lost in the world of change; when it withdraws from the senses, it escapes into that other region of pure, eternal, unchanging being. Plato speaks of the supersensual vision of the philosophers:

'We beheld the beatific vision and were initiated into a mystery which may be truly called most blessed, celebrated by us in our state of innocence, before we had any experience of evils to come, when we were admitted to the sight of apparitions innocent and simple and calm and happy which we beheld shining in pure light; pure ourselves,

[1] Plato's *Apology*, 29 c.

[2] *Ion*, p. 534.

and not yet enshrined in that living tomb which we carry about, now that we are imprisoned in the body like an oyster in his shell.'[1]

Plato gives in the *Phaedo* an account of the life eternal:

'When the soul returns into itself and reflects, it passes into another region, the region of that which is pure and everlasting, immortal and unchangeable; and feeling itself kindred thereto, it dwells there under its own control and has rest from its wanderings, and is constant and one with itself as are the objects with which it deals.'

The truth of things is always in our soul, which is immortal and has been many times reborn. It can recover the memory of what it has formerly known, and in the *Phaedo* this fact of recollection is accepted as the proof for pre-existence. The soul not only has pre-existed but is indestructible. Whatever is composed or put together out of parts is liable to destruction. The incomposite suffers no kind of change.

The soul is for ever travelling through a cycle of necessity where it gets a life agreeable to its desire. Some of the souls go to prisons under the earth, others to heaven, 'to a life suited to the life which they lived while they were in the form of man'. In the famous apologue of Er the Pamphylian with which Plato ends the *Republic*, disembodied souls are represented as choosing their next incarnation at the hands of 'Lachesis, daughter of necessity', which is the law of Karma personified. The human soul is purified through a series of incarnations from which it finally escapes when completely purified. The theory has nothing in common with the popular belief of the nature of the soul as a flimsy double of the body, an unsubstantial shadow which is dissipated when detached from the body. Plato refers his view of pre-existence and rebirth to a 'sacred story'.[2] 'I have heard something from men and women who were wise in sacred lore.'[3]

The dominating thought in Plato is that the ordinary man is not truly awake but is walking about like a somnambulist in pursuit of phantoms.[4] So long as we are subject to passions, dreams are taken for reality. When the truth is realized, the shadows of the night pass away and in the dawn

[1] *Phaedrus*, 250 b, c, Jowett's E.T.

[2] *Ion*, p. 534.

[3] *Phaedo*, 70 c.

[4] *Meno*, 80 e.

of another sun we see no longer in signs and symbols enigmatically, but face to face as the gods see and know. The simile of the cave reminds us of the Hindu doctrine of *māyā*, or appearance. Plato compares the human race to men sitting in a cave, bound, with their backs to the light and fancying that the shadows on the wall before them are not shadows but real objects. We live in the darkness of the cave and require to be led out of it into the sunlight. Again, to the ordinary Greek the body counted for a good deal. To Plato it is a fetter to which we are chained.[1] Our affections must be fixed on a future world in which we will be freed from the body. 'If we would have pure knowledge of anything, we must be quit of the body—the soul in herself must behold things in themselves: and then we shall attain the wisdom which we desire and of which we say that we are lovers: not while we live but after death.'[2] The senses belong to the flesh. When the spirit withdraws from the flesh to think by itself untroubled by the senses, it lays hold upon unseen reality. The pursuit of wisdom is a 'loosing and separation of the spirit from the body'.[3] We have here the possibility of a complete detachment of the thinking self from the body and its senses and passions, and it implies as a consequence the separate existence of the Forms. Such is the view to be found in the earlier Dialogues. They assert that the Forms have an existence separate from things even as the spirit has an existence separate from the body.

'Evil, Theodorus, can never pass away: for there must always remain something which is antagonistic to good. It has no place in heaven, so of necessity it haunts the mortal nature and this earthly sphere. Therefore we ought to escape from earth to heaven as quickly as we can: and to escape is to become like God, as far as possible; and to become like him is to become holy, just and wise. . . . God is never in any way unrighteous—he is perfect righteousness—and those of us who are most righteous are most like him.'[4]

The doctrine that the body is an encumbrance, the source

[1] *Phaedo*, 65–7.

[2] Ibid. 66. Plato attributes the view that the body is a prison or a tomb to the Orphics (*Cratylus*, 400 c).

[3] Ibid. 67 d.

[4] *Theaetetus*, 176.

of evil from which the soul must long to be purified, permeates the *Phaedo*.

It is obvious that here we have a note which is fundamentally opposed to the essentially Greek spirit that learned to delight in all that pleased the senses and satisfied the emotions, that looked upon this world not as a passage to the next but as something which was in itself good and lovely, that life must be lived beautifully as well as worthily, with the strenuous exercise of all the powers of body, mind, and spirit. The sharp separation of the world of the senses from the world of the Ideas should naturally result in a lack of interest in the sensible world and a concentration on the higher, but this consequence is opposed to the natural longing of the Greek to take part in practical affairs. While the Orphic and the Pythagorean teaching set the feet of Plato on the upward path from the cave into the sunlight, his Greek humanism sternly bade him return and help his fellov prisoners still fettered in the darkness of the cave.

We have in Plato, as in the Upaniṣads, the highest God, the Idea of the Good in the *Republic*, the Demiurgus and the Soul of the World in the *Timaeus*.[1] Towards the end of the sixth book of the *Republic* Plato describes the endeavour of philosophy to ascend to the first principle of the universe which transcends all definite existence. The three qualities of *sattva*, *rajas*, and *tamas* have for their equivalents in Plato Logistikon, Thumos, and Epithumia. Epithumia, like *tamas*, represents blind desire with its character of ignorance; Thumos is, like *rajas*, the element of passion and power, standing midway between ignorance and knowledge. The Logistikon, or the rational element, answers to the *sattva* quality, which harmonizes the soul and illumines it. The division of souls into classes based on the preponderance of these psychical elements answers to the divisions of the Indian caste system.

In Book III of the *Republic* Plato criticizes the popular religion as embodied in Homer's poetry, and in Book X he contrasts Homer with Pythagoras. Besides the defects of his moral teaching, he (Homer) has none of the marks of the

[1] The Neoplatonic Trinity is traced by Porphyry to Plato. See Thomas Whittaker, *The Neo-Platonists*, 2nd ed. (1918), p. 36; see also *Enneads*, v. 1. 8.

great teacher. He had no followers; he founded no school; he inspired no disciples; he gave no valid rule of life. The religion of Pythagoras was based on the Orphic teaching with its austere asceticism, its voluntary poverty and community of goods, its belief in rebirth and respect for animal life. Aristotle suggests that Plato follows closely the teaching of the Pythagoreans. He took up Orphic and Pythagorean views and wove them into the texture of his philosophy.

The essential unity of the human and the divine spirit, the immortality of the human soul, the escape from the restless wheel of the troublesome journey, the phenomenality of the world, the contempt for the body, the distinction between knowledge and opinion contradict every single idea of Greek popular religion.[1] They are eccentrics in the sphere of Greek thought.

Empedocles accepts as indefeasible facts the divine nature of the soul and the doctrine of the soul's fall from its original divine condition into the corporeal state in which it must expiate its guilt by a long pilgrimage through the bodies of men, animals, and plants. Asceticism is for him one of the most effective means of delivering the soul from the world of sense. 'Whoever exerteth himself, with toil, him can we release.' The soul at length returns to its divine status and

[1] The contrast between the Greek spirit and Plato's thought is pointed out by Rohde: 'The real first principle of the religion of the Greek people is this—that in the divine ordering of the world, humanity and divinity are absolutely divided in place and nature, so they must ever remain. A deep gulf is fixed between the worlds of mortality and divinity. . . . Poetic fancies about the "Translation" of individual mortals to an unending life enjoyed by the soul still united to the body might make their appeal to popular belief; but such things remained *miracles* in which divine omnipotence had broken down the barriers of the natural order on a special occasion. It was but a miracle too, if the souls of certain mortals were raised to the rank of Heroes, and so promoted to everlasting life. The gulf between the human and the divine is not made any narrower on that account; it remained unbridged, abysmal. . . . Nevertheless, at a certain period in Greek history, and nowhere earlier or more unmistakably than in Greece, appeared the idea of the divinity, and the immortality implicit in the divinity, of the human soul. That idea belonged entirely to *mysticism*' (*Psyche*, E.T. (1925), pp. 253–4). Sir Richard Livingstone writes that 'Plato is the most eminent representative of the heretics'. 'He is the prophet in literature of the Orphic worship, which coming from Thrace in the sixth century, spoke of immortality and rebirth, of intimate union with God, of heaven for the initiate and mud pools for the sinner, preaching asceticism and purity

the wise men who practise such holy living eventually become gods while yet on earth.[1]

The divine origin of the soul, its pre-existence, its fall into corporeality, its judgement after death, its expiatory wanderings through the bodies of animals or men according to its character, its final redemption from the cycle of rebirth and its return to God, are common to the mystery cults and Plato and Empedocles. This tradition is something which Hellenic thought, untouched by alien speculation, was perhaps not very likely to have developed, and we have it in a striking form in Indian religion.

To the student of cultural development it is indifferent whether similarities are due to borrowing or are the result of parallel intellectual evolution; the important thing is that the ideas are similar. They were firmly established in India before the sixth century B.C., and they arise in Greece after that period. History does not repeat itself except with variations. It is idle to look for exact parallels, but we can trace a resemblance between the two systems, the Indian and the Greek. There are some who regard it as derogatory to the Greeks to send them to school to older cultures and assume them to have taken thence some of the sources of their knowledge and belief. But people of their acute intellectual vigour, inquisitiveness, and flexible mind cannot help being influenced by foreigners with whom they come into frequent and intimate contact as soldiers and merchants, as adventurers, seamen, and warlike settlers. When native traditions fail to satisfy increasing curiosity and thirst for knowledge, foreign sources are drawn on more freely. To be a Greek is not to be impervious to every other form of thought.

The spirit of bigotry increased in the West only after Christianity became organized by the Catholic Church. Till

as a road to the former, and somewhat after the fashion of the Egyptian Book of the Dead, giving its votaries elaborate instructions for their behaviour when they found themselves in the lower world' (*Greek Genius and its Meaning to Us*, pp. 197–8). 'The mind of Plato was heavily charged with Orphic mysticism mainly derived from Asiatic sources. India, always the home of mystical devotion, probably contributed the major share' (Stutfield, *Mysticism and Catholicism* (1925), p. 74).

[1] *Fr.* 146.

then the new ideas and worships did not suggest foreign domination or alarm national pride and jealousy. They were freely adopted when old forms were felt to be unsatisfying. The Hindus, on the other hand, have been in all ages preoccupied by religious questions and were, in their vigorous days, interested in the spread of their ideas. The establishment of Hinduism in Java and Indo-China and the spread of Buddhism in large parts of Asia indicate that in wide tracts and long periods the Indians have been culturally enterprising. Up to a point it is a sound principle not to admit that resemblances prove indebtedness unless we can show the exact way in which intercommunication between two cultures took place, but the possibility that all records of such contacts may disappear cannot be ignored. We have little evidence to show how and when the Hindu colonization of Java took place. We are not completely in the dark on the question of Indian influence on Greece. Speaking of ascetic practices in the West, Professor Sir Flinders Petrie observes:

> 'The presence of a large body of Indian troops in the Persian army in Greece in 480 B.C. shows how far West the Indian connections were carried; and the discovery of modelled heads of Indians at Memphis, of about the fifth century B.C., shows that Indians were living there for trade. Hence there is no difficulty in regarding India as the source of the entirely new ideal of asceticism in the West.'[1]

Ascetic practices developed in the tradition represented by the schools associated with the mystery cults, Pythagoras, and Plato, and in it we may suspect the influence of India directly or indirectly through Persia.

Dr. Inge observes that the Platonic or the mystical outlook on life for which religion is at once a philosophy and a discipline 'was first felt in Asia', especially in the Upaniṣads and Buddhism.

> 'This mystical faith appears in Greek lands as Orphism and Pythagoreanism. In Europe as in Asia it was associated with ideas of the transmigration of souls and a universal law of periodical recurrence. But it is in Plato, the disciple of the Pythagoreans as well as of Socrates, who was probably himself the head of a Pythagorean group at Athens,

[1] *Egypt and Israel* (1923), p. 134.

that this conception of an unseen eternal world of which the visible world is only a pale copy, gains a permanent foothold in the West.'[1]

Professor E. R. Dodds insists on the 'Oriental background against which Greek culture arose, and from which it was never completely isolated save in the minds of classical scholars'.[2]

The importance of Indian influence on Greek thought is not to be judged by the amount of information about it which has survived. Eusebius (A.D. 315) preserves a tradition which he attributes to Aristoxenus, the pupil of Aristotle, and a well-known writer on harmonics, that certain learned Indians actually visited Athens and conversed with Socrates.

> 'Aristoxenus the musician tells the following story about the Indians. One of these men met Socrates at Athens, and asked him what was the scope of his philosophy. "An inquiry into human phenomena," replied Socrates. At this the Indian burst out laughing. "How can we inquire into human phenomena," he exclaimed, "when we are ignorant of divine ones?"'[3]

The date of Aristoxenus is 330 B.C. If Eusebius is to be trusted, we have contemporary evidence of the presence in Athens as early as the fourth century B.C. of Indian thinkers. The visit of the Indian to Athens is also mentioned in the fragment of Aristotle[4] preserved in Diogenes Laertius.[5] Even if these stories are apocryphal, they are legendary formulations of the view of the influence of Indian thought generally accepted in the later Academy. At any rate, while the popular religion of the Greeks is united to the Vedic beliefs, the mystic tradition of the Orphic and the Eleusinian cults, Pythagoras and Plato, which has had a great development in Greek and Christian thought, started with certain fundamental principles which are common to Indian and

[1] *The Platonic Tradition in English Religious Thought* (1926), pp. 7 and 9.

[2] *Humanism and Technique in Greek Studies* (1936), p. 11.

[3] *Praeparatio Evangelica*, xi. 3.

[4] 32. 'We find in the fragments of Aristotle's lost dialogues, which were mostly written during his earlier period, a surprising interest in certain features of Oriental religion' (Werner Jaeger, 'Greeks and Jews', *Journal of Religion*, April 1938, p. 128).

[5] ii. 45. Eudoxus, the astronomer and friend of Plato, was greatly interested in Indian thought. See Pliny, *Natural History*, xxx. 3.

Greek mysticism. It gave rise in Christianity to the consciousness of sin and the need of redemption, rewards and punishments after death, the latter both purgatorial and punitive, initiation by sacraments as a passport to a happy life hereafter, the necessity for moral as well as ceremonial purity. Alien in origin, alien to the spirit of Hellenism, predominantly Indian in character and content, walking in the shadow without support from the State, the Orphic, the Eleusinian, the Pythagorean brotherhoods, and Platonic schools prepared the way for the later Platonism and for certain elements in Catholic theology.[1]

[1] Cf. Mayer: 'Egyptian, Persian, and Indian cultural influences were absorbed into the Greek world from very early times' (*Political Thought* (1939), p. 7). As for the influence of Greece on India, it has not been on the deeper levels of life. In the sphere of art the Greek influence was considerable. Perhaps the idea of representing the founder of Buddhism as a man originated with them. Tarn says: 'Considered broadly, what the Asiatic took from the Greek was usually externals only, matters of form; he rarely took substance—civic institutions may be an exception—and never spirit. For in matters of the spirit Asia was quite confident that she could outstay the Greeks; and she did' (*The Greeks in Bactria and India* (1938), p. 67). Again: 'Indian civilisation was strong enough to hold its own against Greek civilisation, but except in the religious sphere, was seemingly not strong enough to influence it as Babylonia did; nevertheless we may find reason for thinking that in certain respects India was the dominant partner' (ibid., pp. 375–6). 'Except for the Buddha-statue the history of India would in all essentials have been precisely what it has been, had Greeks never existed' (ibid., p. 376).

V

INDIA AND WESTERN RELIGIOUS THOUGHT: CHRISTENDOM—I

I

ALEXANDER'S invasion of India in 327 B.C. starts a closer interchange of thought between India and the West. Buddhism must have been prevalent in India for over a century before Alexander's time, and he made an effort to acquaint himself with Hindu and Buddhist thought. He sent a Greek officer named Onesicritus, a disciple of Diogenes the cynic philosopher,[1] to Taxila, the famous seat of learning, and the latter succeeded in getting an ascetic called Kalanos to join Alexander's entourage. In the feast at Susa which he celebrated on his return from India his great dream of the marriage of Europe and Asia took practical shape. He had already married Roxana, a princess from Bactria, and now he took as a second consort Statira, the daughter of Darius. Nearly a hundred of his superior officers and ten thousand of his humbler followers followed the emperor's example and took Asiatic brides.

Pyrrho is said to have taken part in Alexander's expedition to India and acquired a knowledge of Indian thought. In the New Academy we find a blend of the two schools of Plato and Pyrrho and a leaning to negative conclusions. The highest condition of the soul is declared to be imperturbability. The joyousness of the Greek gives place to independence of external circumstances. The religion of the Epicureans, the contemplation of the nature of the gods with a mind at rest, that of the Stoics, who identified God with the living universe, with its reason, and looked upon man as having in him a particle of the divine reason, are in the same line of development. They are both parts of the new world which Alexander had made, produced by the feeling that a man was no longer merely a part of his city-State. Man, with Alexander, ceases to be a fraction of the polis or the city-State. He is an individual bound by relations to the

[1] Strabo, xv, c. 715.

other individuals of the world. Zeus and Athena had been good protectors of the citizens living side by side in a small area, but when this little world grew up into the Oikoumene, the inhabited world as known, they could not serve. It was one of the great moments of history when Alexander, at the famous banquet, prayed for a union of hearts (homonoia) and a joint commonwealth of Macedonians and Persians. He envisaged a brotherhood of man in which there should be neither Greek nor barbarian, though his outlook was more political than spiritual.[1] Zeno responded with alacrity to the appeal of Alexander and in his *Republic* set forth the vision of a world which should no longer be separate States but one great city under one divine law, where all were citizens and members one of another, bound together not by human laws but by their own voluntary adhesion or by love, as he called it.[2] This great hope has never quite left us, though we seem to be as far away from it as in the third century B.C. The Stoic universe is one great city ruled by one supreme power envisaged under many aspects and names, Nature, Law, Destiny, Providence, Zeus. Everything was a derivative of God and so was God. Human minds were sparks of the divine fire, though human body was clay. Wealth and poverty, sickness and health are matters of indifference. The wise man would not worry about such things but attend to the things of the soul. In the realm of spirit men could be equal, whatever their earthly status may be. Both the Stoics and the Epicureans laid full stress on philosophy as a way of life and desired the avoidance of passions and emotions, which bring the unhappiness of unsatisfied desire. Already in the third century B.C. Cleanthes, who succeeded Zeno, identified the traditional deity Zeus with the world god of Stoicism.[3] The anthropo-

[1] See further, pp. 386–7. [2] Cf. Marcus Aurelius (iv. 23): 'A famous one says Dear City of Cecrops and wilt not thou say Dear City of Zeus?'

[3] Most glorious of immortals, Zeus all powerful,
Author of Nature, named by many names, all hail.
Thy law rules all; and the voice of the world may cry to thee
For from thee we are born, and alone of living things
That move on earth are we created in God's image.

The hymn closes with an apostrophe to 'omnipresent law'. (*The Oxford Book of Greek Verse in Translation* (1938), pp. 533 and 535.)

morphic tendency diminishes and Jupiter becomes, not one 'Who hurls the thunderbolts with his own hands', but 'the ruler and guardian of the universe, the mind and spirit of the world' (Seneca).[1] The highest life of man is to live in accordance with the reason which is implanted in him as a part and pattern of the divine reason of the universe. The soul of the individual is not immortal, for it must perish at the general conflagration which is to destroy this sensible world. The fiery element in it will be taken over into the great central fire. The souls retain their individuality until the cycle of time is completed. Marcus Aurelius says: 'You exist as a part of the whole, you will vanish into that which gave you birth or rather you will be taken up by a change into its generative reason.' The Stoics did not reject the gods of the people; they were treated as parts of the world order, 'veils mercifully granted to the common man to spare his eyes the too dazzling nakedness of truth'.[2] We can know God by the practice of introversion. The works of Alexander's companions, Diognetus, Aristobulus, Nearchus, and others, have not come down to us.

Alexander left behind him Greek colonists and soldiers,[3] and in the north-west frontiers for some centuries Greek or semi-Greek principalities continued. In the political unsettlement after Alexander's invasion Chandragupta came to power, overthrew the Macedonian supremacy, and gradually conquered the whole of Hindustan. The Greek prince Seleucus Nikator (third century B.C.) gave one of his daughters in marriage to the Indian sovereign and sent an ambassador to his court at Pātaliputra (Patna), Megasthenes, who gives the West an interesting account of the social and cultural conditions of India during his time. 'In many points', he says, 'their teaching agrees with that of the Greeks.'[3] Megasthenes was succeeded by Daimachus of Plataea, who went on a series of missions from Antiochus I to Bindusāra, the son of Chandragupta. Pliny tells us of a certain Dionysius who was sent to India from Alexandria by Ptolemy Philadelphus (285–247 B.C.).[4] Aśoka, who

[1] Cyril Bailey, *Phases in the Religion of Ancient Rome* (1932), p. 233.

[2] Tarn, *Hellenistic Civilization*, 2nd ed. (1930), pp. 304–5.

[3] *Cambridge History of India*, vol. i (1922), pp. 419–20. [4] *Nat. Hist.* vi. 21.

ascended the throne of Magadha in 270 B.C., held a Council at Pātaliputra, when it was resolved to send missionaries to proclaim the new teaching throughout the world. In accordance with this decision Aśoka sent Buddhistic missions to the sovereigns of the West, Antiochus Theos of Syria, Ptolemy Philadelphus of Egypt, Antigonos Gonatas of Macedonia, Magas of Cyrene, and Alexander of Epirus.[1] From Aśoka's statements it may be inferred that his missions were favourably received in these five countries. Between 190 and 180 B.C. Demetrius extended the Bactrian Kingdom into India and conquered Sind and Kathiawar. The Greeks who settled in India gradually became Indianized. Of the monuments which survive of the Indo-Greek dynasties is a pillar discovered at Besnagar in the extreme south of the Gwalior State (140 B.C.). The inscription on it in Brāhmi characters says: 'This garuḍa column of Vāsudeva [Viṣṇu] was erected here by Heliodorus, son of Dion, a worshipper of Viṣṇu and an inhabitant of Taxila, who came as a Greek ambassador from the great King Antialcidas to King Kāśīputra Bhāgabhadra, the saviour, then reigning prosperously in the fourteenth year of his kingship.'[2] By the time of these inscriptions the Greeks born in India became completely Indianized. The greatest of the Indo-Greek kings was Menander, who was converted to Buddhism by the Buddhist teacher Nāgasena (180–160 B.C.). His conversion is recorded in the famous work *Milindapañha*.[3] About the year 160 B.C. the Scythians, driven from their ancestral homes in central Asia, swept down over the Jaxartes and the Oxus, subdued Kabul and the Panjab, and extended their conquests to and established themselves in the valley of the Ganges. With the conversion of one of their most powerful monarchs, Kaniṣka (first century A.D.), Buddhism entered on a second period of glory and enterprise. Alexander Polyhistor of Asia Minor, according to Cyril of Alexandria, knew a good deal about Buddhism. Clement of Alexandria quotes the work of Polyhistor.[4] According to the *Mahāvaṁśa*, at

[1] Thirteenth Rock Edict.

[2] See further, p. 386.

[3] *Questions of Milinda*, vol. xxv, *Sacred Books of the East*. See, however, Tarn, *The Greeks in Bactria and India* (1938), pp. 268–9. See further p. 386.

[4] *Stromata*, iii. 7. He mentions an Indian order which includes both men

the foundation of the great tope by the king Dutthagāmini in the year 157 B.C. 'the senior priest of Yona from the vicinity of Alasadda [Alexandria] the capital of the Yona country attended accompanied by thirty thousand priests'. The number is, of course, an exaggeration. Strabo states on the authority of Nicolaus of Damascus that an Indian embassy including a thinker who burnt himself to death at Athens in 20 B.C. was sent to Augustus by the Indian king Poros.[1]

During all this period India and the West had extensive trade relations. When Alexander chose in Egypt the site for a city which was destined to perpetuate his name, the preparation for the blending of Eastern and Western cultures started. For a thousand years Alexandria continued to be a centre of intellectual and commercial activity because it was the meeting-place of Jews, Syrians, and Greeks. *Milindapañha* mentions it as one of the places to which the Indians regularly resorted.

II

The facts of religious origin and growth are most important though most uncertain, and one's views can be stated only with great reserve. Most probably Indian religious ideas and legends were well known in the circles in which the accounts of the Gospels originated. The Jewish religion can only be properly understood if its vast background is taken into account, if the non-Semitic influences on Palestine and Syria are considered. Indian or Indo-Iranian groups who worshipped the Vedic deities, Mitra, Varuṇa, Indra, and others, were found in and to the north of Syria in the

and women, who lived in celibacy, devoted themselves to truth, and worshipped pyramids (*stūpa*) which contained the bones of their god. The mass of people worshipped Herakles and Pan. The Brāhinins abstained from animal food and wine.

[1] *Invasion of India by Alexander the Great*, by M'Crindle (1893), p. 389; Strabo, xv. 1. 73; see also Dion Cass. liv. 9. Plutarch refers to the self-immolation in *Vit. Alex.* 69. According to Plutarch, 'the Tomb of the Indian' is one of the sights shown to strangers at Athens. Lightfoot considers that this hero was alluded to by Paul in 1 Corinthians xiii. 3: 'If I give my body to be burned, and have not love, it profiteth me nothing' (*St. Paul's Epistles to the Colossians and to Philemon* (1875), p. 156 n.). Cassius Dio (liv. 9. 10) comments on this self-immolation.

middle of the second millennium B.C. These gods of the *Rg Veda* were known to the Hurrians of Mittani and the Hittites of Anatolia. Professor S. A. Cook writes:

'In what may roughly be called the "Mosaic" age, viz, that illustrated by the Amarna letters and the "Hittite" tablets from Boghaz-Keui, Palestine was exposed to Iranian (Old Persian) or Indo-European influence. This was centuries before the days when it was part of the Persian Empire. . . . In the Mosaic Age, Varuṇa, the remarkable ethical God of ancient India, was known to North Syria, and round about the time of the second Isaiah, the Zoroastrian Ahura-Mazda, doubtless known to the Israelites, was a deity even more spiritual.'[1]

Any interpretation of the Jewish religion which ignores the total environment in which it grew up would be dangerously narrow. Two centuries before the Christian era Buddhism closed in on Palestine.[2] The Essenes, the Mandeans,[3] and the Nazarene sects are filled with its spirit. Philo, writing somewhere about A.D. 20, and Josephus fifty years later relate that the Essenes, though Jews by birth, abjured marriage and practised a form of communism in the matter of worldly goods. They abstained from temple worship, as they objected to animal sacrifices. They were strict vegetarians and they drank no wine.[4] They refrained from trade, owned no slaves, and, according to Philo, there were not among them any makers of warlike weapons. While they

[1] *The Truth of the Bible* (1938), p. 24.

[2] Buddhism and Christianity in later years happen to be confused with each other. Manichaeism is a syncretism of Buddhist, Zoroastrian, and Christian views. Mohammad mixes up the legends of Christ and Buddha. The Buddhist-Christian romance of Baarlam and Joasaph spread from the West from the sixth century onwards until at last in the sixteenth century Buddha was canonized as a Catholic saint. The name Joasaph is derived from Bodhisattva, the technical name for one destined to attain the dignity of a Buddha. See Sir E. A. Wallis Budge, *Baralam and Yewasef, being the Ethiopian version of a Christianised Rescension of the Buddha and the Bodhisattva*, 1923. In the eighth century there was an imperial edict in China forbidding the mixture of the two religions. See Takakusu, *I-Tsing* (1896), p. 224.

[3] The Mandeans flourished in Maišan, which was the gate of entry for Indian trade and commerce with Mesopotamia. Indian tribes colonized Maišan, whose port had an Indian temple. Mandean gnosis is full of Indian ideas.

[4] 'In the asceticism of the Essene we seem to see the germ of that Gnostic dualism which regards matter as the principle, or at least the abode of evil' (Lightfoot, *St. Paul's Epistles to the Colossians and to Philemon* (1875), p. 87).

shared in common with other Jews respect for Moses and the Mosaic Law, they adopted the worship of the Sun, probably as a symbol of the unseen power who gives light and life. They did not believe in the resurrection of the body, but held the view that the soul, now confined in the flesh as in a prison-house, would attain true freedom and immortality when disengaged from these fetters. They accepted the doctrine of the pre-existence of the soul. They also believed in intermediate beings between God and the world, in angels, and were interested in magical arts and occult sciences. They had their mysteries, which they looked upon as the exclusive possession of the privileged few. They held that by mental discipline and concentration we can heal the fissure in our minds. Admission into the sect was both long and difficult, with its careful rites of initiation and solemn oaths by which the members were bound to one another. The Essenes were famous for their powers of endurance, simple piety, and brotherly love.[1]

John the Baptist was an Essene. His time of preparation was spent in the wilderness near the Dead Sea. He preached the Essene tenets of righteousness towards God and mercy towards fellow men. His insistence on baptism was in accord with the practice of the Essenes. Jesus was influenced

[1] Josephus suggests that the Essenes 'practise the mode of life which among the Greeks was introduced by Pythagoras' (*Ant.* xv. 10. 4). Lightfoot criticizes this view, which is supported by Zeller, and holds that the foreign element of Essenism is to be sought in the East, to which also Pythagoreanism may have been indebted. 'The fact that in the legendary accounts, Pythagoras is represented as taking lessons from the Chaldeans, Persians, Brahmins and others may be taken as an evidence that their own philosophy at all events was partially derived from Eastern sources' (*St. Paul's Epistles to the Colossians and to Philemon* (1875), p. 148). He finds broad resemblances between Essenism and the religion of Zoroaster in the matter of dualism, Sun-worship, angelolatry, magic, and striving after purity. Hilgenfeld and Renan suggest Buddhist influence. 'The doctrines of the remoter East had found a welcome reception with the Essene' (Milman, *The History of Christianity* (1867), vol. ii, p. 41).

According to Dr. Moffatt, 'Buddhistic tendencies helped to shape some of the Essenic characteristics' (*Encyclopaedia of Religion and Ethics*, vol. v, p. 401). It is claimed that the Book of Enoch states the Essene views. We have in it a complete cosmogony with references to the mundane egg, angels and their connexion with heavenly bodies, the rebellion of Satan and his host against God, and the fall of the watchers set over the earth.

greatly by the tenets of the Essenes. Before His appearance in Galilee Jesus worked as a disciple of John, and He practised baptism. He looked upon John as His master and forerunner, as the greatest among those born of women. Both preached salvation by the forgiveness of sins. Jesus' emphasis on non-resistance to evil may be due to the Essenes.

The Book of Enoch is a remarkable Hebrew work, written several years before the Christian era, full of non-Jewish speculations.[1] Some of the central features of Jesus' consciousness and teaching may be traced to it. Enoch, the saint of antiquity mentioned in Genesis,[2] preaches the coming world judgement, and proclaims 'the Son of Man' who was to appear in order to rule with the righteous as their head in the time of the new age. The four titles attributed to Jesus in the New Testament—the Christ,[3] the Righteous One,[4] the Elect One,[5] and the Son of Man[6]—are all to be found in the Book of Enoch. Enoch speaks with great conviction and authority: 'Up to the present time there has never been bestowed by the Lord of Spirits such wisdom as I with my insight have received according to the good pleasure of the Lord of Spirits.' He exalts the conception of the Son of Man 'who has righteousness, with whom righteousness dwells and who reveals all the treasures of what is hidden'. Professor Otto is emphatic that this idea of a Son of God who was also a Son of Man is 'certainly not from Israel. . . . The figure of a being who had to do with the world, and who was subordinate to the primary, ineffable, remote, and aboriginal deity is of high antiquity among the Aryans. . . . It may be regarded as indubitable that the phrase "this Son of Man" points back in some way to influences of the Aryan East.'[7] The Son of Man is also 'the Elect One in whom dwells the spirit of those who have

[1] Dr. Charles thinks that the book was composed about 80 B.C. 'It was completed at the latest about the middle of the last century before Christ' (R. Otto, *The Kingdom of God and the Son of Man* (1938), p. 177). Otto finds in it 'speculations (which clearly betray their origin in an Iranian and Chaldean source) about the world and the angels and visions of the supernatural world and its mysteries' (p. 176). In the subsequent pages this indebtedness is worked out.

[2] v. 23

[3] xlviii. 10.

[4] xxxviii. 2.

[5] xl. 5.

[6] xlviii. 4.

[7] Otto, op. cit., p. 187.

fallen asleep in righteousness'.[1] When they rise up into all eternity, they will be clothed with the garment of glory; 'your garments will not grow old and your glory will not pass away'.[2] The metaphor of garments recurs in Paul's eschatology and reminds us of the radiant body made of the element of the pure (*śuddhasattva*) of the Hindu mythology. 'The Elect One will sit upon my Throne.'[3] He is the anointed one.[4] The Messianic idea of the Jews asserts itself here. The political fortunes of Israel and Jerusalem and the return of the scattered tribes are mixed up with the transcendent world catastrophe.

Enoch himself is proclaimed the Son of Man. 'He was taken up on chariots of the Spirit',[5] where he sees 'the patriarchs and the righteous, who have dwelt in that place from time immemorial'.[6] 'Thereafter my spirit was hidden and it ascended into heaven', where he sees angels clothed with the garments of glory.[7] He himself is transformed into an angel: 'And the Lord said unto Michael: Take Enoch and remove his earthly garments and anoint him with good oil and clothe him in glorious garments. I looked upon myself and I was like one of the glorious ones.' Michael leads Enoch by the hand and shows him 'all secrets of mercy and righteousness'. Thereupon 'the spirit transported Enoch to the heaven of heavens',[8] where he saw 'the Aged One [God Himself]. His head was white and pure as wool and his

[1] 'Few could think that anything of the kind could enter the mind of an Israelite. But on Aryan soil the conception that the soul after death enters into its iṣṭadevata goes far back into Vedic times' (p. 189).

[2] lxii. 14.

[3] li. 3. Jesus says the same of Himself. See Luke xxii. 29.

[4] xlv. 3, 4.

[5] lxx. 2 ff.

[6] Cf. the Hindu conception of the *pitṛloka* or the world of manes.

[7] 'Their garments were white and their clothing and countenance bright as snow' Cf. with this the Hindu conception of *devaloka*.

[8] R. Otto asks: 'Whence came these ideas, of which neither the prophets nor the Old Testament as a whole had the slightest notion?' and answers: 'Far off in the Indo-Aryan East, we find the clearest analogy to the process here described of spiritual ascent, of unclothing and reclothing' (pp. 204–5). After a short statement of the Hindu view, he says: 'These materials are found in India in more primitive form not merely at a late period but in the remote pre-Christian *Kauṣītaki Upaniṣad*. That such ancient Aryan conceptions had analogues in Iran is not to be doubted. That they shine through in our *Book of Enoch* is just as certain' (p. 206).

raiment indescribable. . . . When I fell upon my face . . . my whole body melted away, my spirit was transformed. He came to me and greeted me with his voice *You are the Son of Man.*' The predicates which are attributed to Enoch's God are those which are found in the Upaniṣads.[1] The Book of Enoch suggests that out of the illimitable and incomprehensible proceed the limited and comprehensible with its series of aeons, and this account of creation is gnostic in spirit.

What is claimed by Jesus later may be compared with these words: 'All who shall walk in thy ways, thou whom righteousness never forsakes, their dwelling and inheritance will be with thee, and they will never be separated from thee unto all eternity.' We are called upon to walk in His ways, confess Him, and become personal followers of Him, and if we succeed each one of us can be the Son of Man; and now comes the vital conclusion in which God proclaims, 'For I and *my* son will be united with them for ever in the ways of truth.'[2] The Son of Man is the Son of God. He is the saviour: 'He shall be a staff to the righteous whereon to stay themselves, and not fall. And he shall be the light of the Gentiles, and the hope of those that are troubled of heart.'[3] He is pre-existent from the beginning,[4] He possesses universal dominion,[5] and all judgement is committed to Him.[6] When Jesus manifests His spiritual insight by His suffering unto death He inherits the Kingdom. He is the Son of Man and the Son of God. It is the ancient Hindu tradition which Enoch illustrates and Jesus continues.

God together with His Son enters into personal fellowship with those who walk in the ways of truth and righteousness. The souls in the afterworld are separated into three divisions.[7] The first is made for the spirits of the righteous, the second 'for sinners when they die and are buried in the earth

[1] 'The atmosphere of the predicates which describe Enoch's primitive deity is quite Indian' (R. Otto, *The Kingdom of God and the Son of Man* (1938), p. 398).

[2] cv. 2.

[3] xlviii. 4; R. H. Charles (1917), p. 66.

[4] xlviii. 2. 'The Son of Man was previously hidden and the Most High kept him before his power' (lxii. 6). Perhaps he was pre-existent in the sense that he was foreseen and chosen.

[5] lxii. 6.

[6] lxix. 27.

[7] xxii. 9–13.

and judgment has not been executed upon them in their lifetime', and the last 'for the spirits of those who . . . were slain in the days of the sinners. Nor shall they be raised from thence.' The destiny of each soul is defined according to its character on earth. Though immortality is usually reserved for the righteous Jews only, on occasions it is extended to all men. This doctrine and that of rewards and punishments after death influenced considerably the New Testament writers.

Christ's Messianic act in conducting the Lord's Supper may have been suggested by the words: 'The Lord of Spirits will dwell above them, and they will eat with that Son of Man, and lie down and rise up unto all eternity.'[1]

Different views are held in regard to the founder of Christianity. (i) Jesus was the Son of God who came down from heaven, played His assigned part, and then retired. (ii) He was a fanatic whose dominating idea was an early catastrophic last day and Judgement.[2] (iii) He was a great moral teacher who came into the world like other men and became the Son of God much as we become sons of God. He was one of ourselves despite His amazing personality.[3] (iv) He was a prophet like others.[4] (v) Some even deny that He existed at all.[5]

Jesus left nothing written. For some years after His death, His disciples believed that His return as judge and the consummation of this age were imminent. This hope was found even about the end of the first century.[6] The need for compiling trustworthy records of Jesus' life and sayings was felt late in the second generation, and it is difficult to assume that the accounts of the evangelists are historically accurate. They brought together the oral traditions which in transmission were added to and altered. The similarity of the Synoptic Gospels is explained by the hypothesis that Matthew and Luke used Mark and a second source called *Q*, now lost. Latest criticism is of opinion that 'the growth of a New Testament Canon is the result of a long development of which the most important stages lie in the second century although it was only concluded in the

[1] lxii. 14. [2, 3, 4, 5] See further, pp. 387–8.
[6] 2 Peter iii. 3–9.

fifth century or perhaps in a still later period'.[1] The school of criticism which has come to be known as that of *Form-Criticism* argues that the accounts of Jesus transmitted to us by the Evangelists are historically quite untrustworthy. They have been moulded by the devotional needs and spiritual experiences of the early Christian communities. They tell us more of the faith of the Church than of what Jesus actually said and did. We find in the Gospels not so much facts of history as the fancies of the devout.[2] Origen suggests something similar about the method adopted by the Evangelists. It was their purpose, he says, 'to give the truth where possible, at once spiritually and corporeally, but where this was not possible, to prefer the spiritual to the corporeal, the true spiritual meaning being often preserved, as one might say, in the corporeal falsehood'.[3] Naturally the Synoptic Gospels deal with problems which have largely lost their meaning for us. Scholars do not hesitate to say that 'to such an extent are the Synoptic Gospels Jewish books, occupied with problems belonging originally to first century Judaism, that it makes large parts of them difficult to use as books of universal religion'.[4] It is obvious that we have to be very cautious in dealing with the Gospels as historical records. Even if they are the products of fervent devotion, there must have been an historical focus for the pious imaginings, and that, perhaps, was the conviction that those who lived with Jesus felt that they had been in contact with a personality so superior to them as to deserve divine honours. In what does the uniqueness of Jesus lie?

[1] Martin Dibelius, *A Fresh Approach to the New Testament and Early Christian Literature*, E.T. (1936), p. 20; see also R. H. Lightfoot, *History and Interpretation in the Gospels* (1935), p. 1. See further, p. 388.

[2] Cf. 'It seems, then, that the form of the earthly no less than of the heavenly Christ is for the most part hidden from us. For all the inestimable value of the Gospels, they yield us little more than a whisper of his voice; we trace in them but the outskirts of his ways. Only when we see him hereafter in his fulness shall we know him also as he was on earth. And perhaps the more we ponder the matter, the more clearly we shall understand the reason for it, and therefore shall not wish it otherwise. For, probably, we are at present as little prepared for the one as for the other' (R. H. Lightfoot, op. cit., p. 225).

[3] *Commentary on St. John's Gospel*, x. 4.

[4] F. C. Burkitt, *The Earliest Sources of the Life of Jesus* (1910), p. 30.

Jesus gave form and substance to the dreams which had haunted His compatriots for generations, but in this He was greatly influenced by the non-Jewish currents of thought and aspiration which prevailed in His circle during His time.[1] The whole complex of ideas of the coming judgement, of a new age, of the Son of Man who will be transported at the end of His earthly career to God, of the Suffering Servant, of the futility of the earthly kingdom, of the need for self-criticism and discipline, of love and non-resistance filled the air, and in the life and activities of Jesus we find a struggle between the traditional Jewish conceptions which He inherited and the new spiritual outlook to which He laid Himself open. At one period the former tendency predominated, but towards the end the latter prevailed.

If we take the conception of the Kingdom of God, the Hindus, the Buddhists, and the Zoroastrians maintained that the Kingdom of God was not to be identified with an earthly paradise, but is a life which is not of this world. The Hebrews contended that man was to expect and see the Kingdom of God within the limits of this life. An intense nationalism was the dominating feature of the Jewish life, their monotheistic creed being an adjunct of the Nation-State. They employed it to defend themselves against the aggression of foreign imperialists. They developed a catastrophic view of the universe by which history is a succession of crises, a series of supernatural interventions. They looked forward to a great final cataclysm by which they, the chosen people of God, would be restored to their proper place. The last event would close the history of the world and inaugurate a new age and a new society in which Israel would be all-powerful and her enemies nowhere.

There was a period in Jesus' life when this Messianic conception was the dominant one. There are ome who

[1] The New Testament gives us the story of Jesus till the age of thirteen and is silent about the next seventeen years till His appearance at the place of preaching of John the Baptist. Legends that he travelled in the East in the intervening period are sometimes mentioned for which there is no historical evidence. See Eitel, *Three Lectures on Buddhism* (1884), pp. 14 ff.; Jacolliot, *The Bible in India* (1870), p. 289.

think that it was the only impulse in Jesus' life. For them Christianity started as a movement of political revolution against the Roman Empire and its senile supporters, the Jewish priesthood. Jesus does not seem to be speaking of any spiritual change when He refers to the nearness of the impending catastrophe. He does not know when the Son of Man will come: only the Father knows it. He seems to assume a certain interval of time and anticipate wars with the Roman Empire. He observes, with reference to the Temple, that days are coming in which not one stone will be left upon the other. He limits His message at one stage of His career to the Jews only: 'Go not into the way of the Gentiles, and into any city of the Samaritans; but go rather to the lost sheep of the house of Israel.' 'Ye shall not have gone over the cities of Israel, till the Son of Man be come.' 'I am not sent but unto the lost sheep of the house of Israel.'[1] Such passages clearly indicate the predominantly Jewish character of Jesus' message. His task was to prepare the chosen people for the impending coming of the Kingdom. He was destined by God to proclaim to the Jews God's summons to fulfil their vocation. When Jesus announced after His baptism by John the Baptist, 'The Kingdom of heaven is at hand. Repent', His Jewish audience understood it to mean that the great catastrophe was at hand when the Messiah would intervene on behalf of the elect. His disciples suspect that He is the expected Messiah. 'This is that prophet that should come into the world.'[2] Others desired to force Him to assume the role of the King. When he claimed to be the Messiah, the mob understood its revolutionary significance and welcomed him enthusiastically. When He entered Jerusalem He received the homage of His believers. 'Hosanna, blessed is he that cometh in the name of the Lord. Blessed is the Kingdom that cometh, the Kingdom of our father David.'[3] Jesus was to be the King of the Kingdom. This interpretation is supported by many passages. 'There are those who stand here who shall not taste of death until they see the Kingdom of heaven coming in power'; or again: 'This generation shall not pass

[1] Matthew x. 5–6, 23; xv. 24.

[2] John vi. 14.

[3] Mark ix. 9.

away until all these things are fulfilled.' It may be that somewhere about A.D. 30 Jesus marched on Jerusalem with a band of His Galilean followers, seized the Temple, and expelled its occupants by force. His tumultuous entry roused the suspicion of the Roman government, and His act of cleansing the Temple was an attack on the authority of the officials. When Jesus subsequently lost control of the city and retired with His followers to the Mount of Olives, they were surprised by an armed force, having been betrayed by Judas. The Roman opposition to Him could not be on religious grounds. Rome did not persecute other worships with their mysteries and initiations, though each also claimed to be the sole guardian of revealed truth and that its officials held divine commissions to explain their truths to the whole world. The masses who looked for the break-down of the Roman power and the establishment of the Kingdom of God were greatly excited by Jesus' Messianic hopes and His revolutionary message, and He was tried as a political insurgent, a dangerous disturber of peace, a traitor to the Empire. Pilate questioned Him, 'Art thou the King of the Jews?' and He answered, 'Thou sayest.' The death to which He was condemned was that reserved for rebels and traitors.

Before the Sanhedrin He adopted the conception of the Son of Man. At a point in His career, it became clear to Him that an attempt would be made to put Him to death. He claimed the right to interpret the law without reference to tradition. He dispensed men from Sabbath observances on His own authority. He held that obedience to His teaching was of more importance than normal obligations.[1] His claim to interpret the law was offensive to Pharisaic orthodoxy, which valued traditional interpretations, and Sadducee conservatism, which adhered to the letter of the law. This situation suggested to Him that His death was a part of God's plan for the establishment of the Kingdom with power. 'For indeed the Son of Man came not to be served but to serve and to give his life as a ransom for many.'[2] To 'ransom' Israel was a function generally assigned

[1] Matthew viii. 21; Luke ix. 59.

[2] Mark x. 45. In the *Beginnings of Christianity*, edited by Professors Jackson

to the Messiah. It may well be that Jesus expected that His death would be followed by His appearance in clouds of glory, by the overthrow of the forces of evil, and by the judgement of the world. 'Ye shall see the Son of Man sitting at the right hand of power.'[1] Jesus believed that all the early predictions are to be fulfilled in Himself. He had a consciousness of mission, as the inaugurator of a new Kingdom, and felt Himself to be the instrument of its victorious power. This consciousness assumed the form of Messiah—Son of Man—Suffering Servant. It is uncertain whether Jesus knew from the beginning about His suffering unto death. Possibly this knowledge came to Him later, with the failure of the political objective.[2] A crisis in His life put him in mind of the other tradition that the Son of Man must suffer, must be delivered up into men's hands, and they will put Him to death. When Jesus tells His disciples for the first time that He must suffer, Peter reproaches Him: 'Be it far from thee, Lord: this shall not be unto thee', and Jesus repulses him with sharp words: 'Get thee behind me, Satan.'[3] The Gospel tradition shows clearly this change of emphasis in Jesus' teaching, and the new note served to heighten the significance of His message. The intercessory and expiative power of suffering and martyrdom is emphasized in all religions. In Judaism we find that Moses and David are ready to give their lives for Israel. The lives of Jonah and Elijah and the Martyrs of Maccabean times illustrate it. If the Son of Man is to fulfil His vocation, He must be the redemptive suffering servant of God. In the light of His fate, this conception seemed in-

and Lake, the editors were inclined to doubt whether Jesus claimed for Himself the titles of 'Messiah', 'Lord', and even 'Son of Man' (vol. i, pp. 285–94).

[1] Mark xiv. 62.

[2] It is doubtful whether Jesus incurred the suffering of the Cross voluntarily, with the pre-vision of the destiny to which His action was leading. If Jesus went up to Jerusalem convinced that He would be put to death and would rise again, there would not be the consternation among His disciples or the dreadful cry on the Cross which shows that crucifixion was an appalling surprise to Him. M. Loisy thinks that the journey was undertaken in the hope that the divine intervention to terminate the existing world order would take place on His arrival.

[3] Matthew xvi. 21–3.

wardly akin to Him. When He had this perception, Jesus was certain of His exaltation to God through His death.

His is the cause of God, and immediate and complete attachment to His person with the surrender of home, house, and possessions is true worship of God. In the style of Enoch, he says: 'Everyone who shall confess me before men, him shall the Son of Man also confess before the angels of God.'[1] The mystics are persuaded that their knowledge of God is unique and incomparable.[2] 'All things have been delivered unto me of my Father. No one knoweth who the Son is save the Father[3] and who the Father is save the Son, and he to whomsoever the Son willeth to reveal him.' In situations that test us, the depths of life are revealed. Tense moments of crisis are also the moments of grace. Are not the Temptations the impressions that Jesus retained of His interior struggles?

This view that Jesus started with a Jewish nationalist outlook and gradually changed over to a universalist position need not be regarded as derogatory to His greatness or the Church doctrine about Him. The Church insists on the divinity of Jesus as well as His complete and genuine humanity, and looks upon the views of the Arians and the Docetics, the Monophysites and the Nestorians as one-sided. If it is a heresy to look upon Him as 'inferior to the Father', it is equally a heresy to take away anything from His humanity. He was not exempt from feelings incidental to normal humanity—hunger, thirst, weariness, pain, temptation. If it is not derogatory to His nature to think that He felt genuine pain, shed tears at the grave of a friend, or was insulted, beaten, and crucified, and felt the shame and pain of it all, it cannot be derogatory to think that He shared the political passions of His contemporaries and gradually shook them off. It would be to give full weight to Luke's statement that 'Jesus advanced in wisdom and stature'.[4]

From the Synoptic Gospels it is clear that the two currents, the Jewish and the Mystic, the materialistic and the spiritual, were not perfectly reconciled in Jesus' mind. The

[1] Luke xii. 8.

[2] Enoch xxxvii. 4.

[3] Harnack thinks that the words 'No one knoweth who the Son is save the Father' are a later addition.

[4] ii. 52.

Jewish view of the Kingdom is opposed to the conception underlying the words: 'My Kingdom is not of this world.' There is a difference between the traditional interpretation of the Kingdom of God as the continuation of earthly conditions even to the details of eating and drinking, and the mystic view that its nature cannot be indicated in the terms of our empirical existence. The negative descriptions of eternal life which we have in the Upaniṣads and the Buddhist scriptures find their echo in Jesus' declaration that heaven and earth shall pass away, and later sayings: 'It is not yet made manifest what we shall be', and 'Eye hath not seen nor ear heard, neither have entered into the heart of man, the things which God hath prepared for them that love him.' These negations and contrasts suggest the reality of a world which is other than the familiar world of earth. To attain it we have to be reborn, must become 'as the angels in heaven'. It is not possible in an earthly form of existence to be born into the Kingdom of Heaven. It is the wondrous new creation. This is the consummation of the earthly process, this eternal heaven. We can only describe it in words and feelings familiar to us, for we are still in and of the world. So we talk of sitting on thrones, feeding on banquets, and living as angels. All the time we are aware of the inadequacy of these images to the coming of the Kingdom, which is not a mere correction of earthly existence, but a complete transformation of it. But His Jewish audience interpreted the symbolic descriptions as having a reference to the Messianic hope. The Kingdom was to come with flaming lightning, with the appearance of the Son of Man, His angels, and His judgement; starting in Jerusalem, it will go forth extending itself over all the world. The sons of Zebedee ask for the best places in the new Kingdom. The chief aim of the Jew was to save himself from the impending wrath of God. His hopes and prayers were that he belong to the Kingdom of God when it should come. Resurrection is the only way in which the dead could share in the Kingdom. The mystic, however, has the assurance that he has attained security and freedom here and now. If life eternal can be had here and now, there is no point in a resurrection. 'Jesus' preaching of the Kingdom contains elements', says

Professor Rudolph Otto in his last work, 'which are certainly not of Palestinian origin, but point definitely to connections with the Aryan and Iranian East.'[1] While the Messianic conception of the Kingdom belongs to the Palestinian tradition the mystic conception is the development of the Indian idea.

In Jesus' mind universalism and passivism conflict with the exclusiveness and militarism of His Jewish ancestors.[2] He moved forward from the latter and so often came into opposition with the Jews. If some of our theologians explain away Jesus' passivism and arrive at the comforting conclusion that He did not mean what He said or that He acquiesced in armed resistance to evil, as when He used a scourge of small cords in cleansing the Temple in the Johannine account, it is to no small extent due to the struggle in Jesus' own mind. The Gospel according to St. John makes Jesus say, 'I pray not for the world, but for them which thou hast given me.'[3] It is, however, beyond doubt that there was a stage in Jesus' life when He attained a vision of universality and love, and meant literally that 'they that take the sword shall perish by the sword'.

Jesus challenged the Jewish claim to the exclusive right of entry into the Kingdom. While they limited admission to the Kingdom to the righteous, Jesus announced that He had come to call the sinners to repentance. To the question,

[1] *The Kingdom of God and the Son of Man*, E.T. (1938), p. 16.

[2] Dr. Claude Montefiore asks whether as a figure calculated to inspire men to heroic acts of self-sacrifice, the figure of Jesus, detached from what Christians have believed about Him, is adequate. 'What one would have wished to find in the life story of Jesus would be one single incident in which Jesus actually performed a loving deed to one of his Rabbinic antagonists or enemies. That would have been worth all the injunctions of the Sermon on the Mount about the love of enemies put together. Even if such a deed were only reported, and it were of dubious authenticity, how valuable it would be. "Father, forgive them" is of dubious authenticity but it is little the less beautiful and inspiring. Even though it refers only to the Roman soldiers and not to the Jews, it is nevertheless of high ethical import. "The deed! The deed!" as the poet has it. But no such deed is ascribed to Jesus in the Gospels. Towards his enemies, towards those who did not believe in him, whether individuals, groups or cities (Matthew xi. 20–4) only denunciation and bitter words! The injunctions are beautiful, but how much more beautiful would have been a fulfilment of those injunctions by Jesus himself' (*Rabbinic Literature and Gospel Teachings* (1930), p. 104).

[3] xvii. 9.

Who is my neighbour? He answered: any man in trouble, whatever may be his race or nationality.

Jesus protested vehemently against the Jew's exaggerated devotion to ceremonial details. To the Jew the important question is, What am I to do? He insisted on a code of conduct. To the Eastern religions and the mystery cults, the more important question is, What am I to be? The aim is to become something different and not to do something else. Jesus is concerned, not with the wrong we do, but with the corruption of being of which the wrong act is the outcome. We must become different, change our natures, be born again. To be born again is to be initiated into a new life which is not a ceremonial act but a spiritual experience. Rebirth to a higher life, superiority to the bondage of the law, is emphasized by Jesus. We are by birth children of nature, by rebirth sons of God. The pathway to this rebirth is by a life of self-control bordering on asceticism. So far as the Jewish tradition is concerned, there is little or nothing in it of an ascetic character. The Jews have no monks or nuns, people who live apart from the world. For them there is nothing vain and deceitful about the pleasures of the world. Ascetic practices are adopted only as a means for attaining trance conditions, as in the *Martyrdom of Isaiah*, where the prophet and his companions retire to the wilderness clothed with garments of hair and eat nothing but wild herbs. Similarly Ezra was vouchsafed his vision on account of his continence.[1] To prepare for the vision was the object of asceticism. The main Jewish tradition accepted the uninterrupted continuance of the present world order, the doctrine of the goodness of all creation and the duty of peopling the world and reaping the fruits of the earth.[2]

[1] Athanasius in his first festal letter (A.D. 329) writes: 'That great man Moses, when fasting, conversed with God and received the Law. The great and holy Elijah, when fasting was thought worthy of divine visions, and at last was taken up like him who ascended into heaven. And Daniel when fasting, although a very young man, was entrusted with the mystery' (A. Robertson, *Athanasius*, p. 508).

[2] Cf. the famous saying: 'A man will have to give account on the Judgement Day of every good thing which he refused to enjoy when he might have done so' (G. F. Moore, *Judaism, in the First Centuries of the Christian Era* (1927), vol. ii, p. 265.

Wealth is the natural concomitant of righteousness and poverty of sin. The Jewish doctrine of the resurrection of the body implies that the body is not a thing to be condemned. The righteous shall enjoy physical well-being in Paradise. If there would be neither buying nor selling, neither marrying nor giving in marriage, it is because when the day of the Lord comes, the number of the elect is made up and there can be no increase to it. When the goods of nature do not come to our hands unasked, trade and commerce have a place. In the Messianic Kingdom every one will have plenty of good things without labour or barter. The Bishop of Oxford, Dr. Kirk, writes:

'The ascetic outlook of the Gospels is seen to stand out of any recognizable relation with contemporary Judaism. The passages about turning the other cheek, about taking no thought for the morrow, about laying up no treasure on earth, about forsaking parents and possessions, about bearing the Cross are foreign to the genius of the race. The spirit which pervades them constitutes an erratic block in the teaching of Jesus whose provenance—other than in his direct intuition of supernatural truth—must for the moment remain unknown.'[1]

In John the Baptist, in Jesus and Paul, the new current of other-worldliness emerges, and it cannot be accounted for by their Jewish background.

It is interesting to know that the moral teaching of Jesus with its ascetic and other-worldly emphasis has been anticipated several hundred years by the Upaniṣads and Buddha. The late Professor T. W. Rhys Davids observes:

'It is not too much to say that almost the whole of the moral teaching of the Gospels as distinct from the dogmatic teaching, will be found in Buddhist writings, several centuries older than the Gospels; that for instance, of all the moral doctrines collected together in the so-called Sermon on the Mount, all those which can be separated from the theistic dogmas there maintained are found again in the Piṭakas. In the one religion as in the other we find the same exhortations to boundless and indiscriminate giving, the same hatred of pretence, the same regard paid to the spirit as above the letter of the law, the same importance attached to purity, humility, meekness,

[1] *The Vision of God* (1931), p. 63.

gentleness, truth, and love. And the coincidence is not only in the matter; it extends to the manner also in which these doctrines are put forward. Like the Christ, the Buddha was wont to teach in parables, and to use homely figures of speech; and many of the sayings attributed to him are strangely like some of those found in the New Testament.'[1]

It only shows that some of the noblest of the moral lessons usually supposed to be characteristic of Christianity are not characteristic of it alone. They are a necessary consequence of the spiritual life.

On the question of future life, the Christian view was not moulded by the Jewish or the popular Graeco-Roman conceptions. The Jews were satisfied with the conception of Sheol, which, according to the Book of Job, was 'a land of darkness without any order, where the light is as darkness'. As the jurisdiction of Yahweh did not extend to it, all connexion between God and His worshippers ceased at death. In the most literal sense of the word, Yahweh is a 'God not of the dead but of the living'. The earthly life is the most important. The hopes of the Hebrew were for his nation and not for himself.[2] If we leave aside the mystery cults and Pythagoras and Plato, the eschatology of the Greeks was singularly primitive. Homer's faint and cheerless Hades is well known. The Romans did not have a strong belief in immortality. The *Di Manes* were a vague collection and the word had no singular. Faint indications of a more mature view are to be found in the later books of the Old Testament, but there is a vast gulf between them and the elements of Christian eschatology, such as the consciousness of sin, division in the mind of man, the need of healing and redemption, rewards and punishments, both purgatorial and punitive after death. These ideas must have grown up in the little-known period between the Old and the New Testaments. Faith in the high destiny of the human soul is not to be found in the religions of Palestine, Greece, and Rome except in the unofficial and un-Greek mystic cults. The mind of Jesus and His immediate followers on this question must have been shaped in the atmosphere where

[1] *Journal of the Pali Text Society*, 1923, pp. 43–4.

[2] Job xix. 25–7; Psalms xlix. 50; lxxiii. 24; Isaiah xxvi. 19; Daniel xii. 2.

East and West, mystical experience and intellectual speculation, acted and reacted on each other.

The mystery religions revealed things which lay behind the veil of sense and gave hints of the land beyond the grave about which official religions were silent. As geographical barriers broke down and horizons expanded, mystery cults which promised salvation to the soul, release from the burden of sin, and security against judgement, became popular. Even the common people were not insensitive to these cults. Jesus says: 'Unto you is given the mystery of the Kingdom of God; but unto them that are without, all things are done in parables.'[1] 'And with many such parables spake he the word unto them, as they were able to hear it; and without a parable spake he not unto them: but privately to his own disciples he expounded all things.'[2] He said to His disciples: 'I have yet many things to say to you, but ye cannot hear them now.'[3] We have a reference to the spiritual birth after baptism: 'And it came to pass in those days, that Jesus came from Nazareth to Galilee, and was baptized of John in the Jordan. And straightway coming up out of the water, he saw the heavens rent asunder, and the spirit as a dove descending into him: and a voice came out of the heavens, Thou art my beloved son, in thee I am well pleased.'[4] The Christian Eucharist perpetuates the Sacred Meal of the cults of Eleusis and Mithra.[5]

As a Jew, Jesus recognized a corporeal resurrection. At death Lazarus is taken up directly into Paradise and the rich man goes to hell. Jesus' resurrection after three days is probably suggested by Matthew: 'As Jonah was three days and three nights in the belly of the whale: so shall the Son of Man be three days and three nights in the heart of the earth.'[6] This view is in conflict with what Jesus is alleged to have said to the thief on the Cross: 'To-day shalt thou be with me in paradise.' There is immediate entrance into

[1] Mark iv. 11.
[2] Mark iv. 33–4.
[3] John xvi. 12.
[4] Mark i. 9–11. Justin Martyr reads: 'Thou art my beloved son: this day have I begotten Thee' (*Trypho*, 88); see also Luke iii. 22.
[5] The early Christian Fathers Polycarp and Ignatius speak of the Christian mysteries. In the *Stromata* Clement has a chapter on 'The Mysteries of the Faith not to be divulged to all'.
[6] xii. 40.

blessed fellowship with God. The moment of death is the moment of exaltation. We need not confuse the spirit of man with his fleshly covering. Victory over death is the awakening of the spirit from the slumber, that which makes it capable of higher vision. Resurrection is not the revivification of a corpse. The Christian view, that this life is a period of education and testing and we are sojourners in a strange land where we must not expect to see full satisfaction for the deepest interests in life, is not accepted by the orthodox Jew or the normal Greek.

When the prediction of the Kingdom that we would live to see and know Jesus as the exalted Son of God was not fulfilled, the eschatological claim became prominent. The conviction of the exaltation to God through death was the basis of the possibility that Peter and the rest believed after Jesus' death that they saw Him in spiritual vision as living with God. It does not seem to be a question of an empty grave or bodily resurrection. The simple story of the life and activity of Jesus was transformed into an epiphany of a heavenly being who had descended to earth and concealed Himself in robes of flesh. The picture of Jesus of the later Christology blurred the contours of the spiritual God. The Risen Lord takes the place of God and the Church replaces His Kingdom. Even as the Supreme is identified with an historical individual, the Kingdom of God is identified with a concrete empirical structure with its own specific form and organization.

Jesus, as we have seen, enlarges and transforms the Jewish conceptions in the light of His own personal experience. In this process He was helped considerably by His religious environment, which included Indian influences, as the tenets of the Essenes and the Book of Enoch show. In His teaching of the Kingdom of God, life eternal, ascetic emphasis, and even future life, He breaks away from the Jewish tradition and approximates to Hindu and Buddhist thought. Though His teaching is historically continuous with Judaism, it did not develop from it in its essentials. The two tendencies, the Jewish and the mystic, were not perfectly reconciled in Jesus' mind, and the tension has continued in Christian development. We shall now see how the Gospel story bears striking resemblance to the life and teaching of Gautama the Buddha.[1]

Nearly five hundred years before Jesus, Buddha went round the Ganges valley proclaiming a way of life which would deliver men from the bondage of ignorance and sin. In a hundred and fifty years after his death, tradition of his life and passing away became systematized. He was miraculously conceived and wondrously born.[2] His father was informed by angels about it, and, according to *Lalitavistara*, 'the queen was permitted to lead the life of a virgin for thirty-two months'. On the day of his birth a Brāhmin priest predicts his future greatness. Asita is the Buddhist Simeon.[3] He comes through air to visit the infant Gautama. Simeon 'came by the Spirit into the Temple'. When he asks the angels why they rejoice, they answer that they are 'joyful and exceeding glad' as the Buddha to be is born for the weal and welfare in the world of men'.[4] He steadily grew in wisdom and stature. In spite of great efforts to protect him from the sights of sorrow, Buddha found no satisfaction in the life by which he was surrounded. He resolved to flee from the joys of his home. When the tidings reached him that a son was born to him, he observed: 'This is a new and a strong tie that I shall have to break', and he left his home without delay. Early in his career, after a fast of forty-nine days, he was tempted by Māra to give up his quest for truth, with promises of world dominion. The Evil One said unto Buddha: 'So, Lord, if the Lord desired, he could turn the Himalayas, the king of mountains, into very gold, and gold would the mountain be.' Buddha replies: 'He who hath seen pain and the source of pain, how could such a one bow to lusts?' The Evil One vanished unhappy and disconsolate.[5] Buddha overcomes the temptations, persists in his search, meditates for days, and wins enlightenment. Like his conception and birth, Buddha's enlightenment is marked by the

[1] See the writer's *Gautama the Buddha* (1938). [2] *Majjhima Nikāya*, 123. The angels who received the babe held him before his mother, saying: 'All joy be to thee, queen Māyā, rejoice and be glad, for this child thou hast borne is holy.'

[3] See Luke ii. 8–40; *Sutta Nipāta*, 679–700.

[4] *Sutta Nipāta*, 'manussaloke hitasukhataya'.

[5] See Oldenberg, *Buddha* (1882), pp 312 ff.

thirty-two great miracles. The blind receive their sight, the deaf hear, and the lame walk freely. Buddha himself is transfigured, and his body shines with matchless brightness. With a tender compassion for all beings he sets forth 'to establish the kingdom of righteousness, to give light to those enshrouded in darkness and open the gate of immortality to men'.[1] His mission begins. He has twelve disciples whom he sends forth, to carry his message among all classes of men.[2] Buddha heals the sick, is the incomparable physician.[3] In the striking story of the sick brother neglected by the other inmates of the monastery, whom the Buddha washed and tended with his own hands, saying afterwards to the careless monks, who would have been eager enough to serve him, 'Whosoever would wait upon me, let him wait upon the sick',[4] he claims his oneness with humanity so that services to the sick or the destitute are in reality rendered to himself. We have the golden rule in the maxim: 'Doing as one would be done by, kill not nor cause to kill.'[5] 'As a mother would guard the life of her own and only son at the risk of her own, even so let each one practise infinite sympathy toward all beings in all the world.'[6] 'Let goodwill without measure, impartial, unmixed, without enmity, prevail throughout the world, above, beneath, around.'[7] Good conduct and good belief are insisted on.[8] When once we accept Buddha's teaching all other distinctions of caste and status are lost.[9] He converts the robber Angulimāla, has dinner with Ambapāli the harlot,[10] and is accused of living in

[1] See *Mahāvagga*, i. 6. 8.

[2] 'Go forth, O monks, on your journey for the weal and the welfare of much people, out of compassion for the world and for the wealth and the weal and the welfare of angels and mortals. Go no two of you the same [way]' (*Sacred Books of the East*, vol. xiii, p. 112). Mark vi. 7 ff.; Luke x. 1.

[3] *Itivuttaka*, 100; *Sutta Nipāta*, 560.

[4] *Vinaya Texts*, S.B.E., vol. xvii, p. 240. *Mahāvagga*, viii. 26; cf. Matthew xxv. 40: 'Inasmuch as ye have done it unto one of the least of these my brethren, ye have done it unto me.'

[5] 'attānam upamam katvā.' See S.B.E., vol. x, pt. 1, p. 36.

[6] Ibid., vol. x, pt. 2, p. 25.

[7] *Khuddaka Pāṭha*, E.T. by Childers, p. 16.

[8] *Itivuttaka*, 32; see also James ii. 14, 4, 26.

[9] S.B.E., vol. xx, p. 304; see also Galatians iii. 28; Mark iii. 34 and 35.

[10] S.B.E., vol. xvii, p. 105, and vol. xi, p. 30; see Mark ii. 16; Luke vii. 37–9, viii. 102; Matthew xxi. 31 and 32.

abundance.[1] The following sayings of Buddha find their echo in the Gospels:

> 'He abused me, he beat me,
> Overcame me, robbed me.'
> In those who harbour such thoughts
> Their anger is not calmed.
> Not by anger are angers
> In this world ever calmed.
> By meekness are they calmed.[2]

Again:

> Let one conquer wrath by meekness.
> Let one conquer wrong by goodness.
> Let one conquer the mean man by a gift
> And a liar by the truth.[3]
>
> Victory breedeth anger,
> For in pain the vanquished lieth.
> Lieth happy the man of peace
> Renouncing victory and defeat.[4]
>
> Let the wise man do righteousness:
> A treasure that others can share not,
> Which no thief can steal:
> A treasure which passeth not away.[5]

Both Buddha and Jesus bid their disciples lay up for themselves a treasure which neither moth nor rust would corrupt, nor thieves break through and steal. 'A man buries a treasure in a deep pit', Buddha observed, 'which, lying day after day concealed therein, profits him nothing. . . . But there is a treasure that man or woman may possess, a treasure laid up in the heart, a treasure of charity, piety, temperance, soberness. A treasure secure, impregnable, that cannot pass away. When a man leaves the fleeting riches of this world, this he takes with him after death. A treasure unshared with others, a treasure that no thief can steal.'[6]

1 *Majjhima Nikāya*, 26; Matthew xi. 19.
2 S.B.E., vol. x, pt. 1, p. 4.
3 Ibid., p. 58; see also *Majjhima Nikāya*, 21.
4 *Dhammapada*, 201; see also 184, 185, 399.
5 Cf. Matthew vi. 19 and 20.
6 *Khuddaka Pāṭha*, E.T., Childers, p. 13.

What use to thee is matted hair, O fool?
What use the goat-skin garment?
Within thee there is ravening:
The outside thou makest clean.[1]

'Destroying life, killing, cutting, binding, stealing, speaking lies, fraud and deceptions, worthless reading, intercourse with another's wife—this is defilement, but not the eating of flesh.'[2]

Just as Buddha condemns the gloomy ascetic practices which prevailed in ancient India, Jesus goes beyond John the Baptist's emphasis on observances and ascetic rites. Even as Buddha condemns ceremonial religion, emphasizing baptism, Jesus insists less on sacraments and more on the opening of oneself in faith.[3] 'Reverence shown to the righteous is better than sacrifice.'[4] Buddha says: 'Monks, even as a blue lotus, a water rose, or a white lotus is born in the water, grows up in the water, and stands lifted above it, by the water undefiled: even so, monks, does the Tathāgata grow up in the world, by the world undefiled.'[5] 'I am not of the world', says Jesus, according to John.[6]

Buddha has his triumphal entry into his native city of Kapilavastu.[7] As he approaches, marvellous rays proceed from him, lighting up the gates and walls, towers and monuments. The city, like the New Jerusalem illumined by the lamp, is full of light, and all the citizens go forth to meet him. But Buddha remains unmoved. When Buddha is taken to the temple for baptism, he points out that it is unnecessary, as he is superior to the gods, though he conforms to the practice of the world.[8] When a merchant who became his disciple proposed to return to his native town and preach to his people, Buddha said: 'The people of Sunaparanta are exceedingly violent; if they revile you, what will you do?' 'I will make no reply,' said the disciple. 'And if they strike you?' 'I will not strike in return.' 'And if they try to kill you?' 'Death', said the disciple, 'is no evil in

[1] *Dhammapada*, 394; S.B.E., vol. x, pt. 1, p. 90; see also Matthew vii. 15.

[2] S.B.E., vol. x, pt. 2, pp. 40, 41; see Mark vii. 15. For the analogies in the ceremony of baptism see Matthew iii. 14, John iv. 2, and *Mahānibbāna Sutta*, S.B.E., vol. xi, p. 109; see also Introduction to S.B.E., vol. xlv.

[3] Mark i. 15.

[4] *Dhammapada*, 108.

[5] *Saṁyutta Nikāya*, xxii. 94.

[6] John xvii. 14–16.

[7] Cf. Luke ii. 41 f.

[8] See Matthew iii. 13.

itself. Many even desire it, to escape from the vanities of this life; but I shall take no steps either to hasten or delay the time of my departure.' Buddha was satisfied, and the merchant departed.[1] Buddha had his troubles with his disciples. Devadatta, Buddha's cousin, was the Judas among his followers. He once hired thirty bowmen to kill him. But when these came into his presence they were awed by his majesty and fell down at his feet, like the soldiers in the garden of Gethsemane.[2] When all his attempts failed, the faithless disciple entreated Buddha for his forgiveness. Buddha frankly forgave him. On the last day before his death, Buddha's body was again transfigured,[3] and when he died a tremendous earthquake was felt throughout the world.[4]

Many of the parables are common. Buddha is a sower of the word. He feeds his five hundred brethren at once with a small cake which has been put into his begging bowl, and a good deal is left over, which is thrown away.[5] In *Jātaka* 190 we read of an eager disciple who finds no boat to take him across and so walks on the water. In the middle the waves rise and he loses his faith and begins to sink. When he reassures himself with faith in the Buddha, he goes safely to the other side. Max Müller remarks that mere walking on the water is not an uncommon story, but walking by faith and sinking for want of it can only be accounted for by some historical contact or transference, 'and in this case we must remember that the date of the Buddhist parable is chronologically anterior to the date of the Gospel of St. Luke'.[6]

[1] Hardy, *Manual of Buddhism*, p. 259. [2] Ibid., p. 319.
[3] *Mahāparinibbāna Sutta*, p. 46. [4] Ibid., p. 62. [5] *Jātaka* 78.
[6] Max Müller, *Last Essays*, 1st series (1901), p. 285. According to Eusebius the Gospels were published by the Church in the reign of Trajan (A.D. 98–117). Of course they had existed in some form before this, but this was the date of their authoritative redaction. The Canonical works of Buddhism were certainly earlier. In the sixties of the first century Buddha was welcomed officially into China and in that decade a Buddhist work, *The Sutra of 42 Sections*, was compiled in Chinese and a temple built in its honour. This work must have been well known in India at the time of the first Chinese embassy in A.D. 64 and it refers to the 250 rules of *Prātimokṣa* or rules of conventual discipline. A legendary life of Buddha akin to *Lalitavistara* was also translated, and it shows a highly advanced stage of the Buddhist Canon. During the period of Aśoka the bulk of the Canonical works was in existence, for we find from the Bairāt rock inscription that he recommends the study of sever

Though Buddha performs these miracles,[1] he disapproves of them as proofs of his divinity. 'It is because I see the danger in miracles of psychical power and of mind reading that I detest, abhor and despise them.'[2] Buddha denounces suicide except on special occasions: 'Anyone, O Sāriputta, who lays down this body and takes another one, I call blameworthy. But not such was the monk Channa. He committed suicide without blame.'[3] If the physical life is surrendered out of profound inward conviction, that no

different portions of the scripture by monks, nuns, and laymen, five of which are parts of the *Suttapiṭaka* and the two others are found in the *Vinayapiṭaka*. The Ceylon Chronicles declare that the Canon was finally settled at a council called by Aśoka. From the great rail around the tope of Bharahat in Central India, built shortly after the death of Aśoka, about 200 B.C., we learn not only the titles of the scriptures but the names of the Buddhists who are described as 'reciters' 'versed in the dialogues'—'versed in the Baskets', 'versed in the five collections'. See Fergusson, *History of Indian and Eastern Architecture* (1876), p. 85; Cunningham, *The Stupa of Bharhut* (1879). The general agreement of the various lives of Buddha in Pali, Singhalese, and Chinese sources on the incidents of his miraculous birth, his renunciation, his temptation, his enlightenment and subsequent labours as a teacher, and the aims of his mission, points to the existence of a widely diffused tradition in the centuries before the Christian era. The Pāli Canon was settled in Aśoka's time and reduced to writing in the reign of Vattagāmani (88–76 B.C.). Buddhism was in its very nature a missionary religion. In the second century B.C. Buddhist ascetics (*samanas*) were found in western Persia and in the first century B.C. in Bactria.

Garbe assumes direct borrowing from Buddhism in the matter of Simeon, temptations, and the miracles of walking on the water, and loaves and fishes. We have many parallels between Kṛṣṇa and Christ. (1) A marvellous light envelops Mary when Christ is born. A similar light envelops Devakī before Kṛṣṇa is born. (2) There is universal gladness of nature at their birth. (3) Herod inquires of the wise men, 'Where is he that is born King of the Jews?' (Matthew ii. 4); Nārada warns Kaṁsa that Kṛṣṇa will kill him (*Harivaṁśa*, ii. 56). (4) Herod is mocked by the wise men (Matthew, ii. 16) and Kaṁsa is mocked by the demon that takes the place of Yaśoda's infant (ibid. ii. 59). (5) The massacre of the infants is found in both. (6) Joseph came with Mary to Bethlehem to be taxed: Nanda came with Yaśoda to Mathura to pay tribute. (7) The flight into Egypt is similar to that into Braj. The information on the question is so scanty that it is natural that persons approaching the problem with different presuppositions vary a good deal in the conclusions they draw from it.

[1] *Anguttara Nikāya*, iii. 60. For Buddha's power over water, see *Mahāvagga*, i. 20. Cf. Mark iv. 39.

[2] *Dīgha Nikāya*, 11. K. In the *Divyavadāna* Buddha commands his disciples not to work miracles but to hide their good deeds and show their sins.

[3] *Saṁyutta Nikāya*, xxxv. 87.

good can any longer be served by its retention or that it is the higher service to society, it is commended. Buddha's birth stories[1] and the later Mahāyāna exalt his great compassion and renunciation.[2] Buddha is the light of the world (literally Eye of the World), *lokacakṣu*.[3] 'I am a king,' says Buddha, 'an incomparable king of dhamma.'[4] Buddha speaks with an authority on religion and is the lion of his race.[5] He proclaims: 'I, O Vāsettha, know both God and the Kingdom of God and the path that goeth thereto. I know it even as one who hath entered the Kingdom of God (*brahmaloka*) and been born there.'[6] Again: 'He who sees not the dhamma (Truth or doctrine) sees not me. . . . He who sees the dhamma sees me.'[7] 'Those who have merely faith and love toward me', says Buddha, 'are sure of paradise hereafter.'[8] 'Those who believe in me are all assured of final salvation.'[9] But Buddha always puts the practice of the doctrine higher than devotion to himself. While Jesus is angry with the world which will not hear Him, Buddha meets opposition with calm and confidence. He thought of the world as ignorant rather than wicked, as unsatisfactory rather than rebellious. There is therefore no nervous irritability or fierce anger about him. His behaviour is a perfect expression of courtesy and good feeling with a spice of irony in it. Three months after his death Buddha is transfigured. He is identified with the self-existent Supreme. Four centuries after his death he is declared to be a temporary manifestation in an earthly form of the Infinite, accessible at all times to his disciples and promising to make them partakers of his divine nature. By prayer and meditation the pious Buddhist enters into living communion with the heavenly Lord.

[1] *Jātaka* 316.

[2] 'In the whole universe there is not a single spot so small as a mustard seed where he has not surrendered his body for the sake of creatures.' *Saddharmapuṇḍarīka*, E.T., S.B.E., vol. xxi, p. 251.

[3] *Dīgha Nikāya*, 16. Cf. John viii. 12, ix. 5.

[4] *Majjhima Nikāya*, 92; John xviii. 37.

[5] *Anguttara Nikāya*, v. 99; cf. Mark i. 22, and Revelation v. 5.

[6] *Dīgha Nikāya*, 13; cf. John vi. 46, vii. 29, viii. 42 and 55.

[7] *Itivuttaka* 92; cf. John xiv. 6, 9, 18–21.

[8] *Majjhima Nikāya*, 22; cf. John xi. 26.

[9] *Anguttara Nikāya*, x. 64.

To love one's enemies, to bless them that curse, to do good to them that hate, to turn the other cheek, to leave the cloak with him who takes the coat, to give all to him who asks, which are the teachings of Jesus, are precepts not only taught but practised in their extreme rigour by the Buddha in his many lives, according to the *Jātakas*. Buddha revolted against the complexities of the sacrificial religion as Jesus did against Jewish legalism. Both Buddha and Christ, in the spirit of the Upaniṣads, demand the death or the sacrifice of the immediate natural existence as the condition of the new richer life.

The curious may find matter for reflection in these coincidences in the lives of the two teachers. Professor J. Estlin Carpenter writes: 'The lives of the teachers do not essentially differ. It was the mission of both to awaken men out of a state of spiritual indifference, to kindle within them a love of righteousness, to comfort the sorrowful, to reprove as well as to redeem the guilty.'[1] Each of these teachers had his own tradition and grew out of it. This fact leads to certain deep differences beneath the resemblances. Buddha looked upon the Absolute as super-personal spirit, while for Jesus it is a personal God.[2] The theistic emphasis which is very natural in Judaism is lacking in the teaching of Buddha. Apart from the redemptive power of suffering, the special feature of dogmatic Christianity that the world has been saved by the death of Jesus has nothing like it in Buddhism. As for the resemblances, other causes than borrowing may be assigned. If religion is the natural outcome of the human mind, it would be strange if we did not find coincidences. The highest type of self-sacrifice exalted in both may be regarded as common to all lands and ages. The hopes and fears of men, their desires and aspirations, are the same on the banks of the Ganges as on the shores of the Lake of Galilee. If the same examples and modes of illustration are employed, it may be because they are both members of an

[1] 'The Obligations of the New Testament to Buddhism', *Nineteenth Century*, 1880, p. 975; see also A. J. Edmunds, *Buddhist and Christian Gospels* (1908). Many of the parallels collected in this book can be explained without any assumption of borrowing.

[2] See *Indian Philosophy*, vol. i, 2nd ed. (1929), pp. 465 ff., 683 ff.

agricultural society. Possibly some of the incidents, stories, and sayings were common tales of a widespread folk-lore. If both taught in parables, it is because it is the easiest form of teaching for simple men. Making allowance for all these, it is not easy to account for the illustration of two careers with the same legends and embellishments. They cannot be traced to natural evolution. They cannot be accounted for as due to accident. It is no comfort to ascribe them to the Devil, who wished to scandalize us by throwing doubts on our conceptions. But those who are trained in European culture find it somewhat irksome, if not distasteful, to admit the debt of Christian religion to non-Christian sources, especially Hindu and Buddhist. 'In these cases', Max Müller writes, 'our natural inclination would be to suppose that the Buddhist stories were borrowed from our Christian sources and not *vice versa*. But here the conscience of the scholar comes in. Some of these stories are found in the Hīnayāna Buddhist Canon and date, therefore, before the Christian era.'[1] It is not unnatural to suspect that some of

[1] *Last Essays*, 1st series (1901), p. 289. In his *Christian Origins*, E.T. (1906), p. 226, Otto Pfleiderer says: 'These [Buddhist] parallels to the childhood stories of Luke are too striking to be classed as mere chance; some kind of historical connexion must be postulated.'

Speaking of the apocryphal gospels, such a cautious critic as the late Dr. Winternitz says: 'We can point to a series of borrowings from Buddhistic literature which are absolutely beyond all doubt' (*Viśvabhārati Quarterly*, Feb. 1937, p. 14). 'A number of Buddhist legends make their appearance in the Apocryphal gospels and are so obviously Indian in character that it can hardly be maintained that they were invented in Palestine or Egypt and spread thence Eastwards' (Sir Charles Eliot, *Hinduism and Buddhism*, vol. iii (1921), p. 441). Trees bend down before the young Christ and dragons adore Him. At the school He convicts His teacher of ignorance and the latter faints (Gospel of Thomas vi and iv and *Lalitavistara*, x). When He enters a temple in Egypt the images prostrate themselves before Him, and they do the same before the young Gautama in the temple at Kapilavastu (Pseudo-Matthew xxii–xxiv and *Lalitavistara* viii). Mary is luminous before the birth of Christ, which happens without any pain or impurity (Pseudo-Matthew xiii, *Dīgha Nikāya* 14, and *Majjhima Nikāya*, 123). At the moment of nativity all activity of mankind and nature is suddenly interrupted (Gospel of James xviii and *Lalitavistara*, vii). The similarity of Roman Catholic services and ceremonial to the Buddhist is difficult to explain. 'When all allowance is made for similar causes and coincidences, it is hard to believe that a collection of practices such as clerical celibacy, confession, the veneration of relics, the use of the rosary and

the prominent ideas travelled from the older to the younger system. As Christianity arose in a period of eclecticism, it is not impossible for it to have adopted the outlook and legends of the older religion, especially as the latter were accessible at a time when intercourse between India and the Roman Empire was quite common. Let us realize that when Christianity was in a formative stage Buddhism was both settled and enterprising. The affiliation of ideas is a useless pursuit. So long as it is not possible for us to establish with certainty the exact manner in which ideas travelled between India and the West, so long as we do not know who the intermediaries, what the opportunities and times were, it will be unwarrantable optimism to maintain the theory of direct borrowing. Our ignorance of what actually happened need not prevent us from noting the resemblances which strikingly make out that Buddha and Jesus are men of the same brotherhood. Our interest is in the logic of religious experience, and both Buddha and Jesus are eminent witnesses to it. There cannot be any difference of opinion regarding the view of life and the world of thought which seem to be common to Buddhism and Christianity in their early forms. Whether historically connected or not, they are the twin expressions of one great spiritual movement. The verbal parallels and ideal similarities reveal the impressive unity of religious aspiration. Buddha and Jesus are the earlier and later Hindu and Jewish representatives of the same upheaval of the human soul, whose typical expression we have in the Upaniṣads. Whether the two met in early times and one borrowed from the other is of little moment.

Christianity began humbly among a band of disciples who knew and remembered the earthly life of Jesus, the ministry of a revolutionary prophet who announced the speedy coming of the Kingdom and demanded repentance. The Gospels give us what the apostles and the others had to tell of the

bells can have originated independently in both religions' (Sir Charles Eliot, *Hinduism and Buddhism*, vol. iii (1921), p. 443). Many practices common to Indian and Christian worship, such as the tonsure and the altar ritual including incense, flowers, lights, and singing, may have grown independently, but there are some, such as celibacy, relics, and confessions, which are old and established institutions in Buddhism and seem to have no parallels in Jewish, Syrian, or Egyptian antiquity.

life and doctrine of Jesus, or, more accurately, what had been handed down in Christian families and schools as the original teaching of some of the apostles and their friends. While the memory of man is short, his imagination is prolific. The historical facts were soon covered over by the accretions of imagination. Incidents of Jesus' life assumed the form of legends, and it is not improbable that in this work the evangelists were unconsciously influenced by the cult of the Buddha. When Christianity entered the Roman Empire, different streams met, producing many strange eddies of belief and practice.

III

The contacts between India and the West were more frequent in the period of the Roman Empire, especially in the reign of Augustus, Trajan, and Marcus Aurelius. The *Jātakas* contain many references to Buddhist merchants and their adventures in distant lands. Greek and Indian merchants and men of letters met at Antioch, Palmyra, and Alexandria. The Augustan poets refer to the Medes, the Scythians, and the Hindus as being brought under the protecting care of imperial Rome.[1] Indian princes sent embassies to Rome. One of these, from an Indian prince whom Strabo calls Pandion, left Barigaza (Broach) at the mouth of the Narbada and encountered Augustus at Samos four years later.[2] Another Indian embassy went to Rome to congratulate Trajan on his accession in A.D. 99. The Kuṣān kings of India were on excellent terms with Rome. At Antioch the historian Nicolaus of Damascus encountered the three survivors of an embassy from a monarch bearing the historic name of Porus, on their way to Rome. According to the text of the will of Augustus, as it has been restored from a Greek translation on a monument at Ancyra, communications were quite frequent from Indian princes. Pliny refers to an Indian embassy which arrived at Rome in the reign of Claudius.[3] As the commerce between the Mediterranean and the East was considerable, we need not think that it was confined only to material products. The names of the

[1] Horace, *Carm.* iv. 14; Virgil, *Aeneid*, viii. 680 ff.
[2] *Geography*, xv. 73.
[3] *Nat. Hist.* vi. 24.

various imported products—camphor, sulphur, beryl, opal, and the like—show the linguistic influence of India. According to Ptolemy and Dion Cassius, Indians were found in that great emporium of learning, Alexandria.[1] Dion Chrysostom, who lived in the reign of Trajan and died in or after A.D. 117, mentions Indians among those found in Alexandria. In his oration on Homer, he mentions that the Indians, who looked not on the same stars, sang in their own tongue of the woes of Priam and Andromache, of the valour of Hector and Achilles.[2] Apparently he was aware of the existence of the epic *Mahābhārata* and its resemblance in some of its episodes to the incidents of the *Iliad*. Lecturing to an Alexandrian audience, he says: 'I see among you not only Greeks and Italians, Syrians, Libyans and Cilicians and men who dwell more remotely, but also Bactrians, Scythians, Persians and some of the Indians who are among the spectators and are always residing there.'[3] India had a reputation for high philosophy and religion in the middle of the second century A.D., for Lucian makes Demetrius, the Greek philosopher, give up his property and depart for India, there to end his life among the Brāhmins.[4] The travels of Apollonius of Tyana support this tradition. Clement of Alexandria, who died about A.D. 220, knew the distinction between Hinduism and Buddhism. 'There are', he says, 'some Indians who follow the precepts of Boutta, whom, by an excessive reverence, they have exalted into a god.'[5] Clement mentions that Pythagoras learnt from Brāhmins among others.[6] St. Jerome (A.D. 340) mentions Buddha by name and quotes the tradition of his virgin birth.[7] In the reign of Constantine, Metrodorus is said to have journeyed to India to study the science and philosophy of the Hindus. He was followed by his friend Meropius of Tyre and his companions Frumentius and Aedisius. Indian embassies continued to be sent to Constantine, Julian, and Justinian. Damascius mentions, in his life of Isidore, that certain Brāhmins visited Alexandria

[1] *Asiatic Researches*, iii. 53.
[2] *Orat.* liii.
[3] Ibid. xxxii, quoted in M'Crindle, *Ancient India*, pp. 174–8.
[4] *Toxaris*, 34.
[5] *Stromata*, i. 15.
[6] Ibid. i. 15.
[7] St. Jerome, *Contr. Jovin.* i. 26.

(A.D. 500) to learn Alexandrian science. In astronomy and geography the Indians owed a great deal to Western science.

The vast development of material prosperity in the Roman Empire had no spiritual purpose behind it. Its ultimate end seemed to be the satisfaction of selfishness, individual and corporate. In the period preceding the birth of Christ Hellenism weakened the hold of natural religions but stimulated thought and curiosity. The ancestral cults had ceased to hold the larger part of the population in the Roman Empire. The gods of the Greek Olympus and the agricultural deities of the Latins lived in popular fables or poetic literature, but did not represent the religious life of the community. The worship of the Caesars developed the civic virtues, and the worship of law, as with the Stoics, satisfied the highly cultured. They were not essentially religious, though they contained many elements of religion. The religious-minded, for whom the Roman gods had lost their meaning and served only as occasions for civic ceremonial, sought to find spiritual solace outside the life of the society in an esoteric ideal of individual salvation. The people were attracted by the Eastern cults which were streaming into the Empire along the main highways that linked Europe and the Eastern provinces of the Empire, the cults of Isis or Mithras, Jesus or the Orphic mysteries. They all possessed certain features in common—mysticism, asceticism, and superiority to the secular state. The typical Greek may condemn the change as a false turning, a warping of values, but to the men who were dying of despair it seemed to be a vision of reality by which the world can be saved. It filled the aching void in their soul and dissipated despair.

Professor Gilbert Murray tells us that the characteristics of 'indifference to the welfare of the state', 'asceticism, mysticism', are as marked in the Gnostics and the Mithras worshippers as in the Gospels and the Apocalypse, in Julian and Plotinus as in Gregory and Jerome.'[1] 'With all their quackeries,' Professor Gwatkin says, 'these Eastern worships answered the craving for a higher life and for the communion with the unseen powers in a way which the old,

[1] *Five Stages of Greek Religion*, p. 155.

unspiritual worship of the State could not.'[1] They pointed to the need of a wider fellowship than that of the State, a richer life than that of the good citizen. They drew the attention of thinking men to the tragedy of the failure of mere humanism, to the depth of man's longing for the eternal. Every kind of philosophy, every remedy for the troubles of life, found adherents in the Roman Empire in the first century.

The chief cults which vied with Christianity for the spiritual mastery of the world are (1) Mithraism, (2) the Egyptian mysteries, and (3) Alexandrian theology, a curious blend of Greek and Hindu, Jewish and later Christian thought, which developed in Alexandria. When the Roman Empire was consolidated as a political unit, religious unity became essential as its counterpart. The new unitary State required a religion of a more universal character than the polytheistic cults. Mithraism was the first officially recognized monotheistic cult of the Roman world. It brought into religion a soldierly spirit, as it looked upon life as an unending battle between light and darkness. Mithras is the god of light, the representative of deity on earth, the mediator between the high powers of heaven and the human race. His adherents adopted an elaborate system of sacraments and degrees of initiation to secure spiritual blessings and enlightenment.

In the Persian Empire of the Sassanids, Manichaeism was born. Its founder, Mani, was born in A.D. 215 on Babylonian territory and promulgated a creed which was a blend of Zoroastrian dogmas and Gnostic teaching. It held up an ascetic ideal of celibacy, poverty, and fasting. It emphasized the antagonism of the two principles of light and darkness. It spread among all the Christian subjects in Persia who spoke Aramaic. Mani gave a large place to the teaching of Jesus, which caused him to be accepted as a Christian heresiarch. His creed, however, forbade the worship of images, disapproved the killing of animals for sacrifice, and so provoked the wrath of the Roman emperors. It became Buddhist in China and Christian in Europe.

Isis the mother goddess, formed in Ancient Egypt one of the trinity Osiris, Isis, and Horus. She was identi-

[1] *The Knowledge of God*, vol. ii, pp. 143 ff.

fied with many other local goddesses, Ceres, Venus, and Diana.[1] About the period of the rise of Christianity she had become the centre of an elaborate cult of mysticism. She reappears in Christianity as the virgin Mother.

IV

Religious philosophy assumed different forms in Alexandrian circles, where mysticism was the prevailing note.[2] They, however, had certain points in common, such as an abstract notion of God as the transcendent absolute unity, the postulation of intermediary powers to bridge the chasm between the Absolute and the world, the connexion of matter with the principle of evil, and the recognition of ascetic self-discipline as a means to the clearer vision of absolute truths. These are to be found in all the different forms of Alexandrian religious culture, of which the chief are (1) Jewish Platonism, (2) Gnosticism, (3) Neoplatonism, and (4) Christian Platonism. It will be difficult to draw sharp lines of division between these divergent but related phases of religious thought and aspiration. I shall not attempt to deal with these different tendencies except in so far as they are concerned with the problems of the nature of the deity, future life, and the connexion of religion with morality.

In Alexandria, which was the meeting-place of East and West, Philo developed his new interpretation of the Jewish scriptures. It is the most systematic attempt to combine Jewish teaching with Hellenic ideas, to express the religious conceptions of the Jewish prophets in the language of the Greek philosophers. He tried to bring together under the inspiration of his personal experience the dogmas of the Jewish revelation and the results of Greek speculative wisdom. The central and the determining feature of Philo's system is the doctrine of the Logos.

Among the precursors of Philo on the Jewish line are the

[1] An Oxyrhynchus papyrus (No. 1380), assigned on grounds of script to the early second century A.D., gives us a long invocation of Isis, equates her with Maia (Maya) in India, and makes her mistress of the Ganges.

[2] M. Vacherot asserts that the philosophy of the Alexandrians derived nothing from Greek philosophy except its language and its methods. The essentials of its thought are all Eastern. (*Hist. Critique de l'École d'Alexandrie*, vol. iii, p. 250.)

Sibylline Oracles and the Book of Wisdom. The former (*c.* 140 B.C.) call upon the Greek and the Egyptian to renounce their idols and worship the one God, who is conceived as everlasting, imperishable, self-existent. He alone really is, while the world and men under the doom of mortality are nothing. He is wholly invisible to the fleshly eye, though He reveals Himself in the human soul. He creates heaven and earth, the sun, stars, and moon. Unseen Himself, He beholds all things. He is the supreme knower, the witness of everything. Those who honour the true God will inherit eternal life and dwell for all time in Paradise. The specific developments of Philo's doctrine do not find any place here.

The Book of Wisdom, which is undoubtedly earlier than the writings of Philo, makes a distinction between the transcendent God and Wisdom. The former is the eternal self-existent one of whom only being can be predicated. The phenomenal world, on account of its transiency, cannot be regarded as real or ultimate. It points to an unseen reality, the eternal unchangeable ground of all that we behold. He is the eternal light of which the light of stars and sun are but symbol or image. Wisdom is distinguished from the transcendent God. She is 'artificer of all things',[1] an inseparable emanation of the divine essence. She occupies the place of the Logos in Greek philosophy, though its nature is not properly worked out. The Hebrew doctrine of creation out of nothing is not admitted. The universe is made out of a pre-existent material. God 'created the cosmos out of formless matter'.[2] Love is his motive in creation.[3] Man is a self-determining agent with a dual nature, soul and body. Immortality is a purely spiritual survival. To know God is to attain immortality.[4] Plato, it has been suggested, may have inspired the passage, 'The souls of the righteous are in the hand of God.' Pre-existence of souls is assumed.[5]

The Therapeutae or the contemplative monks of Egypt, of whom Philo speaks with great enthusiasm, represent a

[1] vii. 21, viii. 6.
[2] xi. 17.
[3] xi. 24.
[4] xv. 3.
[5] 'I was a child of comely parts and had obtained a good soul, or rather being good, I entered into an undefiled body' (viii. 19 and 20).

blend of Alexandrian Judaism and Hindu beliefs and modes of life.[1]

Philo looked upon himself as a devout orthodox Jew, though his thought is poured into the moulds of Greek philosophy. If the stories of Genesis are to be related to the Platonic doctrine of Ideas, it can only be by the method of allegorical interpretation which Philo adopts. His interpretations may seem to be forced, but they set forth a doctrine of mystic philosophy. The Absolute first principle, which is beyond personality and definite existence, which is immutable and incapable of relations to finite things and expressions in speech, is distinct from the God who makes and sustains the world.

The predicates which it is possible to attach to the Absolute express the contrast of His pure being with the limited and determined nature of finite creatures. Philo says: 'He is full of Himself, and sufficient to Himself, equally before and after the creation of the universe; for He is unchangeable, requiring nothing else at all, so that all things belong to Him, but He strictly speaking belongs to nothing.'[2] We can compare the Absolute to nothing that we know and so must contemplate it in silence. It is not a personal being. To Philo, the anthropomorphism of the Pentateuch is only an accommodation. The free spiritual worship of the Eternal is the goal for which the worship of the personal God is a preparation. He says: 'The two highest statements of the Law concerning the Cause are first, that "God is not as man", second that He is "as man" But the first is guaranteed by the most certain truth; the second is introduced for the instruction of the mass of mankind and not because God is such in His real nature.'[3]

We can apprehend God's existence partly by analogy. Even as we have an invisible mind which is sovereign over the body, so the universe must be guided by an invisible mind which is God. Again, the world shows traces of design,

[1] Dean Mansel finds 'in their ascetic life, in their mortification of the body and their devotion to pure contemplation' the influence of Hindu and Buddhist thought (*The Gnostic Heresies of the First and Second Centuries* (1875), p. 32).

[2] Drummond, *Philo Judaeus* (1888), ii. 48.

[3] Ibid. ii. 14.

but the principle of causality cannot reside in matter which has nothing noble in itself but only the potentiality of becoming all things.

The Absolute godhead, which is perfect, self-existent, and self-sufficient, cannot come into contact with matter; and yet Philo says that out of matter 'God generated all things, not touching it Himself, for it was not right for the wise and blessed to come in contact with indeterminate and mixed matter; but He used the incorporeal powers, whose real name is Ideas, that the fitting form might take possession of each genus'.[1] The Ideas are the archetypal patterns forming an intelligible cosmos, which is the Idea of Ideas. In mediating the relation between the godhead and the universe Philo develops his conception of the Logos and the intermediate powers. He looks on the latter sometimes as personal beings, at other times as impersonal attributes. In one sense the Ideas are identical with God, for, through them, the finite is able to participate in the deity; in another they are different, for the supreme, in spite of this participation, remains free from all contact with the world. God touches matter not through His essence but through His powers. The cosmic process does not add to or take away from the perfection of God. The thoughts are in a sense objective to God, independent of His essential subjectivity, but they are not separate from Him. They are modes of His energy, eternally and inseparably dependent on Him. If He were not, they would not be, even as there would be no rays of light if the central luminary were quenched. They appear as ideal forms in matter, and as thoughts in the human mind. By virtue of their origin they are independent of space and time. The sun is generally taken as the figure, the orb which burns to all appearance eternally, without need of fuel from outside itself. Independent of the world, it sends out its great stream of light and heat which makes possible life on earth. The light is brighter at the source or as one approaches it. The successive stages of diminishing brilliance are marked off as distinct grades of reality, though these grades are said to be only emanations. Philo's account seems to presuppose a distinction between God as He is in Himself

[1] ii. 113.

and God in relation to the cosmos, God the Absolute and God the relative. Dr. Drummond states Philo's view of powers thus:

'They are the connexion between the universe and God, mediating between them, not because they are different from both, but because they are strictly separable from neither. Withdraw them from the mind, and it becomes a nonentity: withdraw them from the material world, and it ceases to be a cosmos: detach them, if that be conceivable, from God, and they will sink into nothingness. They are really divine, and wherever it turns, the seeing soul may discern some thought of God: but they are nowhere exhaustive of the Divine, and it would be wholly false to say that in their totality they were the equivalent of God. Through them God has indeed left no part of the cosmos empty of Himself; but He has not made Himself and the cosmos conterminous and therefore as soon as we endeavour to apprehend Him in the unity of His being, He remains to our thought essentially outside the universe though acting dynamically within it.'[1]

The perceptible universe has invisible patterns working in it. When we survey the cosmos as a whole, we rise to the apprehension of its unity and feel that the different ideas are the varied forms of one ultimate reason. The world is the concrete embodiment of this reason; it is the picture of God's thought. The thought or Logos of God is next only to God Himself. His thought presupposes His being. 'God is the most generic thing,' says Philo, 'and the Logos of God is second.' The Logos is the pervasive law of the universe, the supreme idea impressed on it. As the Idea of Ideas, the most general thought, it is said to be the oldest of things. As thought, it is conceived as produced under the figure of a son. Sometimes in Philo, the Logos is identified with wisdom; the mediating power is symbolized as the mother of the universe, the Śakti of Śaiva and Śākta systems of thought. The Logos is the Platonic Idea of Good, the Stoic world spirit or Reason immanent in creation, which it fosters and sustains. As the mediator between the eternal and the ephemeral, it partakes of both natures. It is neither uncreated like the supreme nor created like the finite creatures. It imparts reality to all lower ideas as they in turn do to sensible things.

[1] *Philo Judaeus*, ii. 116.

Man's material body is the source of evil. By resistance to the allurements of the senses and the active exercise of virtue, man can free himself from bondage to the body, and attain the divine vision when he is 'lifted above and out of himself'. The knowledge of God is attained by vision, the direct personal communion of a soul that no longer reasons and reflects but feels and knows, becomes utterly passive, as in the condition of trance, of which Philo had personal experience.

> 'I will not be ashamed to relate', says Philo, 'what has happened to myself a thousand times. Often when I have come to write out the doctrines of philosophy, though I well knew what I ought to say, I have found my mind dry and barren, and renounced the task in despair. At other times, though I came empty, I was suddenly filled with thoughts showered upon me from above like snowflakes or seed, so that in the heat of divine possession I knew not the place or the company, or myself, what I said or what I wrote.'[1]

We are able to know God, who dwells in us, as He has breathed His nature into us. The inspired soul 'may with good reason be called God'. The different stages for attaining the ecstatic consciousness, the withdrawal from the senses, the abstraction from the intellect, and the flight of the ego are recognized by him. The moral preparation is insisted on. While every good and wise man has the gift of prophecy, it is impossible for a wicked man to become an interpreter of God.

We have in Philo's system a mystic rendering of historical Judaism. His passion for God, the certainty that the pure in heart shall see Him, the conviction that ascetic training alone can lead us to His presence, and his universality make him one of the greatest of mystics.

The only Judaic elements are the insistence on mono-

[1] i. 14–15. Philo says: 'One must first become God—which is impossible—in order to be able to comprehend God. If one will die to the mortal life and live the immortal, he will perhaps see what he has never seen. But even the sharpest vision will be unable to see the Uncreated, for it will first be blinded by the piercing splendour and the rushing torrent of rays, just as fire affords light to those who stand at a proper distance but burns up those who come near' (ii. 17). See also Bigg, *The Christian Platonists of Alexandria* (1886), p. 16.

theism, contempt for image worship, and the claim that the Jews had in the Mosaic revelation the highest religious knowledge. All the other elements of his system are those found in Hindu thought.

'It might almost seem', writes Dean Milman in his *History of Christianity*, 'that there subsisted some secret and indelible congeniality, some latent consanguinity, whether from kindred common descent or from conquest, between the caste divided population on the shores of the Ganges, and the same artificial state of society in the valley of the Nile, so as to assimilate in so remarkable a manner their religion. It is certain that the genuine Indian mysticism first established a permanent Western settlement in the deserts of Egypt. Its first combination seems to have been with the Egyptian Judaism of Alexandria, and to have arisen from the dreamy Platonism, which in the schools of that city had been engrafted on the Mosaic Institutes.'[1]

The mystic tradition is preserved in the Jewish *Kabbala*, whose two chief books are *Sepher Yetzirah*, or the Book of Creation, and *Zohar*, or Light. This system admits the reality of an *En Soph*, which is the highest unity, having no attributes and no definite form of existence, though it comprehends within itself all existence. All that is is contained in it and emanates from it, for since it is infinite nothing can exist beyond it. Its infinity becomes known by a series of emanations or intelligences which are ten in number. These ten *sephiroth* are the attributes of the infinite being, having no reality in themselves but existing in the divine being as their substance. From them arise, directly or remotely, the three worlds of creation, formation, and action. The final destiny of the three worlds, as of all finite existences, is to return to the infinite source from which they all emanated. The souls of men will not return to the infinite till they have developed all the perfections of which they are capable, and if this is not effected in a single life, the soul will migrate into other bodies, until the development is completed. Many features of the *Kabbala*, such as the potency assigned to letters, the use of charms and amulets, the theory of emanation as opposed to creation *ex nihilo*, the doctrine of the correspondence between macrocosm and microcosm, belief in rebirth and a definite pantheistic tendency, are alien to the spirit of orthodox Judaism and akin to that of the Upaniṣads and Tantrism.

V

Gnosticism was a deliberate attempt to fuse Greek (Platonic) and Hindu elements.[1] It is a name for the whole system of syncretistic religious thought, which covers many sects with widely differing tenets which prevailed in the Eastern provinces of the Roman Empire during and prior to the early days of Christianity. It existed long before the Christian era, though Christianity tended to look upon it as heresy. Many of the chief features of Gnosticism are those common to the Upaniṣads and the mystic traditions of Greece. (1) The divine being is indefinable and infinite, exalted above all thought and expression. He is different from the Demiurge or the Creator God. God is separated from His attributes, the aeons of reason and truth. He is eternal silence. (2) If God is the absolute being, how do creation and evil arise? If the world arose out of the sole act of God without any modifying or opposing influence, evil would have been impossible; or we will be driven to the conclusion that God created evil. So an antagonistic principle independent of God by which His creative energy is thwarted and limited is posited. This opposing principle is identified with the world of matter. Gnostic systems do not all agree with regard to the definition of matter. It is looked upon as either a dead passive resistance or a turbulent active power. The resulting dualism is also ambiguous. Evil which is opposed to the divine being has no reality.[2] The

[1] Harnack says: 'The union of the traditions and rites of the Oriental religions, viewed as mysteries with the spirit of Greek philosophy, is the characteristic of the epoch' (*History of Dogma*, vol. i (1894), p. 229). In the technical sense, the term 'gnostic' first appears in 1 Timothy vi. 20.

[2] This led to a denial of the Incarnation of Christ. A divine being cannot assume a body made of evil matter. This view took two forms. The Docetae held that the body of Jesus was an immaterial phantom. The Ebionites affirmed that the spiritual being of Christ was a distinct person from the man Jesus. The former descended upon the latter at the baptism and left Him before crucifixion, never being united to Him in one person. When the Gnostic interprets the dualism as final and ultimate, he departs from the tradition of the Upaniṣads and manifests the influence of Persian dualism. Plotinus criticizes the Gnostic position on this point.

dualism of good and evil is variously interpreted. It is often a temper which accepts the contradictions of experience as ultimate. There is no escape for spirit except in the destruction of matter, no victory for the divine except in the annihilation of the human. Evil is regarded as a part of the constitution, something organic. (3) The infinite principle communicates with the finite by a series of successive emanations. They sink gradually lower and lower in the scale as they are farther removed from their source, until at last contact with matter becomes possible and creation ensues. These emanations, aeons, spirits, or angels are conceived of as more or less concrete or personal forms. (4) The cosmos is a blend of divine and non-divine material principles. It represents the descent of spirit into matter. Matter which was previously insensible is animated into life and activity by the descent of the spirit into it. (5) Deliverance of spirit from its union with matter or the world of sensuality is effected by asceticism and contemplation leading to gnosis or wisdom. (6) Gnosis does not mean intellectual knowledge or logical understanding, but is seeing God, mysterious wisdom. It is reception of the spirit, beatific vision, illumination, deification. It is not imparted to all and sundry. It is esoteric, secret wisdom, accessible only to those who are initiated.[1] For the uninitiated many, faith suffices. There are holy rites and formulas, acts of initiation and consecration. Sacraments such as baptism by water, fire, sacred formulas, names, and symbols play a leading part. Gnosticism assumes that there is a knowledge of God, a science of realities. There is something to be known in religion. Salvation depends on the knowledge of truths, not knowledge *about* but knowledge *of*. Piety becomes gnosis. (7) The perfect Gnostic is the man who is free from the world and master of himself. He is emancipated from the dead letter and outward symbols of religion, having realized the truth. He

[1] In *Pistis Sophia* we have reference to the methods by which ecstatic experiences are obtained. According to it salvation is by a knowledge of the mysteries. It teaches us that we take in evil with our food, which is material, and so it is that we are asked to renounce the world. 'And ye are in great sufferings and great afflictions in your being poured from one into another of different kinds of bodies of the world' (M., p. 248).

lives in God and has life eternal and may be truly said to have passed from death to life, to have risen from the natural and put on the spiritual state. The true nature of resurrection is spiritual. Many of the Gnostic sects believed in pre-existence and rebirth of human souls. They had also a magical theory of the spirit world. The disembodied soul travels by the dark or bright paths[1] and is saved from the perils on the way by the magic word. 'The essential part' of these Gnostic conceptions 'was already in existence and fully developed before Christianity'.[2]

In the first century it became fused with Christian ideas. In the early days Christianity wanted a philosophy which the Gnostics supplied. Harnack is undoubtedly correct in looking upon the Gnostics as 'the theologians of the first century'. He says: 'The Gnostic systems represent the acute secularising or hellenising of Christianity, with the rejection of the Old Testament, while the Catholic system, on the other hand, represents a gradual process of the same kind with the conservation of the Old Testament.'[3] The Church Fathers tell us that the doctrines of Gnosticism are derived from the mystery religions, Pythagoras, and Plato. Gnosticism is by no means a mere attempt to reject the Old Testament and hellenize the Gospels. What it did was to introduce into Christianity not the pure spirit of Greek philosophy but conceptions of Eastern religions which by the first century had taken their place everywhere in the Roman Empire. Its conceptions of dualistic theology, ascetic ethics, ecstatic experience of the real, and redemption from the trammels of flesh are derived from the Eastern cults. 'The first attempts at the intellectual comprehension [of the Christian doctrine], the first efforts of dogma were based on a philosophy profounder and far more venerable than the juvenile wisdom of the Greeks. . . . Gnosticism is not pure Hellenism as some say; it is rather pure orientalism in a Hellenic mask.'[4] By admitting the distinction of the Absolute god-

[1] These answer to the *devayāna* and the *pitṛyāna* of the Upaniṣads. *Bṛhadāraṇyaka Up.* vi. 2. 2.

[2] Professor W. Bousset, 'Gnosticism', *Encyclopaedia Britannica*, 11th ed.

[3] *The History of Dogma*, E.T. (1894), vol. i, pp. 227, 226.

[4] Kennedy, 'Buddhist Gnosticism', *J.R.A.S.* (1902), p. 383.

head and creator spirit, the Gnostics break away from the Old Testament doctrine. The Christian Church stigmatized the Gnostic as the 'first-born of Satan'. Gnosticism is generally regarded as an heretical perversion of Christianity.

The chief document on this subject is the *Philosophumena* or the *Refutation of all Heresies* by Hippolytus, Bishop of Ostia, belonging to the early part of the third century.[1] This book mentions 'The Great Announcement' as containing an account of the pre-Christian teaching of Simon Magus.[2] The Church Fathers describe him as a horrible sorcerer, the parent of all later Gnosticism. The story in Acts viii makes it clear that the sect of which he became the leader was a pre-Christian one. The first cause of all things is said to be Fire.[3] It has a twofold nature, hidden and manifest, apprehended by reason and sense respectively. The cosmos or the ordered universe comes into being from the unbegotten or self-existent Fire by means of six roots called Mind, Thought, Voice, Name, Reason, and Desire. The world is a hebdomad, consisting of seven powers, the six roots with a seventh which is the source of them all. The conception of emanations is adopted. The conception of the Logos or the world soul is also accepted by the Simonians, according to Irenaeus.

The Hermetic tradition of Egypt may be regarded as Gnostic in character. The Hermetic societies grew up in hellenized Egyptian circles where syncretistic cults were the fashion. The latest editor of the Hermetic books observes: 'If one were to try to sum up the Hermetic teaching in one sentence, I can think of none that would serve the purpose better than the sentence, "Blessed are the pure in heart for they shall see God."'[4] Though in their present form they are not earlier than the fourth century, they undoubtedly

[1] E.T., 2 vols., by F. Legge (1921). The author of *Philosophumena* gives an account of Indian thought. The Brāhmins are divided by him into two orders, the householders and the ascetics who live in seclusion and eat only fruits. They designated God under the figure of light, not that of sun or of fire but of the inward reason, the Logos which finds its expression in the knowledge of the wise. We can attain to this wisdom by casting off all vain opinion and controlling our evil passions (i. 21).

[2] See Acts viii. 9–24; Justin Martyr, *Apologia*, i. 26. 56 and ii. 15.

[3] Cf. 'God is a burning and consuming Fire' (Deuteronomy iv. 24).

[4] Scott, *Hermetica* (1924), vol. i, p. 14.

represent an earlier tradition. Perhaps they are a development of the earlier mysteries.[1] They seem to be 'an eclectic combination of Platonic and Oriental doctrines'.[2] They believed in a supreme creator God and many subordinate gods and angels. To account for the emanation of an imperfect and changing world an intermediary, a second god, was accepted. The Lord and Maker of all from Himself made the second god, the visible and perceptible whom He loved as His son. As finite man could not comprehend the infinite, he was made to contemplate the Son. The 'first born' god is named Agatho-Daimon, which was soon identified with the Logos. 'With Logos not with hands did the Creator make the universal cosmos.' Hermes is the messenger of the gods, conveying to us the mystery of the godhead. Contempt for the body as a bond of corruption encourages ascetic practices. The vision of God is attained not through ordinary natural processes but through dreams and divination. The way to worship God is to abstain from evil. No one can be saved until he is born again. '[If you would be born again] you must cleanse yourself from the irrational torments of matter . . . ignorance, incontinent desires, injustice, covetousness, deceitfulness, envy, fraud, rashness, vice. . . . When God has had mercy on a man all these depart from him, and thus is the rebirth accomplished.'[3] Even in this life, we can receive God and achieve immortality. The vision is ordinarily accompanied by ecstatic experiences. 'Father,' the disciple cries, 'God has given me a new being, and I perceive things now not with bodily eyesight but by the working of the mind. I am in heaven and in earth, in water and in air: I am in beasts and plants. . . . I am present everywhere. Father, I see the whole and myself in the mind.' The following is a typical prayer: 'We give thanks to Thee,

[1] Professor Sir Flinders Petrie gives 200 B.C. as the date of the Hermetic books. In the allusions to the destruction of Egyptian temples and worship and the massacre of people by Scythians and Indians, he finds an obvious reference to the second Persian invasion, 342–332 B.C., when the Scythian and Indian were the Western and Eastern branches of the Persian army. He sees in the Hermetic books 'the development of religious thought in Egypt under Persian and Indian influences which formed a basis of later Jewish and Greek developments' (*Egypt and Israel* (1923), p. 113).

[2] Kirk, *The Vision of God* (1931), p. 47.

[3] Ibid., p. 49.

Most High, for by Thy grace we received this light of knowledge. Having been saved by Thee, we rejoice that Thou didst show Thyself to us wholly, that Thou didst deify us in our mortal bodies by the vision of Thyself.'[1] The whole duty of man in the Hermetic writings is declared to be 'to know God and injure no man'.

Plutarch is a cultivated Gnostic of the first century of a tolerant frame of mind. He has no quarrel with any religion that puts God and man in right relation to each other. Bewildered by the problem of evil, he resorts to a dualism and speaks with respect of the Persian doctrine of Ormuz and Ahriman. To make God the author of evil would be to contradict the idea of God. There are two principles hostile to each other. The evil principle is not matter which is characterless and indeterminate but something positive, a spiritual power, an evil world-soul. Matter aspires after the good, but is overcome and dominated by the evil spirit. The dualism in the constitution of the world is reflected in the individual soul, which has two parts opposed to each other. The higher part is not a part or function of the soul, it is something above us. Spirit is immortal. Plutarch believes in the rebirth of souls. The supreme godhead rules through subordinate powers. In the development of his views he was influenced by Greek thought and Egyptian religion.

Apollonius of Tyana is another famous Gnostic. According to the account of Philostratus, he journeyed to India and spent about four months at 'the monastery of the wise men'.[2] Apollonius hated bloody sacrifices and was a strict vegetarian. He was a complete passivist, holding that we have no right to shed blood under any circumstances. He insisted on prayer and contemplation and tried to make men more religious, attempting to alter their ways of worship. Freedom from possessions and needs is the highest value.

Basilides in the first half of the second century A.D.[3] works

[1] Quoted in Kennedy, *St. Paul and the Mystery Religions* (1913), pp. 109–10.

[2] *Apollonius of Tyana*, trans. Phillimore, 1912, bk. iii, chs. 10 and 50.

[3] He is said to have lived immediately prior to Valentinus, and so we may assume that he flourished about A.D. 120 to 130. The chief sources are the *Philosophumena* of Hippolytus and the *Miscellanies* of Clement of Alexandria.

Hindu and Buddhist thought into a Christian framework. He posits the reality of a supreme godhead who is above space, time, consciousness, and even being itself. It is to be worshipped in silence. His conception of God has little in common with the popular Christian view. Dean Mansel writes:

'As a mere system of metaphysics, the theory of Basilides contains the nearest approach to the conception of a logical philosophy of the absolute which the history of ancient thought can furnish, almost rivalling that of Hegel in modern times; but in the same degree in which it elevates God to the position of an absolute first principle, it strips him of those attributes which alone can make him the object of moral obedience or religious worship.'[1]

The will to create the universe arises in this being. In this will is the seed of all universes, which contains everything in itself potentially, even as a grain of mustard seed contains the whole plant. It is the potentiality of all potentialities. The Demiurge, who arises 'thinking it not right that he should be alone, made for himself and brought into existence from the universal seed a son far better and wiser than himself'. Even as man is the crown of the world process, Christ is the crown of manhood. Sonship is the manifestation of the deity. Clement of Alexandria says of Basilides that he 'deified the devil'.[2] The dualism in Basilides is not so ultimate as this comment suggests. In the spirit of Buddhism, Basilides explains suffering as the fundamental principle of all existence and looks upon personality as a complex consisting of five elements. According to Clement, Basilides believes that men suffer for their deeds in former lives. He accepts rebirth in different forms as steps in the purification of the soul.[3] He denies resurrection of the body. He required of his followers a probation of five years of silence.

Though Basilides believed that Christianity was the main factor of his system, there is no doubt that his interpretation of Christianity is profoundly Buddhist.

[1] *The Gnostic Heresies of the First and Second Centuries* (1875), p. 165.

[2] *Stromata*, iv. 12, 85.

[3] In support of the hypothesis of rebirth, Basilides cites Scriptural texts. John ix. 2; Romans vii. 9. Corpocrates adopts the theory of rebirth in a modified form: the soul is imprisoned in the body again and again until it has performed all possible actions. *Irenaeus*, I. xxv.

'All things have their law of being in themselves; suffering is the concomitant of existence, rebirth is the result of former acts and metempsychosis governs men with inflexible justice and with iron necessity. The office of Jesus is the office of the Buddha; the elect alone are saved and the mass of mankind remains content to be born again.'[1]

Valentinus has the reputation of being the greatest of the Gnostics, though our scanty information regarding his life and teaching is from the polemical writings of the Church Fathers. To the nameless being of Basilides he gives the name of Depth. He thus represents the absolute first principle in a positive way as potentially containing all existence rather than as actually determined by none. It is Unspeakable Depth or Unutterable Silence. Its first manifestation is thought preparatory to action, an intellectual process indicated by Nous, whose counterpart is that perfect truth which belongs to divine thought. Then comes speech. Material existence is an error, fall, or degradation.

Theodotus became the leader of the Eastern Valentinians and Clement was familiar with his writings. He taught that Christ came, not for our redemption alone, but for healing the disorders of the whole world. All those who receive Him and in so far as they can receive Him will be saved. There are different kinds of souls: those who have flesh and not soul will perish like the beasts; those who are spiritual are predestined to life eternal. Between these are the psychic, the feminine souls who can win eternal life by faith and discipline. The mingling of spirit, soul, and body is the cause of all evil and suffering, and their final separation is salvation.

Bardesanes the Babylonian (born at Edessa on 11 July A.D. 155) is credited with a work on Indian thought. He met in Babylon some of the members of an embassy addressed to the emperor Antoninus Pius (A.D. 158–81). From two of these, Damadamis and Sandanes, he derived a large amount of information, which Porphyry has preserved in his treatise on *Abstinence*. Bardesanes distinguishes between

[1] Kennedy, 'Buddhist Gnosticism', *J.R.A.S.* (1902), pp. 411–12. 'It is Buddhist pure and simple—Buddhist in its governing ideas, its psychology, its metaphysics' (ibid., p. 383).

the Brāhmins and the Buddhists. He seems to have learnt a good deal about the teaching and mode of life of Hindu and Buddhist thinkers; his work was used by Porphyry.

Marcion cannot be counted among the Gnostics, even though he distinguished between the God of love and the creator of the world, who is a self-contradictory being of limited knowledge and power, and adopts the antithesis of spirit and matter. He assumes three principles: (1) the Supreme God, (2) the Demiurge, and (3) eternal matter. The two latter are imperfect but not essentially evil. He does not admit the theory of emanation for the Supreme principle, which is an essential feature of other Gnostic mysteries. He denies any real assumption by Christ of human nature. Jewish prophecy is not for him a preparation for Christian revelation. He required the Church to reject the Old Testament and thus release it from doctrinal narrowness.[1]

Gnosticism was one of the most powerful currents of thought which influenced Christian doctrine and practice. In the early third century Alexander Severus (A.D. 222–35) paid divine honours to the Gnostic teachers Apollonius and Orpheus. By the command of his mother, Philostratus wrote his *Life of Apollonius*. Gnosticism remained a power down to the fifth century through its alliance with Neoplatonism.

The Gnostics 'approach the problem from a non-Christian point of view and arrive therefore at a non-Christian solution'.[2] But they accept the Christian creed and look upon themselves as Christians. They appealed to Christian scriptures and felt that they had a deeper knowledge of Christian truth. But their teaching was condemned as a heresy. The Gnostic view of creation is opposed to the Christian view as set forth in the first article of the Apostles' Creed: 'I believe in God the Father Almighty, the Maker of heaven and earth.' For the Gnostics creation is not the act of the supreme God but of an inferior demiurge. The god of religion and the god of creation are distinguished. Again, the doctrine of the resurrection of the body is opposed to the Gnostic view, which separates spirit and body. If personal existence is possible only in the body of the flesh, the dead

[1] Loisy, *Hibbert Journal* (July 1938), p. 520.

[2] Bigg, *The Christian Platonists of Alexandria* (1886), p. 29.

will remain dead until the date of the general resurrection. If we cannot exist without the flesh, no one whose flesh is dead can be said to be alive. Its position was not impossible so long as the last day was believed to be imminent, but when it receded into the background the Gnostic view seemed more attractive. For the Gnostic the chief object of man was to set free his spiritual nature from its material imprisonment, and this can be accomplished by gnosis or sacramental rites.

To the careful student, the close similarity between the teaching of the Upaniṣads and early Buddhism and Gnostic theories will be obvious.

'That the seeds of the Gnosis were originally of Indian growth carried so far westward by the influence of that Buddhistic movement which had previously overspread all the East, from Tibet to Ceylon, was the great truth faintly discerned by Matter (in his *Histoire Critique du Gnosticisme*) but which became evident to me upon acquiring even a slight acquaintance with the chief doctrines of Indian theosophy.'[1]

VI

Among the predecessors of Plotinus may be mentioned Poseidonius and Numenius. Poseidonius, the teacher of Cicero, was greatly influenced by the learning of the Chaldeans, and through his advocacy astrology became a popular study. The theory of tempers jovial, mercurial, saturnine, and lunatic and possession by demons, magic, and sorcery favoured the fatalistic attitude and crushed the mind under a load of gloomy and fantastic superstitions. The Gnostic and Neoplatonic speculations by their theory of demons and spiritual agencies did not discourage the spread of these views. But Plotinus reinterpreted the ideal of philosophic unity and transformed the 'return of the soul' from the domain of astral myths to that of experience. Sextus Empiricus[2] quotes a saying of Poseidonius that 'light is appre-

[1] C. W. King, *The Gnostics and Their Remains Ancient and Mediaeval*, 2nd ed. (1887), p. xiv. 'In the history of the Church it is most certain that almost every notion that was subsequently denounced as *heretical* can be traced up to Indian speculative philosophy as its genuine fountain head; how much that was allowed to pass current for *orthodox* had really flowed from the same source, it is neither expedient nor decorous now to inquire' (p. xv).

[2] Ibid. vii. 93.

hended by the light-like power of vision, sound by the air-like one of hearing, and similarly the nature of the universe must be apprehended by reason which is akin to it'. The teaching of Poseidonius himself was much too Stoic in its texture and so could not satisfy an age which demanded a more spiritual conception of God and the soul.

Numenius, whose influence on Plotinus was considerable, 'had directed all his efforts', says Eusebius, 'towards a fusion of Pythagoras and Plato, while seeking for a confirmation of their philosophical doctrines in the religious doctrines of the Brāhmins, the Magi and the Egyptians'. He looked upon Moses as a prophet and called Plato a 'Moses speaking in Attic'. He distinguished the Demiurge or the second god from the supreme being and identified it with the Logos. The creator shares the characteristics of the real and the phenomenal. Our world is the third god. We have three divine hypostases, the supreme godhead, the creator Logos, and the created world. Even as the demiurge is dual in nature, the soul is also dual, or rather there are two souls, the rational and the irrational. Numenius is said to have believed in two world souls, one good, the other bad. The latter is identified with matter. The two souls are in conflict both in man and in the world. Numenius adopts the theory of rebirth.

In the Neoplatonism of Plotinus (A.D. 205–70) we have the fruits of the religious syncretism which arose from the conquests of Alexander the Great and the undertakings of the Roman Empire. It revived the mystic tradition of the Greek cults and its resemblances not only to Alexandrian Judaism but to Vedānta philosophy are well known. Ritter introduces his account of Neoplatonic philosophy with the general title 'Diffusion of Oriental modes of Thought among the Greeks'.[1]

Plotinus, the founder of the Neoplatonic school, was anxious to be instructed in Indian philosophy and with that object he accompanied the expedition of Gordian against Sapor, King of Persia, in A.D. 242, though Gordian's death in Mesopotamia turned him back half-way. The following

[1] Vacherot, Zeller, and Brehier are convinced of Indian influence on Neoplatonism.

are the chief points of the system. The original essence is pure being and absolute causality. It is also the good in so far as everything finite is to find its aim in it and flow back into it. It has no attributes at all; it is a being without magnitude, without life, without thought. One should not even call it existence. It is something above existence and above goodness, and at the same time an operative force without any substratum. As operative force it is continually begetting something else, without being itself changed or moved or diminished. The first principle is perfect self-sufficiency.

There is no good that it should seek to acquire by volition. Why should the one create anything beyond itself? Plotinus answers that since all things, even those without life, impart of themselves what they can, the most perfect cannot remain in itself but must pass over. The first source of all being is compared to an overflowing spring which by its excess gives rise to that which comes after it[1] or a central source of light which illumines all things.[2] The production of the lower is not the aim or motive of the activity of the higher. Creation is not a physical process but an emanation. That which is produced exists only in so far as the originating principle works in it. Everything that has being is directly or indirectly a production of the first principle. Everything so far as it has being is divine, as God is all in all. What is derived is not like the original essence itself. It is an image and reflection of the original essence. The totality of being forms a gradation which loses itself in non-being. Each lower stage is connected with the original essence by means of the higher. Longing for the higher is the general feature of everything derived. The first emanation of the original essence is Nous. It is a complete image of the original essence and archetype of all existing things, for the knowledge of things in their immaterial essence is the things themselves. Mind knows its objects not like perception, as external, but as one with itself.[3] As this unity involves the duality of thinking and being thought, it is not the highest but the second in order of supramundane causes. It is being

[1] *Enneads*, v. 2. 1. Cf. with this the Hindu conception of *līlā*.

[2] Cf. 'tasya bhāsā sarvam idam vibhāti'.

[3] *Enneads*, v. 5. 1.

and thought at the same time. As image the Nous is equal to the original essence. As derived it is completely different from it. It is for Plotinus the highest sphere which the human spirit can reach and at the same time pure thought itself. We are still in the region of eternity. The indivisible unity of the Nous is the archetype of the whole visible world, of all that was or is or will be existent in it. The universal Nous involves the essence of every form of reason. All things are together in it, not only undivided by position in space but without reference to process in time. The characteristic of its logical being is eternity. Eternity belongs to Nous as time belongs to soul.[1]

The Soul is an immaterial substance like Nous, its image and product. It is related to the Nous as the latter is to the primal One. It stands between the Nous and the world of phenomena, a middle term between the unity of self-complete intelligence and the dispersion and change of the sensible world. It is the principle of life and motion in things. In virtue of its nature and destiny it belongs as the single soul of the cosmos to the higher world; but it embraces at the same time the many individual souls. It mediates between the ideal and the sensible worlds. It orders the world in accordance with the general reason of things. The things it produces belong to time and are not imperishable. The individual souls may allow themselves to be ruled by the Nous, or they may be attracted by the sensible and so get lost in the finite. As an active essence the soul belongs to the corporeal world of phenomena. Here there is conflict, growth, and decay. The original cause of this is matter, which lies at the basis of bodies, the obscure, the indefinite, that which is without qualities. As devoid of form and ideal, it is the principle of evil; as capable of form, it is intermediate being. Matter, for Plotinus, is a mere abstraction, a name for the bare receptacle of forms. It is the indeterminate, no thing and yet not nothing. Evil is only a lesser good. Absolute evil, infinite matter symbolized by the limit of the less good, is the last stage of the divine procession.

The theory of emanation is distinguished from creation. The distinction is similar to that between *vivarta* or appear-

[1] *Enneads*, iii. 7. 11.

ance and *pariṇama* or modification. When Plotinus insists on the hypothesis of emanation and the *Advaita Vedānta* suggests the Vivarta view, both are anxious to make out that there is no diremption of the higher principle. God does not disperse Himself in individual things or natural things. There is a continual process from first to last, but the cause remains itself while the effect produced takes on an inferior position.[1] The primal One produces the universal Nous that is one with the Intelligible. The Nous produces the Soul, which in its turn produces all other existences. It is a logical order of causation, not an order in time. Plotinus traces the idea of the causal series to Plato, for whom, he says, the Demiurgus is Nous which is produced by the Good beyond thought and being, which in its turn produces Soul.[2] The *Taittirīya Upaniṣad* makes out that the human soul is a replica of the world and contains the different principles of matter, life, consciousness, intelligence, and spiritual bliss. Plotinus affirms that in the soul are included the principles of unity, of pure intellect, of vital power, and of matter itself. It touches every grade of value and existence. The human souls that are sunk in the material are ensnared by the sensuous and have allowed themselves to be ruled by desire. In attempting to detach themselves entirely from true being and strive after independence they fall into an unreal existence. The soul can return to itself through the practice of virtue and ascetic purification. It can retrace the process of its descent from the divine status, become delivered from corporeality altogether, and be restored to its unity with the absolute One itself. 'Nothing that has real existence can ever perish.' The world of spirit, the kingdom of values, is secure and cannot suffer any final defeat. No noble life can be extinguished by death. The soul exists in its own right. It neither comes into existence nor perishes. The soul which has the capacity to behold and contemplate eternal reality and gaze on the likeness of the supreme spirit, not as something outside itself but as the real in which it shares, which is its own inmost nature, is immortal. Plotinus interprets resurrection not as awakening with the body but as an awakening from it.[3]

[1] *Enneads*, v. 2. 2. [2] Ibid. v. 1. 8. [3] Ibid. iii. 6. 6.

As for the nature of eternal life, it is difficult to be certain of Plotinus's views. As souls are logoi of spirits, each of them represents a distinct entity in the spiritual world. This distinction cannot be destroyed.[1] 'All souls are potentially all things. Each of them is characterized by the faculty which it chiefly exercises. One is united to the spiritual world by activity, another by desire. The souls, thus contemplating different objects, are and become that which they contemplate.'[2] If we wish to know what happens to the souls which have freed themselves from the contamination of the flesh, Plotinus tells us that they dwell in God, where is reality and true being. 'If you ask where they will be, you must ask where the spiritual world is; and you will not find it with your eyes.'[3] 'Spirit in beholding reality beheld itself and in beholding entered into its proper activity, and this activity is itself.'[4] There is no reasoning yonder; nor can there be any memory. Its rest is unimpeded energy, living contemplation. 'We are kings when we are in the Spirit.'[5] We are no longer mere men.

Plotinus believes in rebirth. For him even animals have souls. So long as we do not attain the highest wisdom, we are bound to successive rebirths which are like one dream after another or sleep in different beds.[6] He admits the law of Karma when he says that it is a universal principle, that each soul after death goes where it longs to be.[7] 'Those who have exercised their human faculties are born as men. Those who have lived only the life of the senses, as lower animals.'[8] He also refers to the absorption of disembodied souls in the universal Soul.[9]

The super-rational is the goal of all effort and the ground of all existence. The knowledge we gain by thought is only an intermediate stage between sense perception and super-rational intuition. The intelligible forms are not the highest; they are the media by which the influences of the formless

[1] *Enneads*, vi. 4. 16.
[2] Ibid. iv. 3. 8.
[3] Ibid. iii. 4. 24.
[4] Ibid. v. 3. 5.
[5] Ibid. v. 3. 4.
[6] Ibid. iii. 6. 6.
[7] Ibid. iv 3. 13 and 15.
[8] Ibid. iii. 4. 2. Porphyry and Iamblichus do not admit that human souls are ever sent to inhabit the bodies of beasts and birds.
[9] Ibid. iv. 8. 4; iii. 2. 4.

essence are communicated to the world. The highest reality does not constitute the content of thought but is presupposed and earnestly sought after by man as the unknowable ground of his thought. Man does not live by bread alone or by knowledge alone. Even intellect has a certain duality, for though intelligence and the intelligible are the same, that which thinks distinguishes itself from the object of thought. Beyond thought and the being, which, while identical with it, is distinguishable in apprehension, is the absolute unity that is simply identical with itself. This is other than all being, though the source of it and that to which all things aspire.

Three types of men may achieve the good and obtain a vision of truth—the philosopher, the musician, and the lover.[1] Through the analytic process of the dialectic the mind is able to reach the goal to which its striving has been directed from the start. Having reached this goal the mind becomes quiescent and unified. The highest mode of subjective life is the complete unification in which even thought disappears. Within the soul, at its very centre, is the supreme unity beyond even self-knowledge.

'In the vision of God that which sees is not reason but something greater than and prior to reason, something presupposed by reason as is the object of vision. He who then sees himself, when he sees will see himself as a simple being, will be united to himself as such, will feel himself become such. We ought not even to say that he will *see*, but he will *be* that which he sees, if indeed it is possible any longer to distinguish seer and seen, and not boldly to affirm that the two are one. In this state the seer does not see or distinguish or imagine two things; he becomes another, he ceases to be himself and belong to himself. . . . Therefore his vision is hard to describe. For how can one describe, as other than oneself, that which, when one saw it, seemed to be one with oneself?'[2]

He who attains to a direct contact with reality becomes himself divine. The soul is then in a condition of complete passivity and rest, a state of intense concentration and com-

[1] Ibid. i. 3. 4.

[2] Ibid. vi. 9. 7; Inge, *The Philosophy of Plotinus* (1918), vol. ii, p. 140. Dr. Inge thinks that in Plotinus's theory of vision we have 'the direct influence of Oriental philosophy of the Indian type' (*Christian Mysticism* (1899), p. 98).

plete forgetfulness of all things. It then sees God, the source of life, the principle of being. It enjoys the highest blessedness and is bathed in the light of eternity. 'And this is the life of gods and of godlike and happy men, a deliverance from the other things here, a life untroubled by the pleasures here, a flight of the alone to the alone.'

Neoplatonism believes in the Hindu technique of entering into spiritual consciousness. By meditation we can free the soul from its subjection to the body and attain union with the supreme. Plotinus asks us to strip off everything extraneous till the vision is attained. We must abstract from the body, which does not belong to the true nature of the self, from the soul that shapes the body, from sense, perceptions, appetites, and emotions, and even the intellect with its duality. Then the soul touches and gazes on the supreme light.[1] Neoplatonism, quite as much as the philosophy of the Upaniṣads, has faith in a higher revelation to man in mystical experience. Porphyry tells us that while he was with Plotinus the latter attained four times the end of union with the God who is over all, without form, above the distinctions of intellect.

Even in the spirit of the Upaniṣads, which lay more stress on *jñāna*, wisdom, contemplation, than on *karma* or action, Plotinus looks upon action as an enfeebled product of contemplation. Even those who act do so to possess a good, and the knowledge that they possess it is only in the soul. We must rise above practical activity, which belongs to the world, to self-knowledge. Like all mystic systems, Neoplatonism rose above the political limits of nations and States.

Plotinus has many points in common with the Gnostics. The supreme being is beyond existence. The soul which has lost its way in the dark must return home to God. There is a divine spark in the soul which can serve as the light on the path. Plotinus criticizes the Gnostics for their pessimistic views about the visible world and their impiety in not admitting that the sun and stars are the abodes of God. We cannot exclude divine influence from any part of nature. He objects to their view of the creation of the world in time.

[1] *Enneads*, v. 3. 17. Brehier traces the Plotinian conception of contemplation to Indian sources; see *La Philosophie de Plotin*, 108–9.

Perhaps he was also opposed to their Christian predilections, for, as we saw, the Gnostics considered themselves Christians. Plotinus defends polytheism, which the Gnostics are said to deny.

We have in Plotinus a theory of God which excludes all knowledge of God, answering to the impersonal Brahman of the Upaniṣad, a doctrine of Nous corresponding to the personal Īśvara and the conception of a world soul similar to the hypothesis of Hiraṇyagarbha, intermediate beings through whom God acts on the world of phenomena, faith in ecstatic elevation to be gained by ascetic self-emancipation from the world of the senses. Stutfield maintains that 'Indian mystical thoughts passed over into Africa and western Europe' and 'blossomed forth in Plotinus' and passed into Christian thought through 'the monk mystic and theosophical pantheist, the so-called Dionysus the Areopagite'.[1]

Porphyry (A.D. 230–300) popularized the teachings of Plotinus. For him the aim of philosophy is the salvation of the soul. The source of evil is not so much in the body as in the desires of the soul. Strict asceticism is enjoined. Porphyry advocates abstinence from animal food in his *De Abstinentia*, which is a treatise against the eating of animal food. He gives an account of some Indian views on the authority of Bardesanes, who derived his information from an Indian embassy to the Imperial Court early in the third century.[2] His polemic against Christianity is doctrinal. He held that the Christian view of the creation and destruction of the world in time separated the world from God and required the hypothesis of an Incarnation to bring together the two elements which have been erroneously dissevered. The hypothesis of bodily resurrection seemed to him queer and impossible. He put in a plea for image worship against the Jewish severity on this question.

'Images and temples of the gods', he says, 'have been made from all antiquity for the sake of forming reminders to men. Their object is to make those who draw near them think of God thereby, or to enable them, after ceasing from their work, to address their prayers and vows to him. When any person gets an image or picture of a friend he

[1] *Mysticism and Catholicism* (1925), pp. 34 ff.

[2] iv. 18.

certainly does not believe that the friend is to be found in the image, or that his members exist inside the different parts of the representation. His idea rather is that the honour which he pays to his friend finds expression in the image. And while the sacrifices offered to the gods do not bring them any honour, they are meant as a testimony to the good will and gratitude of the worshippers.'[1]

Iamblichus,[2] who died in the reign of Constantine, about A.D. 330, was considerably influenced by Pythagoras, Plato, and Plotinus, though he converted Neoplatonism into a theurgic spiritualism. He lived at the time of the collapse of the ancient world, when life tended to be oppressive and futile and the sense of man's unworthiness increased. Man could obtain unification with the central source not by his own efforts but by theurgic practices which must be performed correctly. Mystical exercises and even magical ceremonies as expounded by Iamblichus got into the Christian Church and practice.

The most original thinker after Plotinus, however, was Proclus (A.D. 416–85). He is the chief link between ancient and medieval thought.[3] While the *Enneads* of Plotinus are philosophical meditations aiming at spiritual edification, we have in Proclus an ordered exposition of a system, a methodical defence of Neoplatonism. His work is the culmination of the speculative movement extending over five centuries whose direction was motived by speculative and religious interests. It was the aim of Proclus not only to develop a single philosophy which will deal fairly adequately with all that was best in Pythagoras and Plato as well as in Aristotle, but also to provide a scheme of salvation which will meet the supreme religious need of the later Hellenic period. He wished to set forth a religious philosophy within the frame-

[1] Quoted in Harnack, *Expansion of Christianity*, vol. i, p. 376.

[2] 'His works have perished, and we have to get our ideas of his teaching from the references in Proclus and the fragments preserved by Stobaeus and the treatise *On the Mysteries of the Egyptians*.'

[3] Professor E. R. Dodds writes: 'The influence which Proclus exercised upon early mediaeval thought may be called accidental in the sense that it would scarcely have been felt but for the activity of the unknown eccentric who within a generation of Proclus's death conceived the idea of dressing his philosophy in Christian draperies and passing it off as the work of a convert of St. Paul' (*Elements of Theology* (1933), pp. xxvi–xxvii).

work of traditional Greek rationalism, one which can stand comparison with the schemes offered by the mystery religions. While in the main he is true to the intuition of Plotinus, he is considerably influenced by Iamblichus.[1] In his chief works, *Elements of Theology* and *Platonic Theology*, the living experience of Plotinus becomes a fixed tradition. The metaphysics of being is approached by a doctrine of categories. It is assumed that the structure of the cosmos answers to the structure of Greek logic. 'Beyond all bodies', says Proclus, 'is the soul's essence; beyond all souls the intellective principle; and beyond all intellectual substances the One.'[2] The soul is incorporeal and independent of the body and therefore imperishable. To know the self truly is to know it as actually one, as potentially all things and as divine. The Neoplatonic trinity is accepted. The One of Parmenides is identified with the Form of the Good. The demiurge of *Timaeus* is identified with Aristotle's Nous. The world soul of *Timaeus* and *Laws* (x) is assumed.

The existence of the universe outside the One is explained by Proclus on Plotinian lines, that everything which is complete tends to reproduce itself.[3] 'Every productive cause', says Proclus, 'produces the next and all subsequent principles while itself remaining steadfast.'[4] The consequents are brought into existence without any movement on the part of the One. 'For if it create through movement, either the movement is within it, and being moved it will change from being one and so lose its unity; or if the movement be subsequent to it, this movement will itself be derived from the One and either we shall have infinite regress or the One will produce without movement.' Between the pure unity of the One and the minimal unity of matter, intermediate sources are recognized. The descent is not regarded as an error or a punishment but is a necessary cosmic service and a necessary part of education for the soul. The soul's life

[1] Professor Dodds traces his teaching about time and eternity, the classification of gods and of souls, the definite denial that the soul ever attains release from the circle of birth (Prop. 206, *Elements of Theology*), and that only part of it remains above (Prop. 211), to Iamblichus. See E. R. Dodds, op. cit., p. xxi.

[2] Prop. 20.

[3] Prop. 25; see *Enneads*, v. 1. 6.

[4] Prop. 26.

is endless, both ways. Souls have perishable and imperishable vehicles.

Proclus' saying that the philosopher ought not to observe the religious customs of one city or country only but ought to be the common hierophant of the whole world is well known. Ascetic and contemplative virtue is rated higher than the practical. Proclus gave a somewhat devotional orientation to the Neoplatonism of Plotinus. Prayer for Plotinus was the turning of the mind to God; to Proclus it was humble supplication for divine aid. The self-sufficiency for which the attainment of bliss lay in man's unaided capacity gives place to a dependence on God. Proclus found a place for gods above the Nous and immediately below the One. He had superstitious respect for theurgy. He agrees with Iamblichus in thinking that individual things are united to the one by the mysterious operation of the occult 'symbols' which reside in certain stones, herbs, and animals. While Plotinus and Porphyry believe more in human wisdom and spiritual vision, Iamblichus and Proclus are impressed by the blessings of divination and the purifying powers in initiation. Proclus accepts ecstatic experiences. In his commentary on the *Republic* he says: 'Going out of themselves they are wholly established with the gods and possessed by them.'

Neoplatonism was originally regarded as a dangerous adversary to Christianity, and by a decree of the Council of Ephesus (431) and by a law of Theodosius II (448) Porphyry's books were condemned to be burned. About the beginning of the fifth century, Neoplatonism was taught in Athens and at Alexandria by Hypatia. Both schools followed the tradition of Iamblichus and through him Porphyry and Plotinus. The murder of Hypatia put an end to the tradition in Alexandria, and the school of Athens was closed by Justinian in A.D. 529. But Christian theology early absorbed the spirit of Neoplatonism. The thoughts of Plotinus were revived by Boethius and his spirit inspires the writings of Scotus Erigena and Eckhart. At the Renaissance, Neoplatonism again became popular.

VI

INDIA AND WESTERN RELIGIOUS THOUGHT: CHRISTENDOM—II

I

WHEN the Hellenistic Jews in Jerusalem accepted Christianity and the movement spread in the non-Jewish parts of the Roman Empire, it assumed Graeco-Roman and Graeco-Oriental forms of expression. The mystery religions were common to both these types of thinking. In regard to the fundamentals of religious thought and practice, there was agreement. Along with the postulate of an ineffable godhead, they generally accepted the belief that at some epoch of history there had been a great being, who during his life on earth found by personal experience a way out of the difficulties of life and the secret of divine bliss. This wisdom is entrusted to his followers, who accept it in faith and perform certain mysterious acts by which they consciously unite with the purpose and life of God. Primitive Christianity is a mystery religion, a way of living. Early Christians formed a mystery group meeting in secret and having an inner and outer circle.[1] Christ answers to the Gnostic saviour god, the Logos and the Idea of the universe. Legends of the death and resurrection of the suffering deities and heroes, Osiris, Attis, and Adonis, were well known and utilized. The ritual meal of the Mithra cult suggests the love-feast of the early Christian communities. The notion of good and bad demons corresponds closely to the ideas of angels and devils. It is only natural that Christianity grew up in its own environment and couched its beliefs and aspirations in terms familiar to its world. Every religion has to speak the language which its adherents will understand and set its theology in forms which are intelligible to its generation. There is nothing surprising if Christian theology is expressed in the terms of contemporary belief and if its

[1] Mark iv. 10–13; Matthew xiii. 11–17, 26–7. Kirsopp Lake holds that 'Christianity . . . was always, at least in Europe, a mystery religion' (*Earlier Epistles of St. Paul*, p. 215).

ritual is influenced by the mystery religions with which many of the early converts must have been familiar. Besides, the Christian message could not have won its way if it had not found an echo in the religious searchings and beliefs of the time. Christianity developed in the same world and breathed the same air as Alexandrian Judaism, Gnosticism, and Neo-platonism.

St. Paul's training at Tarsus enabled him to know the currents of thought and express his theology in words to which his audience was accustomed. For St. Paul, Jesus is the Christ, the Lord, a phrase used to designate the emperors and the redeemer gods of the mystery cults. For Paul, Jesus is only the Lord and not God. He distinguishes between the heathens, who have 'gods many and lords many', and Christians, who have 'one God—the Father and one Lord—Jesus Christ'. The familiar distinction between godhead and god is here employed. Incorruption, eternity, and invisibility are the characteristics of the godhead. The one God is inconceivable, 'The things of whom knoweth no man', whose judgements are unsearchable, 'his ways past finding out',[1] 'who dwelleth in the light which no man can approach unto, whom no man hath seen or can see'.[2] Jesus becomes the redeemer lord who is the source of salvation both in this world and the world to come. The Messianic idea of the Jews gets mixed up with the Logos of the Greeks. Christ is the 'first born of many brethren'. He is raised from the dead by God as an evidence of His universal mission to men. In the later Epistles He becomes 'the image of the invisible God', the being who is 'before all things' and by whom 'all things consist'.[3] The insistence on the Neo-platonic idea of the Logos is so great as to reduce the human life of Jesus to a mere illusive appearance. If the name of Jesus is employed, it is only in a symbolic way, for St. Paul says[4] how 'all our fathers all drank of the spiritual rock Christ'[5] and Christ can be formed in each of us.[6] He certainly warns us against over-estimating the historical instead of looking upon it as the symbol of metaphysical truth. In

[1] Romans xi. 33.
[2] 1 Timothy vi. 16.
[3] Colossians i. 16 and 17.
[4] 1 Corinthians ii. 16.
[5] Ephesians iv. 13.
[6] Galatians iv. 19.

the Second Epistle to the Corinthians he says: 'Even though we have known Christ after the flesh, yet now we know him so no more.' The Supreme dwells in us. 'Know ye not that ye are the temple of God, and that the Spirit of God dwelleth in you?'[1] Again, St. Paul makes a clear distinction between the conclusions which he reaches by the exercise of his own intellectual powers and the truths revealed to him. We often hear from him the words 'I say this of the Lord', 'I say this of myself'. He speaks of a gnosis or higher knowledge which can be taught only to the initiated. The foundation of St. Paul's Christianity is a vision, not an external revelation. According to the Acts, he saw visions and heard voices in his missionary wanderings and believed himself to be guided by God. In the Second Epistle to the Corinthians he records the ecstatic vision in which he was 'caught up into the third heaven' and saw things unutterable. He is referring to the ineffability of the experience.

In the mystery religions the common facts of daily life are endowed with sacramental significance. They are the divinely instituted means by which man can escape from the snares of the world and attain divine bliss. In St. Paul, Jesus becomes the centre of a cult where baptism and the commemoration of the Last Supper take the place of the sacraments of the mysteries. That communion with deity can be gained through partaking of him is an old doctrine. The rites which circled round the mystic figure of Dionysus-Zagreus in which the bull representing the god himself is killed and devoured assume that in this process his life passes into his votaries.[2] Though they are corporeal in their implications, they denote a change of essence in the adherents, the entrance of God into their persons. The Gospel Christ is a variant of the saviour gods common to earlier faiths.[3]

[1] 1 Corinthians iii. 16; 2 Corinthians vi. 16.

[2] Referring to the old tradition of the crucifixion of Orpheus or Dionysus, Justin Martyr declares (*Apol.* i. 54) that the story was invented by the 'demons' to correspond to the prophecy in the Old Testament in order to bring the true Christ into doubt.

[3] Mr. Edwyn Bevan in his *Hellenism and Christianity* (chap. iv) admits the resemblance between Jesus as a revealer of the divine gnosis and the inspired revealers of the mystery cults. He concedes that 'When the early preachers of Christianity explained the position of Jesus in the totality of

The apotheosis of mortal man through the acquisition of wisdom and immortality is the idea of salvation according to the ancient mysteries, and it is supported by Paul in his Epistle to the Ephesians.[1] We move in a different group of ideas from those of the mystery religions, for Paul knew Jesus to be an historical person who as the result of boundless devotion to the good of His fellows suffered a shameful death in loyalty to His Father's purpose. He looks upon this as the bringing near to man of the redeeming love of God.[2]

Conversion as rebirth is affirmed. 'If any one is in Christ he is a new creation; old things have passed away, behold new things have come into being.'[3] This is possible only with the crucifixion of the flesh. The animal must die that the God may be brought to birth. 'They that are of Christ Jesus have crucified the flesh with the passions and lusts thereof.'[4] Resurrection is the resurrection of the Christ in us from the tomb of our carnal nature, 'the body of sin',[5] 'the body of death',[6] in short, our present, earthly, mortal nature. The higher spiritual self in each of us is buried in

things, they did so in terms which bore a close resemblance to conceptions already current in the heathen and Jewish worlds', but contends that 'the Gnostic Soter was only a prophet while Jesus was a redeemer as well'. In Buddhism, as we have already observed, Buddha, who is recognized as the central object of worship by the first century B.C., is a redeemer deity who has already trodden the difficult way which the faithful have to follow. Again, in Enoch xlviii and li it is said that the righteous shall be saved by the Elect One or the Son of Man.

[1] Loisy gives the following summary of St. Paul's conception of Jesus: 'He was a saviour god, after the manner of an Osiris, an Attis, a Mithra. Like them he belonged by his origin to the celestial world; like them he had made his appearance on the earth; like them, he had accomplished a work of universal redemption, efficacious and typical; like Adonis, Osiris and Attis, he had died a violent death, and like them he had been restored to life; like them he had prefigured in his lot that of the human beings who should take part in his worship, and communicate his mystic enterprise; like them he had predestined, prepared and assured the salvation of those who became partners in his passion' (*Hibbert Journal*, Oct. 1917, p. 51). Loisy concludes 'These are analogous conceptions, dreams of one family, built on the same theme with similar imagery' (ibid., p. 52). I think the parallels between the mythical heroes and the historical Jesus are over-stretched.

[2] Galatians ii. 20, iv. 15. [3] 2 Corinthians v. 17; Galatians vi. 15.

[4] Galatians v. 25. [5] Romans vi. 16. [6] Romans vii. 24.

the tomb of the mortal self, but the grave has no power to hold the divine in it, which must inevitably rise. The life, death, and resurrection of Christ are an illustration of a universal principle. 'We are buried with him through baptism unto death', says Paul to the Romans, 'that like as Christ was raised from the dead through the glory of the Father, so we also might walk in newness of life.' Each of us has 'the mind of Christ',[1] the spark of spirit. It is active even in the ordinary individual at his present stage of evolution, but it can be recovered in all its glory by a knowledge of the mysteries of the Kingdom of Heaven. When the individual is united with the Christ principle, his inward man,[2] his spirit, he realizes to the full his oneness with the Father, the supreme godhead. Each of us can become a perfect man unto 'the measure of the stature of the fullness of Christ'. When the spirit in us is realized, we shall see and know God as He is and knows us, by an immediate vision. 'Now we see through a mirror' in which the reflection will not be clear and distinct, 'but then face to face; now I know in part; but then shall I know even as I am known'.[3] Again, we have the well-known doctrine of the phenomenality of the world (*māyā*) in the saying: 'the things that are seen are temporal but the things that are not seen are eternal'.[4] 'This earthly house of our tabernacle in which we groan' is a phrase nearer to Orphic than to Greek or Jewish thought. We must turn away from material things, for 'flesh and blood cannot inherit the kingdom of God'. We must 'cleanse ourselves from all defilement of flesh and spirit',[5] raise ourselves above the world to be able to assimilate the divine reality. In the spirit of true mysticism he criticizes ceremonial religion. 'Why turn ye back to the weak and beggarly rudiments, whereunto ye desire to be in bondage again? Ye observe days, and months and seasons and years. I am afraid of you, lest I have bestowed labour upon you in vain.'[6] Again, 'Why do ye subject yourselves to ordinances,

[1] 1 Corinthians ii. 16.
[2] Romans viii. 6.
[3] 1 Corinthians xiii. 12. The apostle St. John tells us that we shall see God 'as he is'. 1 John iii. 2.
[4] 2 Corinthians iv. 18.
[5] 2 Corinthians vii. 1.
[6] Galatians iv. 9 ff.

handle not, nor taste nor touch, after the precepts and doctrines of men?'[1] The Platonic words 'fellowship', 'participation', and 'presence' are all in St. Paul. 'I live not but Christ lives in me.' As St. John of the Cross interprets it, 'Each lives in the other, and each is the other, and the two are made one in a transformation of love.' There is the transcending of human personality in the highest life. 'We all, reflecting as in a mirror the glory of the Lord, are transformed into the same image.'[2] 'He that is joined unto the Lord is one Spirit.'[3] There is also suspicion of knowledge. 'Beware lest any man spoil you through philosophy and vain deceit.'[4] His doctrine of the spirit corresponds to the Platonic 'nous'. In Romans i the invisible things are understood through the things that are made. The Logos is the Absolute from the cosmic end, and so when the cosmic process is consummated, when all evil is subdued to good, time will end and the Logos 'will deliver up the Kingdom to God, even the Father', 'that God may be all in all'.[5] The distinctness of perfected souls will be retained until this culmination is reached, when the world is taken over into God the Absolute.

Leaving aside the doctrinal agreements with Gnosticism, we find references to the various orders of angels and worship to be paid to them. Phrases characteristic of Gnosticism such as archons, mystery, and hidden wisdom of God are frequently to be met with.[6] The Epistles to Timothy employ the terminology of Gnosticism. 'We war not against flesh and blood but against the Dominions, the Powers, the Lords of the Darkness, the malevolence of the spirits in the upper region.'[7]

In Paul we find two conceptions of the Supreme, God and Christ, two kinds of knowledge, the reality of mystic experience, the indwelling of God, indifference to ceremonial piety, conversion as rebirth, the need for the crucifixion of

[1] Colossians ii. 20–2.

[2] 2 Corinthians iii. 18.

[3] 1 Corinthians vi. 17.

[4] Colossians ii. 8.

[5] 1 Corinthians xv. 24–8.

[6] See Colossians i. 16–17; ii. 8, 18, 20–3; iii. 3–5; 1 Timothy i. 4.

[7] There is an obvious reference to the mystery religions in 1 Corinthians ii. 6. Loisy thinks that Paul has been the chief factor in transforming the original gospel of Jesus into a 'religion of mystery'.

the flesh, salvation as oneness with Christ, to be transformed into oneness with God with the redemption of the cosmic process. These are all features associated with mystic religion.[1]

In the First Epistle of John, which uses Gnostic phraseology, we find mystic elements more than in the other discourses. God the Father is said to be Light, Love, and Spirit. There is an attempt to identify the human Jesus, 'that which our eyes have seen and our hands have handled of the word of life',[2] with the Greek Logos. Though Jesus never made any claims on this behalf, it is permissible to explain Jesus' personality in terms of a philosophy which He did not use.[3] The divine Logos was identified with the gods of ancient cults, and this general tendency is followed by the writer when he looks upon Jesus as the incarnation, or the manifestation in word and deed, of the eternal Logos by whom the universe had been created and maintained. The writer was apparently familiar with Philo's views.[4] 'The word was made flesh and tabernacled among us.' The pre-existence of Jesus is inferred from such statements as 'And now, O

[1] Dr. Schweitzer in his book *The Mysticism of Paul* argues that 'in Paul there is no God mysticism; only a Christ mysticism by means of which man comes into relation to God'. He looks upon Paul's speech on the Areopagus in Athens which proclaims a God mysticism as unhistorical (E.T. (1931), p. viii). He says that 'the Hellenization of Christianity does not come in with Paul but only after him'.

[2] See also the Epistles to the Colossians and the Hebrews.

[3] Cf. Kirsopp Lake: 'That Jesus did not announce himself publicly as Messiah or Christ is one of the most certain facts in the Gospel narrative. It is obscured if the Fourth Gospel be put on a level with the synoptic gospels, but it can scarcely be doubted if modern synoptic criticisms be accepted.' The Ebionites looked upon Jesus as a wise man or a prophet but only a prophet. He would appear as the Messiah at His second coming. He was a man born as all men, the son of Joseph and Mary. He became a prophet at His baptism when the spirit descended on Him. Jesus was Christ, but so would all men be who fulfilled the law (*The Stewardship of Faith* (1915), p. 42.)

[4] 'There are close and remarkable Philonic parallels and they suggest that John was acquainted with Philo's works. Some will regard them as establishing a real literary dependence of the Fourth Gospel on Philo, but this cannot be regarded as certain' (Bernard, *A Critical and Exegetical Commentary on the Gospel according to St. John* (1928), vol. i, pp. xciii–xciv). For a number of resemblances between the two see p. xciii.

Father, glorify me with thine own self, with the glory which I had with thee before the world was.' 'Before Abraham was, I am.' The Logos is not merely the agency—'by Him are all things made'—but also the sustaining power of the universe. Though the revelation of God in Jesus was complete, it is not intelligible to us without the help of Spirit, which is the living and active principle operating in the hearts of Christians. The many things which Jesus said were not communicated to His disciples, and the Holy Spirit will communicate them to the future generations. Reality diminishes as it recedes from the centre. From the Father the Absolute One arises the Son the divine reason. Though He was with Him from the beginning, He is less than the Absolute: 'My Father is greater than I.' Those who share the divine life and love, the children of God, come next, and last of all the world, the darkness. There is throughout an insistence on the unity of the whole: 'As Thou, Father, art in Me and I in Thee, so may they be in us.' The contrast between flesh and spirit is present in John. 'That which is born of the flesh is flesh, that which is born of the spirit is spirit.'[1] He insists so much on the supernatural aspects of the life of Jesus that in his picture the Son of Man is lost in the Son of God and he is obliged to assert the real humanity of Jesus. The problem of the relation of God and man gave rise to acute controversies in the Church, and it is still with us. 'Jesus said unto them, verily, verily, I say unto you, except ye eat of the flesh of the Son of Man and drink his blood, ye have not life in yourselves.'[2] Flesh and blood here are symbols of spiritual sustenance. If we do not assimilate the spiritual principle, we cannot have any abiding life in us. If this symbolical language is interpreted as the doctrine of the 'real presence', we can only say that the primitive belief that the devotee actually partakes of the nature of God if he eats the flesh and drinks the blood of the sacrificed animal still has its sway over us. Conversion is new birth. 'Except a man be born anew he cannot see the Kingdom of God.' There must be a change from the isolated life of self to the larger one of love. When it is

[1] John iii. 6. Cf. *Itivuttaka*, 100.
[2] vi. 53.

effected, we can say like the blind man who was healed, 'One thing I know, that whereas I was blind, now I see.'[1]

The Epistle to the Hebrews shows the influence of Alexandrian Judaism, and the writer seems to be acquainted with the Book of Wisdom and the writings of Philo. An interesting feature of this writer is that he demands conformity to conventional codes as a preparation for the higher life. When we attain to it we are no longer bound by laws and ordinances. The writer looks upon visible things as symbols of higher truths.

In the epistle attributed to St. James we find the phrase 'wheel of birth', common to the Indians and the Orphics.

Revelation is full of Gnostic ideas. The war in heaven between Michael and his angels and the dragon and his angels, and the departure of the dragon after defeat to the earth, to 'make war with the rest of her seed that keep the commandments of God', are 'Iranian eschatology, applied and conformed to the supposed final fortunes of the Christian Church'.[2] That the redeemed will not return to earth is asserted. 'He that overcometh, I will make him a pillar in the temple of my God and he shall go out thence no more.'[3]

The Apologists tried to persuade their world that Christianity was the highest wisdom and absolute truth and used the concepts of Greek thought for this purpose. While the Gnostics sought to understand and interpret the Christian message and find out how far the Old Testament agreed with it, the Apologists accepted the whole tradition, both

[1] 'It is unquestionable that most of the canonical books of the New Testament, especially the epistles of St. Paul and the Johannine group, do not belong to the Palestinian tradition.' Dieterich is, in my opinion, right when he says that 'for the chief propositions of Pauline and Johannine theology, the basis of Judaism is wanting' (Inge, *The Platonic Tradition in English Religious Thought* (1926), pp. 10–11).

[2] Rudolph Otto, *The Kingdom of God and the Son of Man*, E.T. (1938), p. 99. He says that the fiery dragon is the literal translation of Azhi dahaka (Sanskrit *ahidahaka*), the aboriginal monster against which Trita fought. See also Matthew xii. 25–9, and Otto, op. cit., pp. 99–100.

[3] Revelation iii. 12. Pfleiderer observes: 'Jewish prophecy, Rabbinic teaching, Oriental Gnosis and Greek philosophy had already mingled their colours upon the palette from which the portrait of Christ in the New Testament Scriptures was painted' (*The Early Christian Conception of Christ*, p. 9).

the Old and the New, as ultimate revelation, and so their speculations, though not Greek in character, became the foundation of Church dogma. The certainties were for them in the Christian tradition, though they strove to find confirmation for them in Greek enlightenment. Christianity was represented as the fulfilment of the aspirations of the Platonic and Stoic systems. The chief representative of this tendency is Justin, who regards Jesus as the incarnate reason. 'Christ was and is the Logos who dwells in every man.'[1] By virtue of the participation in reason common to all, we may say that those who have lived with the Logos are Christians. Justin mentions specially Socrates, Plato, and Heraclitus.[2] The highest embodiment of the Logos is, however, in Christ Jesus.[3] Human systems of philosophy may be rational but not completely so, while Christian revelation is the complete truth.[4] The Apologists are agreed that the first principle is the Absolute, self-existing, unchangeable, and eternal, exalted above every name and distinction. This first cause is contrasted with the world, created, conditioned, and transient. It is one and unique, spiritual and perfect. The direct author of the world is 'not God, but the personified power of reason which they perceived in the cosmos'.[5] We have here the transcendent and unchangeable nature of God on the one hand and His creative power on the other. The Logos is the power of reason which preserves the unity and unchangeableness of God in spite of his active manifestation. It is not only the creative principle but also the revealing word. Revelation presupposes a divine person, one who makes himself known on earth. The Logos is often identified with the prophetic spirit. God cannot be without reason, and so He has always Logos in Himself. For the sake of creation He produced the Logos from Himself. The Logos is the visible God in relation to God, a creature, the begotten, the created God. As an emanation He is distinguished from all creatures. He is the principle of vitality and form of everything that is to receive being.[6] The teaching

[1] *Apology*, ii. 10.
[2] Ibid. i. 46.
[3] Ibid. i. 5; ii. 13–15.
[4] Ibid. ii. 15.
[5] Harnack, *History of Dogma*, vol. ii, E.T. (1896), pp. 206–7.
[6] Harnack says: 'Behind this active substitute and vicegerent, the Father

of Christianity becomes with the Apologists revealed doctrine.

While the distinction between godhead and god is preserved by the Apologists, Irenaeus smelt the heresy of Gnosticism in it and so affirmed that the supreme God and the creator of the world are one and the same. He, however, agreed with the Gnostics in looking upon the deification of human nature as the highest blessing. In his present condition man is subject to the power of death. Immortality is God's manner of existence. Man has only the possibility of it. But God intends man to realize it. The only way in which immortality can be attained is by God's uniting Himself with human nature in order to deify it by adoption. If men are to become divine, God must become human. 'By his birth as man the eternal word of God guarantees the inheritance of life to those who in their natural birth have inherited death.'[1] We have here greater stress on the conception of the incarnate God than on the Logos. Revelation is history.

The chief representatives of Alexandrian Christianity are Clement and Origen. Clement wrote his *Stromata* at Alexandria nearly sixty years after the death of Basilides and quotes from the work of the latter.[2] He uses Greek philosophy to interpret Christian tradition even as Philo uses it to expand Judaism. Clement quotes Philo several times. He tells us that God is to be sought in the darkness and reached by way of faith and abstraction.[3] The first cause is above space and time, above speech and thought.

> 'Going forth by analysis to the First Intelligence, taking away depth, breadth, length, and position, leaving a Monad, then abstracting what is material, if we cast ourselves into the vastness of Christ, thence if we proceed forward by holiness into his immensity, we may in some fashion enter into the knowledge of the Almighty, recognizing not what he is, but what he is not.'[4]

stands in the darkness of the incomprehensible, and in the incomprehensible light of perfection as the hidden, unchangeable God' (op. cit., vol. ii, E.T. (1896), p. 212).

[1] Bk. v, Preface. Harnack, op. cit., vol. ii, E.T. (1896), p. 241.

[2] *Stromata*, iii. 7.

[3] Ibid. ii. 2, v. 12.

[4] Ibid. v. 11 (see also ii. 2; v. 12 and 13), quoted in *Encyclopaedia of Religion and Ethics* (1917), vol. ix, p. 91.

He is strictly nameless though we give him names. God has neither unit nor number, neither accident nor substance. We use words and concepts, not because they describe the eternal, but because we require something to lean upon. We cannot reach God except through the Logos. No one comes to the Father except through Christ. The Logos is the rational law of the world. The way to salvation is through gnosis, which is attained by the purifying of the cognitive powers of the soul. The transcendental God is not an object of knowledge but can be approached only by ecstasy. Clement tells us that man may become by virtue like the Son but not like God,[1] and yet for him 'One is the Father of all, One also the word of all'.[2] It is the light that broods over the cosmic process and lights every man that comes into the world. 'The word of God became Man in order that thou also mayest learn from Man, how man becomes God.'[3] Deification was recognized by Clement. 'If anyone knows himself, he shall know God and by knowing God he shall be made like unto him.'[4] 'That man with whom the Logos dwells . . . is made like God . . . that man becomes God.'[5]

Clement was deeply influenced by Basilides and so by Buddhist thought. He refers to the universality of suffering. 'Pain and fear are as inherent in human affairs as rust in iron.'[6] Suffering which accompanies all action is specially the concomitant of sin. 'The Martyrs suffer for their sins.' Children suffer for their sins though they might not be conscious of them. He quotes Basilides on rebirth. 'Basilides lays down that the soul has previously sinned in another life and endures its punishment here, the elect with honour by martyrdom and the rest purified by appropriate punishment.'[7] Every act is fruitful, and if its result does not appear in this life, it will do so in a future life. Soul is not regarded as a simple entity but a compound of various entities. 'It behoves us to rise superior by virtue of our rationality, and to appear triumphant over the baser creature in us.'[8] Again, 'Only let a man will to achieve the good and he will obtain

[1] *Stromata*, vi. 14. 114. [2] Ibid. vi. 7. 58. [3] *Protrept.* i. 8.
[4] *Paed.* i. 3. [5] *Stromata*, i. 5. [6] Ibid. iv. 12. 90.
[7] Ibid. iv. 12. 85. [8] Ibid. ii. 20. 113, 114.

it.'[1] Though the results of our actions are bound to happen, we are free to act.

Clement's interpretation of the Christian tradition was free and liberal. He is conscious of it. 'If the things we say appear to some people to be different from the Scriptures of the Lord, let them know that they draw inspiration and life therefrom, and making these their starting-point give their meaning only, not their letter.'[2] God is known, though imperfectly, in all ages and climes, to those who diligently seek Him, and to the Christian He is revealed in the New Testament as a Triad, Father, Son, and Holy Ghost.[3]

Origen was born A.D. 185–6, probably in Alexandria, of Christian parents. In all his works he thought that he was expounding the orthodox Christian faith, but his system is full of speculations which are of a different origin. He speaks of rising above senses, figures, and shadows to the mystical and unspeakable vision.

The supreme being, for Origen, is the Neoplatonic One beyond being but knowable by man if he free himself from matter. The Father is the fount and the origin of all being, and is pure spirit. The Son is begotten of the Father by an eternal act of will. He is the first-born of all creation.[4] Origen is definite that the Son or Logos is *essentially* God, of the substance and nature of the Father, but sometimes he suggests that the Logos 'possesses Godhead but is not God'. The Spirit and the Son are definitely within the godhead, but the rational souls are outside, though they are also spiritual creatures, made in God's own image. They are limited in number and endowed with free will. Some remained in their original condition, but others fell away from God. The fall necessitated the use of bodies. Different orders of beings with different kinds of bodies arose. He adopts the Gnostic view that heavenly spirits fall from their immaterial bliss into the bondage of matter or into the form of demons. He admits that souls may perhaps be reincarnate in the bodies of animals. He accepted the pre-existence and the future rebirth of souls. 'Every soul has existed from the beginning, it has passed through some worlds already, and

[1] Ibid. iii. 1. 2.
[2] Ibid. vii. 1. 1.
[3] Ibid. v. 14. 103.
[4] Colossians i. 15.

will pass through others before it reaches the final consummation. It comes into this world strengthened by the victories or weakened by the defeats of its previous life.'[1] The matter which is to serve as the basis for bodies is created by God, but it is not eternal. It is such that it can be adapted to a variety of forms and purposes. The sojourn of man in this world is designed to educate him so that he may rise in the scale of being. He may rise to the utmost heights or fall to the lowest depths.[2] There is no limit to human wilfulness and sin, even as there is no limit to God's power and love when once the human soul responds to His healing influence. Salvation is not redemption of the body but the liberation of the soul from the bondage of matter and its gradual return to its original home. He strongly inclined to a universal restitution by which all souls, including the evil angels, would finally return to union with God in the intelligible world of the Logos. He clearly envisaged a time when God should be all in all, and all created spirits would return to that unity and perfection which was theirs at the beginning. 'When the soul is lifted up and follows the Spirit and is separated from the body, and not only follows the Spirit but becomes in the Spirit, must we not say that it puts off its soul-nature, and becomes spiritual?'[3] The Kingdom of God is for Origen a spiritual reality, the supersensuous and intelligible world. The historical facts of Christian revelation are treated by him as symbols of higher immaterial realities. The perfected souls would at the end be absorbed in the divine essence from which they sprang. In Book III, chapter vi, of his *First Principles* he speaks of the ascent of souls and suggests that 'even their bodily nature will assume that supreme condition to which nothing can ever be added'. On this Jerome comments:

'And after a very long discussion, in which he asserts that all bodily nature must be changed into spiritual bodies of extreme fineness and that the whole of matter must be transformed into a single body of the utmost purity, clearer than all brightness and of such a quality as the human mind cannot conceive, at the close he states: And God shall

[1] *First Principles*, 3. 1. 20, 21.

[2] Jerome remarks caustically that for Origen angels might become devils and devils archangels.

[3] *De Oratione*, 10.

be all in all, so that the whole of bodily nature may be resolved into that substance which is superior to all others, namely, into the divine nature than which nothing can be better.'

What, then, is the aim of the cosmic process? It is perhaps a mistake or a meaningless journey since the end will be like the beginning. He reckoned among the angels the spirits of the sun, planets, and stars. Free will and rational illumination are emphasized.

Christ is for him more a teacher than a redeemer. For Origen Jesus also possessed a soul like any other, but He retained His innocence and lived by free choice in close association with the word of God, and by force of habit an indissoluble union was created. This soul, already united with the word of God, took flesh of the Virgin Mary and appeared among men. Origen advocated prayer in the name of Jesus, but rejected direct address to Jesus. He distinguishes two kinds of life, active and contemplative, and prefers the latter. He employs the distinction between a mystery religion for the educated and a mythical religion for the vulgar, and justifies it by appealing to the example of 'the Persians and the Indians'.

The Christian Church abandoned Origen's chief doctrines of the subordinationist conception of trinity, the fall of pre-existent spirits, the denial of bodily resurrection, and final restitution. There is no question that though Origen sincerely believed that he was expounding the Christian faith, 'he ended in speculations which were only remotely connected with it. The real source of these speculations is to be found in the intellectual atmosphere of the time, in which the ideas of Platonists, Stoics and Orientals were mingled.'[1] Porphyry remarks that 'though Origen was a Christian in his manner of life, he was Hellenic in his religious thought and surreptitiously introduced Greek ideas into alien myths'.

This tradition of the liberal Alexandrian school of Clement

[1] G. W. Butterworth, *Origen on First Principles* (1936), p. xxxv. Cf. Harnack: 'The theology of Origen bears the same relation to the New Testament as that of Philo does to the Old. What is here presented as Christianity is in fact the idealistic religious philosophy, attested by divine revelation, made accessible to all by the incarnation of the Logos, and purified from any connexion with Greek mythology and gross polytheism' (*History of Dogma*, E.T., vol. ii (1896), pp. 5–6).

and Origen is continued by the three Cappadocians, Basil of Caesarea and the two Gregorys. For Basil, the Kingdom of Heaven is the contemplation of realities.[1] The Cappadocians are unanimous in asserting the mystery of the divine being. 'We know that he exists but of his essence we cannot deny that we are ignorant.'[2] He is partly known through His creation of the world, but He is best known through the human soul, which is a mirror which reflects the traits of the divine archetype. The Apostrophe to God by St. Gregory of Nazianzen is thoroughly Neoplatonic: 'The end of all art Thou, being One and All and None, being One Thou art not all, being all Thou art not One; all names are Thine, how then shall I invoke Thy Name, Alone, Nameless?'[3] To achieve likeness to God is the aim of man. The best means to it is asceticism. A purified heart aids us in enjoying the vision of uncreated beauty.

Augustine[4] stands at the meeting-point of two worlds, the 'passing of that great order which had controlled the fortunes of the world for five centuries or more and the laying of the foundations of the new world'. He tried to lead his world from the old to the new. Before his conversion to Christianity he was successively a pagan, a Manichaean, and a Neoplatonist. He read Plotinus in a Latin translation and introduced the central principles of Neoplatonism into Christianity. He adopted from Neoplatonism his views on God and matter, freedom and evil, and the relation of God to the world.[5] He used Neoplatonist arguments for defending Christian doctrine. As he expresses it in an early work: 'With me it stands fast never to depart from Christian authority, for I find no stronger. But as for those matters which it is possible to seek out by subtle reasoning, I am confident that I shall find among the Neoplatonists that which does not conflict with our religion.'[6] Philosophy for Augustine meant knowledge of God and his own soul. He

[1] Basil, *Ep.* 8. [2] Ibid. 2. 34.

[3] Quoted in Christopher Dawson, *Progress and Religion*, p. 91.

[4] He was born in Tagaste in Roman Africa in A.D. 354 and died at Hippo in 430. He was Bishop of Hippo from 395 to 430.

[5] See his *Confessions*, vii. 9–21.

[6] *Contra Academicos*, 3. 43, cited in Montgomery, p. 69.

repudiates the arguments of the sceptic as inconsistent. For even while he denies absolute truth, he affirms it. All action depends on knowledge, and scepticism cannot be the basis of conduct. Senses may deceive us; we may dream or walk in our sleep, but the mind has for its proper object the region of the intelligible, the unchanging. There are truths which cannot be doubted. 'It is sufficient for my purpose that Plato felt that there were two worlds: the one intelligible where Truth itself dwelt; the other sensible, which, as is clear, we feel by sight and touch.'[1] In the former sphere the human soul encounters itself and God. There is the noumenon behind the appearances; within us is the soul not visible to the eye of the sense but most evident to us by its own radiance. The existence of the soul is established in the style of Śaṁkara or Descartes.

> 'Everyone who knows himself to be in doubt, knows truth, and is certain about what actually he knows; therefore he is certain about truth. Everyone therefore, who doubts whether there be truth has within himself truth whereby he should not doubt; nor is there anything true which is not true by truth. He therefore that can doubt in any wise should not doubt of truth. Where this is seen, then there is light, pure of all space, be it of places or times, pure too of representation of such a space.'[2]

There is a higher reality to which the human mind is subject, Truth which changes not, God. For Augustine Truth is God. 'The happy life consists of joy in truth for this is a joying in Thee, Who art the Truth, and God, health of my countenance, my God.'[3] The mind of man finds itself in touch with an intelligible world and knows truth. This intelligible world is not a product of the senses or the soul of man. The sensible cannot give birth to the intelligible, which is unchanging, whereas the world is passing. Truth is steady, whereas the soul's glance is unsteady. Truth is found, not made, and the human mind is subject to it.

Augustine is not very clear about the nature of the soul. It is not truth itself, because Truth is immutable and the soul is subject to change. It is not a part of Truth, for it is

[1] *Contra Academicos*, iii. 17. 37.

[2] *De Vera Religione*, xxxix. 73. See D'Arcy in *A Monument to St. Augustine* (1930), pp. 164 ff.

[3] *Confessions*, x. 23. 33.

aware of itself as alive and thinking, and therefore as a substance God sustains it and unites it with Himself in such a way that it perseveres in existence and participates in His thought. Such participation is everlasting, for matter cannot molest the substance of that which is higher, and there is nothing that could conflict with it. As a spiritual being the soul is indivisible, and its spirituality and subsistence are given directly in self-knowledge. It is in the inward self that we find Truth and God.

'I entered into my inward self, Thou being my guide, and beheld with the eye of my soul above my mind the light unchangeable. Thee (my God) when I first knew Thou liftedst me up that I might see there was what I might see, and that I was not yet such as to see. And Thou didst beat back the weakness of my sight streaming forth Thy beams of light upon me most strongly, and I trembled with love and awe, and I perceived myself to be far off from Thee in the region of unlikeness. Thou criedst to me from afar: "Yea, verily I am that I am." And I heard as the heart heareth, nor had I room to doubt and I should sooner doubt that I live than that truth is not.'[1]

Augustine's classic words, 'Thou hast made us for Thyself, and our hearts are restless until they rest in Thee', represent the essence of the religious spirit. Augustine's descriptions of the highest moments of religious experience are in the style and language of Plotinus. In the great passage in which he gives an account of his last conversation with his mother about the life of the redeemed in heaven he repeats the thoughts and almost the very words of Plotinus:

'Suppose all the tumult of the flesh in us were hushed for ever, and all sensible images of earth and sea and air were put to silence; suppose the heavens were still, and even the soul spoke no words to itself, but passed beyond all thought of itself; suppose all dreams and revelations of imagination were hushed with every word and sign and everything that belongs to this transitory world; suppose they were all silenced—though, if they speak to one who hears, what they say is "We made not ourselves, but He made us who abides forever"—yet suppose they only uttered this and then were silent, when they had turned the ears of the hearer to Him who made them, leaving Him to speak alone, not through them but through Himself, so that we could hear His words, not through any tongue of flesh nor by the voice of an angel, nor in thunder, nor in any likeness that hides what it reveals; suppose then

[1] *Confessions*, vii. 16. 23.

that the God whom through such manifestations we have learnt to love, were to be revealed to us directly without any such mediation—just as, but now we reached out of ourselves and touched by a flash of insight the eternal wisdom that abides above all; suppose lastly that this vision of God were to be prolonged forever and all other inferior modes of vision were to be taken away, so that this alone should ravish and absorb the beholder, and entrance him in mystic joy, and our life were forever like the moment of clear insight and inspiration to which we rose—is not this just what is meant by the words "Enter thou into the joy of thy Lord"?'[1]

Augustine is the Christian Plotinus.

The soul can find God by a withdrawing from all things and senses. It is united in the profoundest depths of the heart with the supreme who dwells there. The human heart can find rest in the most hidden point of its sanctified activity, its own nature as a spirit. While the mystic union with the Absolute was regarded by Plotinus as union with the One beyond Nous, for Augustine the Word is itself the Absolute.

Augustine distinguishes between science, which is the work of the lower reason, directed towards the world of action and created things, and wisdom, which is the work of the higher reason directed towards the repose of contemplation. He admits a higher intuition, 'a flash of light to see *that which is*'. He distinguishes the intellectual object of vision from the light by which the soul is enlightened. By means of knowledge we cannot know what God is. 'We can know what God is not but not what He is.'[2] When we have the vision, we are transformed. 'We glow inwardly with Thy fire.' The ascent of the soul is arranged in seven stages, of which the last three are purgation, illumination, and union. The last, 'the vision and contemplation of truth', is the 'goal of the journey'. Augustine's explanation of the Trinity is hardly intelligible. His prayers are to God through Christ but not to Christ Himself.[3]

Augustine is not, however, always loyal to this mystic

[1] Ibid. v. 1. 2. There is a good deal in common between Plotinus and Augustine in the sphere of psychology.

[2] *On the Trinity*, viii. 2.

[3] 'In the personal religion of Western nations, prayer to Christ first wins a prominent place in the early Middle Ages' (Heiler, *Prayer*, E.T. (1932), p. 126).

tradition. The Manichaean dualism operates in his conception of the two cities, the eternal one in heaven and the transitory one on earth. The suggestion is present that the power of evil is independent of and coequal with the power of God. This is not, however, his main tendency. Replying to the comments of the Manichaean Faustus on the lives of the Hebrew patriarchs and judges, Augustine says that their cruelties must have been done in obedience to divine commands and the great Author of moral laws is not Himself subject to them. He can at His pleasure act in ways opposed to His own legislation. Augustine was penetrated by the sense of man's utter impotence to rise of himself, and of his need of divine condescension. Man is divided from God not by external barriers but by a depraved will. Sin is the shadow cast by the light of God.

Yet in the central features of his system, such as the equation between intelligibility and reality, the slow ascent of the soul with increasing likeness to God, the assumption that the soul is the means for the apprehension of truth and God, Augustine remained a Neoplatonist. He observes: 'That which is called the Christian religion existed among the ancients and never did not exist from the beginning of the human race until Christ came in the flesh, at which time the true religion which already existed began to be called Christianity.'[1] This breadth of view is hardly consistent with his conduct as a bishop, when he maintained the right of the Church to persecute heretics. We find in him two currents, the spiritual and the dogmatic. He was at the same time the son of Monica and a bishop of the Orthodox Church. This greatest of the Church Fathers was a Neoplatonist by conviction, and the Christian faith was subordinate in his consciousness to the truth of Neoplatonism.[2]

The writings of Augustine which incorporated the main

[1] *Epis. Retrac.*, lib. I, xiii. 3.

[2] Professor F. Heiler says: 'In this peculiar fusion of the two opposed types of religion, Neo-Platonic mysticism has the precedence. The goal of all prayer for Augustine is the return to the infinite one, the essential unity with the highest good.' He quotes with approval the observation of Scheel: 'Neither in the thought nor in the feeling of Augustine is the first place assigned to specifically Christian ideas. The genuine Augustine is the Neoplatonic Augustine' (Heiler, *Prayer*, E.T. (1932), pp. 126–7).

doctrines of Neoplatonism exercised the most enduring influence on the medieval mind even when the authority of Aristotle was at its strongest.[1]

Boethius (A.D. 480–524) in his *De Consolatione Philosophiae*, a book which was very popular in the Middle Ages, made considerable use of Neoplatonic principles.[2] This book was translated into English by Alfred the Great. Boethius' famous definition of eternal life as the simultaneous and perfect possession of boundless life expresses the spirit of Plotinus's description of eternity.[3] His views on the scale of reality, the primacy of the intelligible and ideal world, the identity of the Good and the One, the deification of the soul by her participation of God, are Neoplatonic.

The writer known by the name of Dionysius the Areopagite is said to be the father of Christian mysticism, and he exercised a decisive influence on the theory and practice of religion in the medieval Church, and he comes from Eastern Christendom, in fact from Syria. He is undoubtedly a Christian Neoplatonist who was familiar with the writings of Proclus, Ignatius, and Clement. As Justinian quotes him, his writings may be assigned to the second quarter of the sixth century. As he was mistaken for St. Paul's Athenian convert, his writings were accepted as the inspired productions of the Apostolic times.[4]

[1] Thomas Aquinas denies knowledge of what God is. He states definitely that 'the Divine Substance by its immensity exceeds every formal principle to which our intelligence can reach, and so we cannot apprehend it by knowing what it is, but we may get a sort of knowledge of it by knowing what it is not'. (*Summa contra Gentiles*, bk. i, chap. xiv). The Thomists postulate a 'gift of higher knowledge' to account for the love which is the most distinctive feature of mystical experience.

[2] Cf. Harnack: Boethius 'in his mode of thought was certainly a Neoplatonist' (*History of Dogma*, vol. i, p. 358).

[3] '*Nous* possesses in itself all things abiding in the same place. It is, ever is and nowhere becomes, nor is ever past, for here nothing passes away but all things are eternally present' (*Enneads*, v. 1. 4).

[4] St. Gregory in the sixth century venerated him. Pope Martin I quoted him textually in the Lateran Council of 640 in defence of Catholic dogma. His words were used in the third Council of Constantinople (692) and at the second Council of Nicea. In the eighth century St. John the Damascene became his follower and accepted his teachings. John Scotus Erigena translated his writings. The Church condemned him in the thirteenth century, but his influence rose again in the mystics of the fourteenth century.

Dionysius refers to his teacher Hierotheus, a Syrian mystic who lived late in the fifth century, as one who 'not only learned, but felt the things of God'. He deals extensively with the adventures of the mind in climbing the ladder of perfection. He professes to have enjoyed ecstatic union and asks us to prepare for it by the method of quietism. 'To me it seems right to speak without words and understand without knowledge; this I apprehend to be nothing but the mysterious silence and the mystical quiet which destroys consciousness and dissolves forms. Seek therefore silently and mystically, that perfect and primitive union with the Archgood.'[1] Commenting on this system Dr. Inge writes: 'It is the ancient religion of the Brāhmins masquerading in clothes borrowed from Jewish allegorists, half Christian Gnostics, Manichaeans, platonising Christians and pagan Neo-platonists.'[2]

In the *Theologia Mystica* and other works ascribed to him[3] he develops the doctrines of Proclus. God is, for him, the nameless supra-essential one, elevated above goodness itself. For him God is the absolute No-thing which is above all existence. He speaks 'of the superlucent darkness of silence' and of the necessity to 'leave behind the senses and the intellectual operations and all things known by senses and intellect'.

> 'And thou, dear Timothy, in thy intent practice of the mystical contemplations, leave behind both thy senses and thy intellectual operations and all things known by sense and intellect, and all things which are not and which are, and set thyself, as far as may be, to unite thyself in unknowing with him who is above all being and knowledge, for by being purely free and absolute, out of self and of all things thou shalt be led up to the ray of divine darkness, stripped of all and loosed from all.'

We must tear aside 'the veil of sensible things', for 'the pre-eminent cause of every object of sensible perception is none of the objects of sensible perception'.[4] We must remove the wrappings of intelligible things, for 'the pre-

[1] Quoted in Inge's *Christian Mysticism* (1899), p. 103.
[2] Ibid., p. 104.
[3] See John Parker's E.T. of the *Works of Dionysius the Areopagite* (1897).
[4] *Ecclesiastical Hierarchy*, vi. 3.

eminent cause of every object of the intelligible perception is none of the objects of intelligible perception'.[1] The real

> 'is neither soul nor mind; nor has imagination nor opinion, nor reason nor conception, neither is expressed nor conceived; neither is number nor order; nor greatness nor littleness; . . . When making the predications and abstractions of things after it, we neither predicate nor abstract from it, since the all perfect and uniform cause of all is both above every definition, and the pre-eminence of him who is absolutely freed from all and beyond the whole, is also above every abstraction.'

We must deny everything about God in order to penetrate into the sublime ignorance, 'divine gloom', which is in verity sovereign knowledge.[2] He uses the image of the sculptor's chisel, removing the covering and 'bringing forth the inner form to view, freeing the hidden beauty by the sole process of curtailment'.[3] He speaks of a power in the soul that makes it able to see eternal verities. When it develops this power, it is deified. '[Preservation] cannot otherwise take place, except those which are being saved are being deified. Now the assimilation to, union with God, as far as attainable, is deification.'[4] Three stages of mystic life are distinguished, purification, illumination, and consummation, in the perfect knowledge of the splendours.[5]

The central problem of Christian Platonism or any mystic religion is the reconciliation of the two presentations of the Supreme, the Absolute One without distinctions and attributes, and the personal God who knows, loves, and freely chooses. Dionysius distinguishes between the Supreme in itself and the Supreme in relation to creatures. While the former is the godhead in its utter transcendence of all created being and its categories, the latter is His manifestation to man in terms of the highest categories of human experience. *Mystical Theology* is concerned with God as He is; *Divine Names* with His partial manifestations in terms of human experience. The theory of the reflection of every degree of

[1] Ibid. v.

[2] Cf. 'Thus delivered from the sensible world and the intellectual alike, the soul enters into the mysterious obscurity of a holy ignorance and, renouncing all the gifts of science, loses itself in Him who can be neither seen nor seized' (i. 3). See Maritain, *The Degrees of Knowledge*, E.T. (1937), p. 18.

[3] *Mystic Theology*, ii. [4] *Ecclesiastical Hierarchy*, i. 3. [5] Ibid. iv.

reality, save the lowest, upon that beneath it gives place in Dionysius to a dynamic conception of a divine Eros, an overflowing love which moves God to create reflections and participants of His bliss and freedom.

'The father is fontal deity but the Lord Jesus and the Spirit are, if one may so speak, God-planted shoots, and as it were Flowers and super-essential Lights of the God-bearing Deity, we have received from the holy oracles; but how these things are, it is neither possible to say, nor to conceive.'[1]

'One Being is said to be fashioned in many forms, by the production from itself of the many beings, whilst it remains undiminished and One in the multiplicity and Unified during the progression, and complete in the distinction, both by being super-essentially exalted above all beings and by the unique production of the whole and by the unlessened stream of his undiminished distributions.'

He is 'undivided in things divided, unified in Himself, both unmingled and unmultiplied in the many'.[2] Dionysius is vague about the nature of evil.

'Evil is non-existing . . . if this be not the case, it is not altogether *evil*, nor non-existing, for the absolutely non-existing will be nothing unless it should be spoken of as in the good super-essentiality.'[3]

Neoplatonism was absorbed by Christianity through his writings. They became, according to Baron von Hügel, 'the great treasure house from which the mystics and also largely the Scholastics throughout the Middle Ages, drew much of their literary material'.[4]

II

When the Arab armies were defeated by Charles Martel near the French town of Poitiers in A.D. 732 they retreated towards Spain. This battle decided the great issue whether

[1] *On Divine Names.*

[2] Ibid., pt. i, pp. 25–6.

[3] Ibid. iv. 19.

[4] *The Mystical Element of Religion*, p. 61. 'The writings of the pseudo-Dionysius contain a gnosis in which, by means of the doctrines of Iamblichus and doctrines like those of Proclus, the dogmatic of the Church is changed into a scholastic mysticism with directions for practical life and worship. . . . The mystical and pietistic devotion of to-day, even in the Protestant Church, draws its nourishment from writings whose connexion with those of the pseudo-Areopagite can still be traced through its various intermediate stages' (Harnack, *History of Dogma*, vol. i, p. 361).

Christian civilization should continue or Islam prevail in Europe. An Arab victory in 732 would have altered the course of European civilization, and Arab civilization in those days was in advance of the European. When Alexandria came to an end in A.D. 642 the Arabs kept up the cultural traditions in schools at Baghdad, Cairo, and Cordova. Baghdad, founded in A.D. 762, was frequented by Greek and Hindu merchants. The Muslim rulers of Baghdad as early as the eighth century had encouraged the translations of Greek thinkers, Plato, Aristotle, and Plotinus, into Arabic. Arab travellers were attracted by Indian civilization. Alberuni accompanied Sultan Mahmud of Ghazni to India and acquired a knowledge of Indian religious classics. Many works, religious and secular, were translated from Sanskrit into Arabic and from Arabic into Latin. The game of chess and many fables, as well as other products of India, were brought by Arabs into western Europe. Towards the end of the twelfth century western Europe acquired the complete body of Aristotle's logical writings in Latin translations made in Spain from the Arabic texts along with the commentaries of Arabian and Jewish philosophers. The writings of Alfarabi (A.D. 950) and Avicenna (A.D. 980–1037) of Baghdad, and Averroes (1126–98) of Spain were known in Europe. A curious blend of Greek, Jewish, and Oriental philosophy entered the Church by means of Arab works. The theism of Aristotle was used as a preparation for the Christian faith. Philosophy was made subservient to orthodoxy. Thomas Aquinas quotes largely from Dionysius. Dante's conception of the beatific vision is identical with that of the intelligible word as figured by Plotinus. He uses the conception of emanation by which the higher cause remains in itself, while producing that which is next to it in the order of being. By means of this idea Dante justifies and explains the varying degrees of perfection in created things. Even before the scholastic system was thoroughly developed it began to break up from within. Thomas Aquinas was followed by John Duns Scotus. Soon after came William of Ockham, and scholasticism flourished during the centuries when Greek thought was not known in its sources. When the classical revival arose along with the impulse towards scientific research, interest in Platonism rapidly developed.

There are great similarities between Hindu, Persian, and Christian forms of mysticism which may be accounted for as products of similar evolution. The Sufis combine Mohammad's prophetic faith in God with the wisdom of the Vedānta and the spiritual discipline of the Yoga. Though the background of Islam is the Mediterranean culture from which the roots of Western civilization derive, and it grew up under the influence of Hellenism and interpreted Hellenism to the medieval world, Christianity dismissed the followers of Islam as infidels, and the later exchanges between East and West were for many centuries confined to exchanges on the battle-field between the forces of Christendom and those of Islam.

Dionysius started the mystical speculations which troubled the orthodox when authority wavered, through the influence of Scotus Erigena. John Scotus Erigena (ninth century) may be regarded as the most profound philosopher of the Middle Ages. Though an Irishman, he belongs in thought to Eastern Christianity. He not only translated the works of Dionysius the Areopagite into Latin, but set himself to elucidate his theories and present them as a systematic whole. He came to be regarded not only as a late Neoplatonist but as the first of the scholastics. His great work, *De Divisione Naturae*, was condemned in 1225 by Pope Honorius III to be burned. In this work he classifies nature, or what we would call Reality, into four kinds: that which creates and is not created; that which creates and is created; that which is created and does not create; that which neither creates nor is created. These are not four different things or classes but four aspects or stages of the one world process. The first deals with God as essence, the ultimate ground of the universe; the second with Divine ideas or First Causes; the third with the created world, and the last with God as the consummation of all things. God alone has true being. God is the beginning of all things and the end, for all things participate in His essence, subsist in and through Him, and are moved towards Him as their last end. While in one sense God is in all things, He is Nothing, for His essence transcends all determination and is inexpressible. The divine being transcends all possible conceptions, and the trinitarian conception is interpreted by him as symbolic. Out of this incorruptible essence the world of ideas is eternally created. This is the Word or Son of God in whom all things exist, so far as they have substantial existence. Creation is an external projection of the ideal order eternally present in God. All existence is a theophany. The soul of man is the reflection of the divine. Erigena revives Origen's universalism and regards the Fall as precosmic.

The teaching of Erigena was condemned as heretical, and he left no important disciples. The tenth century was a dark one, and when philosophical speculations started in the eleventh century, scholastic disputes about the nature of Universals occupied the centre. Peter Abelard was the most renowned dialectician of the twelfth century (died 1142), and he attributes to Plato an anticipation of the Christian doctrine of the Trinity. The One of Plato typifies the Father, the Nous the Son, and the world soul the Holy Ghost. Abelard tried to reconcile Christianity and Platonism.

In the abbey of St. Victor, Hugo and Richard developed the mystical side of the teaching of St. Augustine. 'The way to ascend to God', says Hugo of St. Victor, 'is to descend into oneself.' 'The ascent is through self above self', says Richard of St. Victor. He continues: 'Let him that thirsts to see God clean his mirror, let him make his own spirit bright.' They believe in ecstatic contemplation as the way to the realization of truth.

St. Bonaventure continues the Neoplatonic tradition. For him the soul is the centre and starting-point of human knowledge. Knowledge of the soul and God is obtained without the assistance of the senses. We attain to the knowledge of God through intelligible reflections of the divine ideas displayed to the mind in creatures. In this hierarchy of reflections every degree is a symbol and analogy of its superior. The highest mystical apprehension of God is described in the spirit of Plotinus, though it is to be the gift of God's free grace and beyond man's natural power to obtain.

Albertus Magnus, another great mystic of the age, followed the Dionysian tradition. For him, union with God is the aim of life. Interior contemplation is the way to it. In ordinary life the mind is immersed in what is not itself, in sensible appearances. If we divest the mind of all that is sensible, outward and phenomenal, it rises through the pure intellect to union with divinity.[1]

'When thou prayest, shut thy door, that is, the doors of the senses. Keep them barred and bolted against all phantasms and images. Nothing pleases God more than a mind free from all occupations and distractions. Such a mind is in a manner transformed into God for it can think of nothing, and understand nothing and love nothing except God. He who penetrates into himself and so transcends himself, ascends truly to God.'

St. Thomas Aquinas (1227–74) was a pupil of Albertus Magnus. In the last year of his life he experienced a prolonged ecstasy and refused thereafter to write anything, despite the entreaties of his secretary, Reginald.[2] We preach and talk only till we feel and adore. The mystic tradition is continued by the great German mystics Eckhart and

[1] This great schoolman, who is the master of St. Thomas Aquinas, teaches doctrines 'characteristically Indian' (Kennedy, 'The Gospels of the Infancy', *J.R.A.S.*, 1917, p. 210). 'From what source came this philosophy which Albertus shared with the Gentiles? He got it through the medium of the Arabic: but it is not the intuition or ecstasy of Plotinus. I cannot say whether it is to be found in any of the later Neoplatonists or in the independent speculations of Arabian Metaphysicians: but the ideas are distinctly Indian, and must have come from India to the West' (ibid., p. 212).

[2] Robert Bridges describes this incident in the *Testament of Beauty* (1930):

I am happier in surmizing that his vision at Mass
—in Naples it was when he fell suddenly in trance—
was some disenthralment of his humanity:
for thereafter, whether 'twer Aristotle or Christ
that had appear'd to him then, he nevermore wrote word
neither dictated but laid by inkhorn and pen;
and was as a man out of hearing on thatt day
when Reynaldus, with all the importunity of zeal
and intimacy of friendship, would have recall'd him
to his incompleted SUMMA; and sighing he reply'd
'I wil tell the a secret, my son, constraining thee
lest thou dare impart it to any man while I liv.
My writing is at end. I hav seen such things reveal'd
that what I hav written and taught seemeth to me of small worth.
And hence I hope in my God, that, as of doctrin
ther wil be speedily also an end of Life!'

Tauler, the Spanish St. Theresa and St. John of the Cross, and the English Platonists and numbers of others.

III

The struggle for the Indian market by the European nations began in 1498, when Vasco da Gama discovered the sea-route to India, and in 1509, when the Portuguese took possession of Goa. The lure of the East has not been any spiritual or human appeal but desire for gold and her company as a consumer. Columbus, searching for India, inadvertently discovered America. India has been the prize for competing imperialisms. The Portuguese and the Spaniards, the Dutch, the French, and the English fought with one another for the possession of India, and the conflict ended in 1761 with the decisive victory of England. The scientific study of Indian literature starts from this period. Warren Hastings found it necessary for purposes of administration to study the old Indian law books. In 1785 Charles Wilkins published an English translation of the *Bhagavadgītā*, to which Warren Hastings wrote a preface in which he said that works like the *Bhagavadgītā* 'will survive when the British dominion in India shall have long ceased to exist and when the sources which it once yielded of wealth and power are lost to remembrance'. William Jones published in 1789 his English version of Kālidāsa's *Śakuntalā*. This was translated from English into German by Georg Förster and was enthusiastically welcomed by men like Herder and Goethe. Though Englishmen were naturally the first to make Europe acquainted with the spiritual treasures of India, German scholars soon took the lead.[1] The impulse to Indological studies was first given in Germany by the romanticist Friedrich Schlegel through his book *The Language and Wisdom of the Indians*, which appeared in 1808. August Wilhelm von Schlegel, who became the first German professor of Sanskrit in 1818, in Bonn edited the *Gītā* in 1823. The

[1] Cf. Heine: 'The Portuguese, Dutch and English have been for a long time, year after year, shipping home the treasures of India in their big vessels. We Germans have all along been left to watch it. To-day Schlegel, Bopp, Humboldt, Frank, &c. are our East Indian sailors. Bonn and Munich will be good factories.'

first German translation is dated 1802. It made a great impression on Wilhelm von Humboldt, who said that 'this episode of the *Mahābhārata* was the most beautiful, nay perhaps, the only true philosophical poem which all the literatures known to us can show'.[1] He devoted to it a long treatise in the *Proceedings of the Academy of Berlin* (1825–6).

Schopenhauer became acquainted with the thought of the Upaniṣads through a Latin translation from Persian by a Frenchman, Anquetil Duperron. His eulogy is well known. 'And O! how the mind is here washed clean of all its early ingrafted Jewish superstition! It is the most profitable and most elevating reading which (the original text excepted) is possible in the world. It has been the solace of my life, and will be the solace of my death.'[2] Schopenhauer was greatly influenced by Buddhist ideals also. German transcendentalism was affected by Indian thought through Schopenhauer, Hartmann, and Nietzsche. Richard Wagner became acquainted with Buddhistic ideas through the writings of Schopenhauer. His *Parsifal* arose out of a French translation of a Buddhist legend. To Mathilde Wesendonk, Wagner wrote in the year 1857: 'You know how I have unconsciously become a Buddhist', and again: 'Yes, child, it is a world view, compared with which every other dogma must appear small and narrow.'[3] Even of Heine, Semite though he was, Brandes claims that 'his spiritual home was on the banks of the Ganges'.[4] Through Naumann's German

[1] Letter to Fr. von Gentz, 1827.

[2] *Parerga*, ii, p. 185, quoted in Wallace, *Schopenhauer*, p. 106.

[3] Brunhilde says in Wagner's *Twilight of the Gods*:

> Know ye whither I am going?
> Out of the home of Desire I move away,
> Home of Illusion I fly from for ever;
> The open gates of eternal becoming
> Emancipated from rebirth. The knowing one passes away

Quoted in Winternitz, 'India and the West', *Viśvabhārati Quarterly*, Feb. 1937, p. 19.

[4] *Main Currents of European Literature*, vol. i, p. 126. Amiel refers to the Hindu streak in him. He writes: 'There is a great affinity in me with the Hindu genius—that mind, vast, imaginative, loving, dreamy and speculative, but destitute of ambition, personality and will. Pantheistic disinterestedness, the effacement of the self in the great whole, womanish gentleness, a horror of slaughter, antipathy to action—these are all present in my nature, in the

translations of Buddhist texts Buddhism became popular in Germany. Paul Deussen's translations of the Upaniṣads and scholarly works on Indian philosophy became classics on the subject.

Michelet, speaking about *Rāmāyaṇa*, wrote in 1864: 'Whoever has done or willed too much, let him drink from this deep cup a long draught of life and youth. . . . Everything is narrow in the West—Greece is small and I stifle; Judaea is dry and I pant. Let me look a little towards lofty Asia, the profound East. . . .' Comte's positivism is 'but Buddhism adapted to modern civilization; it is philosophic Buddhism in a slight disguise'.[1]

Edwin Arnold's *Light of Asia* aroused much enthusiasm in England and America. In America Thoreau, Emerson, and Walt Whitman show the influence of Indian thought. Thoreau says: 'The pure Walden water is mingled with the sacred water of the Ganges.' Emerson's Oversoul is the *paramātman* of the Upanisads. Whitman turns to the East in his anxiety to escape from the complexities of civilization and the bewilderments of a baffled intellectualism. The humanism of Irving Babbitt and the writings of Paul Elmer More show the deep influence of Indian thought.

Maeterlinck sets over against each other what he calls the 'Western lobe' and the 'Eastern lobe' of the human brain:

> 'The one here produces reason, science, consciousness; the other yonder secretes intuition, religion, the subconscious. . . . More than once they have endeavoured to penetrate one another, to mingle, to work together; but the Western lobe, at any rate on the most active expanse of our globe, has heretofore paralysed and almost annihilated the efforts of the other. We owe to it extraordinary progress in all material sciences, but also catastrophes, such as those we are undergoing to-day. . . . It is time to awaken the paralysed Eastern lobe.'

nature at least which has been developed by years and circumstances. Still the West has also its part in me. What I have found difficult is to keep up a prejudice in favour of any form, nationality or individuality whatever. Hence my indifference to my own person, my own usefulness, interest or opinions of the moment. What does it all matter?' (*Journal*, pp. 159, 161, 224 ff.). 'It is perhaps not a bad thing', he says, 'that in the midst of the devouring activities of the Western world there should be a few Brāhmanical souls' (p. 269).

[1] Eitel, *Three Lectures on Buddhism* (1884), p. 3.

Romain Rolland, who has been deeply influenced by Indian thought, writes:

> 'There are a certain number of us in Europe for whom the civilization of Europe is no longer enough.'

Keyserling, whose writings breathe the spirit of the East, tells us:

> 'Europe no longer makes me react. This world is too familiar to me to give new shapes to my being: it is too limited. The whole of Europe nowadays is of one mind only. I wish to escape to spaces where my life must needs be transformed if it is to survive.'

The Irish Literary Renaissance, with its central figures of W. B. Yeats and George W. Russell (Æ), is moulded by Eastern conceptions.[1] George Moore, in his novel *The Brook Kerith*, represents Jesus as having survived the Cross and as meeting St. Paul and explaining to him His revised Gospel. 'God', He says, 'is not without but within the universe, part and parcel, not only of the stars and the earth, but of me, yea, even of my sheep on the hillside.' As Paul listens he realizes that this doctrine is the same as was preached by some monks from India to the shepherds among whom, according to this tale, Jesus was living. There are many literary men to-day in Europe and America who are influenced by Indian thought and look to it for inspiration in our present troubles.[2] Sir Charles Eliot observes: 'Let me confess that I cannot share the confidence in the superiority of Europeans and their ways

[1] Æ writes: 'Goethe, Wordsworth, Emerson and Thoreau among moderns have something of this vitality and wisdom, but we can find all they have said and much more in the grand sacred books of the East. The Bhagavadgītā and the Upaniṣads contain such godlike fulness of wisdom on all things that I feel the authors must have looked with calm remembrance back through a thousand passionate lives, full of feverish strife for and with shadows, ere they could have written with such certainty of things which the soul feels to be sure' (*A Memoir of Æ*, by John Eglinton (1937), p. 20).

[2] Mr. Fausset, in his book *A Modern Prelude*, tells how he has travelled from orthodox Christianity to find in 'the inspired pantheism in which the vision and teaching of the Vedānta culminated' what could at least purge and content his unquiet self (p. 258). There the personal God was completed in the 'impersonal God'; there also the Christos or the divine self was known and expressed long before the birth of Jesus. Aldous Huxley in his latest books, *Eyeless in Gaza* and *Ends and Means*, invites our attention to the discipline essential for spiritual insight and argues for the acceptance of the Yoga method. The influence of Indian thought is not so much a model to be copied as a dye which permeates.

which is prevalent in the West. European civilization is not satisfying and Asia can still offer something more attractive to many who are far from Asiatic in spirit.'[1]

There are, however, some in the West who are attracted by the glamour of the exotic, who are carried away by the romantic surface of life. Kipling in some of his moods represents this tendency.[2] The East has ever been a romantic puzzle to the West, the home of adventures like those of *Arabian Nights*, the abode of magic, the land of heart's desire, one to which even men of waning faith may turn for confirmation in the hope that after all the spiritual counts.[3] Theosophical and anthroposophical cults which employ largely Hindu and Buddhist concepts and practices, Neo-Buddhist and Rāmakṛṣṇa societies attract a considerable proportion of religious men in the West.[4] There are some who are obviously uneasy about the spread of Eastern culture in the West.[5] Educated Romans were equally concerned about the spread of Christianity, which they considered a sign of decadence.

[1] *Hinduism and Buddhism*, vol. i, p. xcvi (1921).

[2] In his poem *Mandalay* he writes:

> Slip me somewhere east of Suez where the best is like the worst,
> Where there ain't no Ten Commandments, an' a man can raise a thirst;
> For the temple bells are callin': an' it's there that I would be . . .
> By the old Moulmein pagoda, lookin' lazy at the sea.

Of course, the temple bells mean to the Burman the exact opposite of what they mean to Kipling; be still, not to raise a thirst.

[3] Madame Alice Louis-Barthou writes: 'I look upon the Occident with abomination. It represents for me fog, grayness, chill, machinery, murderous science, factories with all the vices, the triumph of noise, of hustling, of ugliness. . . . The Orient is calm, peace, beauty, colour, mystery, charm, sunlight, joy, ease of life and revery; in fine the exact opposite of our hateful and grotesque civilization. . . . If I had my way, I should have a Chinese wall built between the Orient and the Occident to keep the latter from poisoning the former; I should have the heads of all the giaours cut off, and I should go and live where you can see clearly and where there are no Europeans.'

[4] Cf. 'On the other hand there seems to be an increasing number of persons who have been led by natural and acquired sympathy to adopt in some form one of the Eastern religions' (E. E. Kellett, *A Short Study of Religions*, p. 567). The new German faith is said to have for its main sources of inspiration Eckhart and the *Bhagavadgītā*.

[5] Henri Massis, perturbed by this phenomenon, wrote a work some years ago on *The Defence of the West* (E.T. 1927). See also Wendell Thomas, *Hinduism Invades America*.

VII

GREECE, PALESTINE, AND INDIA

I

TO what is this phenomenon of spiritual waywardness in the West due? May it not be that it is motived by a deep instinct for self-preservation and a longing for world unity? The attraction of Eastern forms may be traced to a failure of nerve akin to what occurred at the beginning of the Christian era, which experienced a similar phenomenon. We seem to be vaguely aware that in spite of our brilliant and heroic achievements we have lost our hold on the primal verities. The instability of life is manifesting itself in many forms. The affirmation of the sovereign State, owing allegiance to none and free to destroy its fellows, itself open to a similar fate without appeal, racial and national idolatries which deny the corporate life of the whole, the growing tyranny of wealth, the conflict between rich and poor, and the destruction of the co-operative spirit threaten the very existence of society. Insecurity of nations and destitution of peoples have always been with us, but periodic sanguinary upheavals have also been with us. The two are different sides of a social order which is really primitive in character. Greek culture was born in strife, in strife of city-States and against foreign foes. The Roman Empire was formed by a series of destructive and often savage wars, though it became the home and cradle of Western civilization. The period of the Middle Ages, when Europe had the formal unity of a common religion, was also the period of the most incessant war. It will not be an over-statement to say that never a day passes but the Great Powers are engaged in wars small or great in some part of their vast dominions. Even now we have the struggle within for juster and better conditions of life, and without for independence. Man has not grown worse. In some points he is an improvement on his predecessors, but we need not exult in it. When Mrs. Rosita Forbes visited the penitentiary at São Paulo she asked if there were many thieves among the inmates. The warden was shocked. 'Oh, no,' he replied, 'Brazilians are very honest. Nearly all these men are murderers.' Augustine quotes with approval the reply of the pirate to Alexander the Great. 'Because I do it with a little ship, I am called a robber, and you because you do it with a great fleet, are called an emperor.' The final test of every social system is the happiness and well-being of men and women. Those who live for economic power and for the State are not concerned with the development of a true quality of life for the people and are obliged to adopt war as a national industry. Our habits of mind and our relations to our neighbours have not altered much, but the mutual antagonisms and reciprocal incomprehensions are turning out most dangerous in a closely knit world with new weapons of destruction. Enormous mechanical progress with spiritual crudity, the love of economic power, and political reaction, with all the injustice that it involves, have suddenly startled us out of our complacency. We are asking ourselves whether the props by which society has hitherto maintained itself precariously are moral at all, whether the present order with its slave basis of society and petty particularism is based on canons of justice. When universal covetousness has outstripped the means of gratifying it; when the unnatural conditions of life demand for their defence the conversion of whole nations into mechanized armies; when the supremacy of power-politics is threatened by its own inherent destructiveness; when the common people feel in their depths 'blessed are the wombs which never bare, the breasts that never gave suck': it is a challenge to our principles and our faith. The perception of the tragic humiliation of mankind must make us think deeply. The world is a moral invalid surrounded by quacks and charlatans, witch-doctors and medicine men who are interested in keeping the patient in the bad habits of centuries. The patient requires drastic treatment. His mind must be led out of the moulds in which it has been congesting and set free to think in a wider ether than before. Ultimate reality cannot be destroyed. Moral laws cannot be mocked. George Macdonald has a parable in which a strong wind tried to blow out the moon, but at the end of it all she remained 'motionless miles above the air', unconscious even that there had been a tempest. It is because we have not developed the spiritual equipment to face facts and initiate policies based on truth and tolerance that we have to secure our injustices by the strength of arms. The alternatives are either a policy of righteousness and a just reorganization of the world or an armed world. That is the issue before us. It is of the utmost seriousness and greatest urgency, for it is even now upon us.

It is a fact of history that civilizations which are based on truly religious forces such as endurance, suffering, passive resistance, understanding, tolerance are long-lived, while those which take their stand exclusively on humanist elements like active reason, power, aggression, progress make for a brilliant display but are short-lived. Compare the relatively long record of China and of India with the eight hundred years or less of the Greeks, the nine hundred years on a most generous estimate of the Romans, and the thousand years of Byzantium. In spite of her great contributions of democracy, individual freedom, intellectual integrity, the Greek civilization passed away as the Greeks could not combine even among themselves on account of their loyalty to the city-States. Their exalted conceptions were not effective forces, and, except those who were brought under the mystery religions, the Greeks never developed a conception of human society in spite of the very valuable contributions of Plato, Aristotle, and the Stoics. The Roman gifts to civilization are of outstanding value, but the structure of the Empire of Rome had completely ceased to exist by A.D. 500. Empires have a tendency to deprive us of our soul. Extension in space is not necessarily a growth in spirit. Peace prevailed under the Roman rule, for none was left strong enough to oppose it. Rome had conquered the world, and had no rival, none to struggle with or struggle for. The *pax Romana* reigned, but it was the peace of the desert, of sullen acquiescence and pathetic enslavement. The cement of the whole structure was the army. The head of the army was the head of the State, the Imperator, answering to our 'Emperor'. In the middle of the third century all manner of upstart soldiers who were able to gather a few followers took over the governments, each in his own region and over his own troops. With the weakening of the Imperial government, moral anarchy increased. With the raids of pirates on the coast and of marauding bands on the frontiers, insecurity was rife. At the end of the third century, Diocletian attempted a reorganization of the whole State, but nothing could arrest the decline in standards.

There are some scholars of the Renaissance who attribute the fall of Rome to the spread of the 'superstition' of Christianity, thus echoing the cry of the Chronicler of the pagan reaction under Julian the Apostate, 'The Christians to whom we owe all our misfortunes . . .'.[1] Possibly the appeal of Christianity grew stronger as outward fortunes sank lower. The fall of Rome is not to be explained solely by the barbarian invasions. Treason from within was its cause quite as much as danger from without.[2] Greed and corruption, growth of vast fortunes and preponderance of slaves threw society out of balance. It was a period of disorder, the collapse of the higher intellectual life and the decline of righteousness. European civilization had fallen so low that many thought that the end of the world was near. 'The whole world groaned at the fall of Rome', said Augustine. 'The human race is included in the ruin; my tongue cleaves to the roof of my mouth and sobs choke my words to think that the city is a captive which led captive the whole world', wrote St. Jerome from his monastery at Bethlehem. To Christian and pagan alike it seemed that the impossible, the unthinkable, had happened. Rome, the dispenser of destiny, the eternal city whose dominion was to have lasted for ever, fell.

The Empire was broken up into two parts, the Western with Rome for its capital and the Eastern with Constantinople. By the end of the fifth century the whole of western and north-western Europe was in the hands of the barbarians. Italy had fallen to the Ostrogoths; Gaul and a large part of

[1] M. Renan says that 'Christianity was a vampire which sucked the life-blood of ancient society and produced that state of general enervation against which patriotic emperors struggled in vain' (*Marc Aurèle*, p. 589).

[2] Mr. Stanley Casson writes: 'The barbarian intrusions were more the consequence than the cause of her sickness. What had happened was that *standards had fallen*. Elements wholly alien to Roman rule and Roman freedom had emerged. In the letters of Sidonius we hear of censorship, of political murder disguised as accident, of bribery and corruption in high places, and even of the persecution of the Jews' (*Progress and Catastrophe* (1937), p. 203).

what is now Germany to the Franks; northern Africa to the Vandals; and Spain to the Visigoths. The Eastern Empire was called the Byzantine, as its capital, Constantinople, was founded by Constantine on the site of the ancient Byzantium, a town formed by nature to be the centre of a great empire. From its seven hills it commanded the approaches to both Europe and Asia. Its narrow straits joined East and West. In all this darkness the single ray of light which remained to kindle civilization once again was preserved within the narrow walls of Byzantium. Theodosius built the great fortress, and Justinian, who succeeded him, rebuilt its institutions. But the fear of attack by barbaric hordes from every part of the world was constantly present,[1] and the values of spirit could not be fostered in an atmosphere of constant fear and imminent catastrophe. Philosophy failed, literature languished, and religion became rigid and superstitious. Before Byzantium fell to the Turks in A.D. 1453 she had succeeded in spreading in the Western world the light of civilization and culture derived from Greece and Rome. And modern civilization, which took its rise after the fall of Byzantium, seems to have worked itself out, for it is exhibiting to-day all the features which are strangely similar to the symptoms which accompany the fall of civilizations: the disappearance of tolerance and of justice; the insensibility to suffering; love of ease and comfort, and selfishness of individuals and groups; the rise of strange cults which exploit not so much the stupidity of man as his unwillingness to use his intellectual powers; the wanton segregation of men into groups based on blood and soil. A world bristling with armaments and gigantic intolerances, where all men, women, and children are so obsessed by the imminence of the catastrophe that streets are provided with underground refuges, that private houses are equipped with gas-proof rooms, that citizens are instructed in the use of gas-masks, is conclusive evidence of the general degradation. Through sheer wickedness, by advocating disruptive forces, not co-operative measures, by allegiance to the ideals

[1] There were attacks by the Persians and the Arabs in A.D. 616, 675, 717, by the Bulgarians in A.D. 813, by the Russians in A.D. 866, 904, 936, 1043.

of power and profit, man is preparing to destroy even the little that his patient ingenuity has built up. Instead of progress in charity we have increase of hostilities. In order to live we seem to have lost the reason for living. World peace is a wild dream, and modern civilization is not worth saving if it continues on its present foundations.

The Chinese and the Hindu civilizations are not great in the high qualities which have made the youthful nations of the West the dynamic force they have been on the arena of world history, the qualities of ambition and adventure, of nobility and courage, of public spirit and social enthusiasm. We do not find their people frequently among those who risk their lives in scientific research, who litter the track to the North or the South Pole, who discover continents, break records, climb mountain heights, and explore unknown regions of the earth's surface. But they have lived long, faced many crises, and preserved their identity. The fact of their age suggests that they seem to have a sound instinct for life, a strange vitality, a staying power which has enabled them to adjust themselves to social, political, and economic changes, which might have meant ruin to less robust civilizations. India, for example, has endured centuries of war and invasion, pestilence, and human misrule. Perhaps one needs a good deal of suffering and sorrow to learn a little understanding and tolerance. On the whole, the Eastern civilizations are interested not so much in improving the actual conditions as in making the best of this imperfect world, in developing the qualities of cheerfulness and contentment, patience and endurance. They are not happy in the prospect of combat. To desire little, to quench the eternal fires, has been their aim. 'To be gentle is to be invincible' (Lao Tze). The needs of life are much fewer than most people suppose. If the Eastern people aim at existence simplified and self-sufficient and beyond the reach of fate, if they wish to develop gentle manners which are inconsistent with inveterate hatreds, we need not look upon them as tepid, anaemic folk, who are eager to retreat into darkness. While the Western races crave for freedom even at the price of conflict, the Easterns stoop to peace even at the price of subjection. They turn their limitations into virtues and adore the man of few longings as the most happy being. Diogenes annoyed Plato with the taunt that if he had learned to live on rough vegetables he would not have needed to flatter despots. The future is hidden from us, but the past warns us that the world in the end belongs to the unworldly. A spiritual attitude to life has nourished the Eastern cultures and given them an unfailing trust in life and a robust common sense in looking at its myriad changes. A purely humanist civilization, with its more military and forceful mode of life like the modern, faced by the risk of annihilation, is turning to the East in a mood of disenchantment. In Greek mythology, young Icarus was made to fly too high until the wax of his wings melted and he fell into the sea, while Daedalus, the old father, flew low but flew safely home. This is not a mere whim. The qualities associated with the Eastern cultures make for life and stability; those characteristic of the West for progress and adventure.

The Eastern civilizations are by no means self-sufficient. They seem to-day to be chaotic, helpless, and incapable of pulling themselves together and forging ahead. Their peoples, unpractical and inefficient, are wandering in their own lands lost and half-alive, with an old-fashioned faith in the triumph of right over might. They suffer from weaknesses which are the symptoms of age, if not senility. Their present listless and disorganized condition is not due to their love of peace and humanity but is the direct outcome of their sad failure to pay the price for defending them. What they have gained in insight they seem to have lost in power. They require to be rejuvenated. So much goodness and constructive endeavour are lost to the world by our partial philosophies of life. If modern civilization, which is so brilliant and heroic, becomes also tolerant and humane, a little more understanding, and a little less self-seeking, it will be the greatest achievement of history.

East and West are both moving out of their historical past towards a way of thinking which shall eventually be shared in common by all mankind even as the material appliances are. We can speak across continents, we can bottle up music for reproduction when desired, animate photographic pictures with life and motion; but these do not touch the foundations of culture, the general configuration of life and mind. These are cast in the old moulds which have never been broken, though new materials have been poured into them. They are now beginning to crack. The rifts which first made their appearance decades ago have now become yawning fissures. With the cracking of the moulds, civilization itself is cracking. Further growth in the old moulds is not possible. We need to-day a proper orientation, literally the values the world derived from the Orient, the truths of inner life. They are as essential for human happiness as outer organization. The restlessness and self-assertion of our civilization are the evidence of its youth, rawness, and immaturity. With its coming of age, they will wear off. The fate of the human race hangs on a rapid assimilation of the qualities associated with the mystic religions of the East. The stage is set for such a process.

Till this era, the world was a large place, and its peoples lived in isolated corners. Lack of established trade-routes and means of communication and transportation and primitive economic development helped to foster an attitude of hostility to strangers, especially those of another race. There has not, therefore, been one continuous stream into which the whole body of human civilization entered. We had a number of independent springs, and the flow was not continuous. Some springs had dried up without passing on any of their waters to the main stream. To-day the whole world is in fusion and all is in motion. East and West are fertilizing each other, not for the first time. May we not strive for a philosophy which will combine the best of European humanism and Asiatic religion, a philosophy profounder and more living than either, endowed with greater spiritual and ethical force, which will conquer the hearts of men and compel peoples to acknowledge its sway?

II

It may be asked whether Western civilization is not also based on religious values. Greek art and culture, Roman law and organization, Christian religion and ethics, and scientific enlightenment are said to be the moulding forces of modern civilization. It will be useful if we consider the exact nature of the religious life of the West and the extent of its influence on Western civilization. At the risk of over-simplification, which is inevitable when we describe the development of centuries in a few paragraphs, it may be said that in the Western religious tradition three currents which frequently cross and re-cross can be traced. We may describe them for the sake of convenience as the Graeco-Roman, the Hebrew, and the Indian.

The Graeco-Roman has for its chief elements rationalism, humanism, and the sovereignty of the State. The spirit of speculation which questioned religious ideas and sought to follow truth regardless of the discomfort it might cause us started with the Greeks. Xenophanes fought hard to emancipate his people from superstition and lies. He preached against belief in gods who could commit acts which would be a disgrace to the worst of men. Democritus found the self-existent in the atom and Heraclitus in fire. The latter said: 'The world was made neither by one of the gods nor by man; and it was, is and ever shall be an ever-living fire, in due measure self-enkindled and in due measure self-extinguished.' Nothing is, everything is becoming. For Protagoras, man is the measure of all things, and as for God, He cannot be found even if He exists. He says: 'Concerning the gods I can say nothing, neither that they exist nor that they do not exist; nor of what form they are; because there are many things which prevent one from knowing that, namely, both the uncertainty of the matter and the shortness of man's life.' For Critias 'nothing is certain except that birth leads to death and that life cannot escape ruin'. According to Gorgias, every man was free to fix his own standard of truth. Unless Plato is wholly unfair, certain of the Sophists were prepared to justify philosophically the doctrine that might is right. The orthodox suspected even Socrates and accused him of impiety and corrupting the youth of Athens. Doubts run through the poetry of Euripides, the rationalism of the Stoics, the schools of the sceptics, and the materialism of the Epicureans. In spite of a different tendency, both the Stoics and the Epicureans adopted physical explanations of the universe. They treated the world, including man's soul, as something material.

Epicurus revived the atomic view of Democritus. He aimed at constructing a world on scientific principles to free men's minds from fear of the gods and the evils of superstition. Man's soul at death dissolves again into the atoms which made it. He conceded to popular beliefs when he admitted the existence of the gods, but they did nothing except serve as models of ideal felicity. They are indifferent to human affairs and so prayers to them are futile. Faith in gods could not last when gods were being made before men's eyes. The Ptolemies of Alexandria were freely spoken of as gods. In an inscription at Calchis as early as 196 B.C. Quinctius Flamininus was associated in inscriptions with Zeus, Apollo, Heracles, and the personified Roma. Julius Caesar received divine honours even in his life; and the day after his death, the Senate decreed that he should be treated as a god; in 44 B.C. a law was passed assigning him the title of *divus*, and the great Augustus dedicated in 29 B.C. the new temple of Divus Julius in the Forum.[1] All this confirmed the scepticism of Euhemerus that the gods were only great men deified.

Though classical Rome was far less speculative than Greece, it produced one of the greatest sceptics of antiquity, Lucretius. With the fervour of a religious enthusiast he attacked religion and hurled defiance and contempt on it. Through his poem *De Rerum Natura* he tried to free men's minds from the fears which beset and haunted them. He accustomed men to the idea of complete annihilation after death. In the early days of the Roman Empire even such an austere Stoic as Marcus Aurelius looked upon the Christian religion with fear and contempt. Independent thought was efficiently suppressed by the tyranny of the Church till the period of the Renaissance, though in the thirteenth century the Emperor Frederick II declared, if the story be true, that the world had been deceived by three impostors, Moses, Jesus, and Mohammad. Roger Bacon was a definitely sceptical thinker. Machiavelli in his *Prince* revived the old conception that religion is an instrument for keeping the people in subjection. He did not disguise his intense dislike

[1] See Cyril Bailey, *Phases in the Religion of Ancient Rome* (1932), pp. 138–40.

of Christianity. Rabelais (1690) was impatient with asceticism and conventional religion. Science in the Middle Ages was largely occultism and magic; nature was full of spirits and to meddle with it was to risk damnation. Friar Bacon was imprisoned as a sorcerer. The scientific movement of the sixteenth and seventeenth centuries, with such names as those of Copernicus, Kepler, Galileo, Harvey, and Newton, discouraged the supernatural explanations of natural phenomena and led to the conception of the universe as a great machine working by rigidly determined laws of causation. The thrill of new discoveries and mental activities raised great expectations. Men seemed to be on the eve of surprising the last secrets of the universe and building a stately fabric of enduring civilization. They seemed to become the lords of creation, though not the heirs of heaven. While some of the leading representatives of the scientific movement, like Descartes and Boyle, Bacon and Newton, were not anti-religious, the movement as a whole encouraged free thinking. The religious conflicts which followed the Reformation contributed to the growth of scepticism and wars. The Church was split up into a number of sects and disputes; persecutions and wars became more frequent. Montaigne (1533–92) was nominally a Catholic but was really an Agnostic. He says: 'Death is no concern of yours either dead or alive: alive because you still *are*; dead because you *are* no longer.' Leonardo da Vinci rejected every dogma that could not be tested and was a complete sceptic. Shakespeare was no better. J. R. Green writes: 'The riddle of life and death he leaves a riddle to the last, without heeding the theological conclusions around him.' For Francis Bacon 'the mysteries of the Deity, of the Creation, of the Redemption' are 'grounded only upon the word and oracle of God, and not upon the light of nature'.[1] Hobbes's scorn of supernaturalism and revealed religion is undisguised. All that we can legitimately say of God is that He is the unknown cause of the natural world, and so our highest duty consists in implicit obedience to the civil law. He reduced religion to a department of State and held that the sovereign power was absolute and irresponsible.[2] Locke defended theism more on

[1] *Advancement of Learning*, ii.

[2] See further, p. 388.

pragmatic grounds. It was necessary for social security. His work on *The Reasonableness of Christianity* aims at proving that the tenets of the Christian religion are in accordance with reason. It is assumed that their rationality is what makes them worthy of acceptance. So for him reason is a completely reliable source of knowledge and an infallible guide in the quest for certainty. But the materials on which reason works are provided not in a rational intuition which penetrates into real being but in sensation and reflection on sense data. If these are the only material for knowledge, it follows that religious truths lie beyond the scope of man's reason. Locke admits the reality of revealed knowledge, though he himself would prefer rational knowledge even in the realm of religion. He believes that the central conceptions of religion can all be proved rationally.[1] Toland, Locke's young Irish disciple, defends the deistic position and finds support for it in the Gospels.[2] 'All men will own the verity I defend if they read the sacred writings with that equity and attention that is due to mere humane works, nor is there any different rule to be followed in the interpretations of scripture from what is common to all other books.' The Deists contend that all the truths necessary for a religious life could be gained rationally and such a natural religion is the only one worthy of the respect of men. 'All the duties of the Christian religion', says Archbishop Tillotson, 'which respect God, are no other but what natural light prompts men to, excepting the two sacraments, and praying to God in the name and by the mediation of Christ.' 'And even these', Anthony Collins observes, 'are of less moment than any of those parts of religion which in their own nature tend to the Happiness of human Society.'[3] We cannot be sure that Christianity is a revealed religion, when no one

[1] 'Since the precepts of natural religion are plain, and very intelligible to all mankind, and seldom seem to be controverted; and other revealed truths which are conveyed to us by books and languages, are liable to the common and natural obscurities and difficulties incident to words: methinks it would become us to be more careful and diligent in observing the former, and less magisterial, positive and imperious in imposing our own sense and interpretations on the latter' (*Essay Concerning Human Understanding*, III. ix. 23).

[2] *Christianity not Mysterious*, II. iii. 22 (1696).

[3] *Discourse of Free-thinking* (1713), p. 136.

seems to know what is revealed or perhaps everybody seems to know that his own version of the faith is the true revelation and everything else a deadly error. The fact that the Bible is an inspired document has not prevented its official interpreters from disagreeing on all fundamentals. Deism developed, and the Deists are rationalists with a feeling for religion. Their rationalism took them away from orthodoxy and their religion kept them from atheism. According to some seventeenth-century Nonconformists a clergyman answered their demand for the scripture texts on which the Thirty-nine Articles were based by quoting 2 Timothy iv. 13: 'The cloak I left at Troas, . . . bring with thee, and the books, but especially the parchments.' If Timothy had not been remiss in executing St. Paul's command we would have had the parchments which provided the missing authority. When Anthony Collins was asked why, holding deistical opinions, he sent his servants to churches, he answered: 'That they may neither rob nor murder me!' Lord Bolingbroke considered Christianity a 'fable', but held that a statesman ought to profess the doctrines of the Church of England.[1] Thomas Woolston in his six *Discourses on the Miracles of Christ* (1727–9) maintained that the Gospel narratives were a 'tissue of absurdities'. Hume declared that miracles were impossible and accepted arguments for the existence of God were untenable. Baron d'Holbach stood for a materialistic conception of the universe and denied the existence of God and the immortality of the soul. Voltaire, Mr. Noyes tells us, was a theist, but there is no doubt that he was a bitter critic of the Church, which he looked upon as the instigator of cruelty, injustice, and inequality. Look at his prayer which breathes the humanitarianism of the French enlightenment:

'Thou hast not given us a heart that we may hate one another, nor hands that we may strangle one another, but that we may help each other to bear the burden of a wearisome and transitory life; that the small distinctions in the dress which covers our weak bodies, in our

[1] Leslie Stephen in his *English Thought in the Eighteenth Century* writes, referring to the later Deistic period: 'Scepticism widely diffused through the upper classes, was of the indolent variety, implying a perfect willingness that the Churches should survive though the Faith should perish' (vol. i, p. 375).

inadequate languages, in our absurd usages, in all our imperfect laws, in all our senseless opinions, in all our social grades, which to our eyes are so different and to thine so alike, that all the fine shades which differentiate the "atoms" called "men" may not be occasions for hate and persecution.'

He was certainly not an orthodox churchman. During an illness towards the close of his life he was visited by a priest, who summoned him to confession. 'From whom do you come?' inquired the sick man. 'From God', was the reply. When Voltaire desired to see his visitor's credentials, the priest could go no farther and withdrew. Diderot and the Encyclopaedists had unqualified contempt for conventional religion. Diderot cried out at the end of his *Interpretation of Nature*:

'O God, I ask nothing from Thee; if Thou art not, the course of nature is an inner necessity; and if Thou art, it is Thy command; O God, I know not whether Thou art, but I will think as though Thou didst look into my soul, I will ask as though I stood in Thy presence. . . . If I am good and kind, what does it matter to any fellow creatures whether I am such because of a happy constitution or by the free act of my own will or by the help of Thy Grace?'

There is little in common between Rousseau's sentimental theism and Christian orthodoxy. Leibniz rejoiced in the 'religion without revelation' of China. Kant tells us that there can be no theoretical demonstration of the existence of God, though we need Him for practical life. Hegelian dialectics have no place for a God to whom we can pray and offer worship. The Prussian State was for him 'the incarnation of the divine idea as it exists on earth'. National Socialism continues the Hegelian tradition and looks upon, not the Prussian State, but the Nordic race, as the ultimate and noblest self-expression of the cosmic intelligence. Its official philosopher, Herr Rosenberg, in his book on *The Myth of the Twentieth Century* (1930), makes it clear that he has no faith in the transcendent God of the theist. His deity is the human spirit and the racial society. Fichte in his *Addresses to the German Nation* developed at length the notion of an 'elect race'. His doctrine is continued in the work of Gobineau and his well-known theory of the inequality of human races. In Houston Stewart Chamberlain's *Foundations of the*

19th Century the racialist legend reappears in a pseudo-scientific setting. Rosenberg's *Myth* is the classic on the question. Each race has its particular soul in which its most intimate being is expressed. Its special virtues are regarded as the specific qualities of the blood. The human species is an abstraction: we have only a number of races determined by differences in the hereditary composition of the blood. Human races are not only diverse but of unequal value. The superior race is the Nordic. Its branches are to be recognized in the Amorites of Egypt, the Aryans of India, the Greeks of the early period, in the ancient Romans, and above all in all the Germanic peoples, whose chief representatives are the Germans. The spirit of this race is personified in the god Wotan, who embodies their spiritual energies. Contamination with inferior races is the great danger which menaces the superior race in all periods of universal history. India and Persia, Greece and Rome are witnesses to the process of racial degeneration. A religion of universalism is foreign to the Nordic race. Catholic religion, Freemasonry, Communism are the enemies of Nordic superiority. The Germanic soul will be manifested in the Third Reich with the symbol of the Swastika in place of the Cross. The aim of the National Socialist Party is to rescue from contamination and develop this precious Nordic element.

Lessing conceives the whole religious history of mankind as an experiment of divine pedagogy. He declares that accidental historical truths can never be the evidence for eternal and necessary rational truths. Hamann observes that Kant's moralism meant the deification of the human will and Lessing's rationalism the deification of man's reason. Nietzsche drew a distinction between the morality of masters and that of slaves. The Romans are for him the strong and the whole, the aristocratic and the noble. Christianity is the moral rebellion of the slaves based upon the resentment of the weak against the strong. Their victory over Rome was the victory of the sick over the healthy, of the slaves over the noble. Out of a feeling of resentment the slave decided to be the first in the Kingdom of Heaven. Auguste Comte put Humanity in the place occupied by God. A morality of service in a godless universe is the ideal of the positivists.

G. H. Romanes (1848–94) in his *A Candid Examination of Theism* writes: 'It is with the utmost sorrow that I find myself compelled to accept the conclusions here worked out: I am not ashamed to confess that, with the virtual negation of God, the universe has lost to me its soul of loveliness.' He later abandoned this position.[1] Even the Christian thinkers themselves tried to reinterpret Christianity. Schleiermacher reduced religion to a feeling of dependence on God. Ritschl meant by redemption the belief that God has revealed an ideal for man to work towards.[2] To many Christians their religion meant only love of man and unselfish service. Even though the orthodox may use the old terminology of grace, communion, and redemption, they stress only pure morality or humanitarian ethics. The works of Strauss and Renan, Karl Marx and Nietzsche, and the scientific doctrines of evolution have made atheism popular. A general tendency to irreligion is in the air. Unbelief is aggressive and ubiquitous.

The strain of scepticism has been a persistent feature of the Western mind. It takes many forms, modernism in religion, scientific humanism, or naturalism. Modernism is not confined to movements which assume that name. All those who wish at the same time to be traditionally religious and rational-minded are modernists in different degrees. In the Introduction to the Report of the Commission on Christian Doctrine in the Church of England the Archbishop of York writes:

> 'In view of my own responsibility in the Church I think it right here to affirm that I wholeheartedly accept as historical facts the Birth of our Lord from a Virgin Mother and the Resurrection of his physical body from death and the tomb. But I fully recognise the position of those who sincerely affirm the reality of our Lord's Incarnation without accepting one or both of these two events as actual historical occurrences, regarding the records rather as parables than as history, a presentation of spiritual truth in narrative form.'[3]

What we accept of revelation depends on our piety and intellectual conscience. The issue, however, relates not to

[1] See p. 389.

[2] 'By the Kingdom', according to Dr. A. E. Garvie, Ritschl means 'the moral ideal for the realization of which the members of the community bind themselves to one another by a definite mode of reciprocal action' (*Encyclopaedia of Religion and Ethics*, vol. x, pp. 812–20).

[3] *Doctrine in the Church of England* (1938), p. 12.

this or that item of belief but the way in which any part of the content of religion is arrived at and justified. It is not a question of the articles of belief but of the intellectual habits and methods. There is only one method for ascertaining fact and truth, the empirical method. While modernism and humanism are more or less compromises, dialectical materialism is its boldest expression. It has its own cosmogony, its own interpretation of the origin and nature of man, its own economic and social scheme, and its own religion. It proclaims a passionate plea for the spread of light steady and serene which will help us to get out of the darkness and barbarism of a monkish and deluded past, to shake off the imbecility of blind faith with its fogs and glooms, and get on to the broad highway of sanity, culture, and civilization. When we speak of heaven and God we 'give to airy nothing a local habitation and a name'. They are outworn superstitions, subjects of antiquarian interest. Religions have rendered a useful service in that they have exhausted all the wrong theories in advance. Everything can be explained in terms of matter and motion. Marx accepts the Hegelian view of an immanent reality unfolding itself by an inner dialectic. But he substitutes matter for Hegel's immanent spirit. Matter is invested with the power of self-movement, auto-dynamism. A self-determining movement whose highest expression is human personality is regarded as material, and the self of man is denied freedom and responsibility. Criminals and sinners who were once upon a time consigned to eternal damnation are capable of being turned into healthy and moral citizens, not by the grace of God, but by a supply of iodine to the thyroid. Hell or heaven depends on the twist of heredity or proportion of phosphorus. Even though man is a product of material forces, he is still deified. As the individual man is obviously too small to be deified, human society gets the honour.

With the Greeks, we reaffirm that the true line of progress lies in positive action, concrete reasoning, and public spirit. We oppose nature to custom and repudiate the latter as a fraud and an imposture. The elaborate framework of customs which we call morality, which we have built up in our rise from savagery, and to which we attribute an absolute value, is dismissed as a convention. Nature knows nothing of justice or mercy. It knows only the power of the stronger. The prospects of peace and brotherhood which religion holds up are only a mirage. To understand the factors and conditions which determine the life and health of societies we must turn to the realms of biology. The behaviour of man is not much different from that of a cell in the human organism. Strife and war are factors in the evolution of mankind. The funeral oration of Pericles sets the tone—the glorification of the State and death on the battle-field. In their argument with the men of Melos the Athenians proclaimed the doctrine that what serves the cause of Athens is not merely expedient but right, making themselves the ultimate arbiters of truth and falsehood, of right and wrong. The Christian religion has not been able to change this habit. 'All cannot be happy at once,' said Sir Thomas Browne in his *Religio Medici*, 'for the glory of one state depends upon the ruin of another.' 'Such is the condition of human affairs', said Voltaire, 'that to wish for the greatness of one's own country is to wish for the harm of its neighbours.' 'Always without exception', said Fichte, 'the most civilised State is the most aggressive.' Treitschke wrote: 'War will endure to the end of history. The laws of human thought and of human nature forbid any alternative, neither is one to be wished for.' 'Man is an animal of prey', says Spengler, and our dictators remind us that 'war is to man what motherhood is to women—a burden, a source of untold suffering and yet a glory'. Mussolini says: 'War alone brings up to its highest tension all human energy and puts the stamp of nobility upon the peoples who have the courage to meet it.' For Dr. Goebbels 'war is the most simple affirmation of life'. In the book *Bio-politics*, which Sir Arthur Keith places by the side of Adam Smith's *Wealth of Nations*,[1] it is said, 'War is unreasonable and so are earthquakes and disease. Profound and lasting peace is death; peace at its best is only an armistice. Peace is a tolerance—a reciprocal endurance.' And again, 'a subdued or latent hostility is a factor in all

[1] In a review of *Bio-politics, An Essay in the physiology, pathology and politics of the Social and Somatic Organism*, by Morley Roberts (*The Observer*, 16 Jan. 1938).

evolutionary progress'. Thus we are accustoming ourselves to the idea of war as a normal part of civilized life.

It is essential to recognize that in a large part of our lives we are materialists. We worship physical force and the machine; we have a passion for power. Power, not spirit, rules our planet. Humanitarianism is a form of self-indulgence, not an ideal. Communism in Russia and Mexico has openly repudiated religion. In Germany a new tribal religion is growing. In England, as usual, nothing is logically carried out. There are no saints as there are no atheists. There is neither active faith nor active unbelief. The cultivated Englishman's attitude to the Church is much the same as his attitude to monarchy. Even if he does not go to church or say his prayers, he respects the Church, as he does the monarchy, as hallowed venerable institutions. Orthodoxy is a matter of prudence. The British are pre-eminently a political people, and their political instinct tells them that old Plutarch was right when he urged that if a city would be an autonomous one, it must possess two things—God and a seat of local government, a church and a town-hall. They respect religion for its political value. If they go to church and kneel down in prayer, it is the tribute they pay to the social order; but such a view is bound to produce religious deadness. God may be or may not be. Either way it does not matter very much. Religious indifference, not denial, is the rule. The cultivated do not interfere with those who believe, even as they do not prevent children from playing nursery games.

III

The second current in Western religious life is the Jewish one. The great prophets are Israel's abiding glory, and their essential contribution to humanity is an ardent monotheism, the conception of the Supreme as a concrete living God whose thoughts and ways are not man's thoughts and ways.[1] The Jews believed not in a metaphysical absolute but in a personal God eternally acting and ceaselessly interested in His creatures, specially bound up with their own history. The spirit of the West with its emphasis on reason and exaltation of the State got mixed up with the Jewish elements and

[1] Isaiah lv. 8.

prevailed over the non-dogmatic and universal sides of the Christian faith which started as a revolt against the tribal and the intellectualist conceptions of the Supreme. The Semitic ideas—exclusiveness and particularism—appealed to the forceful instincts of the Western man, who expressed them in the Greek language and embodied them in Roman organization. For a time when the political fortunes of Europe were down, when the Roman world broke up, involving its populations in heavy losses and miseries, and exposing them to brutal barbarism, fear was on Europe and Christianity appealed to a weary and heavy-laden people. It came with healing in its wings for souls mortally afraid of life. But its whole spirit is foreign to the temper of Europe. The West has always believed that the race is to the swift and the battle to the strong. Meek natures might take refuge in flight or submission, but to the energetic and full-blooded, meekness is a contemptible and dangerous vice. Christianity with its cult of the simple life and emphasis on other-worldliness is the natural refuge of men who have lost faith in the material ends of life but will not give up faith in the spiritual. It caught Europe in a mood of depression and world-weariness, and so its message that the sun still shone in heaven, though on earth it was eclipsed, found a wide welcome. (See further, p. 389.)

Though it has been the religion of Europe all these centuries, it has not yet been perfectly assimilated by it. St. Paul's Epistles to the Corinthians show how far the patience and energy of the earliest apostles were taxed by their attempts to persuade their converts to put away earthly things. The victory of Christianity over the life of the West has always been a remote vision, and the history of the Christian Church is the record of the gradual adaptation of an Eastern religion to the Western spirit. It is not the pale Galilean that has conquered, but the spirit of the West. The ascetic creed of withdrawal from life rather than of participation in its fierce conflicts and competitions has been transformed. The Western races were not prepared to abandon the world or look upon its ends as impermanent. Their energies were too great, the natural man in them unsubduable.[1]

[1] See Dixon, *The Human Situation* (1937), pp. 37–8.

Jesus had an abhorrence of dogma and never encouraged the metaphysical and theological complications which are responsible for a good deal of casuistry, intolerance, and obscurantism. His chief opponents were the high priests and the pharisees, who insisted on salvation by orthodoxy alone. In both the Catholic and the Protestant forms, though in different degrees, Christianity has become a religion of authority, finding its seat in a tradition believed to be supernaturally imparted. Instead of the contemplation of the formless we have the definitization of the deity in the personal God or His incarnation. Instead of indifference to rites and formulas, we have the greatest insistence on them. Though Jesus paid little attention to organization, elaborate ecclesiastical structures have emerged from His teaching. In the effort to establish a kingdom not of this world, the most realistic of ecclesiastical organizations has been built up on earth. The teaching of Jesus had for its aim the making of spiritual souls who are above the battle of creeds and of nations, but it is used to make loyal members of the Church.

There is the emphasis on the material ends of life. Religion is treated as a means for procuring worldly peace and prosperity in this life and escaping hell and winning heaven in the next. The worship of the State has come down to us from Greece and Rome, and we have made religion into a national institution, allying itself with political causes. The interpretation of God's will at the Council of Clermont (A.D. 1095) as a behest to go forth and slaughter the Saracens marks the victory of the European West over the crucified Jesus. Religion is employed to sanctify human passions. The tragedy of man is keenest when his love of power puts on the garb of spiritual dignity. Of all fetters, worldliness assuming the garb of religion is the most difficult to break. It is the unseen enemy of true religion, the invisible assassin who is not recognized as such, and is therefore more subtle and dangerous. A religion ceases to be a universal faith if it does not make universal men.

A contemplative spiritual religion becomes a dogmatic secular one, a system of belief and ceremony, which produces sentiments and emotions but fails to change men's lives. Let us briefly trace the process of this transformation.

When Rome entered into the inheritance of Alexander and his successors and established an empire over all the known Western world, she did not institute any inquisition into men's religious beliefs so long as they did not interfere with the administration of the State. If certain major rules relating to matters of property and contract were observed, and if private wars and brigandage were avoided, men were free to hold any beliefs, and practise any rites they pleased; only they should not outrage the conscience of the ruling caste. There was no worship common to the whole State except that of the emperor. In course of time Christianity, which had all the qualities of a mystery religion, was accepted by the people. Adopting the practice of the mystery cults, the Church, which was endowed with a personality, claimed due authority to teach and admit into its membership by specific forms of initiation those who wished to join it and were found worthy. It traced its foundation to a God-man, and its officers claimed to derive their authority through appointment by the founder, who gathered a small group for that specific purpose. In unbroken succession from this group are descended, it is said, the officers who hold sway over the whole body of Christians. The Church was a strict corporation, a secret society like that for the celebration of the mysteries called *ecclesia*, with its own initiation ceremonies, rites of sacrifice (the Eucharist), baptism, the laying on of hands, and confession. All over the empire a number of small organizations grew up, each called a church, presided over by an Episkopos or bishop. The Church as a whole included them all. Soon the *ecclesia* developed a body of writings which it preserved for the instruction of its members and the continuity of doctrine. When controversies developed in regard to doctrine, the Church had to decide what was the true Christian tradition. These doctrines were later sifted and a certain number of them were accepted as scripture, inspired and authoritative. The process was more spontaneous than deliberate. The Canon of the New Testament included the Four Gospels, a few letters written by the missionaries of the early Church called Epistles, one record of the early Apostolic action called the Acts of the Apostles, and one work of prophetic vision known as the

Apocalypse. When St. Paul and the Apostles refer to the 'scripture' they mean the sacred writings of the Jewish Church known to us as the Old Testament. Free thinking was not encouraged. Tertullian criticizes severely the thesis of Clement of Alexandria that philosophy is a *praeparatio evangelica* as genuine as Old Testament revelation: 'What kinship has the Christian with philosophy,' he exclaims in a well-known passage, 'the Child of God with the Child of Greece?'[1] One of the reasons which led to the success of Christianity was its dogmatism. Men had grown weary and disinclined to seek farther. Any creed that promised to calm the troubled mind, give certainty in place of doubt, a final solution for a host of perplexing problems, found a ready welcome. Sick with the hesitations of thought men turned greedily to a cult which gave them theology instead of philosophy, dogma instead of logic. Reason could not promise or give happiness here or hereafter; religion offered the assurance of happiness, at least beyond the grave. Attempts, however, were made to reconcile Christian tradition with Greek thought, through what has come to be known as the Logos theology. Justin Martyr (*c.* A.D. 155) followed the Fourth Gospel and identified Jesus with the Eternal Logos. This started the theological problem of the person of Jesus and His relation to God. The Logos theology was widely accepted in spite of the difficulties. When the Church became a State within a State, it came into conflict with the civil power. This difficulty disappeared when Constantine accepted Christianity. But a theological crisis arose. Arius, in his anxiety to preserve the unity of the godhead, explained the conception of the Logos in a way which provoked great opposition. He held that the Word was the master of creation and was therefore more than man, and as the creator of all other things He could rightly be called God. But as the Son He was less than the Father. Since He was begotten He was in some sense a creature and was certainly not eternal. Though He was formed before time itself began, yet there must have been a time when He was not. He was obviously subject to pain and change, but remained good by the exercise of His will. Knowing from the beginning that

[1] *Apol.* 46.

this would be so, the Father had adopted Him proleptically as His Son. The Spirit is related to the Son as the Son to the Father. A council of bishops was summoned at Nicea, near Constantinople, to discuss and define the full doctrine of Christ's divinity, for the Arian Controversy split the Church into warring factions. Unity was the essence of the matter and dissent was not tolerated. The enemy of God was looked upon as the enemy of Caesar. Creeds and confessions developed to make sure that new candidates for admission into the *ecclesia* were not tainted with heresy. Athanasius opposed the idea of the created Logos and affirmed that Jesus was God by nature. Faith in God-man was for him the essence of the Christian religion. Here are the words of the Athanasian Creed:

'Furthermore, it is necessary to everlasting salvation: that we also believe rightly the Incarnation of our Lord Jesus Christ.

'For the right Faith is, that we believe and confess: that our Lord Jesus Christ, the Son of God, is God and Man;

'God, of the Substance of the Father, begotten before the worlds: and Man, of the Substance of his Mother, born in the world;

'Perfect God, and perfect Man: of a reasonable soul and human flesh subsisting;

'Equal to the Father, as touching his Godhead; and inferior to the Father, as touching his Manhood.

'But although He be God and Man: Yet he is not two, but one Christ.'

The strife between Arius and Athanasius still continues in the hearts of men. Athanasius weaned the Church from her traditions of tolerance and scholarship, of Clement and Origen. Nicene orthodoxy gained victory over Hellenistic and heretical systems. Those who had a natural bent for speculative doubt exercised their scepticism on Christian dogmas.[1] Soon after, Origen was condemned by the Church. Theological speculation became a servant of the tradition of Justinian, who closed the schools at Athens, codified the law, and restored the Byzantine Church. Learning was lost, and with it the capacity for speculation. In proselytizing the pagans Christianity absorbed many of the pagan beliefs

[1] In the opinion of Chrysostom, Archbishop of Constantinople in the fifth century, the number of Christian bishops who would be saved bore a very small proportion to those who would be damned.

and practices and obscured the simplicity and rationality of the faith of Jesus. In its anxiety to spread, Christianity used the language of every race and class and country.[1] It seemed to be all things to all men. By its sacramental doctrine, its encouragement of relics and charms, by its cults of saints and martyrs it lost its distinctiveness. Its hierarchical organization became stronger in administration than in religion.

In the Dark Ages, which may be regarded as extending from the end of the fifth century to the establishment of feudalism in the eleventh century, Europe weltered in ignorance and misery and lived in constant peril and pressure.

In the Middle Ages, eleventh, twelfth, and thirteenth centuries, faith was dominant and doubt was suppressed. The ecclesiastical tyranny was so ubiquitous that it was perilous to breathe a word against accepted dogmas. Authority was supreme and the Inquisition was actually established at the beginning of the thirteenth century. The heretic was the enemy more than the infidel. In Spain under the Moorish caliphs, Averroes, the Moslem thinker, developed an independent movement which was suppressed by Pope John XXI. The Church endeavoured by the stake and the thumbscrew to preserve the faith once delivered to the saints and became alienated from the spirit of Jesus. If He had returned to Europe in the Middle Ages, He would certainly have been burnt alive for denying the dogmas about His own nature. During three centuries, three hundred thousand persons were put to death for their religious opinions in Madrid alone. The lurid fancies of theologians about the torture chambers of Gehenna did not outrage their moral feelings. Since they thought these were permitted by divine justice, they did not shrink from adopting refinements

[1] 'Except with regard to its fundamental tenets, it adapted itself to the needs and customs of the various nations. In the famine-stricken regions of Anatolia its preachers promised a heaven with ever-bearing fruit trees; for the overworked serfs in Egypt it provided refuges in monasteries; to the Berber mountaineers of Africa it gave a holy cause for crusading, especially against rich and oppressive landowners; to educated Romans, like Minucius Felix and Lactantius, it permitted the reading of Cicero and Virgil, nor did it attempt to deprive the real Greeks of Homer and Plato' (Tenney Frank, *Aspects of Social Behaviour in Ancient Rome*, p. 63).

of cruelty in human affairs. This period saw the rise of the universities, parliaments, and the Gothic cathedrals, as well as the Crusades.

Philosophy in the Middle Ages was scholasticism, and the greatest of the schoolmen was Thomas Aquinas. He attempted to reconcile philosophy with religion, Aristotelian wisdom with Catholic orthodoxy. It is difficult to summarize a metaphysical system which is so massive and closely knit as Thomas's, but its central features may be briefly set down. St. Thomas conceives reality as an ordered hierarchy of existence ranging from God, whose being is wholly from Himself, who is in no sense corporeal, and who is perfect actuality. God alone is pure being, pure Act; all other existents are individual but imperfect and owe their real but limited status to Him who alone truly is. In Him there is neither limitation nor contingency. He exists by His very essence. His being is the condition of all our thinking. From motion and change or becoming we can argue to an unmoved mover, from the causal series to a first cause, from the contingent to independent necessary being, from the gradation of excellences in limited beings to supreme excellence in the highest being, and from the purposiveness and government of the world to the highest person. The existence of matter is wholly dependent on higher orders of being, its essence is pure corporeality, its natural mode is that of wholly undetermined potency. The world is not an undifferentiated chaos or an insuperable dualism. The lower orders of being are not mere shadows or emanations of the reality from which they derive their existence but are distinct and discontinuous. Each order of being has its own characteristic functions and modes. We can argue from one to another only on the principle of analogy, not that of identity. Through this analogical reasoning we can pass from sensible existence to the source of all existence or pure being. Even though we cannot know God by the direct operations of reason, we are not altogether helpless, since analogy provides the means. It follows that we must know the truth about the sensible universe which our minds are capable of fully apprehending, if we would rise to the intelligible. For this reason the entire Aristotelian system is taken over as a complete account of all that reason had hitherto been able to attain by the study of nature. By a consideration of the implications of things we can reach the conception of God, as a metaphysical being with the attributes of intelligence, will, and goodness, but it is only revelation that gives us His triune character.

Man is altogether different from God. His place in the scheme is intermediate between non-intelligent matter, on the one hand, and pure intelligences, on the other. On the principle of analogy, it is asserted that his perfection is wholly distinct from that of the brutes or the angels. As a being composed of soul and body, man should not aim at either an animal or an angelic life. God is the end to which all things move, but each order of existence has its own mode of reaching that perfection. The life of man is incomplete if the faculty of intelligence which he shares with other beings does not attain its natural development. Contemplation of truth is the highest end of man and that requires bodily health, freedom from the disturbance of passions achieved by moral virtues. St. Thomas is definite that a human life is not the divine, and therefore sense-pleasures, though not the whole of human good, are genuinely a part of it. The body is relevant to human perfection. It is by no means a fetter of the soul. He affirms that the beatific vision requires a beatified consciousness (*lumen gloriae*) which is distinct from ordinary consciousness (*lumen naturale*) and prophetic consciousness (*lumen gratiae*). Even then the divine essence will not be comprehended. By the contemplative life, St. Thomas means 'the life of study and passion for truth'.[1] It is not an intuitive vision of the divine essence. On earth it is impossible for us to have a direct vision of God. A partial knowledge of God by mental images (*phantasmata*) is all that can be had. If Moses and St. Paul received the divine vision in their ecstasy, it only shows that ecstasy is not impossible or contrary to nature.[2] Athanasius

[1] Dom Chapman, *Encyclopaedia of Religion and Ethics*, vol. ix, p. 96.

[2] Dr. Kirk says: 'For lesser beings than Moses and St. Paul, such as St. Peter and David, he provides two kinds of ecstasy in which the contemplation of God is less remote from that which the ordinary class may hope to achieve in this life' (*The Vision of God* (1931), p. 392).

admitted that the soul is in its own nature destined for and capable of the direct beatific vision and that its condition is purity of heart.[1] St. Thomas does not agree. For St. Thomas, good life is one of obedience to the law. Wrong-doing is the violation of it. It is assumed that the commands of God are not arbitrary and capricious.

When we look upon morality as mere conformity to commands imposed on us by external authority and obeyed in the last resort not from any sense of the intrinsic goodness of the act commanded, but because it is commanded and disobedience will mean unpleasant consequences, it becomes a species of self-seeking. To make virtue a means to the avoidance of unhappiness in after-life is to degrade it, and that is what the medieval theologians did with their lurid pictures of future torments. Superstitious legends grew up and indulgences were turned into something like a mechanical service. Men believed in buying spiritual benefits as we buy drugs from a store. Ecclesiastical endowments, which covered a good proportion of the surplus wealth of the country, came to be treated as private fortunes in which men could invest as in stocks and shares. They could buy prebends or abbacies for their children.

Scholasticism kept alive intellectual vigour. By its powers of definition and subtle inference, and its intellectual energy, it nourished the roots of scientific culture. Copernicus is said to have conceived the hypothesis of the movement of the earth round the sun as a mere inference from the doctrine of the Trinity. Towards the end of the Middle Ages we have an increasing knowledge of the world by science and discovery. Men were filled with vitality and the spirit of adventure.

At the beginning of the fourteenth century signs of decline of faith became evident and the authority of the Pope was contested. Doubts of doctrine as well as of titles to authority increased, but the dogmatists always are conservative and disciplinary, not progressive and prophetic. Authority, when it is most powerful, acts like a ruthless mechanism, an almost organized opposition to the values of life and spirit. In the fifteenth and sixteenth centuries there was a regular reign of terror in the name of religion.

[1] *Contra Gentes*, 3.

European society became more and more unstable. We find ourselves in a fierce and warring world of jarring sects, furious controversies, and revolting persecutions. The spread of the scientific spirit disturbed men's minds on doctrine even as corruption among the clergy threw doubt on the validity of the sacraments. A sacrament is not valid if the person administering it is not in a state of grace. This led to the belief that the sacramental power of the clergy was an illusion. The movement led by Wycliffe in England was motived by this idea. There was great resentment against the abuse of Church property. Even the masses were affected by doubts of the Real Presence. The cult of relics, payments of alms, abuse of indulgences and masses for the dead suggested to the popular mind a kind of religious barter, the buying and selling of spiritual power. The opposition expressed itself through the Reformation, when Christendom became a house divided against itself. When Luther and other reformers rejected certain doctrines and opposed certain practices maintained by the Roman Church they did so taking their stand on the scripture, especially the New Testament. The controversy revolved round the ground of belief. While the Roman Church maintained that men believed its doctrines because they were declared to be true by an infallible Church interpreting an infallible Book, the Protestant Scholastics rejected the tradition and accepted the Book. They were both agreed on one point, that an infallible external authority is essential for belief. When once this position of the inability of man to interpret for himself the witness of God is accepted, the Catholic position is sounder and truer than the Protestant. We cannot take our stand on a Book, the whole Book, and nothing but the Book. Are its different parts equally inspired and therefore equally authoritative? Are they due to a human author or the inspiration of the Holy Spirit? Do they contain a complete, consistent, and coherent system of doctrine? If so, what is it? Luther said: 'We have a right touchstone for testing all books in observing whether they witness to Christ or not.' Also: 'What does not teach Christ is not apostolic even though St. Peter or Paul teach it. Again, what preaches Christ, that would be apostolic, though Judas,

Hannas, Pilate and Herod did it.' While the Catholic tradition gives us an infallible interpretation of an infallible Book, the Protestant Churches speak in an uncertain voice and give a hundred different answers. They oscillate between two extremes which are both central to their position, unconditional assent to an external authority, and the right of free judgement. The spirit of science requires us to admit that truth is not what is stated in a book or what is asserted by a Church, but what is in accord with reality. The Protestant Reformation was to lead to a new interpretation of the creeds in accordance with the principles of universal religion, to help us to find out what is true and good not by the teachings of tradition but by the light of reason and conscience. This essential trait of the Reformation has not even now fulfilled all its promise. Early Protestantism, however, had for its avowed aim the foundation of a religious system which should be as dogmatic and exclusive as the one which it assailed and which should represent more faithfully the teaching of the early Church. Luther's lecture on *The Epistle to the Romans* (1515–16) begins with the words: 'The essence of this Epistle is the complete destruction and eradication of all wisdom and righteousness of the flesh, however great these may seem in the eyes of man and to ourselves, and however sincere and upright they may be, and the planting and firm establishment of sin whatever the degree of its absence or apparent absence.' To be saved we must learn to despair of ourselves. Dogmatism remains: only the universalism disappears. The Catholic European God became nationalized. Luther asked, 'What have we Germans to do with St. Peter?' God was becoming a German deity. The Churches themselves took on a national colour. Luther's words 'that there is a vast difference between Papists, Turks, Jews, and us who have the word' prove that the spirit of dogmatism was not deficient in him.

Calvin erected a new Church with a well-developed doctrine. The divine will is supreme. Man's good deeds are of no effect towards the salvation of his soul, as they do not proceed from his soul. The sovereignty of God and the predestination of man were Calvin's chief doctrines. The sovereignty of God is pressed to the point of excluding any freedom in man. The individual can do nothing to change his fore-ordained final end. If we are born to be saved, we will respond to the call: if to be damned, we cannot respond. Of his own nature man is inclined only to evil. This view of the total depravity of man's nature logically tended to an exaltation of unnaturalness of living. 'If heaven is our country, what is the earth but our place of exile? If to depart out of the world is to enter into life, what is the world but a sepulchre? What is a continuance in it but absorption in death? We must learn to hate this terrestrial life, that it make us not prisoners to sin.'[1] Calvinism provided the framework of the new Protestant movement which spread over Europe, almost for a time dominating England, and becoming the established system in Scotland.

With the break-up of the feudal organization of society, competitive spirit and the profit motive covered the whole field of man's activities. The early Christian thinkers insist that earthly possessions should be reduced to a minimum and man must learn to despise the vanity of this world, but in the practice of Calvinism the pursuit of wealth, once regarded as perilous to the soul, acquired a new sanctity. Covetousness is not such a great danger to the soul as sloth. Paul's exhortation, 'not slothful in business', was interpreted as meaning that commercial prosperity and not poverty is meritorious. With the rise of the new science, the opportunities for capitalist enterprise increased. A soulless system of economics and the building of empires involving the subjection of vast populations received the blessing of the Church.[2] The use of force in the interests of trade and

[1] *Inst.* iii. 9. 4

[2] Cf. Max Weber, *Protestant Ethics and the Spirit of Capitalism*. This writer argues that the capitalist system of modern days has grown out of the Protestant Reformation, more especially out of the Calvinistic theology and attitude to life. In his Foreword, Professor R. H. Tawney states these conclusions thus: 'The pioneers of the modern economic order were, he argues, parvenus, who elbowed their way to success, in the teeth of the established aristocracy of land and commerce. The tonic that braced them for the conflict was a new conception of religion which taught them to regard the pursuit of wealth as not merely an advantage but a duty. . . . What is significant is not the strength of the motive of economic self-interest, which is a commonplace of all ages and demands no explanation. It is the change of moral standards which converted a natural frailty into an ornament of the spirit, and canonized as the

empire was sanctioned by religion. Cromwell could feel that he was called of God to lead his Ironsides against the tyranny of kings. With the rise of the new machinery and the facilities for transport, social checks on wealth diminished in efficacy, and by the end of the eighteenth century capitalism grew up, and became all powerful in the nineteenth century. The vast masses slowly became conscious of their misery and prepared for revolt. Christianity under Calvin's followers supported the capitalist régime and condoned the growing evils and the mechanization of life.

In religion, hatred of Catholic and Protestant grew up. Wars of religion increased. The savageries of the Inquisition and the massacre of St. Bartholomew and the intrigues of religious teachers such as Luther, Calvin, and Knox showed how religiously Christians could hate one another simply because they bore different labels.

While religion was adjusted in practice to national needs, doctrinally it remained narrow and persecuting. Servetus (1511–33) was burnt alive on a slow fire on the hill of Champel overlooking the lake at Geneva. Protestant leaders who were opposed to Calvin expressed their approval. Even the gentle and humane Melanchthon expressed his delight at the execution of the heretic Servetus as 'a pious and memorable example for all posterity'.[1] Religion became a useful ally of the despotic State. These features of narrowness and intolerance in theory and accommodation to political and economic policies of the State in practice have characterized both the Catholic and the Protestant developments.

Fundamentalism is again to the fore and it is not confined to America. There are new dogmatisms which would rehabilitate the authority of gospel, Church, or creed and effectively quench the spirit. We have in Karl Barth a crusader and a fundamentalist. For him humanism and modernism are the heresies. They seem to commit the grave offence of ignoring the sinfulness of man and the gulf that divides

economic virtues habits which in earlier ages had been denounced as vices. The force which produced it was the creed associated with the name of Calvin. Capitalism was the social counterpart of Calvinistic theology' (p. 2).

[1] See also a letter from Melanchthon to Calvin in J. B. Kidd, *Documents of the Continental Reformation* (1911), p. 647.

him from God. 'For what has actually happened', he says in his *Credo*, 'is that man has made himself master, would like, under the signature "Jesus Christ", to become himself a complete whole, would like himself to speak the creative word and be the living spirit, would like himself to forgive sins and sanctify himself.' And again: 'God never and nowhere becomes world. The world never and nowhere becomes God. God and world remain over against each other.' 'The uniqueness of God is not a religious postulate nor a philosophical idea, but something that corresponds exactly to the uniqueness of God's revelation.'[1] Revelation is God's own self-disclosure. It is something inaccessible except to faith, which is itself a divine gift. Those who adopt this view quote scripture in defence. When Peter confesses, 'You are the Christ, the Son of the living God', Jesus answers, 'You are a blessed man, Simon Barjona, for it was my Father in heaven, not flesh and blood, that revealed this to you.'[2] If flesh and blood could reveal it, it would be human knowledge. It is thus inevitable that Barth should refuse to compromise with modern thought or to bring Christianity 'up to date'. 'It is forced down my throat', he says, 'that the Dogmatic theologian is under the obligation to "justify" himself in his utterances before philosophy. To that my answer is likewise, No. . . . All our activities of thinking and speaking can only have a secondary significance and, as activities of the creature, cannot possibly coincide with the truth of God that is the source of truth in the world.'[3] I do not suppose that any one wishes to exalt the undivine self to the divine status. To realize the self, one requires self-control, self-denial, not self-indulgence. Barth condemns the attempt of theology to satisfy the rational mind of man by reasoned justifications of what it has accepted from faith. For Barth it is a disservice to religion to try to illuminate it by arguments from philosophy. The proper duty of the theologian is to see how far the proclamations of the Church are in conformity with scripture. 'Holy Scripture is the object of our study, and at the same time the criterion of our study of the church's past.

[1] *Credo*, p. 15.
[2] Matthew xvi. 16 and 17.
[3] *Apol.* 46.

As I read the writings of the "fathers", the witness of Holy Scripture stands continually before my eyes; I accept what interprets this witness to me: I reject what contradicts it. So a choice is actually made, certainly not a choice according to my individual taste, but according to my knowledge of Holy Scripture.' These are sentiments that could have been expressed by the first reformers or by Calvin.

Brünner in his *Philosophy of Religion* takes up a stand against Schleiermacher's view that 'the true nature of religion is immediate consciousness of the deity as he is found in ourselves and the world' and defends Protestant dogma. Revelation is the intrusion of divine power into the stream of history. The gulf between God and nature is wide. There are no pathways to God from the side of human nature. Man can only wait for the hour when God in His infinite mercy will claim him as His own. Man is completely alienated from divinity and cannot therefore take even the first steps towards a spiritual life. If ultimate convictions rest on revelation and not reason, it is not easy to distinguish the revelation from its doctrinal setting. The supra-doctrinal character of the prophetic religion of Biblical realism is the faith that Jesus is the Son of the Living God. We know in the Qur'ān, which is the basis of the Muslim faith, Jesus' sonship, his death on the Cross, and such doctrines as the Trinity, Reconciliation, or Atonement are repudiated in the name of Revelation. To reject Christianity is a part of the religious creed of Islam; to admit Christianity would be to repudiate Islam as an error. Such dogmatisms are the vehicles of human pride and not humility. Faith cannot be opposed to reason. It has no power to overrule conscience and intellect.

The weakness of these narrow orthodoxies is a spiritual cowardice, the failure to face realities. They are likely to destroy religion altogether.

The heroic stand which the Confessional Churches are making against the encroachments of the State is much appreciated, but in our admiration we should not forget that under the leadership of Karl Barth the liberal Christianity of the pre-war days which tried to combine the spirit of the Renaissance and the Enlightenment with the legacy of the past is killed. For over a hundred years before the War, under the influence of men like Kant and Hegel, Schleiermacher and Ritschl, Herder and Hermann, Christian theology tried to come to terms with modern thought. For them the knowledge of God was the knowledge of man at his best. Barth declares that Christianity cannot lay claim to absolute supernatural truth so long as it tries to compromise with humanism, liberalism, psychology, and philosophy of religion. Even the Catholic Church tries to build half-way houses between Christianity and Plato (Augustine) or Aristotle (Aquinas). But Barth deprecates all attempts at the adjustment between reason and revelation.

As a Protestant, Barth denies the claims of the Roman Church:

> 'The Tridentinum which recognized tradition as source of revelation in the same manner as Holy Scripture, and the Vaticanum with its dogma of the infallibility of the Pope signify the self-apotheosis of the Church, which is one of the most serious and enormous errors of the Roman Catholic Church. In contrast to that the Reformation Scripture-principle placed the Church permanently under the authority of the prophetic-apostolic Bible-word.'[1]

In spite of their opposition to each other, the Dialectical Theology of Karl Barth and the National Socialism of Hitler are the religious and political expressions of a common reaction against liberalism which is so evident on all sides of German life. Both are based on the Hebrew view of history as a sequence of mighty acts of the Creator leading up to a long-foreseen and intended climax. Barth argues that the highest act of revelation was in Jesus; the Nazi adds that the revelation was not closed then. The type of mind is the same in both. If Barthian theology is less effective than Nazism, it is because its Church has not the temporal authority of a Führer. It calls upon us to cling confidingly to the account of the universe given by the Church, and has little if any conception of the logical and ethical values other than those proper to its own world. The attraction of such a message is natural, though it cannot be lasting. In a world in which there is perpetual unrest and no abiding city, where there are no fixed standards and no goal whither all are striving,

[1] *Credo*, pp. 179–80.

the man of one idea has an opportunity to make his voice heard above the din of the cavalcade, but he will not be heard for long. Heaven is not a totalitarian State with concentration camps for unbelievers. There are many mansions in it to suit different tastes. The new German Faith is an answer to orthodoxy. If only a new and vital form of spiritual Christianity had arisen in Germany to capture the minds of post-war youth, the German Faith movement would not have had such success. National Socialism by its decree of toleration that each can choose his way to blessedness shows itself to be more liberal at least in religious matters than the orthodox Churches.[1]

The revolt against the Church in Germany is not to be explained exclusively by the political motive. Professor Hauer says:

> 'Christianity claims to possess the absolute truth, and with this claim is bound up the idea that men can only achieve salvation in one way, through Christ, and that it must send to the stake those whose faith and life do not conform, or pray for them till they quit the error of their ways for the Kingdom of God. Of course there is a difference between sending men to the stake and praying for them. But the attitude which lies behind both is much the same at bottom. In both cases the whole stress is laid on forcibly rescuing the man of another faith from the peril of hell fire into which the pursuit of his own path would inevitably plunge him.'[2]

Just as these varying creeds divide the world, they divide the people of the countries. We have the conflicts of Hindus and Muslims, Protestants and Catholics. Religion in Germany is represented by two sharply opposed creeds, Catholic and Protestant, which divide men's hearts from their infancy. If the nationalist leaders in their anxiety to weld the people into a unity cry 'a plague on both your houses', it is not unintelligible. Professor Hauer, who spent some years in India as a Christian missionary, is much impressed by the

[1] 'No National Socialist may suffer any detriment on the ground that he does not profess any particular faith or confession, or on the ground that he does not make any religious profession at all. Each man's faith is his own affair for which he answers to his own conscience alone. Compulsion may not be brought to bear in matters of conscience' (Decree of 13 Oct. 1933, *Germany's New Religion* (1937), p. 32). See also Reichsminister Kerrl, *Religion and Philosophy of Life* (1938), p. 3.

[2] *Germany's New Religion*, p. 45.

Hindu attitude of toleration. He says: 'If the attitude and the conviction, that there is only one road to truth and one way to God, form an inalienable characteristic of Christianity, then Christianity is fundamentally opposed to the German genius.'[1] He accepts also the religious presuppositions of this attitude. In Hinduism the attitude of freedom and generosity to other faiths is bound up with the conviction that the religious life has its source and certainty in the eternal deeps of man's soul. Professor Hauer says: 'We who hold the German faith are convinced that men, and especially the Germans, have the capacity for religious independence, since it is true that every one has an immediate relation to God, is, in fact, in the depths of his heart one with the eternal ground of the world.' The doctrines of the completeness of God's transcendence and the corruption of human nature when exclusively stressed do not find an answering echo in the human soul. Possibly the upholders of Dialectical Theology were led to the position when they witnessed the helplessness of man in the last war. We can derive help only from above. A passionate sense of man's weakness led the fundamentalists to doctrinal obscurantism.

But the new German faith reverts to type when it affirms that an individual's religion is determined by his race and stock, and that as long as he follows the peculiar religious instincts of his own race, he achieves as much knowledge of God as is possible for him. Whatever truth this principle has is perverted when attempts are made to purify German life from everything non-Aryan and therefore Semitic Christianity. To hold that the will of the nation is the will of God is opposed to the spirit of religion, though, along with credalism, nationalism has always been imposed on Christianity.

Both the Greek and the Semitic religions look upon God as a useful ally of political groups. Zeus protects the Greeks and Yahweh the Jews. We call upon God to further our plans and frustrate our enemy's. Sophocles makes Philoctetes pray:

> But, O my fatherland
> And all ye gods who look on me, avenge,
> Avenge me on them all in time to come,
> If ye have pity on me.[2]

[1] *Germany's New Religion*, p. 45.

[2] Plumptre's E.T.

Electra cries in the *Choephoroe*: 'Right against the unrighteous I demand, suffering against the wrongdoers.' For the Jews it is well known that God is the Lord of Hosts. Our national anthems breathe the same spirit. Two different lines are adopted in this matter of using religion for our practical ends. If we are a little conscientious and feel the disparity between our professions and practice, we affirm that we should not mix up religion and life. It would be to spoil two good things. But if religion is to live at all, it must be fitted into the framework of life, be in intimate relation with our occupations and judgements. The withdrawal of religion from life does not receive much support.

The more general tendency is to reduce religion to the level of our practice, to argue that the pattern of our civilization is, if not completely religious, at least on the way to it. Even though we have costly and magnificent churches and gorgeous ritual and music, we are not quite so brazen as to say that our commerce and athletics, our selfish nationalism and international anarchy are religious. Among both individuals and nations we admire the rich and the successful, and the strong and the powerful. Any one who has not at least five hundred a year is a figure to be sneered at, and any weak nation which believes in selflessness in others is to be pitied, for it deserves to be wiped out, off the map. If any people are unwilling to convert their corporate manhood into a military arm, they are decadent. To succeed in life, we must believe in life and its values, which are economic success and political power. By a multitude of sophisms we persuade ourselves that God expects us to believe in them and will help us if we pursue them with vigour and enterprise and deceit and cunning, if necessary. Whatever we do, we do in the name of God. We seize our opportunities and thank God for them. We strike down our enemies and thank God for aid. We take risks, meet danger half-way, push our way along, exploit people, and build empires, and thank God for them. The British are committed to the rule of half the world and will fight to defend it, for they are sure that they are doing God's work. If they relinquish their heritage they are not certain that it will get into cleaner hands and the will of God and the ideals of humanity will be better served.

Hitler says: 'The blessing of the Lord is with Germany and not with her enemies.'[1] Whatever he does, he does as the servant of Providence. The devotion in Spain to the bull-ring is so great that the arena is described as 'the sands of God'.[2] Dr. Alfred Rosenberg in *The Myth of the Twentieth Century* rejects the dogmas of the Catholic Church and sets up a new German faith which requires the love of fellow men to be subordinated to the honour of the nation. The Pope blesses the Italian aggression in Abyssinia and shows himself to be a priest, not of the Catholic Church, but of the Italian nation.

A welter of superstitions and taboos, primitive myths and unhistorical traditions, unscientific dogmatisms and national idolatries, constitutes the practising religion of the vast majority of mankind to-day.

IV

It would by no means be a triumph divine or human if atheistic Communism of Russia were to be overcome by the exclusive religions. Opposition to both these extremes is perhaps the greatest tribute that a mind of any spirituality can render to God. If we are to work our way to a larger measure of moral and spiritual unity, we must avoid mere oscillation between the extremes and seek truth in its ultimate depths.

The mystic tradition has been a persistent one in the religious life of the West. Its origins, as we have seen, may possibly be traced to India. Professor F. Heiler observes that

'the history of religion knows only three great independent currents of development, which may possibly go back to two. There runs an unbroken chain from the Ātman-Brahman mysticism of the Vedic upaniṣads to the Vedānta of Śaṁkara on the one side and on the other through the mystical technique of the Yoga system to the Buddhist doctrine of salvation. Another line of development equally continuous leads from the Orphic-Dionysiac mysticism to Plato, Philo and the later Hellenistic mystery cults to the Neoplatonic mysticism

[1] *The Times*, 28 March 1938.

[2] Writing to an American friend after the events of 30 June 1934, a German lady exclaimed: 'Hitler has killed his friends for the sake of Germany. Isn't he wonderful?' The same writer tells us of a German boy whose prayer on making his first communion was 'that he might die with a French bullet in his heart' (Philip Gibbs, *European Journey*).

of the Infinite of Plotinus which in turn is the source of the "mystical theology" of the pseudo-Dionysius the Areopagite. Perhaps this second chain is only an offshoot from the first, since the Eleatic speculations and the cryptic doctrine of redemption have possibly borrowed essential elements from early Indian mysticism. The prophetic religion of the Bible which is poles asunder from mysticism manifests the same continuity. Starting from Moses—perhaps from Abraham—it runs through the prophets and psalmists to its culmination in Jesus and is perpetuated by Paul and John. This line continues in the succeeding Christian centuries though it becomes weaker under the influence of mysticism and a syncretistic ecclesiasticism, until it again finds its pristine strength in the biblical Christianity of the Reformers.'[1]

In other words, he distinguishes two types of religion, the mystic and the prophetic, or the Biblical or evangelical. The former he traces partly to India, though he recognizes that in Indian thought there is a theistic current, which refuses to blur the distinctiveness of individuals and looks upon God not only as immanent but as transcendent, and advocates prayer and personal appeal to the Infinite instead of quiet and contemplation. The *Śvetāśvatara Upaniṣad*, the *Bhagavadgītā*, the theistic reformers such as Rāmānuja and Madhva, and saints such as Tukārām, Tulsīdās, represent this tendency. In them we find a fervent and tender, frank and vigorous life of prayer and communion with a personal God. Yet the other tendency is the more prominent one, and Christian mysticism owes to it a good deal of its development. It need not, however, be assumed that the two are exclusive of each other. As a matter of fact, the Upaniṣads do not look upon them as irreconcilable.[2] The contradiction appears only if we define mysticism in the one-sided way in which Heiler does. For him it is 'that form of intercourse with God in which the world and self are absolutely denied, in which human personality is dissolved, disappears and is absorbed in the infinite unity of the Godhead'.[3] While in the moments of insight the individual is impressed by the community of nature between the soul and God, when he lapses from them a feeling of unworthiness, the desolation of a separate life, disturbs his soul to its depths. He shudders before the awful

[1] *Prayer*, E.T. (1932), pp. 116–17.

[2] See also the writer's *An Idealist View of Life* (1937), 2nd ed., chapters iii and iv.

[3] *Prayer*, E.T., p. 136.

majesty of the great God, quivers in anguish, prays for forgiveness of sins, for aid and protection. The ascent to the supreme light and the prayer for pardon, the joy of the blessed union with the infinite God and the stern, harsh mood of penitence, represent two sides of mystic life. The super-personal and personal aspects of the Supreme may be distinguished in thought but cannot be separated in fact. According to true mysticism, each individual life represents a distinct value, a unique purpose, which will be retained so long as the cosmic process lasts. The ends and values though striven for in time have their source and consummation in eternity. The inner meaning and reality of each individual life remain a distinct fact in the world of spirit, until they are perfected in eternity, when time and the cosmic process terminate.[1] Nor is it fair to contend that in Jesus, John, and Paul the strain of mysticism is not decisive. We have referred to this question in another place. The declaration that the 'Kingdom of God is within you' carries the implication that the Divine King is within us. In the papyrus from Oxyrhynchus, which is assigned to about A.D. 200, there is a saying attributed to Jesus, 'And the Kingdom of Heaven is within you, and whosoever shall know himself shall find it.' Dr. Inge in his *Christian Mysticism* refers to the mystic strain in the early thinkers. He, however, agrees with Heiler in looking upon the negative descriptions of the deity and the world-denying character of ethics as Indian in origin. He says: 'The doctrine that God can be described only by negatives is neither Christian nor Greek, but belongs to the old religion of India.'[2] These are pervasive characteristics of Christian mysticism and show the decisive influence of Indian thought on it. To give a negative account of God is to affirm His immensity of being. When personality is denied to Him, it is only in the interests of super-personality. When we are asked to recognize the ephemeral character of earthly goods, it is to help us to live in the light of the eternal values. This is the lesson of the Upaniṣads and the *Bhagavadgītā*. The unknown author of *Theologia Germanica* describes the soul of Christ as having two eyes. The right

[1] See *An Idealist View of Life*, pp. 303 ff.

[2] *Christian Mysticism* (1899), p. 111.

eye is fixed on eternity and on the Godhead. It has a full intuition and enjoyment of the divine essence and eternal perfection. The left eye sees created things and things of time. While the right eye of His soul remained in full consciousness of His divine nature, the left eye was in possession of His perfect suffering and earthly experience. The created soul of man has also two eyes. One gives him the power of seeing into eternity, and the other helps him to see into time. If the right eye is to see into eternity, the left must be closed. 'Therefore whosoever will have the one must let the other go, for no man can serve two masters.'[1] The author attributes this view to Dionysius the Areopagite.

There is thus enough justification for regarding the mystic element in the West as Indian. This should not lead us to think that there is anything exclusive or peculiar about it. In different places and times, and under the shadow of every religion, mysticism has developed. We may take it that under conditions generally similar, the human mind has expressed itself under similar forms. Though the ways of human thinking are varied and its conclusions often contradictory, if there is anything that can be called universal truth, it is only natural that intuition, philosophy, and ethics should in different conditions sometimes attain similar results. In Indian mysticism this universality is openly acknowledged and a philosophy of religion is built on it. It affirms that the strain of mysticism is everywhere latent in humanity and only requires favouring conditions to reveal itself. To-day, when we are breaking away from incredible beliefs and unsocial traditions, mysticism has a deep appeal to the spiritual-minded.

Science cannot minister to the needs of the soul; dogmatism cannot meet the needs of the intellect. Atheism and dogmatism, scepticism and blind faith, are not the only alternatives. They are the twin fruits on the same branch, the positive and negative poles of the same tendency. We cannot combat the one without combating the other. In the battle-fields of Spain we find massacre, arson, despotic control. Both sides are as ruthless in their action, in their war of creeds, in their determination to stamp out the bestial

[1] viii, Winkworth's E.T.

thing—Marxist atheism or dogmatic Christianity. Is it a matter for surprise that some people believe that a malignant demon sat by the cradle of the unfortunate human race?

We require a religion which is both scientific and humanistic. Religion, science, and humanism were sisters in ancient India; they were allies in Greece. They must combine to-day if we are to attract all those who are equally indifferent to organized religion and atheism, to supernaturalism and nihilism. We need a spiritual home, where we can live without surrendering the rights of reason or the needs of humanity. Reverence for truth is a moral value. It is dearer than Buddha or Jesus. Truth is opposed, not to reason or the Greek spirit, but to dogma and fossilized tradition. We cannot rest the case of religion any more on dogmatic supernaturalism. Celsus tells of many prophets who went about in Syria and Palestine begging and moved as in prophecy:

'It is easy and usual for each to say, I am God or the Son of God or a divine spirit. I have come, for the world is already perishing and you, O men, are going to destruction because of iniquities. I wish to save you, and you shall see me carrying out again with heavenly power. Blessed is he who has worshipped me now; on every one else on cities and lands, I shall cast everlasting fire. And men who do not know the penalties which they incur will in vain repent and groan; but those who have obeyed me I shall keep in eternity.'[1]

When rival creeds appeal to us, are we to leave it to chance which we shall adopt? Celsus asks, 'If they introduce this one [Christ] and others another and all have the common formula ready to hand, Believe if you would be saved or go away; What will be done by those who really wish to be saved? Will they cast dice and so get an omen for the path which they are to take and the people whom they are to join?'[2]

Mysticism takes its stand on verifiable truth and not on the correct solution of credal puzzles. It is not opposed to science and reason. It is not contingent on any events past or future. No scientific criticism or historical discovery can refute it, as it is not dependent on any impossible miracles

[1] Celsus in Origen, *Contra Celsum*, vii. 9.
[2] Quoted in Nock, *Conversion* (1933), p. 206.

or unique historical revelations. Its only apologetic is the testimony of spiritual experience. It is not committed to the authenticity of any documents or the truth of any stories about the beginning of the world or prophecies of its end. Writing to the Corinthians, Paul said: 'God who said "light shall shine out of darkness" has shone within my heart.' Religion is a creative act of power and strength in the soul. If God is not found in each soul, He is unfindable. Religion's standard of values is absolute and eternal. The whole cosmic process has for its consummation a kingdom of ends, whose realization is contingent on human effort.

The code of ethics adopted by mysticism is noble and austere. It insists that suffering and renunciation are the life-blood of religion. In the splendid phrase of Wilamowitz, we must give our blood to the ghosts of our ideals that they may drink and live. The world-accepting suggestions of religions can be easily incorporated in our codes, but the stark element of world renunciation is supremely difficult and we are only too ready to make any shifts and adopt any expedients to eliminate it. In the noble passage with which he concludes his *Ethics* Spinoza writes:

> 'The wise man is scarcely at all perturbed in spirit, but being conscious of himself and of God, and of things, by a certain eternal necessity, never ceases to be but always possesses true acquiescence of his spirit. If the way which I have pointed out as leading to this result seems exceedingly hard, it may, nevertheless, be discovered. Needs must it be hard since it is so seldom found. How would it be possible if salvation were ready to our hand, and could without great labour be found, that it should be by almost all men neglected? But all things excellent are as difficult as they are rare.'

The command to control the fleshly lusts and concentrate our thoughts and affections on things that are good and true and lovely and the cult of the simple life and disinterested love of humanity, which thinks of no reward, appeal to the adherents of all religions. Mysticism finds itself in opposition to all those tendencies which put authority above truths and nation above humanity. It looks upon them as a menace to spiritual life and civilization, and by acquiescing in them we help what is evil to consolidate itself. So it protests often passionately and indignantly against abuses of organized religions. It revolts against institutionalism and stereotyped forms of religious life. The mystics of all religions have at some point or other in their careers protested against outside authority, credal bonds, and spiritual dictatorships.

There is a great European tradition of mysticism which starts from the mystery religions of Greece and develops through Pythagoras and Plato, Alexandrian religious philosophy, Jesus, Paul and John, Clement and Origen, the Neo-platonists, the medieval Christian mystics, the Cambridge Platonists, and scores of others. We need not adopt the official attitude of the Churches to the mystic developments. They may fight furiously about the dogmas of the divinity schools, but the common notions of spiritual religion remain, the plain easy truths, the pure morals, the inward worship, and the world loyalty. This spiritual religion is based on a firm belief in absolute and eternal values as the most real things in the universe, a confidence that these values are knowable by man by a wholehearted consecration of the intellect, will, and affections to the great quest, a complete indifference to the current valuations of tribes, races, and nations, and a devotion to the ideal of a world community. These are of the very stuff of truth, however hostile they may seem to the orthodoxies. They are the common possession of the great religions, though they are often embedded in superstitious accretions and irrelevances. The universality of the great facts of religious experience, their close resemblance under diverse conditions of race and time, attest to the persistent unity of the main spirit.[1] The adherents of this creed are the citizens of the world yet unborn, which is still in the womb of time. They belong to a movement that is world-wide; their temple is not the chapel of a sect but a vast pantheon; the believers in this movement are not eccentric or isolated ones, but are scattered throughout space, though united in their struggles and ideals, and their numbers would increase if vested interests were removed and

[1] 'The mystics form an invisible brotherhood scattered through all lands and times; though separated by space and time they reach hands to each other and agree in saying that God and man are separated only in outer appearance, both are indissolubly one. In spiritual transport they utter the great mystical prayer "I am Thou and Thou art I"' (Heiler, *Prayer*, E.T., p. 191).

if there were no penalties for religious convictions. Mysticism is there latent in the depths of the world's subconsciousness. It is what all sincere people dream of but what earth hath not yet known. It is coming and is well below the horizon.

The modernists in every religion are preparing the way for it. Ernst Troeltsch and Dr. Inge[1] declare that Christianity, if it is to be saved from formalism and excessive institutionalism, must return to the mystic standpoint. In their opinion only such a movement can revitalize Christian life, purify the Christian faith of the deadweight of tradition, stripping off the many lifeless accretions that hamper its progress, and inaugurate a new society based on justice and generosity.

It is unfortunate that, at a time when mysticism is once again coming to its own, a theologian of the eminence of Karl Barth, regarded by some as the 'Church's greatest living thinker',[2] should remain a stranger to its true spirit and implications. If we consider well, we will see that mystic religion has room for some of the fundamental motives of Barth's theological crusade and his criticisms of it are somewhat misdirected. For example, Barth looks upon mystic states as psychopathic conditions, and not states of consciousness in which we are in actual contact with a world of eternal reality. It cannot be denied that some of the manifestations of mysticism have been too emotional. Its defenders have made too much of the unusual and the spectacular. The mystic, it is true, looks to his personal experience, but he speaks of a reality which is over all and yet in all, which is different from the world of space and time and yet its inspiring principle. Barth contends that we are in the region of the subjective in mystic experience and God as the objective will always remain on the other side of experience. So long as we rest in experience, Barth tells us, we have in the place of God 'the questionable figment of our thoughts'. If what Barth calls the 'miracle of the

[1] In his book on *The Platonic Tradition in English Religious Thought* (1926) Dr. Inge pleads 'for the recognition of a third type of Christian thought and belief by the side of the two great types, which for want of better names, are usually called Catholic and Protestant' (p. v).

[2] *Credo*, E.T. (1936), p. vii.

absolute moment' is not subjective, then mystic experience is not. It is the submission of the human to the divine, the turning away from all that is merely human and subjective. From the side of psychology it is a process of self-emptying, when the vacuum is filled with a divine content. The characteristic features which Barth mentions about faith are those to which the mystics bear witness, that it is *sui generis*, that it is its own guarantee. The real which he sees comes from beyond himself, and does not belong to the region of doubt or speculation, hypothesis or opinion. Brünner in his *Theology of Crisis* distinguishes three modes of apprehension: the scientific, which deals with external facts; the metaphysical, which is concerned with underlying principles; and a third mode, 'when one no longer seeks with Philistine concern for practical values; when one seeks not with cold scientific objectivity, or with a serene aesthetic outlook upon the world, but with the passion of a drowning man who desperately cries for help'.[1] It is the burning quest of the total personality on which the mystic also lays stress.

The fundamental emphasis of the Barthian theology is preserved in the mystic religion, for, in all its forms, it insists on a second birth. Even as we were born into our temporal life, we must be 'born again' into the life of spirit. We need not wait for this second birth until the hour of physical death. We can be reborn into eternity while in time. Plato tells us that, if a man is to enter upon the life of immortality, which is a life centred on truth, goodness, and beauty, his whole outlook on the world must be reversed. 'The soul must be turned about', if the rays of the true light are to fall upon it. There must be a conversion, a new creation which is not a mere extension of the old.

The negative descriptions of the Supreme and the doctrine of *māyā* which are said to be the characteristics of Hindu mysticism are employed to denote the distance between time and eternity, between appearance and reality. The passionate antithesis between the real and the unreal, the true and the false, gives the urgency to the religious effort. God is the unknown, the absolutely different, the Beyond who cannot be comprehended by our concepts or recognized by

[1] Lecture II.

our understanding. 'God is ever transcendent to man, new, remote, foreign, surpassing, never in man's sphere, never man's possession: whoso says God says miracle.'[1] Man cannot determine God, for God is the subject, never the predicate. He can only be described negatively or through seemingly contradictory descriptions.

'God, the pure limit and pure beginning of all that we are, have and do, standing over in infinite qualitative difference to man and all that is human, nowhere and never identical with that which we call God, experience, surmise and pray to as God, the unconditioned Halt, as opposed to all human unrest, and the unconditioned Forwards as opposed to all human rest, the Yes in our No and the No in our Yes, the First and the Last, and as such the Unknown, but Nowhere and Never a Magnitude amongst others in the medium known to us, God the Lord, the Creator and Redeemer—that is the true God.'[2]

As God is the totally other, knowledge of God must come from God himself. The Upaniṣad says: 'He whom the Self chooses, by him the self can be gained.'[3] The power of truth is identical with God Himself. The disclosure of this truth is a free gift. It is God's own choice. The only way in which we can prepare for it is by sacrificing our life and all, by standing stripped naked before God. Unless the individual is wholly impoverished, he cannot earn his saving.

Mysticism recognizes the double movement in the religious effort, how the supreme at once fascinates and disturbs, how it is very near and far away, how it is at once the fulfilment of man's nature and its transfiguration. Conflict, distress, sin are possible because we have an apprehension of something absolute. When we struggle against sin and disapprove of it we are not altogether sinful. Even utter despair as echoed by the words 'Why hast thou forsaken me?' is rendered possible by the implicit faith in the Supreme. The infinite imposes on us acute tension and makes us feel how unworthy and carnal-minded we are. It does bring a sword, disruption, and discord. Religion is born in agony. The one cry of the man who has an apprehension of the Absolute and his own distance from it is that he is a sinner, *pāpo'ham*.

[1] Karl Barth, *The Epistle to the Romans*, E.T. by Sir Edwyn Hoskyns (1933), iv. 21.

[2] Ibid., p. 315.

[3] *Kaṭha Up.* i. 2. 23.

When he feels this utter isolation, he is miserable. But this tragedy is also the glory of man. Even at the moment when he feels the utter transcendence of the divine, he is affirming its immanence. The very ability of man to receive and retain an impression of God's revelation, his struggle to give visible expression to the divine life, is the proof of the God in him. It is an exaggeration to assert that 'the power of God can be detected neither in the world of nature nor in the souls of men'.[1] On such a view the human being entirely loses significance. The Catholic Church also holds that man has not the power to attain salvation by his own efforts, but adds that he has the freedom to choose between the acceptance and refusal of grace. Such a view may be illogical, but it is certainly more significant. God is not only the unknown and the inaccessible but one so much within human consciousness that His otherness is vividly felt. He is so terribly near. When we feel our difference from Him, it is His transcendence that strikes us. While the mystic will be ready to grant the infinite qualitative difference between time and eternity and the utter transcendence of God and a sense of his utter unworthiness or depravity in the presence of the Supreme, he will not agree that man is totally depraved and utterly incapable of getting back to God. Even the suffering which crushes all powers of resistance does not necessarily effect the destruction of the sense that he is intended for a higher life. This sense endows the desolation with significance. In the religious effort there are two modes: one in which man is broken from God; another in which he is restored to God. So long as he is in revolt, his creatureliness is a fetter. Death is his fate. When the crisis, which is an essential side of religious life, is overcome, when the man is at one with himself because he is at one with God, he has the consciousness of the indwelling deity. How else can we account for the joy of religious experience of the prophet and the apostle, of the seer and the saint, who feel that they are new men, no more broken in twain, with the duality of their life dissolved? Barth describes it in glowing terms:

'There is here no fear, for perfect love has cast it out. . . . Here is dissolved the terrible weight which infinity imposes on what is finite.

[1] *Romans*, p. 36.

Dissolved also is that embarrassment which everything finite imposes upon infinity. Dissolved is the duality of our life by which at every moment we are pressed up against the narrow gate of critical negation. For it is this duality which gives us to fear, which makes us appalled by the ambiguity of our being and by the riddle of our existence. The Spirit, which we have received and by which we have passed from death to life, brings this duality to an end.'[1]

The Upaniṣad says *brahmābhayam*, there is no fear in God. When the vision is attained, duality is at an end; the otherness of God and our own otherness are overcome. 'God himself and God only. This spirit of sonship, this new man who I am not, is my unobservable existential ego. In the light of this unobservable ego, I must now pass my visible and corporeal life.' Surely it is not necessary to look upon the divine as totally unlike the human, for Barth himself speaks of our present human existence as 'itself not eternity, yet bearing within it eternity unborn'.[2] Eternity and time, 'immortality and death', says the *Mahābhārata*, 'the two together are found in the human being; by delusion we enter into death; by the pursuit of truth we gain life eternal'.[3] Human life is complex, it is both confusion and clarity, sinfulness and hope. When the Upaniṣads speak of 'That thou art', they do not mean that we are divine in an easy and obvious way; they assert that divinity is the manifest destiny of man. 'As that shalt then be manifest with effort and struggle, when you shake off your natural ego. The death of the rebellious ego is the condition of the birth of the Son of God. If there are no crucifixions, there will be no resurrections.

The mystic would agree that creeds and dogmas are not faith but what lead to faith. They must cease to be logical propositions and become living movements. 'Words are weariness', as the Upaniṣad says, if they do not transfigure us. Barth's view that 'the word which enters human ears and is uttered by human lips is the Word of God—only when the miracle takes place; otherwise it is just a human word like any other',[4] is accepted by the mystic. For him

[1] *Romans*, p. 297.
[2] Ibid., p. 301.
[3] amṛtam caiva mṛtyuśca dvayam dehe pratiṣṭhitam
mṛtyur āpadyate mohāt satyenāpadyate amṛtam. (xii. 174. 30.)
[4] *Romans*, p. 366.

the knowledge which is the illumination of the soul is not an addition to his logical knowledge but something which transforms it. When he exalts faith and declares that it is non-ethical,[1] he is referring to the incommensurability of ethical progress and spiritual perfection, what the mystics affirm when they say that the spiritual condition takes us beyond good and evil. The spiritual cannot be achieved by the ethical. *Nāsty akṛtah kṛtena.* All work is dust and ashes for Śaṁkara. Salvation by works is impossible, for all action is empirical and cannot have transcendental consequences. Actions take place in the world of phenomena and can be expiated and atoned for only in the world of phenomena. While all this emphasizes the distance between the empirical and the transcendental, the mystic religion affirms that there is a relation between the two. We can pass from time to eternity, from appearance to reality; otherwise philosophy and religion are an irrelevance and there is no point in such passages as 'Be ye holy even as I am holy' or 'Be ye perfect'. If faith lives by the call to which it responds, the responding itself is human. The capacity to recognize the self-disclosure of the divine is in us. We can understand the Word; we can hear the summons from eternity, and that is due to our participation in the divine spirit. If the world and the soul are the creations of God, will not the Creator's presence be evident in them? Time is the moving image of eternity, and experience is the appearance of the Absolute. If we dig a ditch between the two, there can be no passage from the one to the other. Barth is exaggerating the dualism to its breaking-point when he says: 'Whenever men claim to be able to see the Kingdom of God as a growing organism—or to describe it more suitably—as a growing building, what they see is not the Kingdom of God, but the Tower of Babel.'[2] He makes out that 'evil is the inert mass of human activity as such',[3] and so nothing that we do matters, for nothing depends on us. 'The encounter of grace depends upon no human possessions; for achievement, even awe and

[1] 'Works bring men into relationship with a God whom they can comprehend and such a God is not the God who of necessity doeth miracles' (*Romans*, p. 367).

[2] Ibid., p. 432.

[3] Ibid., p. 467.

awakening—is of no value and has no independent validity in the presence of God.'[1] Barth asserts the utter discontinuity of nature and grace and rejects any shadow of synergism or collaboration of the human soul with God in the realm of faith. Faith is a gift of the grace of God which calls us and at the same time gives us the power to respond. It is a divine miracle, a hidden thing. Naturally Barth, who holds that the finite is incapable of the divine, is inclined to underrate the humanity of Jesus. The Logos constitutes his personality; Virgin Birth and Resurrection become all important. As to why Jesus took over human nature and died on the Cross, it is a mystery unfathomable by man. We can only say that it pleased God so to do. God stands outside the process and calls men according to His purpose. He creates crises in the lives of men and the affairs of mankind. He breaks into the course of events, as He did decisively at that point of history marked by the coming of Jesus Christ. His choosing and being chosen have nothing to do with our growth or response. Grace is superior to nature. We get back to a crude type of Calvinism. 'The Fall, with all its consequences, was predetermined ages before the Creation and was the necessary consequence of that predetermination. The Almighty irrevocably decided the fate of each individual long before he called him into existence and has predestined millions to his hatred and to eternal damnation and with that object he gave them being.'[2]

This despair of human nature which underlies Barthian theology is the reflection of the social situation. Any one who thinks of the way in which the most advanced States of the world are pursuing suicidal policies, with an utter disregard of the lessons of history and the counsels of reason, is likely to lose faith in human nature and talk as if irresistible forces were hurrying us into inevitable disaster. For the blind fate of the materialists Barth substitutes the overruling providence of God. God called Abraham from Ur. He brought up Israel out of Egypt. He gave the law at Sinai. He raised up David to be King. He sent us Jesus Christ. Such a view persuades us to believe that everything that happens is divine, and for effecting changes in the world

[1] Ibid., p. 59.

[2] *Institutes*, iii. 21. 3.

we have to wait for miracles. Faith, however, in the resilience of the human spirit, the responsibility of man for moulding human affairs, is an indispensable mark of true religion. If our situation is desperate to-day, it is only the nemesis of our past mistakes and sins. Self-will and charity are in conflict in our institutions because they are in conflict in ourselves. If civilization has broken down, it is because we still believe and practise the faith that all is fair in the interests of class or nation. Faith in a Kingdom which is not of this world, where life consists, not in meat and drink, but in righteousness, peace, and joy, is what the age needs. With all its ascetic and other-worldly emphasis, mysticism is more adequate to the facts of religious experience and social needs than Barthian theology.

Every attempt on the part of the historical religions to regain universality is bringing them nearer the religions of India. The increasing interest in Indian religions is due to the consciousness that mysticism has had a more successful chance in them.[1] That it originated in India is now practically admitted. That it influenced the Western tradition is not denied by the learned. That the mystical rendering of religion has persisted there for a longer period than anywhere else is common knowledge. If thousands of the more open-minded among Christians and Agnostics find that these new ideas from the East have more power to quicken their religious aspirations, and if they hold that the teaching of Jesus requires reinforcement from these mature conceptions which are by no means unfamiliar to Christendom, it is a matter for rejoicing. Max Müller declared: 'If I were to ask myself, from what literature we here in Europe,—we who have been nurtured almost exclusively on the thoughts of the Greeks and the Romans, and of one Semitic race, the Jewish,—may draw that corrective which is most wanted in order to make our inner life more perfect, more comprehensive, more universal, in fact, more truly human, a life, not for this life alone but a transfigured and eternal life,

[1] I may warn the Western reader against much that passes for Indian wisdom in Europe and America. The highest mysticism of India is thoroughly rational and is associated with a profoundly philosophical culture: it has nothing in common with esoteric quackeries.

again I should point to India.'[1] Perhaps Christianity, which arose out of an Eastern background and early in its career got wedded to Graeco-Roman culture, may find her rebirth to-day in the heritage of India.

The coming together of two great civilizations not so widely separated in some of the main sources of their strength has caused some harsh spiritual discords, political tragedy, and personal agony. It has, however, unrivalled opportunities for the shaping of the future. Indian life and thought have been transformed and her mind has been given a new direction. If, before it is too late, India's legitimate hopes and just aspirations receive their fulfilment, her influence on the British Commonwealth and the world at large will be exerted towards the development of a higher quality of life in the individual and the establishment of a world commonwealth based on the ideals of spirit. Her political subjection has not completely deprived her of her soul. The present Viceroy of India, Lord Linlithgow, addressing the joint meeting of the Indian Science Congress and the British Association of Science in Calcutta early last year, said:

'Even the most enthusiastic believer in Western civilization must feel to-day a certain despondency at the apparent failure of the West to dominate scientific discoveries and to evolve a form of society in which material progress and spiritual freedom march comfortably together. Perhaps the West will find in India's more general emphasis on simplicity and the ultimate spirituality of things, a more positive example of the truths which the most advanced minds of the West are now discovering. Is it too much to hope that you, gentlemen, will be a channel through which India will make in an increasing degree that contribution to Western and to world thought which those of us who know and love India, are confident that she can make in so full a degree?'

[1] Cf. W. J. Grant: 'India indeed has a preciousness which a materialistic age is in danger of missing. Some day the fragrance of her thought will win the hearts of men. This grim chase after our own tails which marks the present age cannot continue for ever. The future contains a new human urge towards the real beauty and holiness of life. When it comes India will be searched by loving eyes and defended by knightly hands.' (*The Spirit of India* (1933), p. vi).

VIII
THE MEETING OF RELIGIONS

I

THE different religions have now come together, and if they are not to continue in a state of conflict or competition, they must develop a spirit of comprehension which will break down prejudice and misunderstanding and bind them together as varied expressions of a single truth. Such a spirit characterized the development of Hinduism, which has not been interrupted for nearly fifty centuries. The past strength and continuity of Hindu culture,[1] as well as its present weakness and disorder, are problems of equal interest. Nor does the weakness really contradict the strength. Hinduism is not based on any racial factor. It is an inheritance of thought and aspiration to which every race in India has made its distinctive contribution.

From the excavations of Harappa and Mohenjo-daro we find the first available evidence on Indian soil of a developed urban life, of images of pottery which show that the human hand has not gained much in dexterity from the lapse of ages. From the skeletal material unearthed there, four different races could be identified, 'proto-Australoid, Mediterranean, Mongolian and Alpine, although the two latter are represented by only one skull of each type'.[2] The inhabitants of the area seem to have led more or less peaceful lives, instead of continually fighting for their existence. 'No evidence exists as in Sumer of the cities being repeatedly sacked and burnt.'[3] Many features of modern Hinduism 'are derived from very primitive sources; they perhaps date back even to a period anterior to that in which the people of Mohenjodaro and Harappa built their great, brick cities'.[4]

[1] 'What peculiarity distinguishes India from the rest of the existing world is the strong survival of direct inheritance from the remote past' (Dodwell, *India* (1936), vol. i, p. 2).

[2] Ernest Mackay, *The Indus Civilisation* (1935), p. 200.

[3] Ibid., p. 14.

[4] Ibid., p. 96; cf. Dodwell: 'Hindu civilisation is the last great civilisation of this kind to survive. Its roots go back into that ancient world which came into being in Sumer and Egypt; and the orthodox Brahmin of to-day would

In the relics we find the figure of Śiva or his ancient prototype. 'The worship of the mother goddess is a very early Indian cult and probably existed in the country long before the arrival of the Indus valley people. It is probably true also of tree worship. . . . Animal worship is also inherent in most primitive communities and has existed in India and elsewhere for so long that its origin is untraceable.'[1] We come across representations of cross-legged figures with worshippers kneeling right and left, *nāgas* (serpents), of pippal tree (*Ficus religiosa*), and of animals, the bull, the elephant, and the rhinoceros, though the last is now extinct in the Indus valley. Obviously the different races and religious cults lived in harmony and adopted an attitude of live and let live.

We are on firmer ground when we pass to the period of the *Ṛg Veda* and the *Atharva Veda*. We find in them echoes of conflicts between different cults and their final reconciliation, an age of intense change in the general outlook and the conditions of life. As the *Ṛg Veda* has it, 'Lo, the supreme light of lights is come, a varied awakening is born, wide manifest'. Before the second millennium B.C. the Dravidians were scattered throughout the continent and had developed a high civilization. The Vedic Aryans had conflicts with the Dāsas, whom they described as noseless (*anāsa*), which is obviously a reference to their racial type. The Vedas mention with disapproval the worshipper of the Phallus. Conflicts between *devas* and *asuras* are frequently mentioned.[2] In *Ṛg Veda*[3] Varuṇa and Mitra are called noble *asuras* (*asurā āryā*). Deities like Indra seem to belong to a rustic, semi-nomadic, half-barbarous people, while Varuṇa and Mitra suggest a somewhat higher level of culture. Ultimately the *devas* drove out the *asuras*, their rivals.[4] In reality, however, they were accepted by the Vedic Aryans. While the Vedas represent the religion of the classes, the masses continued to worship their traditional deities, Yakṣas

probably find far more in common with a priest of Ur or Memphis than with the modern educated European' (*India* (1936), vol. i, p. 1).

[1] Ernest Mackay, *The Indus Civilisation* (1935), p. 97.

[2] *Ṛg Veda*, i. 108. 6, x. 124; *Yajur Veda*, v. 4. 1.

[3] vii. 65. 2; in *Atharva Veda*, i. 10, where Varuṇa is said to be an *asura* ruling over deities. See also *Jaiminīya Brāhmaṇa*, iv. 152.

[4] *Satapatha Brāhmana*, xiii. 8. 2. 1.

and Nāgas. Behind the façade of Vedic orthodoxy and its tendency to abstract symbolism, an extensive and deep-rooted system of popular beliefs and cults and a decided tendency to anthropomorphic presentation prevailed. The Vedic religion, however, absorbed, embodied, and preserved the types and rituals of older cults. Instead of destroying them, it adapted them to its own requirements. It took so much from the social life of the Dravidians and other native inhabitants of India that it is very difficult to disentangle the original Aryan elements from others. The interpenetration has been so complex, subtle, and continuous, with the result that there has grown up a distinct Hindu civilization which is neither Aryan nor Dravidian nor aboriginal. Ever since the dawn of reflection the dream of unity has hovered over the scene and haunted the imagination of the leaders.

A theoretical explanation was put forward in the *Ṛg Veda* for this attitude of acceptance of other cults. 'The real is one, the learned call it by various names, Agni, Yama, Mātariśvan.'[1] Again, 'priests and poets with words make into many the hidden reality which is but one'.[2] The one is spoken of (*vadanti*) or imagined (*kalpayanti*) in different ways. The Upaniṣads adopt the same view. The oneness of the Supreme is insisted on, but variety of description is permitted. The light of absolute truth is said to be refracted as it passes through the distorting medium of human nature. In the boundless being of Brahman are all the living powers that men have worshipped as gods, not as if they were standing side by side in space, but each a facet mirroring the whole. The different deities are symbols of the fathomless.

This liberal attitude is accepted by Buddha. Once upon a time, Buddha relates, a certain king of Benares, desiring to divert himself, gathered together a number of beggars blind from birth and offered a prize to the one who should give him the best account of an elephant. The first beggar who examined the elephant chanced to lay hold on the leg, and reported that an elephant was a tree-trunk; the second, laying hold of the tail, declared that an elephant was like a rope; another, who seized an ear, insisted that an elephant was like a palm-leaf; and so on. The beggars fell to quarrelling with

[1] *Ṛg Veda*, i. 164. 46. [2] Ibid. x. 114.

one another, and the king was greatly amused. Ordinary teachers who have grasped this or that aspect of the truth quarrel with one another, while only a Buddha knows the whole. In theological discussions we are at best blind beggars fighting with one another. The complete vision is difficult and the Buddhas are rare. Aśoka's dictum represents the Buddhist view. 'He who does reverence to his own sect while disparaging the sects of others wholly from attachment to his own, with intent to enhance the splendour of his own sect, in reality, by such conduct inflicts the severest injury on his own sect.'[1]

In China the three religions Taoism, Confucianism, and Buddhism have so far melted into one another that we cannot separate them easily.[2] If the Chinese practise the rites and revere the doctrines of Taoism, Buddhism, and Confucianism without being disturbed by the knowledge that their theologies are mutually contradictory, we need not be puzzled, for this is the great tradition of the East. Three ways to the one goal of spiritual life is quite a reasonable attitude for the cultivated Chinese. The average Japanese worships in a Buddhist tera (temple) as well as in a Shinto miya (shrine).

The spread of Hinduism is described in the epics of the *Rāmāyaṇa* and the *Mahābhārata*. Though in them the facts of history are obscured in a haze of legend, they represent the great age of conflict, emigration, and adjustment out of which a civilization with old ideas but new accents emerges. By the time the cultural conquest of India was over, the

[1] This attitude of Buddhism has not changed. Professor Pratt, after years of study and travel in the East, writes: 'The attitude of the great majority of Buddhists towards Christians and toward Christianity is one of genuine friendliness. If there is to be a fierce and long continued war between the two religions, it will be all the work of Christianity. For its part Buddhism would be only too glad to ratify a treaty of enduring peace, alliance and friendship with its great rival' (*The Pilgrimage of Buddhism*, pp. 735–6).

[2] 'The Scholar followed Confucius, the contemplative recluse sought Buddha in the mountain monasteries, the simple and ignorant populace worshipped the Taoist Queen of Heaven and a multitude of other divinities, to avert calamity' (Fitzgerald, *China* (1935), p. 562). Confucius never pronounced himself in favour of or in opposition to any deity. The Taoists were always ready to acknowledge any deity who commanded popular feeling and accord him a place in their pantheon.

civilization developed altered values. A strong inrush of devotional feeling pervaded the whole atmosphere. Worship was paid to the Supreme under different names. According to the *Bhagavadgītā* the Supreme accepts us as we are, no matter how we approach Him, for all paths in which we may wander are His. In the supreme vision which Arjuna has, he sees the different deities within the boundless form of the Supreme.

The Purāṇas continue the tradition. The Supreme, which is essentially one, according to *Viṣṇu Purāṇa*, assumes the name of Brahmā at the time of creation, of Viṣṇu while maintaining it, and of Śiva at the time of destruction.[1] It is said that the apostle Thomas arrived in India in A.D. 52, and the Syrian Christians of Malabar claim to have descended from Christians converted by St. Thomas. The other account that their Christianity came from Nestorian missionaries is resented by them.[2] Eusebius (A.D. 264–340) in his *Ecclesiastical History*[3] writes that Pantainos, who was sent to India to preach the Gospel of Christ, 'found that the Gospel according to Matthew had been introduced before his arrival, and was in the hands of some of the natives who acknowledged Christ'.[4] Many scholars hold that by India in this passage is meant Southern Arabia. There is a tradition in Malabar that in the middle of the fourth century the 'Katholikos of the East' sent a merchant, Thomas of Jerusalem, to Malabar. Possibly this Thomas was the real founder of the Church who introduced Syrian customs. When in the fourth century the Sassanid Emperor of Persia began a cruel persecution of the Christians, 'a number of them with Bishops and Clergy fled to the more tolerant Hindu princes on the Western coast of India'.[5] There are copper plates now in Kottayam granted by the king of Cranganore, which confer on Christians privileges of the highest caste and freedom of worship. The first Christian

1 sṛṣṭisthityantakaraṇīm brahmaviṣṇuśivābhidhām
sa samjñām yāti bhagavān eka eva janārdanah.

2 'We must leave the apostolic origin of Malabar Christianity as a very doubtful legend' (Adrian Fortescue, *The Lesser Eastern Churches* (1913), p. 356).

3 v. 10.

4 M'Crindle, *Ancient India* (1901), p. 214.

5 Adrian Fortescue, *The Lesser Eastern Churches* (1913), p. 358.

Church in Travancore was built by generous grants from the Hindu king.

Two races of Jews, white and dark, have for long been established on the south-west coast of India and received charters granting them freedom of worship from the Hindu princes.[1] Referring to these charters to the Christians and the Jews, Dr. Fortescue writes: 'both are interesting proofs of the characteristic tolerance of Hindu kings'.[2]

Śaṁkara (eighth century A.D.) is said to have re-established six different religious cults (*ṣaṇmatasthāpanācārya*). To the dogmatic mind Śaṁkara would seem to be either hypocritical, believing in nothing, or essentially lacking in the quality of faith which for some absolutely excludes the possibility of holding two or more religions to be equally valid. Śaṁkara did not believe in a god who denied the existence of his rivals. According to Bāṇa's *Harṣacarita*, in the retreat of Divākaramitra were assembled Jains, Buddhists, materialists, followers of the different philosophies and theistic beliefs. Yuan Chwang relates that King Harṣa installed statues of Buddha, Sun-god, and Śiva. This non-dogmatic attitude has persisted in Hindu religious history. Bilvamaṅgala writes: 'Undoubtedly I am a follower of Śiva. Let there be no doubt of that nor of my due meditation of the five-lettered text sacred to Śiva. Nevertheless my mind constantly revels in recalling the picture of the beautiful face of the child *Kṛṣṇa*, beloved of the gopi maidens.'[3] Appaya Dīkṣita says: 'I do not find any difference in essence between Śiva the lord of the world and Viṣṇu the spirit of the universe. Yet my devotion is given to Śiva.'[4]

[1] *Asiatic Journal*, N.S., vol. vi, pp. 6–14.

[2] *The Lesser Eastern Churches*, p. 363.

[3] śaivāvayam na khalu tatra vicāraṇīyam
pañcākṣarī japaparā nitarām tathāpi
ceto madīyamatasīkusumāvabhāsam
smerānanam smarati gopavadhūkiśoram.

[4] maheśvare va jagatām adhīśvare
janārdane vā jagadantarātmani
na vastubheda pratipattir asti me
tathāpi bhaktis taruṇenduśekhare.

The oneness of the three gods Brahmā, Viṣṇu, and Śiva is brought out by the mystic symbol Aum, where A represents Viṣṇu, U Śiva, and M Brahmā.

The followers of Zoroastrianism, when they were expelled from their country owing to Mohammadan persecution, took shelter in India and to-day they are found nowhere else.[1] They are said to have landed in Sanjan about the year A.D. 716, and the first fire temple was built there through the assistance of the Hindu ruler. While the Parsees came as fugitives, the Muslims and the Christians came as conquerors.

The Hindu attitude to Islam was again the same one of toleration.

> 'The people [of Calicut] are infidels; consequently I [Abdul Razak, Ambassador from the court of Persia about the middle of the fifteenth century] consider myself in an enemy's country, as the Mohammadans consider everyone who has not received the Qur'an. Yet I admit that I meet with perfect toleration, and even favour; we have two mosques and are allowed to pray in public.'[2]

Though the religions of Islam and Christianity by their militant attitude occasionally provoked similar developments in Hinduism, its prevailing note continues to be one of understanding and acceptance of the bona fides of other faiths. Rāmakṛṣṇa experimented with different faiths, tested them in his own person to find out what is of enduring worth in them. He meditated on the Qur'ān and practised the prescribed rites. He studied Christianity, and lived like a Christian anchorite. Buddha, Christ, and Kṛṣṇa, he declared, were forms of the Supreme and they are not all. The monks of the Rāmakṛṣṇa Order join in any worship which is pure and noble and celebrate the birthdays of Kṛṣṇa, Christ, and Buddha. Ram Mohan Roy instructs that the Brāhmo Samāj should be a universal house of prayer open to all men without distinction of caste or colour, race or nation. Over the door of Śāntiniketan, the home of the Tagores, runs an inscription, not only 'In this place no image is to be adored', but also 'And no man's faith is to be despised'. Gandhi says: 'If I were asked to define the Hindu

[1] 'The Persian or Parsi fugitives, after undergoing numerous hardships and nearly incurring destruction succeeded in gaining the shores of India, where the rights of shelter and settlement were conceded by a Hindu ruler' (*History of the Parsis*, by Karaka (1884), vol. i, p. xv).

[2] Murray, *Discoveries and Travels in Asia*, vol. ii, p. 20.

creed, I should simply say: Search after truth through non-violent means. A man may not believe in God and still call himself a Hindu. Hinduism is a relentless pursuit after truth.'[1] Hinduism is 'the religion of truth. Truth is God. Denial of God we have known. Denial of truth we have not known.'[2] He wrote recently in the *Harijan*: 'I believe in the Bible as I believe in the Gītā. I regard all the great faiths of the world as equally true with my own. It hurts me to see any one of them caricatured as they are today by their own followers.' For a true Hindu there are few places dedicated to God in which he may not silently worship, few prayers in which he may not reverently join.

As a result of this tolerant attitude, Hinduism itself has become a mosaic of almost all the types and stages of religious aspiration and endeavour. It has adapted itself with infinite grace to every human need and it has not shrunk from the acceptance of every aspect of God conceived by man, and yet preserved its unity by interpreting the different historical forms as modes, emanations, or aspects of the Supreme.

II

No country and no religion have adopted this attitude of understanding and appreciation of other faiths so persistently and consistently as India and Hinduism and its offshoot of Buddhism. What is this attitude due to? Is it a matter of charity or indifference or policy? The cynicism of Gibbon is well known: 'The various modes of worship which prevailed in the Roman world were all considered by the people as equally true, by the philosophers as equally false, and by the magistrates as equally useful.' The atheist Julius Caesar and the agnostic Tiberius represent the attitude of indifference of the Roman patrician society. The modern critic would say that men so well placed as the aristocrats of Roman society did not need any divine assistance. It is the serfs and the slaves, who are expected to carry out meekly the commands of the rich and the powerful, that require the aid of gods. A Tiberius could say, 'Let the

[1] *Young India*, 24 April 1924.

[2] *Contemporary Indian Philosophy*, ed. by Radhakrishnan and Muirhead (1936), p. 21.

gods attend to their own affairs.' But the suffering masses sunk in misery and servitude who were 'without hope in this world' must be provided with another world in which they can lay their hopes. It is religion that is disbelieved by the classes and forced on the masses that provokes the remark of Karl Marx that 'religion is the soul of soulless conditions, the heart of a heartless world, the opium of the people'.[1] It is the cry of despair wrung out of innumerable suffering souls to whom all earthly happiness is a dream.

The Hindu attitude is not the outcome of scepticism, which despairs of ever reaching any stable truth. If the most we can hope for is a relative truth, a provisional hypothesis, we cannot claim finality or absoluteness for any view. Where nothing is certain, nothing matters. Where there is no depth of conviction, tolerance is easy to attain. If we are impressed by our common ignorance, we may be bound together even though it may be in a feeling of despair. Some modern sceptics who look upon religious views as wish fulfilments reveal our kinship with one another in our deepest needs.

The man of faith, whether he be Hindu or Buddhist, Muslim or Christian, has certainty, and yet there is a difference between the two pairs.[2] The attitude of the cultivated Hindu and the Buddhist to other forms of worship is one of sympathy and respect, and not criticism and contempt for their own sake. This friendly understanding is not inconsistent with deep feeling and thought. Faith for the Hindu does not mean dogmatism. He does not smell heresy in those who are not entirely of his mind. It is not devotion that leads to the assertive temper, but limitation of outlook, hardness, and uncharity. While full of unquestioning belief, the Hindu is at the same time devoid of harsh judgement. It is not historically true that in the knowledge of truth there is of necessity great intolerance.

[1] *Criticism of Hegel's Philosophy of Law.*

[2] Count Hermann Keyserling writes: 'The orthodox Christian in his presumption, which makes him believe that dogma in itself embodies salvation, wants to convert, *coûte que coûte*, everyone who has a different faith, and in the meantime he despises them. I have never met a Hindu who did not believe absolutely in some form of dogma, but on the other hand, I have not met one who wanted to convert anybody, or who despised anyone because of his superstition' (*The Travel Diary of a Philosopher* (1925), vol. i, p. 292).

III

When the Roman Empire had brought under one rule the multitudinous peoples of western Asia, north Africa, and southern and middle Europe, it did not interfere with their beliefs and practices unless it suspected political danger. In the West, toleration prevailed in many periods, but it is traceable to intellectual curiosity and more often to political expediency. Consideration for others is a quality of a cultivated mind. The wisdom of the Athenians, of whom Pericles said, 'We listen gladly to the opinions of others and do not turn sour faces on those who disagree with us', is the product of the good breeding of the mind. The Greeks inherited a tradition of gods and rites which they adopted for the stability of the State. They welcomed other gods so long as the security of the State was unaffected. 'This stranger also, I suppose, prays to the Immortals,' says Peisistratus in the *Odyssey*, 'since all men have need of gods.'[1] Xenophon observes: 'That religion is true for each man which is the religion of his own country.'[2] The Greek temper recognized religious duty, but did not impose religious doctrine. The political bias, however, led to occasional intolerance. The Roman magistrates, according to Gibbon,

> 'encouraged the public festivals which humanise the manners of the people. They managed the arts of divination as convenient instruments of policy; and they respected as the firmest bond of society the useful persuasion that, either in this or a future life, the crime of perjury is most assuredly punished by the avenging gods. But whilst they acknowledged the general advantages of religion, they were convinced that the various modes of worship contributed alike to the same salutary purposes; and that in every country the form of superstition which had received the sanction of time and experience was the best adapted to the climate and to its inhabitants.'[3]

In the second century A.D. a great emperor persecuted Christianity not so much out of love for God as for reasons of State.

The Roman Senate sanctioned in 204 B.C. the orgiastic performances of the Great Mother of the gods which were

[1] iii. 48.
[2] *Mem.* iv. 3. 26.
[3] *Decline and Fall of Rome*, ii.

introduced into Rome from Phrygia. The mystery religions of Isis, of Mithra, of Cybele were established in the eastern part of the Mediterranean. Greek philosophy made itself felt in Rome soon after the close of the second Punic war, and Stoicism was the result. In man dwells the world reason and we all are, in the striking phrase of Epictetus, 'fragments of God'. The Stoic teaching fitted admirably the religious practice of the Roman Empire. If the whole cosmos is animated by the universal reason, every part of it is alive, and we can discern among the different cults the worship of the one Supreme.

> 'There is one supreme god,' said Maximus of Madaura, 'who is, as it were, the God and mighty father of all. The powers of the deity, diffused through the universe which he has made, we worship under many names, as we are all ignorant of his true name. Thus it happens that while in diverse supplications we approach separated as it were certain parts of the Divine being, we are seen in reality to be the worshippers of him in whom all these parts are one.'[1]

The British government in India desires to offend no creed and give no advantage, as far as that is possible, to its own official religion. It is anxious to hold the scales even though it is difficult to say whether it has always been successful. The Hindu view is not motived by any considerations of political expediency. It is bound up with its religion and not its policy.

IV

It is not a mere concession to human imperfection, a vague sentiment for human weakness and sympathy with human error, that makes the Hindu shrink from imposing his views on others. If men feel safe and cosy in their little religious dug-outs, it is not for us to pull them out, though it is a matter for rejoicing that we remain outside: such is not the Hindu view.

V

The Hindu attitude is based on a definite philosophy of life which assumes that religion is a matter of personal realization. Creeds and dogmas, words and symbols have only an instrumental value. Their function is to aid the

[1] Estlin Carpenter, *Comparative Religion* (1916), p. 35.

growth of spirit by supplying supports for a task that is strictly personal. Spirit is free being, and its life consists in breaking free from conventions and penetrating into true being. The formless blaze of spiritual life cannot be expressed in human words. We tread on air so thin and rare that we do not leave any visible footprints. He who has seen the real is lifted above all narrowness, relativities, and contingencies. When we are anchored in spirit we are released, in the words of the *Imitation*, from a multitude of opinions. Authority is no longer binding, and ritual is no longer a support. The name by which we call God and the rite by which we approach Him do not matter much. Karl Heim declares that for the mystic, 'at the peak of ecstatic experience, all thoughts of the person of Jesus are lost and the soul sinks into the ocean of the divine unutterable'.[1] The sense of the present reality of God and the joy of His indwelling make the mystic indifferent to all questions of history. Toleration is the homage which the finite mind pays to the inexhaustibility of the Infinite.

Only in the experience of the greatest contemplatives do we have the pure apprehension of the Absolute, the utter surrender of the creature to the uncreated spirit. The use of symbols and images is forced on us by our nature. Our thinking and feeling are intimately related to the world of things in which we live. By reference to things that are seen we give concrete form to the intuition of the reality that is unseen. Symbolism is an essential part of human life,[2] the only possible response of a creature conditioned by time and space to the timeless and spaceless reality. Whether we pin our faith to stocks and stones or abstract thoughts and notions we are using concrete symbols which are impoverishments of the Supreme. In the fetish we have in a crude form the reinforcement of beliefs by the use of symbolic objects, and it persists even in the highest forms of faith. The highest symbols are only symbols, signs of an enduring

[1] *Spirit and Truth*, p. 106.

[2] Cf. Whitehead: 'Mankind, it seems, has to find a symbol in order to express itself. Indeed, expression is symbolism . . . Symbolism is no mere idle fancy or corrupt degeneration, it is inherent in the very texture of human life. Language itself is symbolism' (*Symbolism* (1928), p. 23).

reality which is larger than man's conception or picture of it. St. Thomas observes:

> 'It is agreed that whatever is received into anything is therein after the mode of the recipient: and consequently the likeness of the divine essence impressed on our intellect will be according to the mode of our intellect: and the mode of our intellect falls short of a perfect reception of the divine likeness; and the lack of perfect likeness may occur in as many ways as unlikeness may occur.'[1]

A system of dogma is nothing less than a closed circle whose more or less narrow limits are determined by the mental scope of its authors. A temporal and finite form of symbolism cannot be regarded as unique, definitive, and absolute.

Though each social group has its symbols and rites, its vision of an ideal society, its City of God in which citizenship is open to all members of the group, we cannot attribute finality to that with which we happen to be familiar. Truth is always greater than man's reach; there is more in God than we know. The seers speak of the 'Divine Dark', and their reverent agnosticism is a more fitting attitude than the flippant vulgarity with which some dogmatists speak of divine mysteries. The Divine Reality is determined by a number of intellectual co-ordinates; and their justification is in those rare moments when the veil is lifted and we catch a glimpse of the Absolute. There are many possible roads from time to eternity and we need to choose one road.

Growth in religion is a vital process. We start with a limited aspect, and if we steadily and with faith pursue it we get to the immeasurable reality. The doctrine we adopt and the philosophy we profess do not matter any more than the language we speak and the clothes we wear. The following texts, which can easily be multiplied, bear out this fact:

> 'Many names have been given to the Absolute by the learned for practical purposes such as Law, Self, Truth.'
>
> 'It is called Person by the Sāṁkhya thinkers, Brahman by the Vedāntins, pure and simple consciousness by the Vijñānavādins, Śūnya by the Nihilists, the Illuminator by the worshippers of the Sun. It is also called the Speaker, the Thinker, the Enjoyer of actions and the Doer of them.'

[1] *Summa Theologica*, iii, q. 92, a. 1.

'Śiva for the worshippers of Śiva, and Time for those who believe in Time alone.'[1]

The *Bhāgavata* says:

'Just as one substance with many qualities becomes manifold through the apprehension of the senses working in different ways, even so the one Supreme is conceived in different ways through different scriptural traditions.'[2]

For the peace of a religious soul it is not necessary that its insight be perfect, but its faith must be sure. We need not be all-knowing, but we cannot remain in doubt of our own belief. According to the *Bhagavadgītā*, even those who worship other gods (*anyadevatāḥ*), ancestral deities, elemental powers, if they do so with faith, then their faith is justified, for the Divine accepts every form conceived by the worshipper. Look at the attitude of Jesus to the Roman centurion: 'I have not found so great faith, no, not in Israel.' Any one who lives in the spirit of profundity, of absolute inner sincerity, will gain in spiritual stature. Luther refers to it in the *Larger Catechism*:

'Only the faith and trust of the heart make either God or Idol. If your faith and trust are right and sincere, you have the true God, and conversely—if your faith and trust are false and wrong, you have not the true God; for these two, God and faith belong together, and must be joined.'

The Danish thinker Kierkegaard says:

'If one who lives in the midst of Christianity goes into God's House —the true God's House—with the true idea of God in his mind and prays but prays in untruth; and if another who lives in a heathen country prays, but with a whole-souled passion for infinity, although his eye rests on an Idol; where then is more truth? The one man

[1] . . . ṛtam ātmā parambrahmā satyam ityādikā budhaih
kalpitā vyavahārārtham tasya saṁjñā mahātmanah
yaḥ pumān sāṁkhyadṛṣṭīnām brahma vedāntavādinām
vijñānamātram vijñānavidām ekāntanirmalam
yaḥ śūnyavādinām śūnyo bhāsako yo'rkatejasām
vaktāmantāṛtam bhoktā draṣṭā kartā sadaiva saḥ
puruṣah sāṁkhyadṛṣṭīnām īśvaro yogavādinām
śivaṁ śaśikalāṇkānām kālaḥ kālaikavādinam . . .
(*Yogavāṣiṣtha*, iii. 1. 12; iii. 5, 6, 7; v. 8. 19.)

[2] yathendriyaiḥ prthagdvāraiḥ arthobahuguṇāśrayah
eko naneyate tadvad bhagavān śāstravartmabhih (iii. 32. 33).

prays to God in truth, though he is worshipping an idol; the other prays to the true God in untruth and therefore in actual truth he worships an idol.'[1]

All sincere religious worship is a worship of the Supreme, who responds to every call to reach His unreachable heights. Even as we approach, so does the Divine receive.

The Hindu welcomes even the atheist into his fold, for if the latter is earnest in his search for truth and gains a true inwardness, he will discover the inadequacy of his faith. Theism and atheism, however antithetic they may seem to be, are equally plausible only at the superficial intellectual level.

No formula, however comprehensive, has absolute value for itself alone. It has to be accepted so long as it creates for those who use it a true path for spiritual life. Its value lies in its suggestive quality, its power to invoke or express the mysterious. If the most childish creations are accepted by the Hindu, it is because he sees in them the effort of man to respond to the unseen spirit. One's religiousness is to be measured not by one's theological affirmations but by the degree to which one brings forth the fruits of the spirit. Who can deny that the great scene of the quiet and glorious martyr-death of Socrates is of immortal value? If the pagan world produces characters full of love and piety, we cannot say that any one religion contains all the truth or goodness that exist. The Psalmist exclaims: 'This is the gate of the Lord: the righteous enter into it.' 'Of a truth', said the amazed St. Peter, 'I perceive that God is no respecter of persons, but in every nation he that feareth Him, and worketh righteousness, is accepted of Him.'[2] The kind Samaritan is a believer in God according to Jesus' declaration: 'He that doeth the Will of God, the same is my brother and my sister and my mother.' The damnatory clauses of the Athanasian Creed are in direct opposition to the simple determination of discipleship which Jesus laid down. We must judge religious men, not by what they say, but by what they do. Even the animistic religions which establish the kinship of man with life and the fertility cults are to be

[1] See Allen, *Kierkegaard: His Life and Thought* (1935), p. 149.
[2] Acts x. 34.

judged, not by the theories and opinions they express, but by the habits and practices they stimulate. If they help their followers to combat the individualistic tendency and overcome the dangers of selfishness, they may not have elevation of thought or sentiment, but they do show evidence of a power at work.[1]

M. Jacques Maritain raises the question of those outside the Christian fold who bear witness to authentic mystical experience and spiritual life, and observes:

'Everything leads us to think that such cases do exist, for we know that the unbaptised, though they lack the seal of unity and cannot participate by virtue of the Church in the proper work of the Church, which is the continuity of redemption, may nevertheless receive without knowing it that supernatural life which is the divine life blood in the veins of the Church and the direction of the Spirit which guides the Church; may belong invisibly to the Church of Christ, and have sanctifying grace and so theological faith and the infused virtues.'

Again:

'Because there is a flock the Shepherd who leads it is also the guide of those "other sheep" who, without knowing him, have also received of his plenitude and who have not yet heard his voice. Because she has received the deposit of revelation in its integrity the Church permits us to honour wheresoever they may be the scattered fragments of that revelation. The saints who belong to the invisible Church enable us to recognise their far-off brothers who are ignorant of her and who belong to her invisibly: St. John of the Cross enables us to do justice to Rāmakṛṣṇa.'[2]

No theory which has held the minds of men for centuries

[1] Cf. Matthew Arnold's lines on Progress:

Children of men! The unseen power whose eye
For ever doth accompany mankind,
Hath looked on no religion scornfully
That man did ever find.
Which has not taught weak wills how much they can?
Which has not fall'n on the dry heart like rain?
Which has not cried to sunk, self-weary man:
Thou must be born again!

[2] *The Degrees of Knowledge*, E.T. (1937), pp. 336, 338. Cf. 'All authentic mysticism which has developed in non-Christian countries, should be regarded as a fruit of the same supernatural life, that supernatural life which Christ, sovereignly generous in his gifts, communicates to those souls of good will who do not visibly belong to his flock' (ibid., p. 357).

producing results that make for pure and devoted living can be wholly devoid of truth. The emphasis on the goal of spiritual life bound together worshippers of many different types and saved the Hindus from spiritual snobbery.

It is argued that this or that religion has been an instrument of greater progress, and so has higher truth. It is represented as the power of a superior type of civilization. It is difficult to determine what constitutes the content of progress or superiority. Assuming that we can do so, it is difficult to say whether the progress of any people is due to their practice or repudiation of religion.[1] Christianity is no doubt the religion of Europe and America, which have today the leadership of the world, but can it be said that their progress is due to the incorporation of Christian principles in their society? The Ethiopians were Christianized earlier than many European races: but the blessings of civilization and progress they had not had until recently. Efficiency is the quality in which the West is supreme. It has worked out methods of increased efficiency in agriculture and industries, in economic affairs and political administration. It has organized efficiently the stores of goodwill and compassion by means of educational institutions, hospitals, and missions to the East. It has sent out to the non-Christian world devoted men and women, specially trained for their tasks, mainly to transplant there a faith, but also to alleviate human suffering and improve material conditions of life. But is this efficiency the expression of religion? Does it follow that we have the best religion simply because we have the most efficient military machine? Or again, are we to adopt the maxim of Patriarch Jacob: 'If the Lord will give me food to eat and raiment to put on, then shall the Lord be my God.' Is God a mere accessory to our needs? The New Testament tells us that it is not possible to serve both God and Mammon, and yet we are told that material prosperity is the chief criterion of success, that material rewards mean moral virtues. Wealthy people imagine that their wealth is a sign of God's favour, while poverty is a sign of moral turpi-

[1] The late Mr. G. Lowes Dickinson writes: 'The Western nations have never really been Christian!' (*Essay on the Civilisations of India, China and Japan* (1914), p. 15).

tude. We miss the true spirit of religion if we recommend it on account of its secular advantages. This ceaseless bribery has nothing in common with the religion which aims at saving the soul, even though we may lose the world. Spiritual goods are not to be confused with the world's currency. Plotinus says with great wisdom: 'If a man seeks from the good life anything beyond itself, it is not the good life that he is seeking.' As students of history, we admire the great empires with their palaces and pyramids. What could have seemed more enduring, more real, more impressive than Babylon and Nineveh, Athens and Rome? Where are they to-day? Again, the dominant peoples of the world centuries ago worshipped other gods. If pagan Greece was great, does it follow that the gods of Olympus deserved worship? Let us frankly recognize that the efficiency of a religion is to be judged by the development of religious qualities such as quiet confidence, inner calm, gentleness of the spirit, love of neighbour, mercy to all creation, destruction of tyrannous desires, and the aspiration for spiritual freedom, and there are no trustworthy statistics to tell us that these qualities are found more in efficient nations.[1]

If we are honest, we will admit that there are defects in the Hindu, the Buddhist, and the Christian societies as they are, and none can be regarded as satisfactory. But we delude ourselves into thinking that defects of our society are peripheral while those of others are central to their religions. The former can be remedied by a stricter adherence to its principles, while the latter can be set right only by an

[1] Mr. Babbitt writes: 'It is difficult to study the ancient records without being convinced that Buddha and many of his earlier followers were not in theory merely but in fact saintly. . . . If I had indeed to give an opinion, I should say, with a full sense of my own fallibility as well as of the prodigious difficulty of holding the balance even in comparisons of this kind, that Buddhism has had as many saints as Christianity and that it has, moreover, been less marred than Christianity by intolerance and fanaticism' (*On Being Creative* (1932), p. xxxiii). Cf. Sir Charles Eliot, who affirms that 'it is clearly absurd for Europe as a whole to pose as a qualified instructor in humanity and civilisation'. He writes: 'If Europeans have any superiority over Asiatics it lies in practical science, finance and administration, not in thought or art. Their gifts are authority and power to organise; in other respects their superiority is imaginary' (*Hinduism and Buddhism*, vol. i (1921), pp. xcvi and xcviii.).

abandonment of their central principles. 'If Christianity were only true to itself it could transform the world; unless Hinduism is splendidly untrue to itself, as one must hope it will be, its world will remain to the end unredeemed!'[1] How certain we are of the truth of our opinions! There is no worse prejudice than a belief in one's own inerrancy.

Unfortunately Christian religion inherited the Semitic creed of the 'jealous God' in the view of Christ as 'the only begotten son of God', and so could not brook any rival near the throne.[2] When Europe accepted the Christian religion, in spite of its own broad humanism, it accepted the fierce intolerance which is the natural result of belief in 'the truth once for all delivered to the saints'. Finality of conviction easily degenerates into the spirit of fanaticism, autocratic, over-positive, and bloodthirsty. It is terribly nervous of free thinking and puts down by force all deviations from ortho-

[1] Macnicol, *Is Christianity Unique?* (1936), p. 52. He writes: 'Christian nations have produced, and indeed produced in the name of Christianity, things even more hateful than the pariah village of India. But if that can be affirmed to be the very offspring of the spirit of Hinduism, as that which, by its nature, drains life of all significance and poisons its springs, whereas on the other hand the gross and evil things that Christians have fashioned flout the whole purpose and challenge of their faith, then the choice between the two types of religion may be in fact a choice between what is false and what is true, between the type of religion that denies the values that enrich life and that which seeks to conserve them' (p. 67).

Dr. Macnicol here distinguishes between the true teaching of Christianity and its actual practice, what Professor H. Frick calls the Gospel and Christianity. He writes: 'Other religions put us to shame by their superiority in many directions. They offer examples of deep religious earnestness, of willing sacrifice for their faith, of noble life, of devout discipline within the community, which strike us Christians dumb. Our arguments break down because our example is shown up in its true colours as the vain work of man, incapable of bearing witness. This failure, which is a fact of experience, demonstrates beyond a doubt that the theoretical separation between Christianity and the Gospel discussed above is right' (*The Gospel, Christianity and other Faiths* (1938), p. 52). If Christianity is different from the Gospel, may not other religions be different from their ideals? If other faiths are able to develop spiritual qualities 'which strike us Christians dumb', is there any need for ousting them?

[2] 'Though we or an angel from heaven should preach any gospel other than that which we preached, let him be anathema.' 'In no other name is there salvation, for neither is there any other name under heaven that is given among men wherein we must be saved.'

doxy. Whatever is in conflict with the closed dogma is said to be unscriptural and therefore false. Evolution is an error and witch-burning a duty. Ancient ignorance is sanctified as revealed truth. The disease of dogmatism, whether in religion or politics or social thought, is inimical to human freedom and progress. The non-Communists in Russia, the non-Fascists in Italy, the Jews and Socialists in Germany, are treated in the same spirit in which the orthodox Churches treated the Dissenters and the Nonconformists.[1]

The modern persecutors who are endeavouring to stamp out all religion, as in Russia, or change its nature, as in Germany, are repeating the old specious arguments which not long ago had wide assent among Christian people.[2] For more than fifteen hundred years Christians have been ready and eager to persecute those who do not share their particular brand of faith. They are ready to adopt a competitive fighting spirit and carry on a crusade against atheistical Russia as against the theistic Islam in the twelfth century. If the Bolshevists adopt similar measures in the interests of their

[1] Speaking of Athanasius, the founder of one kind of orthodoxy, Dr. Stanley says: 'It is a term which implies to a certain extent, narrowness and fixedness, perhaps even hardness of intellect, and deadness of feeling: at times rancorous animosity. His invectives against the Arians prove how far even a heroic soul can be betrayed by party spirit and the violence of the times. Amongst his favourite epithets for them are: devils, antichrists, maniacs, Jews, polytheists, atheists, dogs, wolves, lions, hares, chameleons, hydras, eels, cuttlefish, gnats, beetles, leeches. There may be cases where such language is justifiable but as a general rule and with all respect for him who uses it, this style of controversy can be mentioned, as a warning only, not as an example' (*Lectures on the History of the Eastern Church*, by A. P. Stanley (1862), pp. 246–7).

[2] Fulgentius (A.D. 500) declares that 'without a shadow of doubt, all Jews, heretics and schismatics will go into eternal fire'. Even the gentle St. Louis could say: 'The best answer that a layman can make to a contentious Jew is to run his sword into him as far as it will go.' Luther despaired of the salvation of Zwingli when he heard that the Swiss reformer pictured heaven as 'an assembly of all the saintly, the heroic, the faithful and the virtuous' like Aristides, Socrates, and Cato. Macaulay describes the Catholic theory in these words: 'I am in the right and you are in the wrong. When you are the stronger, you ought to tolerate me, for it is your duty to tolerate truth: But when I am the stronger, I shall persecute you, for it is my duty to persecute error.' One is reminded of the comment made during the World War by a chaplain to a colleague of another denomination: 'You and I are serving the same Master: you in your way, and I in His.'

version of the truth, we cannot say that they are impelled by a fanaticism while our conduct is governed by a philosophy. If we defend persecution in the name of the highest truth entrusted to us, there can be no logical objection to the persecution of all religions in the interests of atheism. The truth is that no doctrine becomes sounder, no truth truer, because it takes the aid of force. Bishop Barnes expresses the root of the matter when he says:

'In spite of the thousand instances in which it can be justified from the Old Testament, notwithstanding that it seems the natural product of the deepest piety, true though it may be that since the time of Constantine it has been practised by every great branch of the Christian Church, persecution in however mild a form, is usually both a mistake and a crime. It is a mistake because it so rarely succeeds.[1] It is a crime because in the name of virtue you unchain the baser passions of mankind.'[2]

History and geography, time and place affect our natural and spiritual existence. Ideas do not come to birth *in vacuo*. Their growth is moulded by the kind of mind that thinks them and the conditions in which they are thought, even as the plants and animals of a particular geographical area are determined by the physical conditions, soil, climate, &c. After all, our obligation to our religion or nation is not generally a matter of will or choice but one of blind fate or herd infection.[3] If the Hindu chants the Vedas on the banks

[1] Persecution is not always unsuccessful. It drove out Christianity from North Africa. The Albigenses were crushed by it. It banished from Spain every vestige of Protestantism. Lecky tells us that the essential catholicity of France was due mainly to the massacre of St. Bartholomew's Day and the revocation of the Edict of Nantes. The sword of the Christian converted thousands to the faith and strengthened the power of the Church against the heresies that threatened her.

[2] *Should Such a Faith Offend?*, p. xxvii.

[3] Cf. Tolstoi's letter to the painter Jan Styka, reprinted in *Le Théosophe* (6 Jan. 1911): 'The doctrine of Jesus is to me only one of the beautiful doctrines which we have received from the ancient civilisations of Egypt, Israel, Hindustan, China, Greece. The two great principles of Jesus; the love of God, that is, of absolute perfection, and the love of one's neighbour, that is, of all men without distinction, have been preached by all the sages of the world. . . . I have no predilection for Christianity. If I have been particularly attracted by the teaching of Jesus it is (1) because I was born and lived among Christians and (2) because I have found a great spiritual joy in disentangling the pure doctrine from the astonishing falsification created by the Churches.'

of the Ganges, if the Chinese meditates on the Analects, if the Japanese worships the image of Buddha, if the European is convinced of Christ's mediatorship, if the Arab reads the Qur'ān in his mosque, and if the African bows down to a fetish, each one of them has exactly the same reason for his particular confidence. Each form of faith appeals in precisely the same way to the inner certitude and devotion of its followers. It is their deepest apprehension of God and God's fullest revelation to them. The claim of any religion to validity is the fact that only through it have its followers become what they are. They have grown up with it and it has become a part of their being.

'It is God's countenance as revealed to us; it is the way in which, being what we are, we receive and react to, the revelation of God. It is binding upon us, and it brings us deliverance. It is final and unconditional for us, because we have nothing else, and because in what we have we can recognise the accents of the divine voice. But this does not preclude the possibility that other racial groups, living under entirely different cultural conditions may experience their contact with the Divine life in quite a different way, and may themselves also possess a religion which has grown up with them, and from which they cannot sever themselves so long as they remain what they are. And they may quite sincerely regard this as absolutely valid for them, and give expression to this absolute validity according to the demands of their own religious feeling.'[1]

The different creeds are the historical formulations of the formless truth. While the treasure is one and inviolable, the earthen vessel that contains it takes the shape and the colour of its time and environment. Every historical view is a possible, perfect expression of the Divine, capable, not in spite of but because of its peculiarity, of leading us to the highest. The distinctiveness has a special appeal to the group. Dr. Inge says that no Englishman can be a Roman Catholic: Santayana writes a commentary on this text:

'If the Englishman likes to call himself a Catholic, it is a fad like a thousand others, to which his inner man so seriously playful, is prone to lend itself. He may go over to Rome on a spiritual tour: but if he is converted really and becomes a Catholic at heart, he is no longer the man he was. Words cannot measure the chasm which must henceforth separate him from everything at home. For a modern Englishman with freedom and experiment and reserve in his blood, to go over to Rome

[1] Troeltsch, *Christian Thought* (1923), pp. 26–7.

is essentially suicide: the inner man must succumb first. Such an Englishman might become a saint but only by becoming a foreigner.' The change is not an organic one but a displacement of one nature by another. Religion is like the string of a violin: if removed from its resonant body, it will give the wrong tone, if any.

Even as human personality depends on the persistence of memory, social life depends on the persistence of tradition. Tradition is society's memory of its own past. If we tear up the individual from his traditional roots he becomes abstract and aberrant. Those who believe in conversion look upon the historical process as a tyranny imposed on man from without, and assume that the choice of a religion is made by a process not different from spinning a coin. History is something organic, a phase of man's terrestrial destiny as essential for him as memory is for personal identity. It is the triumph of memory over the spirit of corruption. To forget our social past is to forget our descent. It would be, therefore, as difficult to separate a man's religion from the rest of his life as it would be to separate a vein of gold from the rock in which it is embedded. The *Bhagavad-gītā*, with a clear grasp of the historical, warns us against taking away the psychological comfort of people by unsettling their faiths.[1] We are required to confirm the faith of others even though we may not have any share in it.[2] Human nature is not a clean slate, a blackboard on which we can scribble anything with a piece of chalk and then wipe it off with a sponge. It is a sensitive spirit in which subtlest impressions are recorded. We must have a clear notion of what it costs to produce a social order, maintain an equilibrium between freedom and stability, without which there is no decent life. As every religion aims at social cohesion, and gives it to a degree, to replace it by a rival religion is

[1] iii. 26.

[2] Robert Louis Stevenson once wrote to a lady missionary: 'Forget wholly and for ever all small pruderies and remember that you cannot change ancestral feelings of right and wrong without what is practically murder. Barbarous as they may seem, always bear them with patience, always judge them with gentleness, always find in them some seed of good: see that you always develop them: remember that all you can do is to civilise the man in the line of his own civilisation, such as it is.'

to be attempted with great caution. Besides, an outrage on others' convictions cannot be a triumph for any religion. It is not blind caprice that inclines us to prefer in religion symbols that are ancient, emblems that are moss-grown. Novelties may rouse our sense of curiosity, but the deeper emotional levels are stirred by older impulses whose echoes go back to the childhood of the individual and the race. Modernity may bring new awakenings, but old memories rouse powerful dreams. The author of the *Bhagavadgītā* realized that the crudest of sensible images and the most primitive gestures of worship are means of apprehending the holy. Though none of these ideas, affections, and imaginations is adequate to the ineffable object of our worship, the discipline of religion demands that we should be willing to worship where we are and as we can. The different symbols, however remote from reality, wake up and nourish a rich religious experience. As a means of creative religion the native cult has an absolute advantage over any imported religion,[1] for a convert to a new religion feels an utter stranger to himself. He feels like an illegitimate child with no heritage, no link with the men who preceded him. What in other people is a habit or an instinct seems to be with him a pose or an affectation. There is no inner development or natural progress to the new religion. It does not arise out of the old, but falls from one knows not where.

Unfortunately, even as faith in one's nation kills faith in mankind, faith in one religion seems to kill faith in others. The followers of each religion feel called upon to make their religion an article of export quite as much as Chinese porce-

[1] Gandhi writes: 'In the matter of religion I must restrict myself to my ancestral religion; that is, the use of my immediate surroundings in religion. If I find my religion defective, I should serve it by purifying it of defects.' He told the Christian missionaries: 'it is no part of your call, I assure you, to tear up the lives of the people of the East by the roots' (C. F. Andrews, *Mahatma Gandhi's Ideas*, p. 96). The famous anthropologist Pitt-Rivers writes: 'The public at home probably does not appreciate how strongly the majority of field ethnographers, sympathetically anxious to learn all about the customs and religion of the people and working in all parts of the world, have been driven, often against their inclinations, to the conclusion that Christian proselytism has done irretrievable harm to native races by disintegrating their culture and to us also by the unrest and antagonism the process evokes' (*The Clash of Culture and Contact of Races*, p. 240).

lain or Japanese colour-prints. They would drive all souls into the same spiritual enclosure. They are unaware of the great loss to humanity which would follow the imposition of any common creed on all. The supersession of the different religious traditions would make this world into a poor place. Have we the right to destroy what we have not learnt to appreciate? To drag into the dust what is precious to the soul of a people, what has been laboriously built up by the wisdom of ages, is spiritual vandalism. Among the inspiring treasures of the human spirit is the memory of Gautama the Buddha. Its hold over the imagination of millions of our fellow beings is immense; its inspiration to braver and nobler living for centuries is incalculable; its contribution to the refining of the spirit of man and the humanizing of his social relations is impressive. And yet attempts are made by men fighting under other flags, earnest lovers of their kind, no doubt, to destroy the memory of that great soul, to terminate his influence. We can only attribute it to blind prejudice, to pitiful ignorance. A religion which can develop such hardness of heart, which can look with equanimity on such a racial calamity, is hardly worth the name. 'Think not', says Jesus, 'that I come to destroy the law or the prophets: I am not come to destroy but to fulfil.'[1] He tells us not to put out the smoking flax, not to break the bruised reed.

As every religion is a living movement, no one phase or form of it can lay claim to finality. No historical religion can be regarded as truth absolute and changeless. After all, even man's history on earth is inconsiderable when compared to the age of the oldest rocks, and the career of any particular religion is still less important if we judge by its age, and it is presumptuous to assume that in this short period we have arrived at truth absolute and final.

We may assume that God is not only inalienably immanent in man by virtue of his first creation, but is also energizing in him. He holds us by the roots of our being, however abandoned we may seem. He is everywhere sustaining by His spirit the tottering footsteps of all mankind in its toilsome ascent towards spiritual heights. We cannot rush nature, though we can help its activities. If we are so

[1] Matthew v. 17.

priggish as to strip a religion of everything of sense and imagination instead of quietly awaiting the stripping action of God, we may end by leaving nothing on which our sense-conditioned minds and passion-limited hearts can lay hold.

Those who believe in an immanent Logos are obliged to admit the value of other faiths. While the apostles recognized the natural impulse in man to seek after God, and declared that the Divine is not without its witness in the minds of the heathens, they regarded the rites and beliefs of the Gentiles as the products of superstition and error. St. Paul had the contempt of the Hebrew prophets for the 'idols of the heathen'. Justin Martyr (A.D. 150) held that those who lived with reason as Socrates and Heraclitus did were Christians. Clement of Alexandria maintained that philosophy was a *paidagogos* to bring the Greeks to Christ even as the Law was for the Jews. St. Augustine held that all good men from the beginning of the human race have Christ for their head.

This whole order of ideas derived from the Logos doctrine is wrecked by the Jewish inheritance.[1] For the Jews Yahweh was the God, and all other gods were the gods of their enemies. The Jews were the chosen people who had their own system of laws and taboos. The great sin was to break the laws, desert their own true God, and go after others. For a religion like Hinduism, which emphasizes Divine Immanence, the chosen people embraces all mankind. If we have something to teach our neighbours we have also something to learn from them. The Hindu sage is aware that the road to reality which he himself has taken is altogether too steep and perhaps not easy to follow for the vast multitudes who form the bulk of Hindu society and who yet have a sense of religion. They have their rights, too, though they cannot be expected to move at the pace of the enlightened, as they have not had his advantages. They must be led to the same goal, but along their own paths.

[1] Professor Angus, after stating that 'never was there a more tolerant age than that in which Christianity appeared', observes: 'In the matter of intolerance, Christianity differed from all pagan religions, and surpassed Judaism: in that respect it stood in direct opposition to the spirit of the age' (*The Mystery Religions and Christianity*, pp. 277–8).

There are two rival philosophies of life, which may be stated in the words of Plato and Rousseau. Plato says:

> 'He [the lawgiver] need only tax his invention to discover what convictions would be most beneficial to a city, and then combine all manner of devices to ensure that the whole of such a community shall treat the topic in one single and selfsame lifelong tone, alike in song, in story and in discourse.'[1]

Rousseau says:

> 'The only man who does his own will is he who has no need, in order to do it, to put the arms of another to it as well as his own; whence it follows that the first of all good things is not authority but liberty. The man truly free wants only what he can have and does what pleases himself. There you have my fundamental maxim.'[2]

Uncertainty between these naturally hostile views of human life is written across the history of man's pilgrimage down the centuries. The one assumes that man has no instinct for truth and his own reason is likely to do him wrong, and he must be compelled to see the truth and do the right. Let us breed human beings like guinea-pigs, mould them like clay, condition their reflexes, and determine their thought and life. This view of man justifies Fascist and Communist indoctrination, while the other supports the methods of democracy and liberalism. It regards man, not as a chained brute, but as a potential spirit. It is all the difference between force and freedom, uniformity and individuality, conversion and growth. Religion at least must remain the home of liberty. It cannot be forced on us from without by machinery. The law of the soul's growth is different from the law of things, where we are the victims of the deceptive bondage of possession. The seed must grow until it forces the fulfilment from within. Truth is as much a quality of the mind that seeks it as of the things in which it finds it. The search is as important as the discovery. Truth can never be enforced. We can by force make others pretend and behave, but cannot make them accept and believe. We can impose the forms and the outward apparatus, but cannot impart the secret life. The latter lives on under imported forms. Christians in East and West may use the same forms, the same words, and yet give different meanings and have

[1] *Laws*, A. E. Taylor's E.T. [2] *Émile*.

different experiences. When the West took over Christianity, the essentials of it never became its inward property. It fashioned out a new mode of religious expression, accepted some aspects of it which appealed to it, and dropped out or misunderstood others. When we change our religion we do not change our habits of mind and practices of life.[1]

Religious life is not exempt from the laws which govern our mental activity. We comprehend and assimilate a new

[1] 'The Indians of Guatemala really hardly know whether they are praying to their god Gucumatz or to Jesus Christ. The ceremonies are half pagan, half Christian and no Catholic priest would venture during "Holy Week" to forbid the Indians their masked dances, in honour not of Christ but of Judas. The parish money would not come in if the priest were to forbid the Indians in their dramas, to stage the escape of St. John and the divine maiden on the night of the Crucifixion deceiving their Lord most sinfully' (*The Savage Hits Back*, by Julius E. Lips (1937), p. 22).

Mr. Aldous Huxley writes: 'The Catholic pantheon has received the most surprising additions, the Gospel story been treated to all kinds of the oddest emendations. There are villages, for example, where Judas instead of being burnt on Easter Saturday, as is the case in the more orthodox cities, is worshipped as a god. At Atitlan, according to S. K. Lothrop, it is currently believed that St. John and the Virgin had a love affair on the night of the crucifixion. To prevent a repetition of this event, their images are locked up on Good Friday in separate cells of the town prison. The next morning, their respective confraternities come, and for a couple of hundred pesos a piece bail them out of captivity. Honour is safe for another year; the saints are taken back to their altars.' After giving a detailed description of their religious forms, he concludes: 'Christianity for these people of the Guatemalan highlands is no more than an equivalent alternative to the aboriginal religions. Their catholicism is just an affair of magic, fetishism and sociable activity' (*Beyond the Mexique Bay* (1934), pp. 160 and 163). It is well known that many Indian converts to Christianity adopt Hindu beliefs and practices. In an article in the *Baptist Missionary Review*, April 1937, a number of lady missionaries deplore the prevalence of aboriginal practices among Christian women. 'It is amazing to enter a Christian village and to observe upon the necks of women and children all sorts of charms. The children especially wear as many as six or seven separate necklaces of silver, horsehair, black strands of hemp or of common cord. On each of these will be a flat piece of silver with the crudely engraved image of the monkey-god or a small roll sealed at the ends which will contain the dried body of a spider or lizard's tail or perhaps a bit of parchment upon which a mantram has been inscribed. The temptation of Christians to take part in Hindu festivals is very real.' Mass conversions on a large scale are Hinduizing Christianity. Hindu beliefs and practices are given Christian labels. Again, 'it is certain that the mass of the Chinese people still regard Christianity as essentially a foreign religion, as being indeed the religion of the West: and there are grounds for doubting whether any considerable

view in accordance with our own intellectual potentialities.[1] Many of the ideas and symbols of Christianity can be traced to earlier periods. Sir Arthur Evans, while conducting the excavations at the Knossos palace in the island of Crete, found a cross of fine-grained dark marble, and a priest of the Greek Orthodox Church who happened to be present reverently worshipped it, refusing to believe that it was not a Christian cross but some other earlier by three thousand years than the Cross of Calvary.[2] The hieroglyphic inscription of Akhnaton, 'the first individual in history' according to J. H. Breasted, reads: 'Thou, Father, art in my heart. There is no other who knoweth Thee except me, Thy son.' The mystery religions fashioned saviour gods and offered

section of the three millions who make up the Christian community have really come to feel at home in their new faith' (Hughes, *The Invasion of China by the Western World* (1937), pp. 54–5).

[1] Marc Connelly's Negro play *The Green Pastures* makes us wonder about our inborn certainty of the colour of the godhead. His God is the God of the Negroes, black and comfortable. Dressed like a Negro preacher He lives surrounded by dusky angels and archangels in a heaven which is an ornate happy place with gilded fencing and pillow-soft clouds, with swings for the cherubs, green lawns for picnicking, custards for every one, and an enormous fish-fry. 'De Lawd' is kind but just and careful. He keeps the heavenly accounts accurately with the help of the archangel Gabriel. His study is swept out daily by cleaning angels, with checked aprons tied over their wings. He is not, however, free from worry. He bothers about the sun and the moon and the little planet called the earth which He once made with a bit of extra firmament. And every thousand years or so He opens the Golden Gates and climbs down the big staircase to see how Adam and all his children are getting on down below on the earth, which is peopled with Negro children of Israel in modern clothes. He finds all kinds of sin and trouble, and is moved to raise up some good man or other to lead the world to repentance. The first time it is Noah, a harassed little Negro preacher, who is worried about the 'allicats' and the bed bugs and particularly the snakes in the Ark, and considers forty days of flood 'a complete rain'. Next time it is Moses, a simple shepherd in Egypt, who is charmed at the thought of becoming 'a great tricker' in theory, but apologetic before all his major miracles. 'I am sorry Pharaoh, but you can't fight the Lord. Let my people go.' Then it is Joshua, blowing his trumpets jubilantly before the walls of Jericho, and lastly the apocryphal Hezdrel, 'a man nobody ain't ever heard of', who worries De Lawd and harasses Him in prayer until He comes down and saves Jerusalem, teaching Him, in a curious and disturbing exchange of dialogue, that the God of vengeance must be the God of mercy too. It is an ideal picture which strikes at nothing in faith which is real and deeply rooted. The actual religion of the Negro is not quite so neat.

[2] *The Palace of Minos at Knossos*, p. 517.

a parallel to the Messianic expectations of the Jews. When Christianity moved out of purely Jewish surroundings it made terms with the religious beliefs and practices of the Graeco-Roman world. Christmas is in its origins the pagan festival of the winter solstice. Its association with trees goes back to the days when trees were endowed with sentient life and made the oracles of the will and wisdom of the gods. The toys that we hang on the Christmas tree for the children remind us of that passage in the *Georgics* of Virgil where he tells us how the peasants of his day would 'hang puppet faces on tall pine to swing' in honour of the god Bacchus. The Logos conception was taken over by the author of the Fourth Gospel from Greek philosophy. Catholic worship in some of its aspects reminds us of the cult of the Alexandrian divinity, Isis. The worship of the Mother and the many saints of the Roman calendar takes us to the pagan world. In the accepted texts of Jesus' teaching we find little support for the worship of the Mother. At Eleusis a church of St. Demetrius was built on the site of Demeter's temple. No one who is familiar with the Latin, Russian, and Eastern forms of Christianity can fail to be impressed by its compromises with the religious systems which preceded Christianity. This generosity is only justice and not mere pandering to the unregenerate instincts of the primitive pagans.

VI

All this does not mean that there is no such thing as religious reform or growth. Loyalty to tradition does not exclude adaptation. Hinduism recognizes that each religion is inextricably bound up with its culture and can grow organically. While it is aware that all religions have not attained to the same level of truth and goodness, it insists that they all have a right to express themselves. Religions reform themselves by interpretation and adjustment to one another. The Hindu attitude is one of positive fellowship, not negative tolerance. The different cults are brought into mutually helpful relations. Hinduism and its offshoot Buddhism spread over a large part of Asia, not only in Kashmir and Assam, Burma and Ceylon, but also in China and Cambodia, Korea and Japan. The movement found its way northwards into Bactria, and beyond that to Chinese Turkestan, Tibet, and Mongolia. The permeation of the Indian religious spirit from the Pacific Ocean almost to the Mediterranean is not based on a conviction of the finality of its particular faith and the futility of the rest. Hinduism and Buddhism do not work from outward to inward, but work from within outwards. They do not change the label and wait for a change in life, but change the life while retaining the labels.[1] Words form the thread on which we string our experiences. Rememberable words give continuity and direction to our lives and thoughts. Every group has a natural prejudice in favour of the words and symbols through which its experience attains clarification and communal expression. All the religions in the world, like all the women in the world, do not compare with the one that is our own. If strangers are sceptical it is because they do not know. Hinduism respects this sentiment and effects the change in the essentials. We can understand only so much of the divine truth as has some correspondence with our own nature and its past development. Man cannot be remade overnight. By a practical deepening of experience we alter the ideas. The nobler the man, the worthier is his conception of God and the purer his worship. By raising the standard of religious life we clarify the vision. When you let in strong sunlight, cobwebs disappear. Beliefs which are irrational and practices which are repugnant to our conscience get transformed in the new atmosphere into which they are brought. Falsehood carries within itself the seed of its own decay, so that if you give it time, it will surely perish. If we substitute one form of words for another the new form points to no objective and significant reality to

[1] 'Brahmanism is one of the greatest assimilants that the world has known' (F. W. Thomas, *The Mutual Influence of Mohamadans and Hindus* (1892), p. 2). 'It is infinitely absorbent like the ocean. At all events until the coming of the Muslims, fierce and warlike tribes, again and again invaded its northern plains, overthrew its princes, captured and laid waste its cities, set up new states and built new capitals of their own and then vanished into that great tide of humanity, leaving to their descendants nothing but a swiftly diluted strain of alien blood and a few shreds of alien custom that were soon transformed into something cognate with their overmastering surroundings' (Dodwell, *India* (1936), vol. i, p. 2).

the old man. A vital process must happen before the new form acquires meaning.

While the Hindu teachers admit the crude beliefs of primitive peoples as the truth narrowed down to their limited understanding, they insist on their raising themselves to the comprehension of the highest. We have no right to prostrate ourselves before any being than whom we are able to conceive one that is higher. 'Thou shalt have no other God before me' means really 'thou shalt not convert life into something that is dead or suffer a known semblance of reality to be put in the place of reality'. Faith is a living responding of the soul to God. It is ceaseless action, perpetual renewal. A man lives by running: when we stand still, we are almost dead. Unless we are straining towards perfection, we have forfeited our manhood. The strain is the highest thing in life. The universal prayer of the Hindus coeval with India's cultural history, open to all men and women, high and low, without limit of time or place, is the Gāyatrī.[1] It asks us to seek the truth fearlessly and with single-minded sincerity. It assumes faith in the strength of the human soul and in an end to human effort. For a religious soul there is no rest from the striving to see what he cannot yet see and to become what as yet he is not. Those who tell us that, if only we believe our mental histories will end, our spiritual journeys will be over, do not understand the life of religion. 'Whosoever is unflagging in his striving for ever, him we can redeem.'[2] The prayer requires us, not to lose ourselves, but to find our true self, naked and without the mask of falsehood, to live our lives on the highest plane of self-criticism and human aspiration. Buddha warns us against mental sloth or stupidity. We must examine daily our life and thought in the light of truth, and throw away whatever is false or has served its day. Truth requires no other authority than that which it contains within itself. Only, we must not forget that the commandment to love one another is itself

[1] Though it may have started as a primitive form of sun-worship, its content was refined very early. It was taught to the non-Indian non-Hindus of Java, though to-day it is unfortunately restricted to the upper classes and men only. See Sarkar, *Indian Influences on the Literatures of Java and Bali*, pp. 70–1.

[2] Goethe's *Faust*, Pt. II, Act v.

part of the truth which must be held at all costs. The greatest requirement of human life is to be loyal to truth as one sees it. Above all, one must learn to be loyal to the spirit of loyalty in other people, even when we do not share their visions of truth. The supreme object of loyalty is the spirit of loyalty. This world loyalty is the essence of religion. It is the deepest truth and the widest charity. The greatest contribution we can make to religious growth is to impart the inquiring spirit, the spirit of devotion to truth which is larger than any tradition or system of beliefs and symbols. Religious life becomes a co-operative enterprise binding together different traditions and perspectives to the end of attaining a clearer vision of the perfect reality.

The triumphs of this method of religious reform have been striking: no less so are its failures. After these many centuries, Hinduism, like the curate's egg, is good only in parts. It is admirable and abhorrent, saintly and savage, beautifully wise and dangerously silly, generous beyond measure and mean beyond all example. It is strange how long primitive superstitions will last, if we do not handle them roughly. When they were taken over by Hinduism, they were given added respectability. It is not easy to move men to quit their old ways, overcome indolence and inertia, and venture on new paths. Though the most revolting practices of cannibalism, polyandry, and human sacrifices were soon abolished, others, such as animal sacrifices, repugnant to our moral sentiments still persist. While we may criticize the cheap assurance of reformers, they are morally a force to be greatly welcomed, for they have the quality of a faith that moves mountains. The Hindu method, being a democratic one, is more expensive and wasteful. Reform by consent is slower than reform by compulsion in religion as in politics, but it has the human touch. Life is a school of patience and 'charity suffereth long'. An extensive application of the principle of liberty, equality, and fraternity has made Hinduism the most elastic of all religions, the most capable of adapting itself to new conditions. It is less dependent on historical facts, is freer from authority. Its gods form no exclusive group. Its pantheon has stood wide open for the admission of new deities who are always naturalized as aspects of the Supreme godhead. The danger of the Hindu attitude is that what is may be accepted because it is, and progress may be infinitely delayed.

VII

The other religions which came into India are influenced by the Hindu spirit. While Hinduism is a large synthesis achieved in the course of centuries, Islam is the creation of a single mind and is expressed in a single sentence. 'There is one God and Mohammad is his prophet.' Mohammad claims to be the final link of the great chain from Adam through Noah, Moses, and Jesus. His simple faith, with its real brotherhood and hatred of idolatry, hurled itself on the world, bidding it choose between conversion and subjection. It claimed world dominion. Before his death Mohammad saw himself master of Arabia and had already begun to assail his neighbours. Four years later, in A.D. 636, the power of Persia was shattered at the battle of Kadisiya. A century from the Hijra the northern frontier had been advanced to the Jaxartes and the conquest of Sindh had brought Islam into contact with Hinduism. In the West, Antioch fell in 638 and Alexandria in 648. Carthage was torn from the empire sixty years later and Spain was invaded in 710. This triumphal progress was checked by the youthful vigour of the West under Charles Martel on the momentous battle-field of Tours. Militant and inelastic, Islam frames the same dogmas, prescribes the same laws, upholds the same constitution, and enforces the same customs. It borrowed its idea of Messiah from Judaism, its dogmatism and asceticism from Christianity, its philosophy from Greece, and its mysticism from India and Alexandria.

The Indian form of Islam is moulded by Hindu beliefs and practices. Popular Islam shows the influence of Hinduism. The Shiahs are much nearer Hinduism than the Sunnis. The Khojas, whose tenets are a mixture of Vaiṣṇava and Shi'a doctrines, hold that Ali is the tenth incarnation of Viṣṇu. Sufism is akin to Advaita Vedānta. It believes in the non-dual Absolute and looks upon the world as the reflection of God, who is conceived as light. The Sufis abstain from animal food and believe in rebirth and incarnation.[1] The dogmatism of Islam was toned down in India. The emperor Akbar was led to give up his faith in the absoluteness of Islam and declare that 'there are sensible men in all religions, and abstemious thinkers and men endowed with miraculous powers among all nations'. He says: 'Each person, according to his condition, gives the supreme being a name, but in reality to name the unknowable is vain.'[2] He is, according to Max Müller, 'the first who ventured on a comparative study of the religions of the world'.[3] He was not, however, lacking in the spirit of religion. Akbar, whatever may have been the extent of his failing in practice, was a sincerely religious man. Jahangir declares that his father 'never for one moment forgot God'. That testimony is corroborated by Abul Fazl, who avers that his sovereign 'passes every moment of his life in self-examination or in adoration of God'. Jahangir said of the Hindu anchorite Jadrup that he had 'thoroughly mastered the science of the Vedānta, which is the science of Sufism'.[4] Dara Shikoh, the eldest son of Shah Jahan, is the author of a treatise designed to prove that the differences between Hindu and Muslim were matters only of language and expression. Kabīr, Nānak, Dādu, and a host of others point to a blend of Hindu and Muslim religious doctrines. Bahaism stands up for a free religious fellowship. Baha'u'llah's advice to his apostles has nothing in common with fanaticism.

'O Children of Baha! Have intercourse with all the peoples of the world, with the disciples of all religions in the spirit of complete joyfulness. Remind them of what is good for them all, but beware of making the word of God the stumbling block of friction or the source of mutual hatred. If ye know what the other does not know, tell him with the tongue of friendliness and love. If he accepts it and takes it up, then the aim has been attained, if he rejects it, pray for him and leave him to himself; ye may never importune him'.

[1] *Dabistan*, E.T. by Shea and Troyer, vol. iii, p. 281. A celebrated Sufi of the seventeenth century, by name Sabjani, it is said, 'abstained from flesh, venerated the mosques, performed in houses of idols according to the usage of the Hindus, religious rites in mosques, worship (pūja) and prostration after the manner of the Mussulmans' (pp. 301–2).

[2] Vincent Smith, *Akbar the Great Moghul* (1917), pp. 349–50.

[3] *Introduction to the Science of Religion*, p. 68.

[4] *Memoirs of Jahangir*, E.T. by Beveridge, vol. i, p. 356.

The conflicts between Hindus and Muslims, which have become more frequent in recent times, fill one with shame and grief. Political and economic considerations are mixed up with religious questions. The New Indian Constitution, which has arranged political power and influence in proportion to numbers, has added to the tension. The bid for souls and the scramble for posts are getting confused.

VIII

The influence on Christianity is a more interesting study, indicating the conflict between tradition and experiment in the Christian mind. The traditional attitude is the one expressed in Bishop Heber's hymn. It has had a long history. It used political power for religious propaganda.[1] It is represented to-day by Karl Barth of 'Dialectical Theology' fame. He brands non-Christian religions as foes to Christendom, which must in no circumstances 'howl with [those] wolves'. A true Christian's response to other faiths must be an intolerant No! He writes: 'Does Christendom know how near to her lies the temptation, by a slight betrayal of her proper business, to escape such an imminent conflict with these alien religions? Does she know that this must not happen? We can only ask: Does she know that under no circumstances must she howl with the wolves?' Any attempt to see anything valuable in other religions 'must be abandoned without reserve. Christendom should advance right into the midst of those religions whatever their names may be, and let come what will, deliver her message of the one God and of His compassion for men forlorn, without yielding by a hairbreadth to their "daemons".'[2] The other

[1] St. Francis Xavier wrote from Cochin on 20 Jan. 1548 to King John III of Portugal, 'You must declare as plainly as possible . . . that the only way of escaping your wrath and obtaining your favour is to make as many Christians as possible in the countries over which they rule.' See Macnicol, *The Living Religions of India* (1934), p. 268 n. The African explorer H. M. Stanley remarked, when he inspected the original maxim gun, 'What a splendid instrument for spreading Christianity and civilization among the savage races of Africa!'

[2] Quoted in Macnicol's *Is Christianity Unique?* (1936), pp. 168–9. The Bishop of London in his work on *Why am I a Christian?* writes: 'I have been round the world and seen at close quarters the other religions of the world. They have certainly got no candle to light them on the way' (p. 32).

religions are, in fact, untouchable. The Report of the Commission on Christian Higher Education in India, presided over by Dr. A. D. Lindsay, expresses the Christian motive thus:

'The Christians are convinced that they have a message which alone is a solution for the problems of humanity and therefore of India. They believe themselves to be bearers of good news which they wish to share with others. Their hope and desire is that India may become Christian. They can never acquiesce in the position that different religions are good for different communities, that all religions are fundamentally the same and that it is for each religious community to seek to make the best of the possibilities of its own religion.'[1]

This is a paraphrase of Karl Barth's attitude in milder terms, for the Report continues: 'there is little in either Hinduism or Islam which can resist the irreligious influence of economic and psychological determinism'.[2] The Report notes that 'the characteristic note of modern Hinduism is its undiscriminating comprehensiveness'.[3]

Even though this view has high authority and age to back it, it does not receive general support. Even from the official biographies of Jesus we learn that He is more considerate and compassionate than His followers.

We cannot dismiss as negligible the sense of the majesty of God and consequent reverence in worship which are conspicuous in Islam, the deep sympathy for the world's sorrow and unselfish search for a way of escape in Buddhism, the desire for contact with ultimate reality in Hinduism, the belief in a moral order in the universe and consequent insistence on moral conduct in Confucius. It is difficult for

Augustine adopted a very different and more liberal attitude: 'If those who are called philosophers, and especially the Platonists, have said aught that is true and in harmony with our faith, we must not shrink from it, but claim it for our use as from those who possess it unlawfully . . . heathen learning is not all made up of false and superstitious fancies' (Kirk, *The Vision of God* (1931), p. 334). The late Canon H. R. L. Sheppard wrote: 'The intolerable idea that God only revealed himself to one people and left all the others in darkness is vanished save in the least enlightened circles' (*The Impatience of a Parson*, p. 107).

[1] p. 136.

[2] p. 148.

[3] p. 147. Referring to this feature Dr. L. P. Jacks writes: 'The spiritual men of India, a great and watchful multitude whose spiritual status is unattainable, are many of them catholics in a deeper sense than we of the West have yet given to the word . . .' (*Two Letters* (1934), p. 26).

us at this time of the day to believe that only one religion provides divine revelation and others have nothing of it.

IX

Karl Barth is definite that the glimpses and intuitions of God found in other religions are not a preparation for the full revelation in Christ but are misdirections. In this matter Karl Barth may have the support of rigid minds, but the general Christian tradition is not with him. Even in the Old Testament the local cults were not destroyed, but reformed. The prophets, it is true, repudiated the cult of the Queen of Heaven, but she has returned in the Virgin Mother. Adherents of Trinitarian religions persuade themselves by a jugglery of words that they believe in one God, and the best that has been said on the subject is that it is a mystery of which no rational explanation is possible. It is difficult to know the real distinction between praying to the Madonna, Saints, and Angels and worshipping minor deities as symbols of the Supreme. The Christian doctrine did not grow up in a vacuum, in a straight encounter between God and soul. It arose in a world full of warring sects and rival faiths, and used whatever was at hand. Palestine gave morality and monotheism, Greece art and philosophy, Rome order and organization, and the East mysticism and a gift for worship. The great Church Fathers did not repudiate the non-Christian faiths in the Barthian way. Clement was not only a Christian Father but a learned philosopher, who clothed the new religion in the amenities of Greek thought. Origen said in reply to Celsus' criticism: 'When God sent Jesus to the human race, it was not as though He had just awakened from a long sleep. Jesus has at all times been doing good to the human race. No noble deed amongst men has ever been done without the Divine word visiting the souls of those who even for a brief space were able to receive its operations.'[1] 'That which is called the Christian religion', says Augustine, 'existed among the ancients, and never did not exist, from the beginning of the human race until Christ came in the flesh, at which time the true religion which already existed began to be called Christianity.'[2]

[1] *Contra Celsum*, vi. 78.

[2] *Epis. Retract.*, bk. i.

The second view recognizes the divine element in the other religions of the world, but contends that Christianity is the peak of the development of religion. It is the crown and completion of the religion of humanity, the standard by which all others are judged.[1] While on the first view no recognition is given to the workings of the spirit in other religions, here it is conceded that others also sought to know God and do His will, but they are merely preparations for the Christian religion, which is unique.

The difference between Christianity and any other religion is that of the best and the good, and the good is the enemy of the best. 'God, having of old time spoken . . . by divers portions and in divers manners, hath at the end of these days spoken unto us in His son',[2] that is to say, spoken perfectly and finally. 'Christ is indeed the true light, light of light eternal, while all of us children of men, have had kindled within us—just because we are children of men—flickering candles, smoking flax, lit all alike at the first by the divine Hand, but now, poor dim guttering lamps that can only shine again if they are kindled anew, if they can have their oil replenished from the source.'[3] Those, like Dr. Macnicol and the late Dr. Farquhar, who maintain this view would use the scriptures of the Indian people and their rites in their attempts to naturalize Christianity. But at a certain stage in this process they feel that they come up against a rock which they have no right to ignore. 'There is a core of adamant in our Christian faith that is not any one's private property to barter or to buy or to sell.'[4] Truth and falsehood are embattled opposites. While Christianity need not stand solitary apart from other religions, it is not to be regarded as merely relatively excellent, one among many efforts of human beings.

These two attitudes are common to all missionary religions.

[1] Cf. 'It is the Christian religion which is the perfect religion, the religion which represents the Being of Spirit in a realised form, or for itself, the religion in which religion has itself become objective in relation to itself' (Hegel, *The Philosophy of Religion*, E.T. (1895), vol. ii, p. 330).

[2] Hebrews i. 1, 2.

[3] Macnicol, *Is Christianity Unique?* (1936), p. 166.

[4] Ibid., p. 19. Dr. Frick writes in the *International Review of Missions* (Oct. 1926): 'As long as we claim to be Christians in deed and truth, we must cultivate a certain consciousness of superiority' (p. 10).

Each claims with absolute sincerity that it alone is the true light while others are will-o'-the-wisps that blind us to the truth and lure us away from it. When it attempts to be a little more understanding, it affirms that the light of its religion is to that of others as the sun is to the stars, and the minor lights may be tolerated so long as they accept their position of subordination.

X

An increasing number of Christians adopt a third attitude, the Hindu one, which is definitely against proselytism. The Syrian Christians, who have the longest Christian tradition in India, are opposed to proselytism. Among the later converts to Christianity, this attitude is gaining acceptance.[1] The International Missionary Council at its Jerusalem meeting held in 1928 declared: 'We would repudiate any symptoms of a religious imperialism that would desire to impose beliefs and practices on others in order to manage their souls in their supposed interests. We obey a God who respects our wills and we desire to respect those of others.'[2] The

[1] Rājkumāri Amrit Kaur writes: 'The conversion or the desire to impel another person to change his faith has always savoured of an arrogance tantamount to a violent attitude of mind which must surely be against that very doctrine of love for which I believe that Christ lived and died. . . . While there has been no conscious effort to purge the Indian Church of the taint of untouchability that exists within its own doors, the untouchability that exists in Hinduism has been exploited to the extent of attempted mass and wholesale conversions to so-called Christianity of the Depressed Classes. I say "so-called Christianity" advisedly, because I know not one of these poor people to whom I have spoken—and I have spoken to many—who has been able to tell me anything of the spiritual implications of his change of faith . . . Is there not room for Jesus in Hinduism? There must be. I cannot believe that any who seek to worship God in spirit and in truth are outside the pale of any of the great religions which draw their inspiration from Him who is the fountain-head of all truth. I am sure that I am not the only Indian born in the Christian faith who holds these views' (*The Harijan*, 30 Jan. 1937).

[2] *The World Mission of Christianity*, p. 10. Mr. Bernard Lucas in his book *Our Task in India* draws a distinction between proselytism and evangelism. The former is what Jesus condemned when he said: 'Woe unto you Scribes and Pharisees, hypocrites! for ye compass sea and land to make one proselyte; and when he is become so ye make him twofold more a son of Gehenna than yourselves' (St. Matthew). The latter is, for Mr. Lucas, what is implied in the words 'But go then and publish abroad the Kingdom of God' (St. Luke). Commenting on the latter, Mr. Lucas writes: 'The standpoint of evangelism

Report calls upon non-Christian religions to join forces with Christianity in resisting the attacks of those who deny God and the world of spirit. 'We call on the followers of the non-Christian religions to hold fast to faith in the unseen and eternal, in face of the growing materialism of the world and to co-operate with us against all the evils of secularism.'[1] It has a perception of the desperate need of the world as well as of the fellowship of all believers in God, in the deep places of the spirit. The Report of the American Commission of Laymen affirms that it is unwise to undermine men's faith in their traditions. 'There is a real danger that the sound elements of tradition will be discarded with its abuses and that nothing will be adequate to take the place of the restraints of the older cultures, which, however misconceived, at least maintained a social order.'[2] The task of the missionary would be to pool his religion along with others. 'Perhaps the chief hope for an important deepening of self-knowledge on the part of Christendom is by way of a more thorough-going sharing of its life with the life of the Orient. The relations between religions must take increasingly hereafter the form of a common search for truth. A growing apprehension of truth is effected by the creative interaction of different minds and their insights, by the mutual criticism and enlargement which result from a fuller appreciation of

recognises the value of the law of heredity in the religious development of the race. There is a distinct type of religious thought and life in India which God has been evolving through the centuries and this must be saved for India and for the world.' He adds that if India loses her distinctive religious genius it would be an irretrievable and incalculable loss to the world. 'The Hindu must be saved as a Hindu.' Dr. D. J. Fleming in his book on *Whither Bound in Missions* (1925) pleads for a 'mutuality in giving and receiving'. He argues that there is a just resentment at the imperialist type of missionary endeavour. He feels that we must be impartial enough to recognize that each race has its special gift and its special contribution to civilization. His first chapter is entitled 'Eradicating a Sense of Superiority'.

[1] *The World Mission of Christianity*, p. 14.

[2] There are Christian missionaries who adopt and advocate this view. Rev. Verrier Elwin says: 'I live among the Gonds and love them. I have never interfered with their religion and when any of them ask me to make them Christian, I refuse. I think myself, that it would be better for all to adopt a similar attitude of detachment and leave their ancestral faith alone' (*Indian Social Reformer*, 2 Nov. 1935, p. 136).

other systems of thought and culture. 'All fences and private properties in truth are futile; the final truth whatever it may be is the New Testament of every existing faith.' There is a common ethical and religious ideal influencing the whole civilized world, and each people tries to find it in its own religion and does find it there. In other words, this Report admits that no religion in its present form is final and every religion is seeking for a better expression. It looks forward to a time when 'the names that now separate men may lose their divisive meaning'.[1] 'Supposing they worship a Being with the same attributes,' Dr. Inge says, 'it does not very much matter whether they call him Buddha or Christ. We must look to things rather than to words.'[2]

There are thus three different attitudes, right, centre, and left, which Christian missionaries adopt towards other religions. Here, as elsewhere, the hopes of the future are under the left wing of liberals and not with the reactionaries or conservatives. If we do not bring together in love those who sincerely believe in God and seek to do His will, if we persist in killing one another theologically, we shall only weaken men's faith in God. If the great religions continue to waste their energies in a fratricidal war instead of looking upon themselves as friendly partners in the supreme task of nourishing the spiritual life of mankind, the swift advance of secular humanism and moral materialism is assured. In a restless and disordered world which is unbelieving to an extent which we have all too little realized, where sinister superstitions are setting forth their rival claims to the allegiance of men, we cannot afford to waver in our determination that the whole of humanity shall remain a united people, where Muslim and Christian, Buddhist and Hindu shall stand together bound by common devotion, not to something behind but to something ahead, not to a racial past or a geographical unit, but to a great dream of a world society with a universal religion of which the historical faiths are but branches. We must recognize humbly the partial and defective character of our isolated traditions and seek their source in the generic tradition from which they all have sprung.[3]

[1] (1932) pp. 44, 46, 47, 58.

[2] *Inquirer*, 12 June 1926.

[3] Cf. Professor Hocking: 'We have to recognise that a *world religion exists*.

Each religion has sat at the feet of teachers that never bowed to its authority, and this process is taking place to-day on a scale unprecedented in the history of humanity and will have most profound effects upon religion. In their wide environment, religions are assisting each other to find their own souls and grow to their full stature. Owing to a cross-fertilization of ideas and insights, behind which lie centuries of racial and cultural tradition and earnest endeavour, a great unification is taking place in the deeper fabric of men's thoughts. Unconsciously perhaps, respect for other points of view, appreciation of the treasures of other cultures, confidence in one another's unselfish motives are growing. We are slowly realizing that believers with different opinions and convictions are necessary to each other to work out the larger synthesis which alone can give the spiritual basis to a world brought together into intimate oneness by man's mechanical ingenuity.

We give religious systems separate names, but they are not separate; they are not closed globules. They merge in the universal human faith in the divine being'—quoted in Basil Mathews, *Roads to the City of God* (1928), p. 43.

IX

THE INDIVIDUAL AND THE SOCIAL ORDER IN HINDUISM

I

THE last fifty years have seen the most revolutionary changes of any period in human history.[1] The inventions of science have put an end to human isolation and provided marvellous opportunities for the realization of the dream of ages, the building of a great society on earth, whose vision has inspired the seers and prophets of all races and nations. The social and ethical issues raised by the spread of science and technology and the new contacts of races and cultures are common to both East and West. We must now learn to live together and understand one another.

The chief obstacle to mutual understanding has been an almost mystical faith in the superiority of this or that race and the historic missions of nations. Napoleonic France felt called to sow the seeds of revolution in the soil of Europe, Imperialistic Britain to carry the white man's burden of civilizing, for a consideration, the backward peoples, Soviet Russia to liberate the proletariat from bondage to capitalism, and Nordic Germany to save the world from the antichrist of communism. This conceit of the legendary destinies of nations is not confined to the West. There are Indians who believe that true spirituality has never appeared anywhere in the world save on the sacred soil of India. There are Chinese who imagine that they alone are civilized. Public men in Japan often use the language of the Shinto divine Hirata of a hundred years ago, that the Japanese are the descendants of the gods, different in kind rather than degree from all other nations, and the Mikado, the son of heaven, is entitled to rule them all. If in ancient times the groups claimed to be under special divine protection, they now employ scientific jargon by declaring that they are in line with

[1] 'From the stone age to the death of Queen Victoria is one era; we are now living in the second' (Gerald Heard, *These Hurrying Years* (1933), p. 1).

the development of evolution, with the unrolling of history. They solemnize their desires and organize their hatreds by propounding the theory of the predestination of races. This pernicious doctrine of fundamental racial differences and national missions is preventing the development of a true human community in spite of the closer linking up of interests and the growing uniformity of customs and forms of life. Science, however, supports the very different view that the fundamental structure of the human mind is uniform in all races. The varied cultures are but dialects of a single speech of the soul. The differences are due to accents, historical circumstances, and stages of development. If we are to find a solution for the differences which divide races and nations to-day, it must be through the recognition of the essential oneness of the modern world, spiritually and socially, economically and politically.

Some of those whose tradition and training are limited to the European are apt to imagine that before the great Greek thinkers, Socrates, Plato, and Aristotle, there was a crude confusion of thought, a sort of chaos without form and void. Such a view becomes almost a provincialism when we realize that systems of thought which influenced countless millions of human beings had been elaborated by people who never heard the names of the Greek thinkers. The Hindu sages had formulated systems of philosophy and conduct, the Jews had developed a lofty monotheism, Zarathustra had proclaimed the universe to be an ever increasing kingdom of righteousness, and Buddha had taught the way of enlightenment. The Chinese had records of a civilization that was even then two thousand years old, and the pyramids of Egypt and the palaces of Babylon were antiquities in the eyes of men of that period. If we leave aside the great civilizations of Egypt, Assyria, Knossos, and others whose influence on the modern world is more indirect than direct, the outstanding developments prior to 500 B.C. were the emergence of the prophetic school in Israel, of Confucianism in China, and of Brahmanism and Buddhism in India. The present state of the world is largely conditioned by the philosophies of life that had been worked out by then. The opportunities for these different tendencies to weave themselves into the warp and woof of world history are now available. Even if some of them are unsuited to modern conditions, the story of man's gradual rise and progress cannot be without its interest to all those who have faith in the solidarity of man. It is therefore a matter of significance that in these lectures we are taking up one important problem and viewing it from different historical standpoints.

II

In dealing with any social organization we must inquire into the essential ideas on which it is founded, the conception of life which inspires it, and the forms which these ideas of life assume. The inspiring ideas are always larger than the historical forms which embody them. The Hindu view of the individual and his relation to society can be best brought out by a reference to the synthesis and gradation of (i) the fourfold object of life (*puruṣārtha*), desire and enjoyment (*kāma*), interest (*artha*), ethical living (*dharma*), and spiritual freedom (*mokṣa*); (ii) the fourfold order of society (*varṇa*), the man of learning (*Brāhmin*), of power (*Kṣatriya*), of skilled productivity (*Vaiśya*), and of service (*Śūdra*); and (iii) the fourfold succession of the stages of life (*āśrama*), student (*brahmacārī*), householder (*grihastha*), forest recluse (*vānaprastha*), and the free supersocial man (*saññyāsin*). By means of this threefold discipline the Hindu strives to reach his destiny, which is to change body into soul, to discover the world's potentiality for virtue, and derive happiness from it. It used to be said that God created the universe in order that He might apprehend Himself. Whatever we may feel about it, it is beyond question that the world exists in order that we may apprehend ourselves, attaining our full selfhood through response to whatever in it corresponds to the developing personality. The approach to this goal must not be too sudden and immediate for all individuals. It has to be reached through a progressive training, a gradual enlarging of the natural life accompanied by an uplifting of all its motives. The rule, the training, and the result differ with the type of the individual, his bent of life and degree of development. Life is much too complex for an ideal simplicity.

III

The Four Ends of Life

1. *Mokṣa*. The chief end of man is the development of the individual. The Upaniṣad tells us that there is nothing higher than the person.[1] But man is not an assemblage of body, life, and mind born of and subject to physical nature. The natural half-animal being with which he confuses himself is not his whole or real being. It is but an instrument for the use of spirit which is the truth of his being. To find the real self, to exceed his apparent, outward self, is the greatness of which man alone of all beings is capable.[2] 'Verily, O Gārgī, he who departs from this world without knowing this Imperishable one is a vile and wretched creature.'[3] To inquire into his true self, to live in and from it, to determine by its own energy what it shall be inwardly and what it shall make of its outward circumstances, to found the whole life on the power and truth of spirit, is *mokṣa* or spiritual freedom. To be shut up in one's own ego, to rest in the apparent self and mistake it for the real, is the root of all unrest to which man is exposed by reason of his mentality. To aspire to a universality (*sarvātmabhāva*) through his mind and reason, through his heart and love, through his will and power, is the high sense of his humanity.

2. *Kāma*. Is this perfection consistent with normal living? There is a prevalent idea that the Hindu view concedes no reality to life, that it despises vital aims and satisfactions, that it gives no inspiring motive to human effort. If spirit and life were unrelated, spiritual freedom would become an unattainable ideal, a remote passion of a few visionaries. There is little in Hindu thought to support the view that one has to attain spiritual freedom by means of a violent rupture with ordinary life. On the other hand, it lays down that we must pass through the normal life conscientiously and with knowledge, work out its values, and accept its enjoyments. Spiritual life is an integration of man's being,

[1] 'puruṣān na param kiñcit'.

[2] The *Bhāgavata* says, 'The chief end of life here is not the attainment of heaven popularly known to be the result of pious duties. It is the desire to enquire into truth' (i. 2. 10).

[3] *Bṛhadāraṇyaka Up.* iii. 8. 10.

in its depth and breadth, in its capacity for deep meditation as well as reckless transport. *Kāma* refers to the emotional being of man, his feelings and desires.[1] If man is denied his emotional life, he becomes a prey to repressive introspection and lives under a continual strain of moral torture. When the reaction sets in, he will give way to a wildness of ecstasy which is ruinous to his sanity and health.

3. *Artha*. The third end relates to wealth and material well-being. Though it is not its own end, it helps to sustain and enrich life. There was never in India a national ideal of poverty or squalor. Spiritual life finds full scope only in communities of a certain degree of freedom from sordidness. Lives that are strained and starved cannot be religious except in a rudimentary way. Economic insecurity and individual freedom do not go together.

4. *Dharma*. While the spontaneous activities of interest and desire are to be accepted, their full values cannot be realized if their action is unrestrained. There must be a rule, a guidance, a restraint. *Dharma* gives coherence and direction to the different activities of life. It is not a religious creed or cult imposing an ethical or social rule. It is the complete rule of life, the harmony of the whole man who finds a right and just law of his living. Each man and group, each activity of soul, mind, life, and body, has its *dharma*. While man is justified in satisfying his desires, which is essential for the expression of life, to conform to the dictates of his desires is not the law of his being. He will not get the best out of them if he does not conform to the *dharma* or the rule of right practice. A famous verse of the *Mahābhārata* says: 'I cry with arm uplifted, yet none heedeth. From righteousness (*dharma*) flow forth pleasure and profit. Why then do ye not follow righteousness?'[2] *Dharma* tells us that while our life is in the first instance for our own satisfaction, it is more essentially for the community and most of all for that universal self which is in each of us and all beings. Ethical life is the means to spiritual freedom, as well as its expression on earth.

[1] *Bhāgavata*, i. 2. 10.

[2] ūrdhvabāhur viraumyeṣaḥ na hi kaścit cchruṇoti mām.
dharmād arthaśca kāmaśca sa kim artham na sevyate.

The *dharma* and its observance are neither the beginning nor the end of human life, for beyond the law is spiritual freedom, not merely a noble manhood but universality, the aim which ennobles the whole life of the individual and the whole order of society. Man's whole life is to be passed in the implicit consciousness of this mysterious background.

The four ends of life point to the different sides of human nature, the instinctive and the emotional, the economic, the intellectual and the ethical, and the spiritual. There is implanted in man's fundamental being a spiritual capacity. He becomes completely human only when his sensibility to spirit is awakened. So long as man's life is limited to science and art, technical invention, and social programmes, he is incomplete and not truly human. If we are insolent and base, unfair and unkind to one another, unhappy in personal relationships, and lacking in mutual understanding, it is because we remain too much on the surface of life and have lost contact with the depths. When the fountains of spirit from which creative life of the individual and society is fed dry up, diseases of every description, intellectual, moral, and social, break out. The everlasting vagrancy of thought, the contemporary muddle of conflicting philosophies, the rival ideologies which cut through national frontiers and geographical divisions, are a sign of spiritual homelessness. The unrest is in a sense sacred, for it is the confession of the failure of a self-sufficient humanism with no outlook beyond the world. We cannot find peace on earth through economic planning or political arrangement.. Only the pure in heart by fostering the mystical accord of minds can establish justice and love. Man's true and essential greatness is individual. The scriptures could point out the road but each man must travel it for himself. The law of *karma* affirms the responsibility of each individual for his life. 'The sins ye do by two and two, ye shall pay for one by one,' as Kipling called Beelzebub to remark. There is no salvation by proxy or in herds. In primitive societies there is collective responsibility, but on the hypothesis of rebirth, the guilt of an action attaches to its author. The punishment must fall on the individual, if not in this life, then in the next or perhaps in a later. The dignity and responsibility of the individual soul are recognized.

IV

The Four Classes[1]

The aim of *dharma* is to take the natural life of man and subject it to control without unduly interfering with its largeness, freedom, and variety. It has two sides: the social and the individual, the *varṇa dharma*, which deals with the duties assigned to men's position in society as determined by their character(*guṇa*) and function (*karma*); the *āśrama dharma*, which deals with the duties relevant to the stage of life, youth, manhood, or old age. We may deal with the theory of the four classes from three different standpoints, the spiritual-social, the ethical-psychological, and the conventional.

1. The earliest reference to the four classes is in the *Puruṣa Sūkta* of the *Ṛg Veda*,[2] where they are described as having sprung from the body of the creative spirit, from his head, arms, thighs, and feet. This poetical image is intended to convey the organic character of society. Man is not only himself, but is in solidarity with all of his kind. The stress of the universal in its movement towards the goal of the world is the source of man's sociality. Society is not something alien, imposed on man, crushing him, against which he rebels in knowledge and action. There is a profound integration of the social destiny with that of the individual. Human society is an attempt to express in social life the cosmic purpose which has other ways of expression in the material and the supramaterial planes.

Between the individual and the totality of mankind are set up smaller groups as aids, though they often turn out obstacles, to the larger unity of mankind. The difficulties of distance and organization, the limitations of the human heart, as well as the variety and richness of life, are responsible for the smaller groups, which are meant to be used as means to a larger universality. Even if humanity becomes a more manageable unit of life, intermediate groups are bound to exist for the development of varying tendencies in the total human aggregate. The family, the tribe, the clan, the nation,

[1] See Bhagavan Das, *Hindu Social Organization* (1932); Aurobindo Ghose, *The Psychology of Social Development*; G. H. Mees, *Dharma and Society* (1935).

[2] x. 90.

are successive stages in this constant approach to universality. The individual thus belongs not only to humanity but to a class or country, race or religion. The group, which is midway between the individual and humanity, exists not merely for itself but for the one and the other, helping them to fulfil each other.

If the limited group, religious, political, or economic, regards itself as absolute and self-sufficient and demands the total service and life of the individual for its own development, it arrogates to itself claims which it does not possess. Even as the individual has no right to look upon himself as the final end of existence and claim the right to live for himself, without taking into account the needs of society, the social group has no right to demand the absolute surrender of the individual's rights. The two principles which must govern all group life are the free and unfettered development of the individual and the healthy growth of society. The individual and the society are interdependent. The sound development of the individual is the best condition for the growth of the society, and a healthy condition of society is the best condition for the growth of the individual. An ant-heap or a beehive is not the model for a human commonwealth. No harmony is to be achieved by the enslavement of the individual.

Man is not an abstract individual. He belongs to a certain social group by virtue of his character, behaviour, and function in the community. When the fourfold division of society is regarded as the ordinance of God or the dispensation of the spirit, the suggestion is that spiritual wisdom, executive power, skilled production, and devoted service are the indispensable elements of any social order. It is the function of the wise to plan the social order, of the powerful to sanction it, i.e. back it by authority which has force behind it, of the skilled to execute it or carry it out with the help of the devoted workers. The fourfold classification is conceived in the interests of world progress.[1] It is not intended specially for the Hindus, but applies to the whole human race, which has one destiny which it seeks and increasingly attains through the countless millenniums of history. The

[1] 'lokānām tu vivṛddhyartham'.

true object of all human action is *lokasamgraha* or the holding together of the human race in its evolution. In pursuance of such a view, Hindu leaders accepted primitive societies and foreign settlers such as the Greeks and the Scythians into the Hindu fold and recognized their priestly families as Brāhmins and their fighting men as Kṣatriyas.

2. As the individual is a social being, society is the necessary means by which he attains the development of his personality. A secure place must be found for him in the community so that he can derive the utmost help from it. By his nature, man falls into four types, the man of learning and knowledge, the man of power and action, the skilled craftsman, and the labourer. The types are determined by the prominent elements of man's active nature.

Those who are pre-eminently intellectual are the Brāhmins, whose function it is to seek and find knowledge, communicate it to others, and make it prevail in the world. Their activity is not the pursuit of practical aims in the narrow sense. They seek their joy in the practice of an art, a science, or a philosophy and set an example of attachment to disinterested pursuits of the mind. The perversions of this type are a mere intellectuality or curiosity for ideas without an accompanying ethical elevation, a narrow specialization without the requisite openness of mind, a thirst for novelty, a tendency to imitate current fashions, an ineffective idealism without any hold on life. The true Brāhmin is said to be one who has sensed the deepest self and acts out of that consciousness.[1] He is expected to embody the law of self-dedicating love, the grace and joy of souls in the consciousness of the service, free, high, and daring, of the humanity of the future, where hate, violence, and fanaticism will be unknown. The Brāhmins give moral guidance. They reveal but do not enforce. Practical administration is not their task. They keep clear of the love of power as well as the pressure of immediate needs. Plato affirms that kings must be philosophers. In the allegory of the Cave the wise man who has escaped into the daylight must not stay there but must go back to teach others. 'We shall compel him

[1] 'yaḥ kaścid ātmānam aparokṣīkṛtya kritārthatayā vartata sa eva brāhmaṇaḥ'. *Vajrasūcika Up.*

to go back though we do him an injustice.' The Hindu believes that any one immediately and deeply concerned with the exercise of power cannot be completely objective. The rulers will be concerned with government and the thinkers with values. If society is not to be led by the blind, we must have the contemplative thinkers at the top. Every society needs to have a class which is freed from material cares, competitive life, and is without obligations to it. Freedom is of the essence of the higher life and the great values cannot be achieved under a compulsion or a sense of duty.

A dry spirit of detachment and disconnexion from immediate surroundings are essential qualities for those engaged in the pursuit of truth. An invincible patience, a contempt of all little and feeble enjoyments, humility without any baseness, an infinite hope, and a high fearlessness are the qualities that mark the seeker of truth.[1] These, which fit them for their vocation, unfit them for success in life. If their claims on society are not sufficiently safeguarded, they will be doomed to loneliness and not seldom to starvation. Their very strength prevents them from compromising with the things they despise. A class of disinterested seekers of truth supported by society, influencing it, and placed above the corrupting tendency of power, is the very life of social stability and growth. After all, civilization is based on a vision.

If a Brāhmin class was found necessary even in those less organized and complicated times, it is much more necessary to-day, when there is a widespread tendency to confuse national interests with objective truth. Our intellectuals today with rare exceptions are camp followers of political rulers. When Hegel saw Napoleon on horseback at the head of his army, he said, 'I saw the world soul riding.' The thinkers betray their function when they descend to the market-place to serve the passions of race, class, or nation. When they let their spirits get enclosed in the mentality of politics, when they fail to give to society a vision of humanity and civilization, the whole social structure will totter. Those who belong to the spiritual ministry of society must guard

[1] Cf. Vaśiṣṭha:

yogas tapo damo dānam satyam śáucam dayā śrutam
vidyā vijñānam āstikyam etat brāhmaṇalakṣaṇam.

their integrity of mind as a sacred possession, be completely masters of themselves, and proclaim the truth that all cities, all States, all kingdoms are mortal, and only the spirit of man immortal. Thucydides contemplates the image of a world in which Athens should have ceased to exist. Polybius shows us the conqueror of Carthage meditating over the burning town. 'And Rome too shall meet her fateful hour.'[1]

The Brāhmins will now be considered to be receivers of unearned income. Even as it is the function of the State to support schools and colleges, museums and picture-galleries, it must also support a leisured class. In the world to-day the leisured are those who inherit wealth, though there is no reason to suppose that the children of rich parents are exceptionally intelligent and sensitive. In China, boys and girls used to be selected for this class on the results of competitive examinations. But the special training cannot be postponed till the age of examinations. If the training is to start early enough we must choose the members soon after birth. Is it to be by lot? The Hindu assumed that birth in a family which had the traditions of the leisured class might offer the best solution.

While it is the business of the Brāhmin to lay down the science of values, draw out the blueprints for social reconstruction, and persuade the world to accept the high ends of life, it is the business of the Kṣatriya to devise the means for gaining the ends. Not only in the ancient epics but in the recent history of Rajput chivalry do we find Kṣatriya princes cast in the heroic mould, the limits of whose fame are the stars, men whom no fear could terrify, no difficulty could daunt, men for whom retreat was more bitter than death. The qualities that mark the Kṣatriya type are a heroic determination from which no danger or difficulty can distract them, a dynamic daring which shrinks from no adventure, a nobility of soul which would do nothing sordid or mean, and an unflinching resistance to injustice and oppression. The worshippers of power, the men of brute force, the selfish tyrants are the perversions of this type. The qualities of the Kṣatriya are as necessary as those of the Brāhmin for the perfection of human nature.

[1] Julian Benda, *The Great Betrayal*, E.T. (1928).

The political is not the highest category. The State exists in order that its members may have a good life. It is a social convenience. It is not the judge of its own conduct. Though righteousness depends on force, 'it is wrong to say that it is the will of the strong'.[1] The State is not above ethics. It exists essentially for the good of the individual and has therefore no right to demand the sacrifice of the individual, though it has every right to demand the conditions essential for the performance of its task. The worship of the God-State with which we are familiar to-day, that the State is the creator of right and wrong, that reasons of State justify any crime, that ethics are a purely individual matter, are flatly opposed to the Hindu view. Rāma tells Lakṣmaṇa: 'I bear arms for the sake of truth. It is not difficult for me to gain this whole universe but I desire not even the suzerainty of the heavens if it is to be through unrighteousness.'[2] The State finds its justification according to the measure in which it pursues and protects the full development of the human person. The end is personal liberty and happiness, and all government is a convenient means to this end.

The Hegelian theory that what is is right, and that the Prussian military State is the highest form of 'the Spirit' on earth, is in practice a denial of moral authority. It confuses the good with the real and reduces the distinction between right and wrong to one of strong and weak. Force is what counts, and not right, which is only another name for superior force. On this view, no government has any moral authority, and conflicts between classes and nations can only be decided by force. The League of Nations is suspected to be another power system, not an alternative to war but only an excuse for a holy war. The League has failed not because it was lacking in armed force but because it had no moral authority. Only an earnest application of the democratic tradition in the relations between States and a rearrangement of the world on that basis can give the needed authority to the

[1] *Mahābhārata*, iii. 134. 3.

[2] . . . satyena āyudham ālabhe
neyam mama mahī saumya durlabhā sāgarāmbarā
na hī ccheyam adharmeṇa śakratvam api lakṣmaṇa.
(*Rāmāyaṇa*, ii. 97. 6–7.)

League. The great task of our generation is to embody real democracy in the material structure of our civilization, to work for a world community far richer in its cultural opportunities for all men, and far more brotherly in its relationships.

The Hindu scheme permits the use of force for the maintenance of order and enforcement of law, occasionally even to the point of the destruction of human life. In a perfect society where every one is naturally unselfish and loving, there would be no need for government or force, but so perfect a condition is perhaps not suited to mere men. In the actual imperfect conditions the State will have to exercise force on recalcitrant individuals. The need for force is, however, a sign of imperfection. In principle anything which has the taint of coercion is to that extent lacking in perfection, as the *Mahābhārata* has it.[1] We may feel that we are justified in using force to restrain the evil-doer. This very necessary coercion results in two disadvantages. It tempts the user to its unrighteous use and causes resentment in those against whom it is used. While we cannot obviate the necessity for the use of coercion in political arrangements, so long as sinful ambition, pride, lust, and greed are operative in human nature, it is essential to guard against its abuses and remember that there is a higher obligation of love that transcends the requirements of mere justice, in the light of which all codes of justice are to be judged. The ideal is the Brāhminic one of non-resistance, for the means are as important as the end.[2] In this imperfect world, however, the non-resisters are able to practise their convictions only because they owe their security to the maintenance by others of the principles which they repudiate.

[1] 'hiṁsayā samyutam dharmam adharmam ca vidur budhāh'. Again, 'The victory that is achieved without war is much superior to the victory that is achieved through war' (xii. 94. 1). Aśoka in Rock Edict XIII writes: 'In order that my sons and grandsons should not regard it as their duty to make a new conquest . . . they should take pleasure in patience and gentleness and regard as the only true conquest the conquest won by piety' (*The Edicts of Aśoka*, by Vincent A. Smith (1909), p. 21).

[2] Cf. these well-known sayings from the *Mahābhārata*:

ahiṁsān sarvabhūteṣu dharmam jyāyas taram viduh
tasya ca brāhmaṇo mūlam . . .;
yad ayuddhena labhyeta tat te bahumatam bhavet.

The use of force is limited to occasions where it is the only alternative and is applied for the sake of creating a more suitable environment for the growth of moral values and not for activities which can hardly fail to result in social chaos. Force, when unavoidable, must be employed in an ethical spirit. The use of force does not become permissible simply because it has an ethical aim. It must be applied in an ethical way.[1] The users of force are not the ones to judge the causes for which it has to be employed. The Kṣatriyas rule only as the guardians and servants of the law. They have an executive power over the community which is valid only so long as they carry out the law, which is placed under the control of the Brāhmins and the seers and protected from interference by political or economic power. The function of the State is limited to the protection of the law and defence. People were allowed to manage their affairs in accordance with the traditional rules and customs. They did not care who the rulers were so long as their lives were undisturbed. One flag was as good as another, if social life was carried on in the same way. This attitude has made the country a prey to invaders. The enforcement of moral laws is what gives a king his glory. This is evident from the description of the king who could say: 'In my realm there is neither thief nor miser, nor drunkard, nor one who is altarless, nor any ignoramus, nor any unchaste man or woman.'[2]

As in all ancient societies, only the fighting classes took part in wars. The motive was more monarchical loyalty than national pride. Even when tribes were at war, the non-combatants were little affected. Megasthenes writes: 'If the Indians are at war with one another, it is not customary for

[1] War has its rules of right behaviour which must be observed by the king. He must not permit the use of poisoned arrows or concealed weapons or the slaying of a man who is asleep or a suppliant or a fugitive. He must not as a victor destroy fine architecture or extirpate the family of the defeated dead but invest a suitable prince of that family with royal dignity (*Mahābhārata*, xii. 100. 5). Though political weapons are employed for gaining their ends, the rulers should not allow their aims to be distorted by revenge or vindictiveness. For Kauṭilya the preservation of the State is the highest duty of the king and any course which saves the kingdom is justified.

[2] *Chāndogya Up.* v. 11. 5.

them to touch those who are tilling the land, but the one group may be engaged in battle . . . but the other is peacefully engaged in ploughing or reaping or pruning or mowing nearby.'[1] These principles were laid down at a time when wars were fought according to strict rules by small professional armies. In modern wars whole populations are involved and there are no non-combatants. The forces must act with efficiency and indiscrimination. They may kill and maim, starve and ruin millions of human beings who are absolutely innocent. An indiscriminate massacre of masses will be disastrous to the whole society, and by no stretch of imagination can it be said that it will protect the interests of the community. There is much to be said for those who believe that complete pacifism is the only attitude to wars under modern conditions that can be adopted by those who have faith in the fundamental unity of all being. Yet we live, not in a perfect universe, but only in an improving one at best.

The third class of *vaiśyas* brings into relief the tendency of life to possess and enjoy, to give and take. In its outward action, this power appears as the utilitarian, practical mind engaged in commerce and industry. Though bent on the efficient exploitation of the natural resources, this type is also marked by humanity and ordered benevolence. Though the members of this class are engaged in pursuits where the temptations to the acquisition of wealth are real, they are expected to develop qualities of humanity and neighbourly service. If they are keen on wealth for its own sake, they are to be 'detested'.[2] It is not their main function to contribute to the spiritual welfare of society or its political power, yet we cannot have these without their co-operation. Practical intelligence and adaptive skill are their chief marks. The perversions of this type are familiar to us, as our age is pre-eminently a commercial one. Armament manufacturers foment discords between nations for the sake of profits. The records of the League of Nations show how merchants, European and Asiatic, have been making mil-

[1] Arrian, *Indika*, 11. 9. See also *Bhāgavata*, 1. 7. 36.

[2] Cf. *Rāmāyaṇa*, ii. 21. 58. 'dveṣyo bhavati arthaparo hi loke'. Similarly we fail if we are addicted to enjoyment. 'kāmātmatā khalv api na praśastā.'

lions through the sale of vile drugs that destroy the body, mind, and soul of the people. In some countries those who purchase the drug are given free the hypodermic syringe with which to inject it. For the lust of gold man hurls his fellow men over these precipices of war between races and nations, of drunkenness and drug-addiction. Commerce and industry, which are the life-blood of the human race, are perverted from their proper use by a false standard of values. Property, according to the Hindu view, is a mandate held by its possessors for the common use and benefit of the commonwealth. The *Bhāgavata* tells us that we have a claim only to so much as would satisfy our hunger. If any one desires more, he is a thief deserving punishment.[1] To gain wealth and power at the expense of society is a social crime. To destroy surplus products simply because we cannot sell them for profit is an outrage on humanity.

A fourth variety of human nature finds its outlet in work and service. Labour is the basis of all human relations. While the first three classes are said to be twice born, the fourth is said to be once born and so inferior. It only means that the activities of the members of the fourth class are instinctive and not governed by ideals of knowledge, strength, or mutual service. While the seeker of wisdom works for the joy of the search, the hero of action works from a sense of honour, the artist and the skilled craftsman are impelled by a love of their art, and even the lowest worker has a sense of the dignity of labour. Though all these are impressed by the social code with a sense of their social value, the lowest classes are not generally aware of the plan of the social order and their place in it. They fulfil their duties for the satisfaction of their primary needs, and when these are gratified, they tend to lapse into a life of indolence and inertia. An instinctive obedience and a mechanical discharge of duty are their chief contributions.

It is not to be assumed that the qualities which are predominant in each of the four classes are exclusive of one another. As a matter of fact there is no individual who does not possess all these essentials. Classes are marked as wise

[1] yāvad mṛyeta jaṭharam tāvat svattvam hi dehinām
adhikam yo 'bhimanyeta sa steno daṇḍam arhati (vii. 14. 8).

or heroic, skilled or unskilled, according as one or the other predominates in them. None of these can be regarded as complete. The Brāhmin cannot serve truth with freedom if he has not moral courage and heroism, if he has not the practical sense to adapt the highest truth to the conditions of actual life and the needs of the different classes of society, if he has not the sense of service to humanity. Even the man of action, though he is not engaged in the pursuit of wisdom, has a sense of the direction of society, the aims it has, and the way in which he has to sanction the details essential for the realization of those aims. He uses his power for the service of the society. The man of practical ability is called upon to devote his skill and possessions to the good of society. He has a general idea of the nature of the social good, has the courage and the enterprise essential for the exploitation of natural resources, and is anxious to improve the material conditions of life in every conceivable way. Even the man of labour is not a social drudge. As a part of the social order, he strives to serve society through his special function with knowledge, honour, and skill. The fourfold spirit is present in every member of society and its fruitful development is the test of each one's efficiency. There is no life, in so far as it is human, which is not at the same time an inquiry into truth, a struggle with forces inward and outward, a practical adaptation of the truth to the conditions of life and a service of society. Every one in his own way aims at being a sage, a hero, an artist, and a servant. But the conditions of life demand specialization within limits. Each one cannot develop within his single life the different types of excellence. As a rule one type of excellence or perfection is attainable only at the expense of another. We cannot erect on the same site both a Greek temple and a Gothic cathedral, though each has its own loveliness. 'The ascetic virtues cannot flourish side by side with the social and the domestic. If you choose to be an anchorite, you cannot be a statesman.'[1] A hermit does not know what human love is. A social worker cannot devote his strength to the advancement of knowledge. But wherever we may start, it is open to us to reach the highest perfection, and man reaches perfection by each being intent on his own

[1] See Dixon, *The Human Situation* (1937), p. 294.

duty.[1] 'Men of all classes, if they fulfil their assigned duties, enjoy the highest imperishable bliss.'[2]

While, from a spiritual standpoint, all work has in it the power to lead to perfection, a natural hierarchy binding the position in society with the cultural development of the individual arises. Life is a staircase with steps leading to a goal and no man can rest satisfied until he reaches the top. Not the stage reached but the movement upwards is of importance. The road is better than the resting-place.[3] Hierarchy is not coercion but a law of nature. The four classes represent four stages of development in our manhood. Every human being starts with a heavy load of ignorance and inertia. His first stage is one of toil demanded by the needs of the body, the impulse of life, and the law of society. Manu tells us that all men are born Śūdras and become Brāhmins by regeneration through ethical and spiritual culture. From the lowest stage we rise into a higher type when we are driven by the instinct for useful creation. We have here the vital man. At a higher level, we have the active man with ambition and will power. Highest of all is the Brāhmin, who brings a spiritual rule into life. Though something of all these four is found in all men in different degrees of development, one or the other tends to predominate in the dealings of the soul with its embodied nature, and that becomes the basis for future development. As he unfolds and grows man changes his status and class.[4] Growth is ordinarily gradual. Nature cannot be rushed. The seer's vision is the ideal for the active man; while he can trust the seer, the lower ones may not be able to do so. They look to the practical men. We can only understand and follow those who are just a step beyond ourselves. The distant scene is practically out of sight. The social order is intended to produce the type and provide for growth beyond it.

If one who is of a lower nature desires to perform the

[1] *Bhagavadgītā*, xviii. 45. [2] *Āpastamba*, ii. 1. 2. 2.

[3] 'All men must serve those who belong to the higher classes.' *Gautama*, x. 66.

[4] 'A man whether he be a Brāhmin, Kṣatriya, Vaiśya or Śūdra is such by nature. By evil deed does a twice-born man fall from his position. The Kṣatriya or a Vaiśya who lives in the condition of a Brāhmin by practising the duties of one attains to Brāhminhood' (*Mahābhārata*, Anuśāsanaparva, 143. 6).

social tasks of a higher class, before he has attained the answering capacities, social order will be disturbed. To fight is a sin for a Brāhmin but not for a Ksatriya, whose function is to fight without ill will for a righteous cause, when there is no other course.[1] Arjuna in the *Bhagavadgītā* is required to follow his own nature. To follow the law of another's nature is dangerous. The bent of Arjuna's nature was to fight; to run away from the battle-field would be a flight from his nature. Man cannot ordinarily transcend his psychological endowment. In the actual social order, there may be people who consider it right to fight and others to abstain, and both are justified. The fourfold classification is against modern notions of conscription where every one is obliged to take to military service or universal suffrage where ruling power is distributed among all. In the natural hierarchy there cannot be one moral standard for all. The higher a person is in the social scale, the greater are the obligations. The tendency to judge others by our own standards must be tempered by a greater understanding of each one's special work and place in society.

Individuals and classes were bound to one another by what is called the spirit of status and not terminable contract. Every man had his place in society and fixed duties attached to it. The social organism expected from each man his duties but guaranteed to each subsistence and opportunity for self-expression. The spirit of competition was unknown. Regulated control, even if coercive, is less tyrannical than blind competition. It secures for the largest number of individuals effective freedom in non-economic and cultural spheres. Regulation in the interests of a fuller measure of freedom is not the same as the total subjection of the individual to the State.

In a real sense, the fourfold scheme is democratic. Firstly, it insists on the spiritual equality of all men. It assumes that within every human creature there is a self which has the right to grow in its own way, to find itself, and make its life a full and satisfied image and instrument of its being. Secondly, it makes for individuality in the positive sense.

[1] 'If thou wilt not carry on this righteous warfare, then casting away thine own dharma and thine honour, thou wilt incur sin' (*Bhagavadgītā*, ii. 33).

Individuality is attained not through an escape from limitations but through the willing acceptance of obligations. It is erroneous to assume that only the aberrant or the anarchical is the true individual. Thirdly, it points out that all work is socially useful and from an economic standpoint equally important. Fourthly, social justice is not a scheme of rights but of opportunities. It is wrong to assume that democracy requires all men to be alike. Society is a pattern or an organism in which different organs play different parts. Excellence is specific and cannot be universal. Equality refers to opportunity and not to capacity. While it recognizes that men are unequal in scale and quality, it insists that every human being shall have the right and the opportunity to contribute to human achievement, as far as his capacity goes. Society must be so organized as to give individuals sufficient scope to exercise their natural energies without being interfered with by others. Even Marx does not accept the view that all men are born equal with an inherent right to identical shares in the commodities produced by the community. An assertion of abstract equality is not the same as the principle from each according to his capacity and to each according to his requirements. There is no attempt to equalize capacities or level up the requirements.[1] Fifthly, the essence of democracy is consideration for others. Freedom for the individual means restrictions on absolute power. No one class can make unlimited claims. The State, the Church, and other organizations must limit themselves and leave room for those who neither think nor feel as they do.

[1] Stalin, in his address to the Seventeenth Congress of the Communist Party, defines the position thus: 'By equality Marxism means not only equality in personal requirements and personal life, but the abolition of class, i.e. (*a*) the equal emancipation of all toilers from exploitation, after the capitalists have been overthrown and expropriated; (*b*) the equal abolition for all of private property in the means of production, after they have been transformed into the property of the whole society; (*c*) the equal duty of all to work according to their ability and the equal right of all toilers to receive according to the amount of work they have done (socialist society); (*d*) the equal duty of all to work according to their ability and the equal right of all toilers to receive according to their requirements (communist society). And Marxism starts out with the assumption that people's abilities and requirements are not, and cannot be, equal in quality or in quantity, either in the period of socialism or in the period of communism.' (Webb, *Soviet Russia* (1936), vol. ii, p. 702.)

Spiritual power, political power, and economic power must be properly adjusted in a well-ordered society. Democracy is not to be confused with mutual rivalries. Kauṭilya's *Arthaśāstra* discusses the theory of social contract to enforce the duties and rights of the State and the individual. While the rulers are obliged to abide by the rules of *dharma*, the citizens pay the taxes in return for the protection they receive. Monarchy was not the only type of government. Republican constitutions were well known. Representative self-governing institutions operated in India even by the time of Megasthenes. Village communities presided over by councils of elders chosen from all castes and representing all interests maintained peace and order, controlled taxation, settled disputes, and preserved intact the internal economy of the country. Trade-guilds were also managed on similar lines, protecting the professional interests and regulating working hours and wages. The peasant worked the land to maintain himself and the family and contribute a little to the community. The craftsman fashioned the tools and the clothing necessary for the community, and was in turn provided with the food and shelter necessary. This system prevailed even after the British rule started. Sir William Hunter observed: 'The trade guilds in the cities, and the village community in the country, act, together with caste, as mutual assurance societies, and under normal conditions allow none of their members to starve. Caste, and the trading or agricultural guilds concurrent with it, take the place of a poor law in India.'[1] Land became a commodity to be bought and sold for the first time in the administration of Warren Hastings. The new economy of the private ownership of land, with the zamindar as the permanent landlord, a sort of middleman between the State and the peasant, the divorce of industry from agriculture, and large-scale production in factories have brought about a social revolution. Under the centralized administration of the British, local self-government and autonomous village organization disappeared. A strange impression prevails that in India caste prevented the development of democratic institutions. In the administration of villages and towns, caste and trade-guilds, provinces

[1] *Indian Empire*, p. 199.

and even federations, the democratic principle where every individual is both sovereign and subject is affirmed. Even such details as the rules of elections, division into electoral units, rules of procedure and debate do not escape notice.[1] Representative democracy or the *pañchāyat* system is native to the Indian temperament. Sixthly, the general tendency of men of all classes to strive to the summit is due to the impression that the position at the top is one of pleasure, profit, and power. To obtain these, every one wishes to climb the social ladder. But in the Hindu scheme life becomes more difficult as we rise higher. A Brāhmin should do nothing for the sake of enjoyment. If we realize the increase of social responsibility and the diminution of the personal enjoyments of life as we rise in the social ladder, we will be more satisfied with our own place and work in society. Those who seek the higher place will lead a life of simplicity and self-denial.

Within this fourfold scheme each individual has to follow his own nature and arrive at his possible perfection by a growth from within. The individual is not a mere cell of the body or a stone of the edifice, a mere passive instrument of its collective life. Man is not a thing or a piece of machinery which can be owned. The question of property, of the man over the woman, of the father over the child, of the State over the individual must be given up. The individual's action must be determined by his own essential quality.[2] Through the fulfilment of his nature he contributes to the good of the society, though he may not intend it. We must

[1] The Marquis of Zetland writes: 'And it may come as a surprise to many to learn that in the Assemblies of the Buddhists in India two thousand years and more ago are to be found the rudiments of our own parliamentary practice of the present day. The dignity of the Assembly was preserved by the appointment of a special officer—the embryo of "Mr. Speaker" in the House of Commons. A second officer was appointed whose duty it was to see that when necessary a quorum was secured—the prototype of the Parliamentary Chief Whip in our own system. A member initiating business did so in the form of a motion which was then open to discussion. In some cases this was done once only, in others three times, thus anticipating the practice of parliament in requiring that a Bill be read a third time before it becomes law. If discussion disclosed a difference of opinion the matter was decided by the vote of the majority, the voting being by ballot' (*The Legacy of India*, p. xi (1937)).

[2] 'svabhāvaniyatamkarma'.

avoid the cant of the preacher who appeals to us for the deep-sea fishermen on the ground that they are daily risking their lives that we may have fish for our breakfasts and dinners. They are doing nothing of the kind. They go to sea for themselves and their families, not for our breakfasts and dinners. Our convenience happily is a by-product of their labours.

True law which develops from within is not a check on liberty but its outward image, its visible expression. Human society progresses really and vitally only when law becomes the expression of freedom. It will reach its perfection when man having learned to know becomes spiritually one with his fellow men. The law of society exists only as the outward mould of his inner nature. The true man conforms to law simply because he cannot help it.[1] When Draupadī blames her husband for obeying the law when it has led him into difficulties, he replies that he does not observe it in expectation of any reward but because his mind has become fixed on it.[2] Man helps the world by his life and growth only in proportion as he can be more freely himself, using the ideals and the opportunities which he finds in his way. He can use them effectively only if they are not burdens to be borne by him, but means towards his growth. By gathering the materials from the minds and lives of his fellow men and making the most of the experience of humanity's past ages, he expands his own mind and pushes society forward. Social order (*kṣema*) and progress (*yoga*) are thus safeguarded.

3. When birth acquired greater importance classes degenerated into castes. The chief features of caste are: (i) *Heredity*. One cannot change one's caste. (ii) *Endogamy*. Every member of a caste must marry a member of the same caste and may not marry outside it. (iii) *Commensal restrictions*. Regulations are imposed regarding the acceptance of food and drink from members of other castes. The caste scheme recognizes the individuality of the group. When

[1] na dhanārtham yaśo 'rtham vā dharmas tesām yudhiṣṭhira
avaśyam kāryaity eva śarīrasya kriyās tathā.
(*Mahābhārata*, Śāntiparva, 158. 29.)

[2] nāhamdharmaphalākānkṣī rājaputri carāmyuta
dharma eva manaḥ kṛṣṇe svabhāvāccaiva me dhritam.

aboriginal deities were taken over into the Hindu pantheon, the priesthoods attached to them were accepted as Brāhmins even as the ruling families of the tribe were accepted as Kṣatriyas. Hence arose innumerable subdivisions. The beliefs and practices which the different groups developed in the course of ages were recognized as valid and relations among groups regulated in accordance with them.

In the period of the Vedic hymns (1500 B.C. to 600 B.C.), there were classes and not castes. We do not find any reference to connubial or commensal restrictions. The occupations were by no means hereditary. There is, however, a marked differentiation between the fair-skinned Aryans and the dark-skinned Dasyus. This racial distinction faded into the background in the early Buddhist times (600 B.C. to 300 B.C.). In the *Jātakas* the four classes are mentioned and the Ksatriyas are said to be the highest. Any one who took to the priestly way of life became a Brāhmin. There were no endogamous restrictions. According to one *Jātaka*, Buddha himself though a Kṣatriya married a poor farmer's daughter. Though marriages within the same class were encouraged, intermarriages were by no means unusual or forbidden. Function in the trade-guilds became before long hereditary. Megasthenes tells us that there were seven castes, that intermarriages between them were forbidden, and that function was hereditary though the philosophers were exempt from these restrictions. His observations can be accepted only with caution. Chandragupta himself was of mixed descent. Megasthenes' account shows, however, that mixed marriages were exceptional even in the fourth century B.C., though they continued to occur in later times.[1] Caste in its rigour became established by the time of Manu and the Purānas, which belong to the period of the Gupta kings (A.D. 330 to 450). The great invaders, the Sakas, the Yavanas, the Pahlavas, and the Kushans, were accepted as Hindus. It is said in *Mudrārākṣasā* that Chandragupta was opposed by a force under the command of 'the great monarch of the barbarian

[1] According to *Mālavikāgnimitra*, Agnimitra, a king of the Sunga dynasty (*circa* 150 B.C.), married a woman of an inferior caste. In the *Mrcchaghaṭika*, the hero Cārudatta, who is a Brāhmin by birth and a merchant by profession, married a courtesan.

tribes'[1] who had in his army members of the foreign tribes. Yuan Chwang's account of the bloodthirsty Hunnish tyrant Mihiragula shows that the Huns were savages from the central Asian steppes. When these tribes were taken over into Hinduism an unusually strong disinclination to intermarriage developed. The endogamous custom which was encouraged in the Buddhist period and became the usual practice in the time of Megasthenes was made the rule by Manu, who regulated carefully exceptions to it. Caste was the Hindu answer to the challenge of society in which different races had to live together without merging into one.[2] The difficulty of determining the psychological basis led to the acceptance of birth as the criterion. Society, being a machine, inclines to accept an outer sign or standard. The tendency of a conventional society is to fix firmly and formalize a system of grades and hierarchies. Besides, as the types fix themselves, their maintenance by education and tradition becomes necessary and hereditary grooves are formed.

While there are only four classes, the castes are innumerable. We have tribal, functional, sectarian castes, as well as outcastes. There are references to the untouchables in the *Jātakas*.[3] Fa Hien, the Chinese pilgrim (A.D. 405 to 411), describes how the Caṇḍālas had to live apart and give notice of their approach on entering a town by striking a piece of wood. The untouchables mainly included some who were on the outskirts of civilization and were left unabsorbed by the Hindu faith and others who performed duties which were regarded as low. In the class scheme there was no fifth class of untouchables.[4]

The substitution of the principle of birth for virtue and valour has been the main factor in the process of social crystallization and caste separatism. Birth is said to indicate real, permanent differences in the mental attitudes of men though they cannot be easily measured by the rough and

[1] mahatamleccharājena.

[2] See *The Hindu View of Life*, 5th impression, pp. 93 ff.

[3] See *Śetaketu Jātaka*, iii. 233; *Mātanga Jātaka*, iv. 358; *Cittasambhūta Jātaka*, iv. 391.

[4] triṣu varneṣu jāto'hi brāhmanābrāhmano bhavet,
smṛtāś catvarnāh catvārah pañcamo nādhigamyate.
(*Mahābhārata*, Anuśāsanaparva, 44.)

ready methods of anthropologists. The theory of rebirth by which man's inborn nature and course of life are determined by his own past lives gives additional support to the view that man is born to the social function which is natural to him. It is not realized that the fact of ancestry, parentage, and physical birth may not always indicate the true nature of the individual. When the obligations of the classes do not spring spontaneously from their inner life, they become mere conventions, departing largely from the maintenance of ethical types. The son of a Brāhmin is always a Brāhmin though he may have nothing of the Brāhmin in him. The individual does not fall naturally into his place in society but is thrust into it by an external power. Any system where an abstract power, caste, or Church decides a person's profession and place is an unnatural one. As the individuals are esteemed high or low, not by the degree of their sociality but by their profession, wealth, or power, class conflicts arise where all desire power and privilege. In the class scheme the social duty of the individual is insisted on, not his personal rights. In caste, privilege is more important. In the class order any one who has the courage to undergo the discipline, the strength to deny himself the pleasures of life, and the capacity to develop his powers is free to rise to the top; not so in the caste scheme, which does not allow for the free play of man's creative energies. While the man of the higher caste is left to his sense of duty and conscience, the weaker ones with their anti-social tendencies are made to feel the weight of punishment. In actual practice the setting up of different standards of punishment for offenders of different castes is the weakest part of the system. In fairness to the lawgivers, it may be said that they made out that the higher the caste the greater is the offence when moral rules are violated.[1]

The disparity between the hereditary function and the individual's nature was reduced to some extent by education and training. And so the scriptures while recognizing the hereditary practice insist that character and capacity

[1] Gautama, xii. 17. Manu says that a king should be fined a thousand times as much as a common man for the same offence (viii. 336), The *Mahābhārata* is even stronger. Even priests should be punished; the weightier the men, the weightier should be their punishment (xii. 268. 15).

are the real basis and without them the social status is meaningless.

When the Brāhmin looked upon his position as one of easy privilege and not arduous obligation, protests were uttered. Manu and others contrast the ideal Brāhmin who has the ethical quality with the actual who bases his claim on birth.[1] In *Śuddhārthacintāmani* it is said that the three features of a Brāhmin are austerity, learning, and birth, and one who has the third and not the first two qualities is only a Brāhmin by caste.[2] Again, Kauśika received instruction from a meat-seller and said to him: 'In my opinion you are a Brāhmin even in this life. Because a Brāhmin who is haughty and who is addicted to degrading vices is no better than a Śūdra, and a Śūdra who restrains his passions and is ever devoted to truth and morality I look upon as a Brāhmin, inasmuch as character is the basis of Brāhminhood.'[3] *Chāndogya Upaniṣad* gives the story of Satyakāma, the son of Jābālā who approached Gautama Haridrumata and said to him, 'I wish to become a student with you, sir; may I come to you?' He said to him, 'Of what family are you, my friend?' He replied, 'I do not know, sir, of what family I am. I asked my mother and she answered, "In my youth when I had to move about much as a servant, I conceived thee. I do not know of what family thou art. I am Jābālā by name and thou art Satyakāma", therefore I am Satyakāma Jābālā, sir.' He said to him, 'No one but a true Brāhmin would thus speak out. Go and fetch fuel, friend. I shall initiate you; you have not swerved from the truth.'[4] Even after caste became conventional, Kavaṣa, the son of a slave girl, was accepted as a Brāhmin.[5] To minimize the rigours of caste the relative character of caste distinctions is frequently emphasized. The

[1] 'Whether a Brāhmin performs rites or neglects them he who befriends all creatures is said to be a Brāhmin' (*Manu*, ii. 87). 'The panegyrists, the flatterers, the cheats, those who act harshly and those who are avaricious—these five kinds of Brāhmins should never be adored, even if they are equal to Brihaspati in learning' (*Atri*, 379).

[2] tapaśśrutam ca yoniśca trayam brāhmaṇya kāraṇam
tapaśśrutābhyām yo hīno jātibrāhmaṇi eva saḥ.

[3] *Mahābhārata*, Vanaparva, iii. 75–84.

[4] iv. 4. 1–5.

[5] *Aitareya Brāhmaṇa*, ii. 19.

Rāmāyaṇa tells us that there were only Brāhmins in the Kritayuga and all people were of one class.[1]

Though theistic movements from the Āḷvārs and Rāmānuja, though Rāmānanda and Kabīr, Nānak and Caitanya, Nāmdev and Eknāth protest against caste inequalities, they have not disappeared as yet. Even Christian churches in their anxiety to propagate their faith compromise with it. Pope Gregory XV published a bull sanctioning caste regulations in the Christian Church of India.[2] The general effect of the impact of the West has been in the direction of liberalizing the institution. The rise of nationalism is the direct result of the incorporation of Western ideals in the thought and life of the country. The hostile judgement on British rule in India is based on conceptions of justice and freedom for which the British are, in the main, responsible. The Britisher's interest in India is more the permanence of his rule than the reform of Indian society. His attitude and policy are best expressed in the statement of James Kerr, the principal of the Hindu College at Calcutta, who said as far back as 1865, 'It may be doubted if the existence of caste is on the whole unfavourable to the permanence of our rule. It may even be considered favourable to it, provided we act with prudence and forbearance. Its spirit is opposed to national union.'[3] The recent constitutional changes stereotype communal divisions and caste distinctions. Though measures which provide for the special representation of certain classes of people are adopted in the name of social justice, they are calculated to retard the growth of national unity. Hindu reform movements are impelled by the conviction that caste is an anachronism in our present conditions, and that it persists through sheer inertia.

Those who defy caste rules are outcasted, and this punishment till recently made the influence of caste virtually irresistible. The freedom of the individual, however, was not completely suppressed. The rules of caste were quite flexible. There was no attempt to crystallize morals. Those who demand a radical reform might form themselves into a new

[1] Uttarakāṇḍa, 74. 9–11; 30. 19. See also *Bhāgavata*, xi. 17. 10–11; *Manu*, i. 83. [2] *Encyclopaedia Britannica*, 11th ed., vol. v, p. 468.

[3] Ghurye, *Caste and Race in India* (1932), p. 164.

caste. The laws were there, but they were admitted to be relative and susceptible to change. The law books declare that the sources of *dharma* are the scriptures, the sayings and doings of those who know the scripture, the practice of the virtuous and the approval of the enlightened conscience.[1] The texts indicate the framework, and within their limits ample liberty of interpretation is allowed. As the texts themselves are often conflicting,[2] one is obliged to use one's own reason and conscience. Men of moral insight and uprightness could depart from the established usage and alter customary law. Āpastamba says, 'Right and wrong do not go about proclaiming "here we are"; nor do gods, angels and the manes say "this is right and that is wrong", but right is what the Aryans praise and wrong is what they blame.'[3] In the *Taittirīya Upaniṣad* the teacher gives the young man at the end of years of study a general rule of conduct.

> 'Speak the truth, practise virtue; neglect not the sacrifices due to gods and manes: let thy mother be to thee as a divinity, also thy father, thy spiritual teacher and thy guest; whatever actions are blameless, not others, shouldst thou perform; good deeds, not others, shouldst thou commend; whatsoever thou givest give with faith, with grace, with modesty, with respect, with sympathy.'

How is the student to know what is right? Ordinarily custom is a sufficient guide, but in cases of doubt the young man is invited to take as his model what is done in similar circumstances by Brāhmins 'competent to judge, apt and devoted, but not harsh lovers of virtue'. If the learned doctors differ, one has to consult one's own conscience.[4] Rules are made for man, and the conventions, not the moral principles, may be set aside in emergencies. A saint declared that he would eat beef if he chose, and another satisfied his

[1] vedo'khilo dharmamūlam smritiśileca tad vidām
ācāraścaiva sādhūnām ātmanastṛptir eva ca.

[2] srutis ca bhinnā smṛtayas ca bhinnāḥ, mahārṣiṇām matayas ca bhinnāḥ.

[3] i. 20. 6.

[4] In Kālidāsa's *Śakuntalā* the hero falls in love with Śakuntalā and declares that it cannot be wrong, for in matters of doubt the voice of conscience is an unerring guide.

asaṃśayam kṣatraparigrahakṣamā yad āryam asyām abhilāṣi me manaḥ
satāmhi sandehapadeṣu vastuṣu pramāṇam antaḥkaraṇapravṛttayaḥ.
(Act 1.)

hunger with dog's meat received from an impure low-caste man. 'A saint can eat anything,' he said, 'and when a man is as hungry as I am, one kind of meat is as good as another.' He enunciates a rule that 'it is not a serious matter if one eats unclean food, provided one does not tell a lie about it'.[1] The former is a matter of convention, the latter relates to ethical life. The independence of the individual became fettered when the law with this fourfold basis became codified and required for changes legislative enactments.

The truth underlying the system is the conception of right action as a rightly ordered expression of the nature of the individual being. Nature assigns to each of us our line and scope in life according to inborn quality and self-expressive function. Nowhere is it suggested that one should follow one's hereditary occupation without regard to one's personal bent and capacities. The caste system is a degeneration of the class idea. It does not admit that the individual has the right to determine his future and pursue his interests. Though idealistic in its origin, beneficent in large tracts of its history, still helpful in some ways, it has grown out of harmony with our present conditions, owing to arrested development and lack of elasticity. The compulsory degradation of a large part of mankind is revolting to the refined natures who have a sense of the dignity of man and respect for the preciousness of human life. The right of every human soul to enter into the full spiritual heritage of the race must be recognized. Caste is a source of discord and mischief, and if it persists in its present form, it will affect with weakness and falsehood the people that cling to it.

V

The Four Stages of Life

The Hindu scheme does not leave the growth of the individual entirely to his unaided initiative but gives him a framework for guidance. Human life is represented as consisting of four consecutive stages, of which the first three fall within the jurisdiction of class or caste.[2]

[1] *Mahābhārata*, xii. 298. 7.

[2] *Bṛhadāraṇyaka Up.* iv. 4. 22; *Chāndogya Up.* ii. 23. 1; *Jābāla Up.* 4.

1. *The Student.* Human offspring are the most helpless of all living creatures. In the absence of parental care, their chances of survival are little. The tending will have to be continued for a long period, till the child reaches the status of man. The higher the cultural level the longer is the period required for education.

The aim of education is not to pour knowledge into the resisting brain and impose a stereotyped rule of conduct on his struggling impulses: it is to help the child to develop his nature, to change him from within rather than crush him from without. The education imparted not only fits man for his role in life but gives him a general idea of the conditions of spiritual life.

2. *The Householder.* By filling his place in social life, by helping its maintenance and continuity, the individual not only fulfils the law of his own being but makes his contribution to society. Man attains his full being only by living in harmonious social relationships. Sex is a normal human function concerned with the perpetuation of the race. Marriage, love, and motherhood are glorified. The wife has an equal position with the husband in all domestic and religious concerns. Every woman has a right to marry and have a home. Celibacy is the rarest of sexual aberrations. Any preoccupation with the flesh is in itself an evil even though it may be for purposes of crucifying it. Soul and body, however different, are yet closely bound together. The things of spirit are in part dependent on the satisfaction of the body. The physical and the economic, though they may not be important in themselves, are important as means to the life of spirit.

One must learn the social and spiritual lessons of the earlier stages before one can pass on to the later. One must learn to be sober before striving to become a saint. He who does not know what it is to love as a child or a husband or a parent cannot pretend to the love which contains them all. To withdraw the noblest elements of humanity from the married state to monkhood is biologically and socially unhealthy. The state of the householder is the mainstay of social life. It is said that the householder shall have his life established in the supreme reality, shall be devoted to the pursuit of truth, and shall dedicate to the Eternal Being whatever activities he undertakes.[1] Hinduism does not demand withdrawal from life into mountain tops or gloomy caves as an essential condition for spiritual life. The way to a higher life is normally through the world.

3. *The Forest Dweller.* To be, for man, is not merely to be born, to grow up, marry, earn his livelihood, found a family, and support it and pass away. That would be a human edition of the animal life. It is rather to grow upward exceeding his animal beginnings. By fulfilling his function in society, the individual begins to feel the greatness of the soul which is behind the veils of nature and longs to reach his true universality. When the children get settled and no more want his attention, he retires probably with his wife to a quiet place in the country to lead a life of inquiry and meditation and work out within himself the truth of his being, in an atmosphere of freedom from the strife of social bonds. The mystery of life, as of death, each one has to discover for himself. We can sing and taste with no tongues but our own. Though each one has to attain his purpose by his separate encounter, the result is of universal significance.

4. *The Monk.* A *saññyāsin* renounces all possessions, distinctions of caste, and practices of religion. As he has perfected himself, he is able to give his soul the largest scope, throw all his powers into the free movement of the world and compel its transfiguration. He does not merely formulate the conception of high living but lives it, adhering to the famous rule, 'The world is my country; to do good my religion'. 'Regarding all with an equal eye he must be friendly to all living beings. And being devoted, he must not injure any living creature, human or animal, either in act, word, or thought, and renounce all attachments.'[2] A freedom and fearlessness of spirit, an immensity of courage, which no defeat or obstacle can touch, a faith in the power that works in the universe, a love that lavishes itself without demand of return and makes life a free servitude to the universal spirit,

[1] brahmaniṣṭho grihasthah syāt tattvajñānaparāyaṇaḥ
yadyat karma prakurvīta tad brahmaṇi samarpayet.

[2] *Viṣṇu Purāṇa*, iii. 9.

are the signs of the perfected man. The *saññyāsin* is a super-social man, a *parivrājaka*, a wandering teacher who influences spiritual standards though he may live apart from society. The difference between a Brāhmin and a *saññyāsin* is that while the former is a full member of society, living with wife and children in a well-regulated but simple home, and performing religious rites, the latter is a celibate, homeless and wandering, if he does not live in a monastery, who has renounced all rites and ceremonies. He belongs neither to his language nor to his race but only to himself and therefore to the whole world.[1] This order is recruited from members of all castes and both sexes. As the life of the *saññyāsin* is the goal of man, those who live it obtain the allegiance of society. Kālidāsa, the great Indian poet, describes this supreme ideal of life as 'owning the whole world while disowning oneself'.[2]

Hinduism has given us in the form of the *saññyāsin* its picture of the ideal man. He carries within himself the dynamism of spirit, its flame-like mobility. He has no fixed abode and is bound to no stable form of living. He is released from every form of selfishness: individual, social, and national. He does not make compromises for the sake of power, individual or collective. His behaviour is unpredictable, for he does not act in obedience to the laws of the social group or the State. He is master of his own conduct. He is not subject to rules, for he has realized in himself the life which is the source of all rules and which is not itself subject to rules. The quietude of his soul is strange, for though he is tranquil within, everything about him is restless and dynamic. His element is fire, his mark is movement.

The ideal man of India is not the magnanimous man of Greece or the valiant knight of medieval Europe, but the free man of spirit who has attained insight into the universal source by rigid discipline and practice of disinterested virtues, who has freed himself from the prejudices of his time and place. It is India's pride that she has clung fast to this ideal and produced in every generation and in every part of the country from the time of the Rṣis of the Upaniṣads

[1] When his colleagues boasted that they were native to the soil Antisthenes replied that they shared this honour with slugs and grasshoppers.

[2] *Mālavikāgnimitra*, i. 1.

and Buddha to Rāmakṛṣṇa and Gandhi, men who strove successfully to realize this ideal.

The ideal of the *saññyāsin* has still an appeal to the Indian mind. When Gandhi wants the political leaders to break all the ties that hold them to the world, to be ascetics owning nothing and vowed to celibacy, when he tells them that the prison should be their monastery, the coarse jail dress their religious habit, fetters and handcuffs their hair shirt and scourge, he is applying the ideal of renunciation in the political sphere.

The scheme of classes and stages is helpful but not indispensable. Mandana[1] tells us that it is like a saddle horse which helps a man to reach his goal easily and quickly, but even without it man can arrive there. Life is a progress through stages. The race is a long one, and society should not lay on any one a burden too heavy to bear. The higher flights are not to be attempted until we train ourselves on the lower ones. We should not, however, be content to remain for all time on the lower stages. That would not be to live up to the ideal demanded of us. The goal is the vision of God and it is open to all. The world and its activities are no barriers to it but constitute the training ground.

VI

The scheme of the ends of life, classes, and stages has for its aim the development of the individual. It helps him to order and organize his life instead of leaving it as a bundle of incompatible desires. It looks upon him not as a mere specimen of a zoological species but as a member of a social group which reflects in its organization the scheme of values for the realization of which the group exists. By education and social discipline the individual is helped to develop the inner conviction essential for social stability. But throughout there is insistence on the fact that the highest values are supernational and truly universal. The activities and achievements of art and science, of morality and religion, are the highest manifestations of the human spirit assimilable and communicable across barriers of blood and race. This is not to deny or underrate the importance of the group life, but the

[1] *Brahmasiddhi*, p. 37. I owe this correction to my friend Mr. S. S. Swiyanarayana Sastri of Madras University.

highest values of art and literature, science and philosophy, have, in principle, a universal appeal. The higher the individual the more free is he of the social order. The highest is the most universal, having transcended the need for discipline by the social scheme (*ativarṇāśrami*). He is a king among men, being a king over himself, *svayam eva rājā*. He is a citizen of the world and speaks a language that can be understood by all who call themselves men. Of the four ends the highest is spiritual freedom; of the four classes, the Brāhmin engaged in spiritual pursuits is the highest; of the four stages, that of *saññyāsa* is the most exalted. The meaning of human existence is in a larger consciousness which man does not enter so long as he remains confined in his individuality. The limitations of family life and social obedience embarrass the spirit in its main purpose of advancing into a life of unity with all being. The negative method of asceticism by which the individual mortifies his body, gives up all possessions, and breaks all social connexions is not the Hindu view, which requires us to grow into the larger freedom of spirit, the super-individuality, by developing each side of our life until it transcends its limits. In this fatal hour of twilight, of tragic conflict between light and darkness, it is the duty of the free men of the spirit, who have seen the real beyond the clouds, to do their best to ward off the darkness, and if that is not possible to light their lamps and get ready to help us to see when the night falls.

VII

We are at a gloomy moment in history. Never has the future seemed so incalculable. With a dreary fatality the tragedy moves on. The world of nations seems to be like a nursery full of perverse, bumptious, ill-tempered children, nagging one another and making a display of their toys of earthly possessions, thrilled by mere size. This is true of all countries. It is not a question of East or West, of Asia or Europe. No intelligent Asiatic can help admiring and reverencing the great races that live in Europe and their noble and exalted achievements. His heart is wrung when he sees dark clouds massing on the horizon. There is something coarse at the very centre of our civilization by which it is betrayed again and again. No civilization, however brilliant, can stand up against the social resentments and class conflicts which accompany a maladjustment of wealth, labour, and leisure. Perpetual disturbance will be our doom if we do not recognize that the world is one and interdependent.[1] If we do not alter the framework of the social system and the international order, which are based on force and the exploitation of the inferior individuals and backward nations, world peace will be a wild dream. While resolved to renounce nothing, this generation wishes to enjoy the fruits of renunciation.

The *Imitation* has a profoundly significant sentence. 'All men desire peace, but very few desire those things which make for peace.' We are not prepared to pay the price for peace, the renunciation of empires, the abandonment of the policy of economic nationalism, the rearrangement of the world on a basis of racial equality and freedom and devotion to world community. It is obvious common sense, but for it to dawn on the general mind, a mental and moral revolution is necessary. Peace demands a revolutionary desire, a new simplicity, a new asceticism. If men conquer their own inordinate desires, this inner victory will show forth in their outer relations. In the third century B.C. Aśoka succeeded to a realm more extensive than modern British India. He achieved in early life a reputation as a military hero. The spectacle of the misery caused by war filled him with remorse and he became a man of peace and an enthusiastic disciple of Buddha. The results of his conversion may be told in his own words as they appeared in the edicts which he caused to be carved on rocks and pillars throughout his vast empire. In one of them he tells us of his profound sorrow at the thousands who had been slain in his war on the Kalingas and at the misery inflicted on the non-combatants. 'If a hundredth or a thousandth part of these were now to suffer the same fate, it would be a matter of deep sorrow to his majesty. Though one should do him an injury, his majesty now holds that it must be patiently borne, so far as it

[1] 'The world of mortals is an interdependent organism':
'sanghātavan martyalokaḥ parasparam apāśritah'.
(*Mahābhārata*, xii. 298. 17)

can possibly be borne.'[1] Here was a mighty emperor who not only repented of his lust for dominion but had his repentance cut in rocks for the instruction of future ages. If science and machinery get into other hands than those of warring Caesars and despotic Tamerlanes, if enough men and women arise in each community who are free from the fanaticisms of religion and of politics, who will oppose strenuously every kind of mental and moral tyranny, who will develop in place of an angular national spirit a rounded world view, what might not be done?

[1] Rock Edict XIII. See Vincent A. Smith, *The Edicts of Aśoka*, p. 19 (1909).

APPENDIX

Note to page 154

To understand the importance of Alexander's achievement which is a milestone in human progress, it is essential to know how far he has travelled from his teacher Aristotle. The Greek distinction between Hellenes and Barbarians is not found in Homer. When he speaks of the Carians as barbarophōnoi, he means that they speak a different language and are foreigners and not that they are uncivilized or unworthy of fair treatment. The Ionian philosophers maintained that mankind was one by 'nature' and distinctions of Greek and barbarian, slave and free were founded on 'convention'. After the sixth century B.C., however, the stranger is treated as an enemy. The strange or the utterly different inspires fear; from fear follows hatred and from hatred contempt. Plato says of the Barbarians that they are enemies by nature (*Republic*, 5. 470). Aristotle holds that there are slaves by 'nature' and war against Barbarians is 'natural'. (Augustine called the Devil the barbarian of the universe—'barbarus mundi'—*Sermon* I. 2.) Alexander ignored the teaching of Aristotle and held that the distinction was not a racial one between the Greeks and the Barbarians but a moral one between the good and the cultured and the evil and the uncultured. 'Towards the end of his treatise,' says Strabo of the Alexandrian Eratosthenes who was born about 70 years later than Alexander, 'after refusing to praise those who divide the whole mass of mankind into two groups, namely Greeks and Barbarians as well as those who advised Alexander to treat the Greeks as friends and the Barbarians as foes, Eratosthenes goes on to say that it would be better to make such divisions according to virtue and vice; for not only are many of the Greeks bad, but many of the Barbarians are cultured; for example, Indians and Ariyans, and further, Romans and Carthaginians whose governments are admirable. And this, he says, is the reason why Alexander disregarding his advisers welcomed as many as he could of the men of good repute and did them good services.' (*Geography* I. 66, quoted in Haarhoff, *The Stranger at the Gate* (1938).) Alexander's will, as given by Diodorus, has little documentary value, but it probably contains ideas mentioned or discussed by him. It deals, among other things, with the transplanting of men and women both from Asia to Europe and from Europe to Asia, the encouragement of inter-marriage to produce oneness of spirit (homonoia), and friendship that springs from family ties. Plutarch tells us that it was Alexander's intention to establish unity (homonoia), partnership (koinōnia), and peace (eirēnē) in the world as a whole. He wished all men to be obedient to the universal principal of reason (logos) and a single constitution. If Plutarch is to be trusted, Alexander believed that he had a mission from God to bring men into unity and reconcile different parts of the world (*The Life of Alexander*, 27). He believed himself to be the descendant of Achilles, the passionate and the swift-footed. Plutarch adds that 'he bade all men regard the inhabited world (oikoumenē) as their fatherland'. At any rate he was the first person to endeavour to translate the high ideal of 'on earth one family' into practical achievement. (Professor Tarn states that Alexander 'was the pioneer of one of the supreme revolutions in the world's outlook, the first man known to us who contemplated the brotherhood of man or the unity of mankind'—*Alexander and Unity of Mankind*, p. 28.)

Note [2] *to page 156*

We have a Kharoṣṭhi inscription, on a vase from Swat, of the Greek meridarch Theodorus, who, as a Buddhist, deals with the establishment of some relics of Buddha, and this inscription is probably of the early part of the first century B.C.

Note [3] *to page 156*

Some of the Greeks in India adopted Buddhism or at any rate took such keen interest in it as to place their artistic skill at its service. It has been well said that the art of Gāndhāra was born of Buddhist piety utilizing Greek technique. This influence continued from the first century B.C. into the Kushan period and even after it, when it became completely Indianized.

Note [2] *to page 163*

He was condemned to death for his more or less seditious activities, though his fanatic followers elevated Him to the rank of God.

Note [3] *to page 163*

Such a view was held in antiquity by Tacitus, Celsus, and Porphyry and by the Jews and Muslims.

Note [4] *to page 163*

Renan looks upon Jesus as the greatest of the prophets. In the words of Sainte-Beuve, Jesus is offered a seat at the summit of humanity on condition of his abdication from the throne of God.

Note [5] *to page 163*

M. Couchoud: *Jésus le Dieu fait Homme*. Doubt about the existence of Jesus was first raised in Alexandria in the third century of the Christian era by Celsus and it has been expressed since by thousands. While we know a good deal about Julius Caesar, who was assassinated only about 50 years before the birth of Jesus, of Antony and Cleopatra, who died 25 years earlier, of Augustus and Tiberias, who were Jesus' contemporaries, we have very little contemporary evidence about Jesus himself. Joesphus, born in Jerusalem only six years after the Crucifixion, wrote a history of the Jews in which there is only one mention of Jesus and even that is regarded as an interpolation by a later writer. Plutarch and Philo do not allude to him. From all this M. Couchoud infers that Jesus was at first to St. Paul and his followers the name of a God who was later in the second century transferred into the name of a man who was unknown as an historical person until then. The Jesus of Paul's inspiration was not so much an historical person as a spirit akin to

Socrates' 'daimon'. The existing general tradition about God became associated with the name of Jesus. The Book of Enoch has the conception of a Heavenly man who would be near to the throne of God and receive a mandate to judge and destroy the world in God's place. The pagan environment was full of stories of divine beings such as Coré, Dionysus Zagreus, Osiris, Attis, who had died and come to life again. All these mysteries offer salvation to men by intimate communion with a divine being who had triumphed over death. M. Couchoud affirms that 'Jesus is misclassed when placed in the series of great religious reformers, Zoroaster, Confucius, Mani, Mahomet, Luther. His true place is among the resurrection gods, his predecessors and inferior brethren, Demeter, Dionysus, Osiris, Attis, Mithra, whose mysteries before his, but with lesser power, had offered to men the great hope of winning the victory over death.' (See 'The Historicity of Jesus', *Hibbert Journal*, Jan. 1939.)

Continuation of note [1] to page 164

There is no agreement among the critics about the historic facts about Jesus to be gathered from the Gospels. In an arbitrary way, each critic reduces the historic kernel to what pleases him. M. Loisy, for example, accepts little more than the crucifixion and the name of Jesus. Nearly everything in the Gospels seems to be a product of faith.

Note [2] to page 262

As regards scripture, Hobbes contends that sovereigns are the sole judges as to which books are canonical and how they should be interpreted. Of all the abuses that constitute the kingdom of darkness, the greatest arise from the false doctrine that 'the present Church now militant on earth is the Kingdom of God'. 'The papacy is no other than the ghost of the deceased Roman Empire, sitting crowned upon the grave thereof.' The Cambridge Platonists laid stress on the moral and spiritual factors in religion and claimed that true religion must harmonize with rational truth. They were opposed to all claims of private inspiration. Benjamin Whichcote (1610–83) writes: 'If you say you have a revelation from God, I must have a revelation from God too before I can believe you.' God reveals Himself in the mind of man 'more than in any part of the world besides'. This revelation cannot conflict with universal reason of mankind. The only thing which is unalterable and final is the ethical side of religion. We may dispute doctrines of theology but not the laws of morality. 'I will not', he said, 'break the certain laws of charity for a doubtful doctrine or of uncertain truth.' Nathanael Culverwel observes: 'The Church hath more security in resting upon genuine reason than in relying upon some spurious traditions.' Two propositions sum up his doctrine: '1. That all the moral law is founded in natural and common light, in the light of reason; and 2. That there is nothing in the mysteries of the Gospel contrary to the light of reason.' Culverwel is an earnest rationalist, though he holds that reason needs illumination from faith.

Note [1] *to page 267*

W. K. Clifford (1845–79) was a fanatic in his unbelief. He raged against Church and Creed and denounced Christianity as 'a terrible plague which has destroyed two civilisations'. He put man in place of God and his faith and he concluded his essay on *Cosmic Emotion* with the words, 'Those who can read the signs of the times read in them that the Kingdom of man has come.'

Note to page 271

'One thing is clear: the victory of Christianity indicates a break with the past and a changed attitude in the history of the human mind. Men had grown weary and unwilling to seek further. They turned greedily to a creed that promised to calm the troubled mind, that could give certainty in place of doubt, a final solution for a host of problems, and theology instead of science and logic. Unable and unwilling to direct their own inner life, they were ready to surrender the control to a superior being, incommensurable with themselves. Reason neither gave nor promised happiness to mankind: but especially the Christian religion gave man the assurance of happiness beyond the grave. Thus the centre of gravity was shifted and men's hopes and expectations were transferred to that future life. They were content to submit and suffer in this life in order to find the life hereafter. Such an attitude of mind was entirely foreign to the ancient world, even to the earlier nations of the East, not to speak of the Greeks and Romans. To a Greek the future life was something shadowy and formidable; life one earth alone was prized by him.' Rostovtzeff, *A History of the Ancient World*, vol. ii, *Rome* (1927), p. 350.

INDEX

DATE DUE

Demco, Inc. 38-293